Property and Human Flourishing

Property and Human Flourishing

Gregory S. Alexander

OXFORD
UNIVERSITY PRESS

OXFORD
UNIVERSITY PRESS

Oxford University Press is a department of the University of Oxford. It furthers the University's objective of excellence in research, scholarship, and education by publishing worldwide. Oxford is a registered trademark of Oxford University Press in the UK and certain other countries.

Published in the United States of America by Oxford University Press
198 Madison Avenue, New York, NY 10016, United States of America.

Library of Congress Cataloging-in-Publication Data

Names: Alexander, Gregory S., 1948–, author.
Title: Property and human flourishing / Gregory S. Alexander.
Description: New York : Oxford University Press, 2018. | Includes bibliographical references and index.
Identifiers: LCCN 2017041342 | ISBN 9780190860745 ((hardback) : alk. paper)
Subjects: LCSH: Right of property—Philosophy. | Property. | Obligations (Law).
Classification: LCC K721.5 .A94 2018 | DDC 306.3/201—dc23
LC record available at https://lccn.loc.gov/2017041342

9 8 7 6 5 4 3 2 1

Printed by Edwards Brothers Malloy, United States of America

Note to Readers
This publication is designed to provide accurate and authoritative information in regard to the subject matter covered. It is based upon sources believed to be accurate and reliable and is intended to be current as of the time it was written. It is sold with the understanding that the publisher is not engaged in rendering legal, accounting, or other professional services. If legal advice or other expert assistance is required, the services of a competent professional person should be sought. Also, to confirm that the information has not been affected or changed by recent developments, traditional legal research techniques should be used, including checking primary sources where appropriate.

(Based on the Declaration of Principles jointly adopted by a Committee of the American Bar Association and a Committee of Publishers and Associations.)

To Andre van der Walt,

whose work and life continue to inspire me

CONTENTS

PREFACE

This preface provides the rationale for another book on property theory. It briefly explains the human flourishing theory and what distinguishes that theory from other property theories currently available in the literature. It provides a brief synopsis of the book's argument and states both goals and the limits of the human flourishing theory.

It is a fair question to ask what, if anything, justifies this book. Do we really need another book on property theory? After all, it isn't as though we lack books elaborating one property theory or another. There are many fine ones available.[1] I believe this book is justified. What justifies it is that it offers an entirely novel theory of ownership, one that I have been developing in a series of articles over the past several years. This theory, which I call the human flourishing theory, is an alternative to the two theories that now dominate Anglo-American writing about what ownership means: the utilitarian/information-cost theory and the Kantian rights theory. In North America, the leading proponents of the former

1. I hesitate to identify any for fear to overlooking, and thereby insulting, any worthy candidates, but here goes: Hanoch Dagan, Property: Values and Institutions (2011); Peter M. Gerhart, Property Law and Social Morality (2013); J.W. Harris, Property & Justice (1996); Adam J. Macleod, Property and Practical Reason (2016); Ben McFarlane, The Structure of Property Law (2008); Eduardo M. Peñalver & Sonia Katyal, Property Outlaws (2010); J.E. Penner, The Idea of Property in Law (1997); Jedediah Purdy, The Meaning of Property: Freedom, Community, and the Legal Imagination (2011); Carol M. Rose, Property and Persuasion (1994); Joseph William Singer, Entitlement: The Paradoxes of Property (2000); Laura Underkuffler, The Idea of Property: Its Meaning and Power (2003); Andre van der Walt, Property in the Margins (2009).

are Thomas Merrill and Henry Smith,[2] and the leading spokesmen for the latter are Ernest Weinrib[3] and Arthur Ripstein.[4]

I said that the human flourishing theory is an alternative to those theories, but in fact it does not reject them completely. Rather, finding them radically incomplete, it incorporates aspects of both into a much richer and morally satisfying approach to explaining what private ownership means and what its limits are. From the information-cost theory, it integrates the idea that information efficiency is important. As I explain in Chapter One, human flourishing is a pluralistic concept that includes multiple values, including cost-minimization. The difference between information-cost theory and the human flourishing theory is that the latter, unlike the former, does not suppose that information alone does or should decide cases.

Like Kantian rights theory, the theory I develop here recognizes the importance of personal autonomy and self-governance. Unlike Kantianism, however, the human flourishing does not consider individual autonomy to be the singular value foundation of all of private law, including property law. Its moral foundation is human flourishing, and, again, human flourishing is pluralistic, including multiple values. Those values are not only multiple but incommensurate, and in many (likely most) cases, there are multiple values at stake that compete with each other. In Chapter Six I discuss how rational choices can be made between competing incommensurate values.

The human flourishing theory is novel, but it draws on several sources of inspiration. As the term "human flourishing" suggests, its origins are, broadly speaking, Aristotelian, although it cannot be called an Aristotelian theory, speaking strictly. For one, my understanding of human flourishing, which I explain in detail in Chapter One, differs in important respects from that of Aristotle. What is important, however, is its insistence on the inherently social character of humans and the implications that each person's dependence on other human beings have for the substantive content of ownership. What also connects the theory to Aristotle is the claim that property's moral foundation is human flourishing.

2. *See, e.g.*, Thomas Merrill & Henry E. Smith, *What Happened to Property in Law and Economics?*, 111 Yale L.J. 357 (2001); Thomas Merrill & Henry E. Smith, *Optimal Standardization: The Numerus Clausus Principle*, 110 Yale L.J. 1 (2000).

3. *See* Ernest J. Weinrib, Corrective Justice (2012); Ernest J. Weinrib, The Idea of Private Law (2012).

4. *See* Arthur Ripstein, Private Wrong (2016); Arthur Ripstein, Force and Freedom: Kant's Legal and Political Philosophy (2009).

That is, private ownership is justified insofar as it facilitates the opportunity of individuals to live well-lived lives.

The theory that I develop here has other sources as well. It draws principally on two sources of inspiration. First, Charles Taylor's social thesis provides the foundation for the conception of the self upon which the human flourishing theory is based. Second, the capabilities approach of Amartya Sen and Martha Nussbaum is the source of the human flourishing theory's focus on developing capabilities rather than resources as such.

The human flourishing theory draws inspiration from legal sources as well. For a number of years now, my work has been part of what has come to be known as progressive property theory.[5] Contributors to this theory whose work has greatly influenced my thinking include Eduardo Peñalver,[6] Joseph Singer,[7] and Laura Underkuffler.[8] Foreign contributors to this body of work include Hanoch Dagan,[9] Kevin and Susan Gray,[10] and Andre van der Walt.[11] My human flourishing theory

5. *See, e.g.*, Gregory S. Alexander et al., *A Statement of Progressive Property*, 94 Cornell. L. Rev. 743 (2009).

6. *See, e.g.*, Eduardo M. Peñalver, *Land Virtues*, 94 Cornell L. Rev. 821 (2009); Eduardo M. Peñalver, *Property as Entrance*, 91 Va. L. Rev. 1889 (2005).

7. *See, e.g.*, Joseph William Singer, Entitlement: The Paradoxes of Property (2000); Joseph William Singer, *Should We Call Ahead? Property, Democracy*, 5 Brigham-Kanner Prop. Rts. Conf. J. 1 (2016); Joseph William Singer, *Democratic Estates: Property Law in a Free and Democratic Society*, 94 Cornell L. Rev. 1009 (2009).

8. *See, e.g.*, Laura Underkuffler, The Idea of Property: Its Meaning and Power (2003); Laura Underkuffler, *The Politics of Property and Need*, 20 Cornell J. L. & Pub. Pol. 363 (2010); Laura Underkuffler, *Property as Constitutional Myth: Utilities and Dangers*, 92 Cornell L. Rev. 1239 (2007).

9. *See, e.g.*, Hanoch Dagan, Property: Values and Institutions (2011); Hanoch Dagan, *The Public Dimension of Private Property*, 24 King's L.J. 260 (2013); Hanoch Dagan, *Pluralism and Perfectionism in Private Law*, 112 Colum. L. Rev. 1409 (2012).

10. *See, e.g.*, Kevin & Susan Gray, Elements of Land Law (5th ed. 2009); Kevin & Susan Gray, *Civil Rights, Civil Wrongs and Quasi-Public Space*, 4 Eur. Hum. Rts. L. Rev. 46 (1999); Kevin & Susan Gray, *Private Property and Public Propriety*, *in* Property and the Constitution 11 (Janet McLean ed., 1999).

11. *See, e.g.*, A.J. van der Walt, Property in the Margins (2009); A.J. van der Walt, *Property and Marginality*, *in* Property and Community 81 (Gregory S. Alexander & Eduardo M. Peñalver eds., 2010); A.J. van der Walt, *Property, Social Justice and Citizenship: The Transformation of Property Law in Post-Apartheid South Africa*, 19 Stellenbosch L. Rev. 325 (2008); A.J. van der Walt, *Normative Pluralism and Anarchy: Reflections on the 2007 Term*, 1 Constitutional Court Rev. 77 (2008).

differs from their work in various respects, but the basic thrust of our ideas is the same.

The term "communitarian" has been thrown around so much in current writing, both by academics and journalists, that I am not entirely sure what it means. Whatever its meaning, I do not think such a term is a fitting label for the human flourishing theory, if labels are what we seek. Although communities play an important role in the theory, the individual person is by no means sublimated. To the contrary, human flourishing requires that individuals have control over the choice among their possible future life horizons. To flourish, they must be autonomous. But I do not mean autonomy in the Kantian sense, which is limited to constraints on the conduct of others.[12] Rather, I mean it in the sense that a person is able to exercise self-governance and to be able to choose which paths they wish to pursue.[13] This is a capability that is essential to living a flourishing life. What the theory rejects, however, is a view of the self that Taylor calls "atomistic."[14] As I have indicated, humans are inherently social creatures and, more, inherently dependent on others in the process of developing the capabilities that every person requires to live a fulfilling life. This dependency extends to the very idea of what it means to be an autonomous human being. Personal autonomy is possible only in the context of dependence upon communities of other persons who facilitate the development of the capabilities which together are necessary for autonomy as self-governance.

A brief synopsis of the argument may be helpful at the outset. The core claim is that the vital purpose of property is to enable individuals to live a flourishing life. Flourishing is a matter of what a person is able to do rather than what she has. That is, the well-lived life should be measured by a person's capabilities rather than by a person's possession or by the satisfaction of his subjective preferences. Flourishing, as I define it, has two key characteristics. First, as I have already indicated, it is pluralistic, meaning that it rejects the notion that there exists a single irreducible fundamental moral value to which all other moral values may be reduced. Rather, it conceives of human flourishing as including (but not limited to) individual autonomy, personal security/privacy, personhood, self-determination, community, and equal dignity. These values cannot be reduced to a single basic value because they are incommensurable; there is no available metric by which one can commensurate goods such as equality and personhood.

12. *See* Ripstein, Force and Freedom, *supra* note 4, at 14, 34, 45.

13. This conception of autonomy fits with that of Hanoch Dagan. *See* Hanoch Dagan, *Pluralism and Perfectionism*, 112 Colum. L. Rev. 1409 (2012). *See also* Joseph Raz, The Morality of Freedom 372, 381, 395, 398–99 (1986).

14. *See* Charles Taylor, *Atomism*, *in* Charles Taylor, Philosophical Papers, vol. 2, 185 (1985).

The second defining characteristic of flourishing is that it is objective. This is why "flourishing" is a better translation of *eudaimonia* than "happiness" is. The problem with "happiness" is that it connotes something which is subjectively determined. It is for me, not for you, to pronounce on whether I am happy, or on whether my life, as a whole, has been a happy one.

Human flourishing, unlike welfarism, is not a desire-fulfillment theory of how a person's life can go maximally well. It is an objective theory. That is, it contends that "certain things are good or bad for us, whether or not we want to have the good things, or to avoid the bad things."[15] This does mean that the theory claims that there is one and only way to live a life that goes maximally well. There are many diverse paths to lead a fulfilling life, many ways of flourishing.

A person's life cannot go well unless he at least possesses certain essential capabilities, such as health, security, autonomy, and sociability. No one can develop these capabilities alone. We are inevitably and inherently dependent on others to cultivate the necessary capacities. Indeed, we are dependent on others for our ability to function as free and rational agents.

Communities, including but not limited to the state, are the mediating vehicles through which we come to acquire the resources we need to flourish and to become fully socialized into the exercise of our capabilities. Even as free and rational persons, we never cease to operate within and depend upon the matrices of the many communities in which we find ourselves in association.

Our dependence on others and on the various communities of which we are members creates an obligation not only to participate in but also to support the social networks and structures that enable us to develop those human capabilities that make human flourishing possible. This obligation is not based on reciprocity, and it is not contractarian. Rather, it is based on the obligation each of us owes to ourselves to live well. If I value my life (as presumably I do), then I must maintain the conditions that make my life as good as possible. Those conditions include the communities to which I belong and without which my living well—indeed, my life itself—would not exist.

The communities that enable our capabilities require resources so that they may also continue to flourish. My obligation to support these communities has consequences for me as a property owner. It means that I owe certain duties, some of which are negative, others affirmative, to members of my communities to facilitate development of their necessary capabilities. These duties not imposed externally by the state. Rather, they are inherent in what it means to own property, just in the way that the duties not to commit waste and nuisance are.

They are, that is, conceptually entailed in ownership.

15. Derek Parfit, Reasons and Persons 493 (1984).

These duties are not unlimited. They are limited by the same demands generated by the capabilities that facilitate human flourishing—health, personal security, sociability, and so forth. Owners as well as nonowners have capability-related needs. Disputes between owners and nonowner will invariably involve the multiple values that underlie human flourishing, and choices must be made between these values. Despite the fact that these conflicting values are incommensurate, rational choices between them can and are made. The fact that people disagree about how such choices should be made does not make them any less rational.

As this summary indicates, this book operates at both a conceptual and a normative level.

Conceptually, it elucidates the concept of ownership and what it means to own property. Normatively, the book develops a theory that is more morally appealing than those already available in the literature. It is more appealing morally because it takes into account all the values that comprise a well-lived life, and it is rejects the implausible belief that values such as friendship and honesty can somehow be measured against each other by some neutral metric like Bentham's fanciful "utils."[16] It stresses the social condition of humanity and the social context within which private ownership exists, and it faces up to the fact that out of this social web certain obligations attach to private ownership. They inhere in private ownership. The theory elucidates the parameters of those obligations and provides guidance for owners, nonowners, and decision makers.

The book is normative also at the basic level of seeking to change results, indeed, change the law. The human flourishing theory would not change results in all of the cases mentioned in this book, but it would change some, as I discuss in subsequent chapters. To pick just one example (which I select not because it has widespread practical importance for lives of many people—it does not—but because it neatly frames issues about the relationship between owners and neighbors), in disputes over public access to private beaches, the theory would support the decisions of the New Jersey Supreme Court recognizing the public's right to "reasonable access" of the beach.[17] In other states, where owners still exercise a strong right to exclude their neighbors, theory would change the law. It would have implications also for other controversial topics, including the public use requirement in eminent domain law, historic preservation, destruction of human reproductive material, homelessness and access to affordable housing,

16. "Utils" were the unit of measuring pleasure or pain in Bentham's felicific calculus. *See* Jeremy Bentham, An Introduction to the Principles of Morals and Legislation (2007).

17. *See* Raleigh Avenue Beach Ass'n v. Atlantis Beach Club, 879 A.2d 112 (N.J. 2005); Matthews v. Bay Head Improvement Ass'n, 471 A.2d 355, cert. denied, 469 U.S. 821 (1984).

and reparations to African Americans. In other words, the theory is not strictly theoretical; it has practical consequences for improving people's lives.

At the same time, the human flourishing theory has limits to what it can immediately accomplish. It is in the first instance a theory of private law, and as such, its immediate applications are in that realm. Although I certainly do not hold that any rigid categorical separation between the public and private realms is tenable, I do consider that the distinction between public and private law is a meaningful convention. More to the point, the human flourishing theory cannot provide direct solutions to problems such as homelessness. As I discuss at greater length in Chapter Ten, homelessness is a systemic and structural problem that requires a comparable solution. We cannot end homelessness simply by recognizing the obligations that individual owners owe to others. Solutions to problems such as homelessness require complex public responses involving legislation and administrative action. At the same time, the human flourishing theory can provide inspiration both to justify the needed public efforts and to identify the actions that should be taken. In this context, that is, the theory serves as an inspiration, not a roadmap.

In Chapter Five, I sketch a methodology that decision makers may use in applying the theory to decide property disputes. This methodology does not consist of bright-line rules. This may result in a sacrifice of information efficiency, which is certainly one value, among several others, underlying property law. But information costs alone should not determine the method by which property law disputes are resolved. As Seana Shiffrin has argued, "The superficial opacity of standards is often a virtue."[18] The opacity of standards induces citizens to deliberate about whether they are acting reasonably, in good faith, and according to similar standards. Moreover, it requires them to deliberate about the meaning of the moral concepts that most standards incorporate.[19] Deliberation of this kind is itself a capability that contributes to a well-lived life, and it requires exercise. Jeremy Waldron considers the capacity to deliberate about the meaning of open-ended norms an aspect of human dignity,[20] but it is also an aspect of human flourishing. Deliberation of this sort is an integral aspect of practical reasoning and sociability. A norm that relies on a standard such as reasonableness requires the actor's exercise of practical reasoning in the context of the circumstances set out in the norm. Moreover, by deliberating about the content of open-ended moral

18. Seana Valentine Shiffrin, *Inducing Moral Deliberation: On the Occasional Virtues of Fog*, 123 Harv. L. Rev. 1214, 1214 (2010).

19. *See id.* at 1217.

20. *See* Jeremy Waldron, *Vagueness and the Guidance of Action*, 6. (NYU Public Law & Legal Theory Research Paper Series Working Paper No. 10-81), *available at* http://ssrn.co,/abstract+1699963.

standards such as good faith, we necessarily make judgments within the social context of such actions, taking into account the perceptions and evaluations that others may have about actions and the social norms of those contexts.

Advocates of bright-line rules often claim that whatever gains standards achieve come at the expense of predictability.[21] This is a false trade-off. Flexible standards may be and commonly are applied in ways that result in relative predictability. Over a period of time, the results of cases in which courts apply standards form patterns from which results in future disputes may be predicted with a fairly high degree of accuracy.

A series of trespass cases from the New Jersey Supreme Court illustrates this tendency.[22] The New Jersey court applies a kind of sliding-scale approach to decide a wide variety of trespass cases, taking into account multiple factors to decide whether and when private owners might rightfully exclude members of the public from entering their property. In our book,[23] Eduardo Peñalver and I plotted the results of these cases on a graph, the horizontal axis of which represents the degree to which the owner had invited the public onto her property. Under the New Jersey approach, this variable is inversely related to the objective weight of the owner's interest in being able to exclude those seeking entry to the property against the owner's will.

The vertical axis represents the importance of the values (which is not the same as the intensity of the preferences) that would be vindicated by granting the entrant access to the property. The cases revealed a clear pattern: The more the owner has opened up her property to the public, the stronger the entrant's claim to access; conversely, the more private the owner's actual use and possession of her property and the less urgent the entrant's need, the weaker the entrant's claim.[24] The pattern, although not based on the mechanical application of any single rule, is consistent with the result of cases in which courts have applied more formal rules.[25] The result helps to avoid the high information costs

21. *See, e.g.*, Henry Smith, *Mind the Gap: The Indirect Relation between Ends and Means in American Property Law*, 94 Cornell L. Rev. 959 (2009).

22. *See Matthews, supra* note 17; Uston v. Resorts Int'l Hotel, Inc., 445 A.2d 370 (N.J. 1982); New Jersey Coalition Against War in the Middle East v. J.M.B. Realty Corp., 650 A.2d 757 (N.J. 1994); State v. Schmid, 423 A.2d 615 (1980).

23. Gregory S. Alexander & Eduardo M. Peñalver, An Introduction to Property (2012).

24. *See id.* at 143.

25. *See, e.g.*, Jacque v. Steenberg Homes, Inc., 563 N.W.2d 154 (Wis. 1997).

that proponents of formal rules predict will result from embracing this approach to trespass disputes.

The defender of the New Jersey approach can go even further. The charge of ad hocery can be leveled at the traditional trespass rule which I discuss in Chapter Six. As I explain there, that rule is subject to so many exceptions, built into the common law of property, that justifying the status quo as a bright-line rule requires a great deal of special pleading.

Critics have read the human flourishing theory as a resource-redistributive theory.[26] This is a misreading. It is important that I be clear now what its redistributive aims are and are not.

The theory is not intended as a theory advocating redistribution of resources. At least that is not its main aim and not its main effect. The theory is not primarily resource-redistributive for two reasons. First, critics have read it as involving redistribution of property entitlements from owners to nonowners.[27] What the theory actually does, however, and is intended to do, is to recognize duties that already exist for owners. These duties inhere in ownership itself. The human flourishing theory is not a matter of creating new duties and imposing them ex post on owners. Rather, it is a matter of recognizing duties that exist ex ante as an aspect of owning property, just in the way that the duties to avoid waste and not to commit nuisance are inherent in what the common law means by private ownership. Some property scholars believe that the common law recognizes only a very small, clearly defined number of ownership duties, but this is incorrect. Concepts such as trespass do not have such hard-edged and immortal boundaries.

So, when courts recognize duties such as the beach owner's duty to provide the public with "reasonable access" to the beach,[28] they are providing definition to the concept of ownership by recognizing, not creating, a duty that inheres in the situation of an owner of beachfront property where beach access is limited and demand is high. The question had not come up in the past, and the court is simply now providing greater definition to what ownership means in that situation.

The second reason why it would be erroneous to characterize the human flourishing theory as resource-redistributive is that its focus is not on resources directly but on capabilities. It seeks to provide members of communities with the capabilities that are essential for them to live well-lived lives. Those capabilities will at times require resources, of course, and the human flourishing theory

26. *See* Robert C. Ellickson, *The Affirmative Duties of Property Owners: An Essay for Tom Merrill*, 3 Brigham-Kanner Prop. Rts. Conf. J. 43 (2014).

27. *See id.*

28. *See Matthews, supra* note 17.

is not indifferent to the distribution of resources. The key point, though, is that provision of resources is a derivative not primary task. It only serves the interest of capabilities, which are the main good that the theory seeks to provide persons. The difference between capabilities and resources is the focal point of departure between Sen's theory and that of Rawls, whose theory of justice[29] is a theory about redistribution of resources as such.[30] Sen's great insight was that well-being is better defined according to and measured by human capabilities than by holdings.[31] I follow Sen in this respect.

The book has three parts. Parts I and II are theoretical and foundational. Part I explains in detail my conception of human flourishing. Chapter One distinguishes what I mean by human flourishing and welfare, as welfare theorists use that term. Chapter Two is the theoretical heart of the book. It lays out the theory that connects ownership with the obligations that owners owe to members of their communities and establishes the foundation for those obligations. The chapter considers, and rejects, alternative possible bases for the obligations that property owners owe to others, particularly contract and reciprocity. Instead, the argument here is that the obligations that inhere in ownership derive from dependency that is an inevitable condition of humanity. Chapter Three considers in some detail what I mean by community. Given the importance that communities play in the human flourishing theory, clarity on just what community means is critical to the theory. Too often, writing about community has been abstract and vague. I have tried to avoid that deficiency by explaining what I mean by communities to which we belong in concrete terms.

Part III turns from theory to applications. Each chapter considers the implications of the human flourishing theory for various issues that are important in the property literature or in society. The range of topics is broad and eclectic. I selected them either because they have raised controversy among property scholars or because they are highly important in American society today. Chapter Four provides a segue between Chapter Three and Part III. It takes up the topic of obligations between generations and asks whether those who came before us and who come after us are members of our communities to whom we owe obligations and, if so, of what sorts?

Chapter Five continues with intertemporal questions by considering the topic of land reparations, that is, specific restitution of land wrongfully dispossessed in

29. *See* John Rawls, A Theory of Justice (1971).

30. *See, e.g.*, G.A. Cohen, *Equality of What? On Welfare, Goods, and Capabilities*, *in* The Quality of Life (Martha Nussbaum & Amartya Sen eds., 1993).

31. *See, e.g.*, Amartya Sen, Development as Freedom (2000); Amartya Sen, Commodities and Capabilities (1999).

the past. Chapter Six examines the right to exclude. This topic has been widely debated in the property literature in recent years, and Chapter Six analyzes the scope and significance of the right to exclude from the perspective of the human flourishing theory.

In Chapter Seven, I consider one aspect of the impossibly broad takings topic, examining the public use requirement both from a comparative and a human flourishing perspective. The public use requirement remains controversial after the Supreme Court decision in *Kelo*,[32] and this chapter looks to German law to find an approach that is more analytically and normatively satisfying than the Court's. Chapter Eight takes up another twig in the proverbial bundle that constitutes ownership—the right to destroy. My concern is with the duty to conserve. The question whether the owner has a duty to consider some asset she owns comes up in a surprisingly wide range of occasions, from historic preservation of buildings to artwork to human reproductive material. I develop an approach to such problems on the basis of human flourishing.

Chapters Nine and Ten are concerned with broader social problems of far more pressing concern. In Chapter Nine, I return to the subject of membership in communities by asking what obligations, if any, institutions and perhaps even individuals owe to members of the African American community. The chapter begins by focusing on the case of Georgetown University, which owned and sold slaves in the antebellum nineteenth century and has now taken certain reparative steps. I move from that example to broader questions of obligations, both institutional and individual, membership in the black community, and the basis for such obligations. Chapter Ten ends the book with an examination of the housing problems now facing the country. The main point of the chapter is that the human flourishing theory is incapable of directly contributing to solutions of the problems of homelessness, eviction, lack of affordable housing, and so on, because those problems are by nature structural and systemic. What the human flourishing theory can do is to contribute inspiration for understanding why those problems must be perceived as urgent and for focusing on the connection between safe and decent housing and the capabilities that are essential to a meaningful life.

There certainly are many other property-related topics that I might have considered here, but I had to make choices. I chose what I considered a sufficiently wide and diverse range of topics to illustrate how the human flourishing theory applies in concrete contexts. My aim was to show that the theory is not confined to the world of abstract ideas but has practical implication, both direct and indirect, for property-related problems. I leave it to others to judge my success in this respect.

32. Kelo v. City of New London, 545 U.S. 469 (2005).

Although the cases and problems that I discuss are American, I do not mean to suggest that the human flourishing theory is relevant only to American property law. Far to the contrary, it is equally relevant to all common-law jurisdictions around the world, from the United Kingdom to Australia. I see no reason why it should not be relevant in the civil-law world as well. In fact, my hope is that it opens a dialogue with civilian colleagues over what ownership means and the basis of obligations of ownership.

My greatest ambition is twofold: to emphasize the fact that ownership comes with obligations which are inherent in ownership itself, and, second, to establish human flourishing as the moral foundation of private ownership of property. Both points are certainly contestable, and I welcome debate on them. My sincerest hope is that I have made a useful contribution to the property literature.

ACKNOWLEDGMENTS

This book emphasizes the important role played by communities in the lives of every person, and I am certainly no exception. In my scholarly life, I have been blessed with many friends and people who have supported my work. Several of them have been kind enough to have contributed their valuable time to read and critique various chapters of this book, and I am immeasurably grateful to them for their efforts. Their input has saved me from many errors and misjudgments and has certainly made this a better book than it would otherwise have been.

The remaining weaknesses of the book—and doubtless they are legion—owe strictly to my own ignorance. I am grateful to my Cornell colleagues Eduardo Peñalver, Laura Underkuffler, Bob Hockett, George Hay, Jim Henderson, Mike Dorf, Sherry Colb, Annelise Riles, Josh Chafetz, and Emily Sherwin. Outside the walls of Myron Taylor Hall, many friends and critics have come to my aid: Joe Singer, Jed Purdy, Hanoch Dagan, Larissa Katz, Bernadette Atuahene, David Lametti, Eric Freyfogle, Mike Frakes, Chuck Geisler, Jeremy Waldron, Seana Shiffrin, Katrina Wyman, Eric Claeys, Molly van Houweling, Cui Zhuiyan, Yifat Holzman-Gazit, Rod McDonald, Shelly Kreiczer-Levy, Avihay Dorfman, Daphna Lewinsohn-Zamir, Kevin Gray, and Hanri Mostert. I am also grateful to critics from both political flanks who have been generous enough to read my earlier work, portions of which I have worked into this book, and commented on it. Although I do not always agree with them, this book is stronger because of their insights and criticisms. I am especially grateful to Henry Smith and Ezra Rosser. I am also grateful to two anonymous reviewers, who provided excellent comments and suggestions on several chapters. My assistant, Mrs. Ernestine da Silva, has worked harder on this book than I have. I am immensely indebted to her.

This book would not have been possible without the intellectual contribution and other support of my Cornell colleague, coauthor, and friend, Eduardo Peñalver. Our earlier work together and our friendship has literally paved the path for this project.

It should go without saying that I owe an immense debt to my wife, Kim. Throughout this project, she has shown patience, tolerance, and understanding, all born of love. For all of this, and more, I am in her debt more than I could possibly express.

This book is dedicated to the memory of Andre van der Walt. Andre inspired me in so many ways, through his prodigious and pathbreaking scholarship, his unstinting generosity, and his profound commitment to equality and human dignity. I shall truly miss him.

I have previously presented portions of this book in various venues, including: The South Africa Research Chair in Property Law International Conference in Property Law on "Property Law in the New Constitutional Dispensation," in Stellenbosch, South Africa, August 2017; a conference on constitutional property law, held at the National Autonomous University, Mexico; a conference on constitutional property law, held at Diego Portales University, Santiago, Chile; a conference on "Intergenerational Justice," held at the College of Law & Business, in Ramat Gan, Israel, in January 2013; a conference on "Competing Histories and Conflicted Spaces: Property, Ethnicity and Contested Memory in Post-War Societies," held at the University of Haifa and the Hebrew University of Jerusalem, Israel, in October 2012; a lecture at the University of Hong Kong; a lecture at Trinity College, Dublin, Ireland; a panel at the Law & Society Association annual meeting, in Hawaii.

Excellent comments and suggestions were provided at faculty workshops at Cornell (both in the Law School and the Department of Rural Sociology), UCLA, the University of Kansas, Tel Aviv University, the Hebrew University of Jerusalem, the Chinese University of Hong Kong, and Tulane Law School.

All or portions of some chapters have been previously published. These are:

Gregory S. Alexander, "The Social Obligation Norm in American Property Law," 94 *Cornell Law Review* 745 (2012).

CHAPTER FOUR

Gregory S. Alexander, "Intergenerational Communities," De Gruyter *Law & Ethics of Human Rights* 25, Walter De Gruyter GmbH Berlin Boston, 2014. Copyright and all rights reserved. Material from this publication has been used with the permission of Walter De Gruyter GmbH.

CHAPTER FIVE

Gregory S. Alexander, "The Complexities of Land Reparations," 39 *Law & Social Inquiry* 874. (Edited by Christopher W. Schmidt). ©American Bar Foundation, 2014. Published by John Wiley & Sons. Copyright and all rights reserved. Material from this publication has been used with permission.

I am grateful to the publishers of these journals for granting the right to republish here.

PART ONE

Human Flourishing

1

Flourishing and Welfare

Property serves human values,[1] but just what those values are is less clear. Property theorists differ in their accounts of the moral underpinnings of property,[2] and some do not clearly identify, let alone analyze, the values that constitute the moral foundation of their theories. The purpose of this chapter is to define as clearly as possible the value theory that I take to be the moral foundation of property law. In identifying human flourishing as property's moral foundation, my claim is both positive and normative. That is, a theory of human flourishing provides the best account of the value constitution that underpins the structure of modern property law. It is also the most morally attractive justification of property.

1. *See* State v. Shack, 277 A.2d 369 (N.J. 1971).

2. In the United States, the dominant theory is utilitarianism or some variant thereof, including law and economics. *See, e.g.*, Guido Calabresi & A. Douglas Melamed, *Property Rules, Liability Rules, and Inalienability: One View of the Cathedral*, 85 Harv. L. Rev. 1089 (1972); Harold Demsetz, *Toward a Theory of Property Rights*, 57 Am. Econ. Rev. 347 (1967). Other theories include Hegelian (*see* Alan Brudner, The Unity of the Common Law: Studies in Hegelian Jurisprudence (1995)), Kantian (*see* Arthur Ripstein, Force and Freedom: Kant's Legal and Political Philosophy (2009)), and libertarian (*see* Richard A. Epstein, Takings (1985); Robert Nozick, Anarchy, State and Utopia (1974)).

Property and Human Flourishing. Gregory S. Alexander.

I stress three points here: First, human flourishing, although overlapping at times with the concept of welfare, is fundamentally different from welfare and welfarism.[3] Second, human flourishing is a value-plural concept, encompassing multiple and incommensurable moral values or ends; hence property has multiple ends. Third, property's pluralistic moral foundation does not mean that rationality and consistency must be sacrificed when property's various ends come into conflict in particular disputes. Value pluralism is reconcilable with both rational choice and rule-of-law values such as consistency.

HUMAN FLOURISHING

In moral philosophy the concept of human flourishing is one of the main concepts in virtue ethics, the approach to normative ethics commonly associated with Aristotle.[4] Virtue ethics is distinguished from the other two main approaches to normative ethics, deontology and consequentialism, by emphasizing a person's virtues or moral character. That is, it says that actions should be guided not by duties or rules (deontology) or by the consequences of one's actions (consequentialism) but by whether an action would be virtuous.

Although the theory that I shall develop here is one that is based on human flourishing, it is not a virtue theory. Rather, it is consequentialist. It contends that the moral foundation of property, both as a concept and as an institution, is human flourishing; hence, human flourishing is the consequence, or goal, that property law strives to realize. In this sense human flourishing operates as a value term, like well-being.

The meaning of human flourishing has been the subject of a very wide range of responses in modern philosophical literature.[5] In its broadest sense, the concept of flourishing means that a person's life is good, or worthwhile. I shall refer to human flourishing in a particular sense here, however. According to the specific

3. It is worth noting that welfare differs from Aristotelian *eudaimonia* in that welfare pertains to states of affairs whereas *eudaimonia* describes actions. *See* Bernard Williams, Ethics and the Limits of Philosophy 79 (1985). This distinction accords with Aristotle's generally action-centered ethics.

4. Aristotle's term was *eudaimonia,* which is commonly translated as "happiness." "Human flourishing" is a better translation of *eudaimonia,* however, for reasons I will explain later. *See infra.*

5. Some idea of this diversity can be gleaned from the following very truncated list of sources discussing the question: Julia Annas, The Morality of Happiness (1993); William Galston, Justice and the Human Good (1980); James Griffin, Well-Being (1986); Martha Nussbaum, The Fragility of Goodness (1986); Joseph Raz, The Morality of Freedom (1986); Michael Slote, Goods and Virtues (1983); Charles Taylor, Sources of the Self: The Making of the Modern Identity (1989); Bernard Williams, Moral Luck (1981); Richard Wollheim, The Thread of Life (1984).

conception of human flourishing that I shall use here, a person's life flourishes when it goes as well as possible, that is, when the person lives a life of dignity, self-respect, and satisfaction of basic material needs.

There are two important characteristics of this conception of human flourishing. First, it is morally pluralistic; that is, it rejects the notion that there exists a single irreducible fundamental moral value to which all other moral values may be reduced (value monism). Rather, it conceives of human flourishing as including, but not limited to, individual autonomy, personal security/privacy, personhood, self-determination, community, and equality. These values cannot be reduced to a single basic value because they are incommensurable; that is, there is no available metric by which one can commensurate goods such as equality and personhood. (It is as if one states that Einstein's genius was "better than" Mother Theresa's compassion—the comparison makes no sense.) They are all aspects of human flourishing and cannot be balanced one against the other, although rational choices can be made between them in cases where they come into conflict with each other.

The second defining characteristic of flourishing is that it is objective. This is why "flourishing" is a better translation of *eudaimonia* than "happiness." The problem with "happiness" is that it connotes something that is subjectively determined. It is for me, not for you, to pronounce on whether I am happy, or on whether my life, as a whole, has been a happy one.

Contrast my being healthy or flourishing. Here we have no difficulty in recognizing that I might think I was healthy, either physically or psychologically, or think that I was flourishing and just be plain wrong. It is all too easy for me to be mistaken about whether my life is *eudaimon* not simply because it is easy to deceive oneself, but because it is easy to have a mistaken conception of *eudaimonia,* or of what it is to live well as a human being, believing it to consist largely in physical pleasure or luxury, for example.

As an objective theory, the human flourishing theory contends that "certain things are good or bad for us, whether or not we want to have the good things, or to avoid the bad things."[6] Stated even more strongly, some things can be intrinsically good for me even though I may hate it. Some people regard such a view as strange or counterintuitive. They consider well-being to be a matter of subjective judgment, that is, a thing is not good for a person unless that person endorses it. Subjectivists contend that welfare is a matter of subjective psychological states, or attitudes, like pleasure or desire.[7]

6. Derek Parfit, Reasons and Persons 493 (1984).

7. *See* Dan Haybron, The Pursuit of Unhappiness 13 (2008). Some subjective psychological states can themselves be good for a person. It is possible that pleasure itself contributes to a person's well-being.

Now, it is important to emphasize that in characterizing the human flourishing theory as an objective theory, this does mean that the theory claims that there is one and only way to live a life that goes maximally well. Far from it. There are many diverse paths to lead a fulfilling life, many ways of flourishing. At the same time, not every way of living that a person may choose to pursue, no matter how excellent an individual may become at his chosen path, is one that maximizes his well-being. For a Nazi SS officer, a life devoted to murdering Jews, no matter how excellently performed, is not a well-lived life.

HUMAN FLOURISHING AND CAPABILITIES

How can one measure human flourishing? Economists and others committed to welfare measure that value, of course, in terms of resources.[8] For welfarists, human welfare is a matter of satisfying subjective individual preferences, revealed through exchange transactions.[9] In recent years, Amartya Sen has developed an alternative approach to measuring well-being, one that does not focus on resources.[10] Sen's insight is that flourishing is a matter of what a person is able to do rather than what he has. That is, the well-lived life should be measured by a

8. *See, e.g.*, Louis Kaplow & Steven Shavell, Fairness versus Welfare (2002).

9. *See, e.g.*, Harold Demsetz, *Toward a Theory of Property Rights*, 57 Am. Econ. Rev. 347 (1967). This is not to say that welfarists are indifferent to the social good. Far from it; their objective is precisely to maximize aggregate social welfare. Hence, the human flourishing theory and welfarism, which derives from classical utilitarianism, share common ground insofar as they both hold a basic concern with the well-being of society. The two theories part company on two important points. The first point concerns the standard by which one measures well-being.

Welfarism measures it on the basis of what is commonly called revealed preferences, that is, the actual choices a person makes between resources. According to this theory, a society is better off to the extent that it maximizes the aggregate revealed preferences of its members. *See* Robert Sugden, *Welfare, Resources, and Capabilities*, 31 J. Econ. Literature 1947 (1993). The human flourishing theory, drawing upon Sen's work, rejects revealed preferences in favor of looking at the capabilities that are necessary for a person to flourish, that is, to live a well-lived life.

The second, and related, point of difference is that welfarism holds a conception of the common good that is subjective, whereas the human flourishing theory's conception is objective. As Sugden states, "Revealed preference welfarism purports to evaluate each person's circumstances in terms of that person's own system of values, without even asking what those values are. An aggregation of such independent valuations cannot be any kind of valuation at all." *Id.* By contrast, the human flourishing theory contends that although there are many ways of living a well-lived life, not every way a person may happen to choose to spend his life is good. The common good must have an objective dimension in the sense of filtering certain values, certain choices, or certain ways of living that are intrinsically bad.

10. *See* Amartya Sen, Commodities and Capabilities (1999); Amartya Sen, Development as Freedom (1999).

person's capabilities rather than by a person's possessions or by the satisfaction of his subjective preferences. What a person actually does with his capabilities is up to him, but his life simply cannot go well unless he at least possesses certain essential capabilities.

We could debate endlessly what capabilities are essential to be in a position to live a fulfilling life. Various philosophers, including Sen, have their own preferred lists of capabilities.[11] But four such essential capabilities seem uncontroversial. These are *life,* understood to include certain subsidiary values such health; *freedom,* understood as including the freedom to make deliberate choices among alternative life horizons; *practical reasoning*; and *sociability*.

No one can develop these capabilities by himself. The physical process of human development makes us dependent on others to cultivate the necessary capacities. Indeed, we are dependent on others for our ability to function as free and rational agents.[12] Our dependence on others is deeper. This form of dependence is perhaps most clear with respect to life and its subsidiary goods. We enter the world utterly dependent on others for our physical survival.[13] Even upon reaching adulthood, we continue to place at least partial physical dependence (and even emotional or psychological dependence) on others as we move through a dangerous world. Often, little more than dumb luck separates the independent adult from the dependent one. And, as we reach the final years of our lives, the possibility of physical dependence once again looms ever larger.

Life, freedom, practical rationality, and sociality can meaningfully exist only within a matrix of social structures and practices. Even the most seemingly solitary and socially threatened of these capabilities, freedom, depends upon a richly social, cultural, and institutional context; the free individual must rely upon others to provide this context. From the earliest age and well into adulthood, if not for our entire lives, we receive from and we rely on parents, teachers and mentors, and friends for lessons about planning and evaluation, causes and consequences, self-restraint and discipline: These are the raw materials from which the capability of practical reasoning emerges. We are, in short, inevitably dependent upon communities, both chosen and unchosen, not only for our physical survival but also for our ability to function as free and rational agents.

11. *Compare, e.g.,* Martha Nussbaum, Women and Human Development: The Capabilities Approach 78–80 (2000), *with* Sen, Development as Freedom, *supra* note 10, at 286–87.

12. Charles Taylor, *Atomism, in* Charles Taylor, Philosophical Papers: Philosophy and the Human Sciences, vol. 2, at 205 (1985).

13. *See* Alasdair MacIntyre, Dependent Rational Animals: Why Human Beings Need the Virtues 71–74 (1999).

Communities, including but not limited to the state, are the mediating vehicles through which we come to acquire the resources we need to flourish and to become fully socialized into the exercise of our capabilities.[14] Even as free, rational persons, we never cease to operate within and depend upon the matrices of the many communities in which we find ourselves in association. Each of our identities is inextricably connected in some sense to others with whom we are connected as members of multiple communities. Our identities are literally constituted by the communities of which we are members. Asked who we are, we inevitably talk about the communities where we were born and raised, our nation, our family, where we attended school, our friends, our religious communities and clubs. Indeed, individuals and communities interpenetrate one another so completely that they can never be fully separated.[15]

The communities in which we find ourselves play crucial roles in the formation of our preferences, the extent of our expectations, and the scope of our aspirations. The homeless person, accustomed to receiving little more than abuse or neglect, may come to expect little more out of life.[16] Similarly, although membership in certain communities can obviously be based upon contract or voluntary agreement, the very possibility of these voluntarily associative relationships depends upon our prior and continuing (and typically involuntary) participation in or exposure to communal institutions. These institutions impart to us the information and capacities that give us the tools needed to permit us to understand and engage in voluntary choosing at all.[17]

Beyond nurturing the individual capabilities necessary for flourishing, communities of all varieties serve another, equally important function. Community is necessary to create and foster a certain sort of society, one that is characterized above all by just social relations within it.[18] By "just social relations," I mean a society in which individuals can interact with each other in a manner consistent with norms of equality, dignity, respect, and justice as well as freedom and

14. The conception of community that I hold is more fully explicated in ROSALIND HURSTHOUSE, ON VIRTUE ETHICS (1999); MACINTYRE, DEPENDENT RATIONAL ANIMALS, *supra* note 13. *See* Chapter Three.

15. For an elaboration of this idea, *see* Gregory S. Alexander, *Dilemmas of Group Autonomy: Residential Associations and Community*, 75 CORNELL L. REV. 1, 21–28 (1989).

16. *See* SEN, COMMODITIES AND CAPABILITIES, *supra* note 10, at 21 ("A person who is ill-fed, undernourished, unsheltered and ill can still be high up in the scale of happiness or desire-fulfillment if he or she has learned to have 'realistic' desires and to take pleasure in small mercies.").

17. *See* TAYLOR, PHILOSOPHICAL PAPERS, *supra* note 12, at 196–98.

18. *See* Alexander, *Dilemmas of Group Autonomy*, *supra* note 15, at 1–3, *passim*.

autonomy.[19] Communities foster just relations with societies by shaping social norms, not simply individual interests.[20]

Precisely because capabilities are essential to flourishing in a distinctively human way, development of one's capabilities is an objective human good, something that we ought (insofar as we accept these particular capabilities as intrinsically valuable) to promote as a good in and of itself. As a matter of human dignity, every person is equally entitled to flourish. This being so, every person must be equally entitled to those things essential for human flourishing, that is, the capabilities that are the foundation of flourishing and the material resources required to nurture those capabilities. In the absence of these capabilities and supporting resources, recognition of the entitlement to flourish is simply an empty gesture. But not every society will be equally conducive to human flourishing. The cultivation of the capabilities necessary for flourishing depends upon social matrices, and the condition of those matrices varies among societies, sometimes quite widely. A society that fosters those capabilities that are necessary for human flourishing is morally better than one that is either indifferent or (even worse) hostile to their manifestation.

HUMAN FLOURISHING AND WELFARE DISTINGUISHED

The two defining characteristics of the human flourishing concept as I conceive of it—pluralism and objectivity—distinguish it from the concept of welfare, at least as modern economists and law-and-economics analysts use that term. Legal welfarists sometimes suppose that the concepts of welfare and human flourishing are synonymous,[21] but they are not, at least not in the sense in which law-and-economics analysts refer to welfare.[22] To see why, we need to dwell a bit on each of the two characteristics that distinguish the concept of human flourishing from welfare.

19. An alternative formulation for such a society is one that borrows from the South African Constitution, which refers to "an open and democratic society based on human dignity, equality and freedom." S. Afr. Const. 1996 § 36(1).

20. Of course, this is not to say that all communities promote just social relations. Many examples, past and present, exemplify communities that do not promote just social relations. The point that I am making is that communities have the capacity to do so by virtue of their social-norm-shaping function.

21. *See* John O'Neill, Ecology, Policy And Politics 71 (1993).

22. *See* Kaplow & Shavell, Fairness versus Welfare, *supra* note 8.

Value Pluralism vs. Value Monism

Welfare is an imprecise term, and it certainly could be understood to have the same meaning as flourishing. After all, welfare seems to mean "faring well," which is more or less what flourishing is all about. But the question is, faring well in what sense or what respect? Law-and-economics analysts define "faring well" in a particular way—whether one's personal preferences, taken as givens, are satisfied. One fares more or less well according to the degree to which one is able to maximize the satisfaction of one's personal preferences. Welfarism, in this sense, supposes that there is one and only one good—maximization of preference satisfaction.[23] All other values can be reduced to that single, irreducible value. Such a theory is a value-monist theory. Welfarism, specifically preference-satisfaction theory, appears to be a value-monist theory, although as I will discuss later, there is some uncertainty about that.

The human flourishing theory, by contrast, is unambiguously value pluralist. It rejects the view that the good can be reduced to one ultimate value, defining the good life instead as comprising multiple irreducible goods. As I discuss later, human flourishing itself does not constitute a unitary foundational value, one to which all other values are reducible.

Value pluralism is sometimes confused with political pluralism, and it is important to keep the two terms separate. Political pluralism is sometimes called value pluralism, but what I am calling value pluralism is a moral, not a political, theory. Political pluralism, which is often associated with Isaiah Berlin, is based on the premises that many diverse value systems exist throughout the world and that these value systems are presumptively entitled to respect and protection. For political pluralists, the question is what restrictions the state may legitimately place on differing values that individuals hold. Value pluralism, by contrast, is about values rather than value systems.[24] The question is whether the many different values that exist are really all reducible to one basic value.

The debate between value monism and value pluralism is about the structure of moral values. Moral theory recognizes many values, of course, but the relevant question is how these values relate to each other. In ordinary conversation, we commonly speak of many values that matter to us in our lives—love, friendship, happiness, freedom, beauty, justice, and so on—and we talk as though they are

23. *See* Daniel M. Hausman & Michael S. McPherson, *Preference Satisfaction and Welfare Economics*, 25 Econ. & Phil. 1 (2009).

24. *See* Elinor Mason, *Value Pluralism*, Stanford Encyclopedia of Philosophy (July 29, 2011), *available at* http://plato.stanford.edu/archives/fall2011/entries/value-pluralism.

all different from each other. In value theory terms, the question is whether all of these values can really be reduced to one basic value or whether instead they really are distinct from each other.[25]

The monist-pluralist dichotomy cuts across another set of distinctions that is familiar in moral theory, the three basic approaches to normative moral theory. These approaches are, of course, consequentialism, deontology, and virtue ethics.[26] There is no necessary correlation between any of these approaches and either of the ways of thinking about values, so in theory a monist could be a consequentialist, deontologist, or virtue ethics proponent. Similarly, a pluralist could subscribe to any one of the three moral theories. No moral theory has its own unique or distinctive way of looking at values. There are differences, however, in the ways in which adherents of the three types of moral theory look at the nature of value itself. Consequentialists look at value in terms of goods, such as knowledge, beauty, health, and so on.[27] They see value as residing in such goods. Consequentialists are not the only moral theorists to perceive values in these terms; virtue ethicists hold this understanding of values as well.[28] Deontologists, however, do not. Rather than translating values into goods, their vocabulary is one of rules and principles.[29] They ask about a plurality of principles, or a single overarching principle, rather than values or goods.

Regardless of their understanding of values, monists make the same basic claim. There is, they claim, only one fundamental value, whether that value is framed in terms of goods or principles. So, for example, Kant was a deontologist, and he was also a monist, for he argued that all moral principles are based on a single, objective moral value, namely, humanity (or human dignity), which he describes as having "absolute" and "objective" worth as an end in itself.[30] Similarly, utilitarians are monists, although they take a consequentialist, rather than a deontological, meta-ethical position. Utilitarians usually insist that there

25. *See id.*

26. Rosalind Hursthouse, *Virtue Ethics*, Stanford Encyclopedia of Philosophy (July 18, 2007), http://plato.stanford.edu/archives/fall2011/entries/ethics-virtue/.

27. *See* Walter Sinnott-Armstrong, *Consequentialism*, Stanford Encyclopedia of Philosophy (Feb. 9, 2006), http://plato.stanford.edu/archives/fall2011/entries//#WhaGooHedVsPluCon (citing G.E. Moore, Principia Ethica 83–85, 194 (1903)).

28. *See* Mason, *Value Pluralism, supra* note 24.

29. *See* Hursthouse, *Virtue Ethics, supra* note 26.

30. Immanuel Kant, *Groundwork of the Metaphysic of Morals*, *in* The Cambridge Edition of the Works of Immanuel Kant: Practical Philosophy 37, 78 [4:428–29] (Mary J. Gregor ed. & trans., 1996).

is only one moral value, variously termed as pleasure, happiness, social utility, or welfare.[31] They recognize that other goods—such as friendship, honor, and knowledge—exist, but they argue that all such goods are merely instrumental goods insofar as they serve to achieve the same basic good.

Pluralists resist such reductionism. They hold that there may be multiple values that are equally valid and equally fundamental and that these values sometimes conflict with each other.[32] Moreover, as we shall later see, pluralists often regard conflicting yet equally valid moral values to be incommensurable in the sense that there is no possible hierarchical ordering of them in terms of importance or weight.

Different forms, or levels, of pluralism must be distinguished from each other. At the bottom level, in the sense of being most singular, is foundational pluralism. This view holds that pluralism exists all the way down to the most basic level so that there is no single value by which we can judge the goodness of all other values.[33] The best example of conflicting views regarding foundational pluralism comes from articles by G.E. Moore and Judith Jarvis Thomson. Moore argued that goodness is unanalyzable.[34] He contended that when a person says that something is "good" the meaning is not purely descriptive, such as the thing contributes to happiness.[35] There is no getting beneath good; it is intrinsically basic. Thomson replied that there is a basic plurality of ways of being good. If I say that the movie was good, there are a number of different senses or ways in which the movie could be good, and these different senses of the movie's goodness are sufficiently distinct from each other that they cannot all be reduced to something that they all share in common.[36]

At the next level up is normative pluralism, sometimes called preference pluralism. This view rejects the claim that one moral value prevails over all others (e.g., autonomy over equality).[37] The normative pluralist denies that there is any one unitary normative standpoint from which all possible different moral values, which one might think of as "good-transmitters," might themselves be evaluated.

31. Moore, *supra* note 27, at 107; *see also* Amartya Sen, *Capability and Well-Being, in* The Quality of Life 30, 32–33 (Martha Nussbaum & Amartya Sen eds., 1993).

32. *See* Mason, *Value Pluralism, supra* note 24.

33. *See id.*, §1.1.

34. *See* Moore, Principia Ethica, *supra* note 27, at 6–16.

35. *Id.*

36. *See* Judith Jarvis Thomson, *The Right and the Good*, 94 J. Phil. 273, 275–76 (1997).

37. *See* Mason, *Value Pluralism, supra* note 24, § 1.1.

There is a plurality of good-transmitters, or value-bearers, but only one foundational good that they all bear.[38] Thus, one may think that aggregate well-being is the foundational intrinsic good but also believe that there are many bearers of well-being.

The final rung in the ladder of value pluralism is decision proceduralism. This view distinguishes between criteria of right action and decision procedures.[39] According to this view, which is held mainly by consequentialists, criteria of right action, like utility, are not intended to serve as decision procedures.[40] Rather, they claim, utility or other such consequentialist end is only a standard of what is morally right. An agent need not be able to calculate in advance whether all of the conditions necessary for the right action have been met. One could be a value monist in every other way but with respect to decisional procedures, choosing whichever one is most advantageous. This is the least demanding form of pluralism, then.

Finally, it is important that we be clear about distinguishing between a term that applies to a group of values and a term meant to suggest only one unitary value. The former meaning is consistent with pluralism, whereas the latter is consistent only with monism. Human flourishing is an example of the former meaning. It is a blanket term used to cover multiple irreducible values. This is why it is not a value-monist theory.

Welfarists have not always been clear in which sense they use the term "welfare." Is welfare a term that covers a number of different values which in these theorists' view cannot be ordered (meaning that welfare theorists are pluralists)? Or do they regard welfare as a single unitary value, in which case they are monists? Economists and law-and-economics analysts are preference-satisfaction welfarists, for whom the good consists of maximizing satisfaction of individual preferences. But if the good consists of whatever subjective preferences different people have, then in what sense is it unitary? The problem threatens to turn what appears to be a monist theory into a pluralist one. People, of course, have very different preferences. I prefer opera; you prefer NASCAR racing. These are quite different kinds of things, so since preference-satisfaction welfarism admits that all of these are equally valid, does this mean that it is really a form of value pluralism?

38. This does not preclude the possibility that goodness itself might be foundational, or a priori, meaning that a moral theorist could combine foundational pluralism with normative pluralism. Such was the case with G.E. Moore. Moore thought that although bearers of value possessed the same foundational value, they were plural with respect to the amount of that good. *See id.* § 1.1.

39. *See id.*

40. *See* R. Eugene Bales, *Act-Utilitarianism: Account of Right-Making Characteristics or Decision-Making Procedures?*, 8 AM. PHIL. Q. 257, 261–63 (1971).

On one view, all welfarists, including preference-satisfaction welfarists, are both foundational and normative (preference) monists because there is only one irreducible good (welfare); all other goods are merely instrumental and therefore not really independent goods at all. On another view, preference-satisfaction welfarists are foundational monists but normative (preference) pluralists by virtue of their commitment to preference satisfaction. From this perspective, only one thing—aggregate social welfare—is the intrinsic foundational good, but there are many agents the satisfaction of whose preferences contribute to social welfare. Stated differently, only one thing—welfare—is the ultimate value, but many things—satisfying the preferences that individual agents have—bestow value. It seems clear, at least, that preference-satisfaction welfarism is some version of monism. I shall have more to say about preference-satisfaction theory a bit later in this chapter.

Burnishing welfarism's monist credentials further is welfarist theory's ancestral roots in utilitarianism. Utilitarianism is a monist theory, and it is perhaps the most familiar example of such a moral theory. Although there are, of course, many varieties of utilitarianism (e.g., hedonism, preference-utilitarianism) all of its adherents agree that the right action is what maximizes the good, that is, utility. Economists and law-and-economics scholars distinguish between welfarism and utilitarianism.[41] Welfare economics, unlike utilitarianism, they claim, is a matter of description, not justification. In welfare economics a higher utility ranking does not justify individual choice. Rather, it is simply a convenient way of describing that choice.[42] Sen explains the distinction clearly:[43]

> [T]o say that [a] state of affairs with torture is better than a state of affairs without it, is not the same as saying that [a] policeman . . . *should* undertake this torture. That would be a judgment about actions, not about states of affairs as such, and the link between the two must depend on whether a consequentialist view is taken, and even if consequentialism were accepted, it would depend on the *version* of consequentialism to be used.

Many other scholars, however, equate welfarism with some form of utilitarianism.[44] To them, welfarism is not simply a descriptive theory but a moral theory, specifically, a theory that provide reasons or justifications for actions.

41. *See, e.g.*, Richard Craswell, *Incommensurability, Welfare, Economics, and the Law*, 146 U. Pa. L. Rev. 1419, 1424 (1998).

42. *See id.*

43. Amartya Sen, *Utilitarianism and Welfarism*, 76 J. Phil. 463, 474 (1979).

44. *See, e.g.*, Shelley Kagan, Normative Ethics 48 (1998); Roger Crisp, *Well-Being*, Stanford Encyclopedia of Philosophy, *available at* https://plato.stanford.edu/entries/well-being (last

Preference Satisfaction as a Value-Monist Theory

As a moral theory, welfarism, including both hedonism and preference satisfaction, is a value-monist theory.[45] It holds that welfare is the singular moral value to which all other values may be reduced. Welfarist theorists recognize other values, of course, but they maintain that all of those values are secondary, that is, they are merely instrumental to welfare itself.

It is difficult to justify welfare as a unitary value. A main, perhaps the main, objection to value monism is that it is implausibly reductive. Monists attempt to reduce all moral goods to some single irreducible evaluative standpoint, such as pleasure or desire. This attempt simply does not square with our everyday experiences. As Elizabeth Anderson states, "Our evaluative experiences, and the judgments based on them, are deeply pluralistic."[46]

How do we respond to situations in which we are faced with multiple, competing goods, like equality and autonomy? Utilitarians and welfarists respond by weighing the competing goods against each other. In doing so, they assume that the nature of the difference between the competing goods is simply quantitative and that, this being so, the rational solution to such dilemmas is to subject them to weighing by a common scale or metric, which, they assume, is readily available. This is a strategy of monism, and it is deeply flawed.

Many defenses of moral pluralism have been offered, most of them basically arguing that there is an irreducible heterogeneity of goods (e.g., knowledge, love, integrity, personal autonomy, etc.). I find particularly attractive Elizabeth Anderson's argument, which points out that there exists what I will call a pluralism of pluralisms,[47] and I shall rely substantially on her theory, along with Charles Taylor's.

The common denominator of all versions of value pluralism is their claim that apparently different moral values really are different from each other and irreducibly so. But values can differ from each other in more than one respect. What is attractive about Anderson's defense of pluralism is that it takes seriously everyday experiences, specifically, attitudes along with practices that reflect values. By examining such attitudes and practices, we can recognize

visited July 8, 2017); Patrick Moyes & Nicolas Gravel, *Utilitarianism or Welfarism: Does It Make a Difference?*, Cahier du GREThA no. 2011-30, *available at* http://www.vcharite.univ-mrs.fr/pp/Gravel/UtilWelf%20DT%20version.pdf.

45. *See* Chris Heathwood, *Monism and Pluralism About Value*, *in* THE OXFORD HANDBOOK OF VALUE THEORY 136, 140 (Iwao Hirose & Jonas Olson eds., 2015).

46. ELIZABETH ANDERSON, VALUE IN ETHICS AND ECONOMICS 1 (1993).

47. *See id.* at 14.

the multiplicity of differences among differences in moral values. Much in the way that ordinary language philosophy successfully draws conceptual insights from everyday expressive practices, ordinary attitudes and practices regarding moral values are a useful and reliable source of knowledge concerning moral questions.[48]

Looking to the evaluative attitudes and practices of everyday life, we can see how the differentiation of goods proceeds along multiple vectors. One vector concerns the modes of valuation.[49] Anderson points out that we employ distinctive evaluative attitudes toward different goods.[50] This is saying more than that different kinds of goods are different in different ways. It is saying that in our everyday practices we use different kinds of standards to evaluate different kinds of goods. When I say, "The Dalai Lama is a good man," I don't mean "good" in the same sense as when I say, "This cake is good." The standards I use in valuing the Dalai Lama and cake are quite distinct and resist reduction to any single or unitary standard. We have, in other words, a plurality of evaluative attitudes and standards in addition to a plurality of goods.

But in valuing something—persons, objects, whatever—that is, judging it to be good, we do not always employ standards. Sometimes we value people or things intrinsically, that is, simply for who or what they are.[51] Most parents value their children this way. This is partly what it means to say that we love our children unconditionally. But at other times we value things or persons because they meet a certain preexisting standard that we have. I value my favorite bakery's cake because it meets a certain standard of taste that I use in judging cakes, not because I value cakes intrinsically.

These two different ways of valuing things leads Anderson to observe that there are two conceptions of good. Although these two conceptions overlap with each other, they do not coincide perfectly. The broader sense is captured when we say that something is good simply when it is appropriately valued.[52] The second, narrower conception of good means that a person or thing is good because

48. This approach, relying as it does on everyday attitudes and practices, is not an intuitive approach. It differs from an intuitive approach in at least two respects: First, an intuitive approach does not identify the source of our intuitions; second, this method is more social than the intuitional method insofar as it concerns societal rather than individual attitudes and practices.

49. *See* ANDERSON, VALUE IN ETHICS AND ECONOMICS, *supra* note 46, at 8–11.

50. *See id.* at 8–16.

51. Goods may be valued either intrinsically, that is, for who or what they are, or instrumentally, that is, for what they can obtain or lead to.

52. *See* ANDERSON, VALUE IN ETHICS AND ECONOMICS, *supra* note 46, at 2.

it merits being valued by virtue of meeting certain preexisting standards of value that we have.[53]

As Anderson explains, these two different conceptions of good lead to two different conceptions of a plurality of goods. One conception is the idea that we value goods in different ways, ways that are irreducibly different.[54] The second form of pluralism concerns evaluative standards.[55] There exists an irreducible plurality of evaluative standards according to which we judge whether something is good or not. The standard(s) I use in judging whether or not a cake is good are irreducibly different than the evaluative norms that lead me to declare a Mahler symphony good.

Another vector of differentiation concerns the social dimension of valuation.[56] As Anderson notes, "[I]ndividuals are not self-sufficient in their capacity to value things in different ways."[57] The different ways in which we value things emerge from social settings which sustain the different modes of valuation. Anderson states, "To care about something in a distinctive way, one must participate in a social practice of valuation governed by norms for its sensible expression."[58] For example, the appropriate mode of expressing valuation of symphonic music in the United States is applause, that is, clapping one's hands together, and this distinct mode is learned in a social setting. The appropriate mode of expressing valuation of an oral presentation of a scholarly paper at a university setting in Germany is rapping one's fingers or knuckles on the table, a different mode that is also learned in a social setting.

A final vector of differentiation of goods involves the relationship between goods and self-image.[59] Our self-perceptions, of what kind of persons we are and what we would like to be, inform our perceptions of values. My desire to be an excellent scholar implicitly means that I value certain goods, goods which I strive to attain—to be clear, insightful, careful, and honest in my work. It means, moreover, that I have become acculturated in the norms of a particular community that has educated me about what goods are valued in the relevant social group of scholars of which I am a member.

53. *See id.* at 4.

54. *See id.* at 4–5.

55. *See id.*

56. *See id.* at 11–16.

57. *Id.* at 11–12.

58. *Id.* at 12.

59. *See id.* at 5–8.

Monism attempts to bypass these several levels of differences among goods by reducing them all to one fundamental value. This attempt ignores the evaluative attitudes and practices of everyday life, which inform us that we use multiple and fundamentally diverse standards when coming to value the variety of goods that we encounter in the diverse realms of our lives. It also denies the dependency of our evaluative standards on the particularity and diversity of social settings in which we deploy those standards. It implausibly supposes that one unitary fundamental value cuts across all social and cultural contexts.

As Anderson suggests, one way to test monist theories against pluralist theories is through ordinary experience.[60] Can the monist theory in question satisfactorily account for the entire range of ordinary evaluative experience? This means whether the theory can account for the variety of standards we ordinarily deploy when valuing people, things, and so on, in different spheres of social life. Can it account for all of the many goods, and the many kinds of goods, as we experience them, that we value in ordinary life? Elaborating on this last point, do those things that are valued as good by the theory match up with just those things that our experience gives us good reasons to value?

The version of monist value theory that is most common in property scholarship (and perhaps most common generally) is preference-satisfaction theory, which, as we have seen, lies at the heart of modern welfarism. Preference-satisfaction theory is a variant of rational-desire theory, which posits that what is good for a person is what she rationally desires.[61] Preference-satisfaction theory, or at least the most robust versions thereof, depart from rational-desire theory by dropping the condition of rationality. What is good for a person, what that person values, is what she or he actually prefers. Welfare economics, which posits a cruder version of this theory,[62] considers such preferences to be the actual preferences a person has as they are revealed through actual behavior. It is worth comparing the more sophisticated rational desire understanding of the good with the pluralist theory just described.

Although the pluralist theory and rational desire theory agree in identifying the good with the subject of a person's positive evaluations in everyday life, they part company from that point on. The first point of difference concerns rational

60. *See id.* at 118–19.

61. *See generally* RICHARD BRANDT, A THEORY OF THE GOOD AND THE RIGHT (1979).

62. *See generally* KAPLOW & SHAVELL, FAIRNESS VERSUS WELFARE, *supra* note 8. Whether objectionable actual preferences, say, racist preferences, should be ignored or cleansed in the welfare calculus is a controversial topic among welfarists. *Compare, e.g.,* JON ELSTER, SOUR GRAPES 20–24 (1983) (advocating elimination of improper preferences from welfare calculation), *with* KAPLOW & SHAVELL, FAIRNESS VERSUS WELFARE, *supra* note 8, at 422 (arguing that purging any preferences conflicts with individuals' basic autonomy and freedom).

desire theory's identification of the good with preferences. Rational desire theory does not account for all goods. It is not so much wrong as it is incomplete.[63] Objects of desire are aims that we wish to bring about or to obtain. Not everything that people value is something that we wish to bring about. Indeed, some of the most valuable goods to a person are not aims at all. A person values them intrinsically rather than desiring them in some motivational sense. Think of one's children, for example. A theory of the good that defines the good exclusively in terms of preferences or rational desires cannot capture most people's experience of valuing their children. Some additional value besides preference satisfaction, a value not reducible to preference satisfaction, must be at work to explain people's positive evaluations of their children.

The second respect in which value pluralism and rational desire theory differ is the inverse of the first point of difference. The category of desired or preferred objects is overinclusive in the sense that not all preferences are goods. This is so because of the logic of preference theory, which is maximization of preference satisfaction. If maximization of preference satisfaction is to serve as the sole basis of the good, then we must be able to represent preferences in a "single, complete, transitive preference ordering."[64] If a person's preferences can be represented, at least at times, only by multiple conflicting preference orderings, then some value other than preference satisfaction must be at work to determine which preferences indicate value.[65] In fact, preferences often do conflict. This occurs partly because preferences arise from multiple and diverse sources, ranging from rational evaluation to whim to habits and even compulsion. One possible response to the problem of conflicting preferences is to identify the strongest preference as the authoritative one, measuring strength on the basis of either experienced intensity or motivational effectiveness.[66] But this solution will not work. The problem with relying on felt intensity as the benchmark of strength is that it is very misleading. Often the desires that a person feels most intensely are compulsions or obsessions. If we define rational desire on the basis of what states of affairs on reflection we seek to secure for ourselves, then intensely felt desires will sometimes fail to meet the test of a rational desire.

If we use motivational effectiveness as the yardstick by which to measure intensity of desire, we encounter other problems. The motivational effectiveness

63. *See* Anderson, Value in Ethics and Economics, *supra* note 46, at 129–30.

64. *Id.* at 132.

65. *See id.*

66. *See id.* at 136.

measure endorses whatever desire actually leads a person to action, but such desires sometimes are the result of weakness of will. By this standard, people who are addicted to nicotine and who are trying unsuccessfully to quit have stronger preferences for cigarettes than they do for good health. But surely that is a misleading conclusion to draw regarding which preference is that person's authoritative preference. When preferences conflict, no intrinsic attribute of preference can tell us which preference is the authoritative index of value. We must look to some source outside of preference to determine that index.

THE INADEQUACIES OF VALUE MONISM OF PROPERTY THEORY

Value monism can be found in various forms throughout modern property theory.

Probably the best example is, as I have already indicated, welfarism; specifically, preference-satisfaction theory, the value theory that is the foundation of law and economics. Because I have already discussed some of the problems that confront welfarism and its theory of value, preference satisfaction, I will briefly examine two other monist property theories in this section: libertarianism and the neo-Hegelian personhood theory. Two problems appear in monist property theories. First, they do not maintain their monist character. That is, they both tend to slide into pluralism insofar as they introduce other values. Second, the preferred value of monist property theories does not account for all of property law but only for selected parts.

Consider first libertarianism. Perhaps the best-known spokesperson celebrating individual liberty as the single foundational value grounding all of property law is Richard Epstein, and among his vast body of property writings, the best exemplar of his libertarian view is his famous book *Takings*.[67] Epstein's book has attracted more than its share of critics, and one of the common threads of criticism is that Epstein does not consistently hew to his rights-based libertarian line. He blends libertarianism with more than a few doses of welfarist consequentialism. Epstein claims, for example, that his theory strictly protects property as a classically liberal natural right. But in explaining the foundation of this natural right, Epstein rejects the divine origin theory of Locke and Kant's pure reason theory in favor of utility maximization.[68] This move—attempting to marry individual

67. Richard A. Epstein, Takings: Private Property and the Power of Eminent Domain (1985).

68. *See* Thomas C. Grey, *The Malthusian Constitution*, 41 U. Miami L. Rev. 21, 36 (1986); *see also* Margaret Jane Radin, *The Consequences of Conceptualism*, 41 U. Miami L. Rev. 239, 242 (1986).

liberty as the fundamental value with utilitarian or welfarist constraints—is characteristic of much of Epstein's property scholarship.[69]

Epstein is not the only libertarian who fails to maintain a consistent commitment to individual liberty as the sole foundational value that does or ought to undergird all of property law. Barbara Fried has argued that the same problem besets Robert Nozick's theory of property.[70] Fried contends that in *Anarchy, State and Utopia*, Nozick actually has three theories, which she considers mutually exclusive—Lockean libertarian, utilitarian, and "anything goes, provided that citizens have some unspecified level of choice among legal regimes."[71] To the extent that any one of them predominates, Fried suggests, it is utilitarianism. Indeed, Fried goes on to suggest that most deontologists have not been able to provide detailed solutions to everyday moral problems on the basis of their deontological premises alone; rather, they have usually relied on assistance from welfarism.[72]

Not only do monist property theories tend to fail in their commitment to a single, unitary value as the foundation of property law, they also fail as comprehensive theories of property.

That is, they account only for limited parts of property law, conceding (usually implicitly) that the remainder of property law rests on other values. Margaret Jane Radin's personhood theory illustrates this problem. This limitation of Radin's personhood theory is indicated by the very fact that Radin herself concedes that her neo-Hegelian theory is not a general theory of property.[73] It applies only to those assets and those forms of social life that are (or should be) beyond the reach of the market. Even if we significantly reduce the market's realm, removing from it a number of assets or interests that may legally be the subject of market exchanges under current law, we would still be left with an enormous area of social life and an enormous part of property law about which Radin's personhood theory has nothing to say.

Both Epstein's and Radin's efforts tell us something important about the moral foundation of property law. It is too heterogeneous to be reduced to a

69. *See, e.g.*, Robert C. Ellickson, *Adverse Possession and Perpetuities Law: Two Dents in the Libertarian Model of Property Rights*, 64 Wash. U. L.Q. 723 (1986); Radin, *The Consequences of Conceptualism*, *supra* note 68, at103.

70. *See generally* Barbara Fried, *Does Nozick Have a Theory of Property Rights?* (Stanford Pub. L. & Legal Theory Working Papers Series, Research Paper No. 1782031, 2011), *available at* http://ssrn.com.abstract+1782031.

71. *Id.* at 4.

72. *Id.* at 27–28.

73. *See* Margaret Jane Radin, *Property and Personhood*, 34 Stan. L. Rev. 957, 958, 991, 1013.

single, all-encompassing moral value. Property law's heterogeneity has at least two dimensions. Radin's dichotomy between "personal" property and "fungible" property points to one dimension—the heterogeneity among types of assets (especially viewed in context).[74] As Radin wonderfully shows, although people experience many assets as market commodities, viewing them for their capacity to create wealth, they experience other types of assets in a fundamentally different way, reflecting a different valuation. It is different not in the sense of being higher or lower but in the sense of being an altogether different form or dimension of valuation. They value these "personal" assets for their contribution to and relationship with the construction of the owner's identity.

A second dimension of heterogeneity is social context. Here, I have in mind less the discrete realms of social activity (e.g., the family, the workplace, politics, etc.) that Michael Walzer famously described[75] than I do the myriad forms and means of social interaction. Epstein's inability to maintain a single-minded commitment to individual liberty illustrates, for example, how the passage of time not only affects the relations between past and present possessors of land but also implicates other goods—including wealth-maximization, the self-identity that accompanies long-term possession, and so on—beyond individual liberty in disputes between those possessors.[76] More broadly, recent judicial applications of the public trust doctrine to contexts in which recreation is the use in question illustrates how courts have recognized the importance of goods other than those expressed by the right to exclude.[77] These goods notably include friendship, sociality, and tolerance.[78] Goods such as these cannot be reduced to mere preferences. They are not simply objects of desire, the conditions of which can be specified in strictly nonevaluative terms, something we either have or do not have ("I just do.").[79] Rather, as we experience such goods, we recognize that in identifying them as valuable to us, we must employ standards that are evaluative, even emotional in nature. The need to use evaluative or emotional standards in identifying goods is one basis for distinguishing mere preferences from pluralist goods.

74. *See id.* at 960.

75. *See generally* Michael Walzer, Spheres of Justice (1983).

76. *See* Richard A. Epstein, *Past and Future: The Temporal Dimension in the Law of Property*, 64 Wash. U. L.Q. 667 (1986).

77. *See* Glass v. Goeckel, 703 N.W.2d 58 (Mich. 2005); Raleigh Ave. Beach Ass'n v. Atlantis Beach Club, 879 A.2d 112 (N.J. 2005).

78. *See* Carol Rose, *The Comedy of the Commons: Custom, Commerce, and Inherently Public Property*, 53 U. Chi. L. Rev. 711, 779–80 (1986).

79. *See* Anderson, Value in Ethics and Economics, *supra* note 46, 129.

Hanoch Dagan has pointed out that in property theory monism takes a structural form as well as a value form.[80] By structural pluralism he means the multiplicity of realms of social activity and corresponding legal doctrines and institutions with attending value foundations.

Thus, with respect to the family home, in relations between the owner and outsiders, the right to exclude is indeed paramount and appropriately so. In this realm, the law values individual autonomy and personal security. But in the context of marriage and marital property, a very different set of values prevails. Here, sharing, community, and cooperation are the values that are normative guideposts for the law. Individual autonomy and security are inappropriate as normative foundations for an intimate social relationship like marriage. This institutional multiplicity can be seen in further detail as we look at social organizations ranging from common-interest communities to partnerships.

What needs emphasis is the fact that beneath the structural multiplicity lies value pluralism that is both foundational and normative.[81] The existence of multiple social spheres each with attendant legal institutions and doctrines expresses the pluralism of moral values. The various legal institutions and norms embody the basic moral values that are at work in the social spheres that the legal institutions regulate. That the law creates such multiple and diverse institutions and norms is itself prima facie evidence that the underlying values are genuinely diverse and plural. Moreover, even within the same social sphere and same attendant legal institution or set of institutions, there may well be multiple and diverse fundamental values that conflict with each other or at least are potentially in tension with each other. Some property institutions may express both individual autonomy and cooperation or sharing, for example. In such situations we will need to determine whether the fundamental values are incommensurable and if so, whether a rational choice between them is possible.

PLURALISM AND VALUE INCOMMENSURABILITY

Value pluralism is often associated with the problem of incommensurability.[82] Some theorists suppose that if values are plural they must be

80. *See* Hanoch Dagan, *Pluralism and Perfectionism in Private Law*, 112 Colum. L. Rev. 1409, 1410 (2012). *See generally* Hanoch Dagan, Reconstructing American Legal Realism & Rethinking Private Law Theory (2013).

81. *See id.* at 1413–15.

82. For an argument that value pluralism does not necessarily involve incomparability qua incommensurability, *see* Ruth Chang, *Introduction*, Incommensurability, Incomparability, and Practical Reason 14–16 (Ruth Chang ed., 1997).

incommensurate.[83] But we need to be clear about just what we mean by incommensurate, for there is disagreement about its meaning.[84] One meaning is that incommensurable objects cannot be measured by a single common scalar metric. In this sense it does appear that plural values involve incommensurability. But others use the term "incommensurable" (or "incommensurate") as being synonymous with *incomparable*.[85] Strictly speaking, the two are not identical.[86] Incommensurables can be comparable. The side and diagonal of a square are incommensurable but comparable.[87] However, even if plurality does not entail incomparability, the plural (and incommensurate) moral values at conflict in a given situation may still be regarded as incomparable, raising the problem of whether rational choice between (or among) them is possible.[88] This is the problem that critics of pluralism commonly raise, and it is the one I wish to address. Hence, I will, following Joseph Raz,[89] treat incommensurability as synonymous with incomparability, which I think is the more serious problem.

Let us define two incommensurate goods as two goods about which no positive value relation between them holds. A positive value relation means that we can say that *x* is *better than y*, or *x* is *less than y*, or *x* is *equal to y*. If we can say none of those things about the relation between x and y, then they are incommensurate.[90] One can commensurate two or more values only in relation to what Ruth Chang calls a "covering value," that is, some valuable respect or consideration that they share in common.[91] So, two intrinsically valuable goods such as Bach's musical genius and Mother Theresa's kindness are incommensurate because they are valuable in fundamentally different respects. There is no covering value that enables

83. *See* Michael Stocker, *Abstract and Concrete Value: Plurality, Conflict, and Maximization, in* INCOMMENSURABILITY, INCOMPARABILITY, AND PRACTICAL REASON, *supra* note 82, at 196, 203.

84. *See* Chang, *Introduction, supra* note 82, at 1.

85. *See* RAZ, THE MORALITY OF FREEDOM, *supra* note 5, at 322.

86. Comparison does not require any single scalar metric of measurement. One alternative can be better than another in a relevant sense (e.g., moral) without being a certain number of units better. Items that are comparable can be ordinally ranked, that is, ranked on a list, but need not be cardinally ranked, that is, precisely ranked on the basis of a certain number of units of some scalar metric. *See* Chang, *Introduction, supra* note 82, at 2.

87. Stocker, *Abstract and Concrete Value, supra* note 83, at 203.

88. *Id.*

89. *See supra* note 56 and accompanying text.

90. *See* Elizabeth Anderson, *Practical Reason and Incommensurable Goods, in* INCOMMENSURABILITY, INCOMPARABILITY, AND PRACTICAL REASON, *supra* note 82, at 90,

91. Chang, *Introduction, supra* note 82, at 34.

any statement of a positive value relation between them to be made. Where there is a covering value, Elizabeth Anderson has developed a three-part test for incommensurability. Sharing a covering value, multiple goods are still incommensurable, she suggests, if (1) they both meet the standards measured by some scale but do so in very different ways; (2) there are no great differences in the extent to which each good meets the standards in its own way; and (3) meeting the standards in one way is not categorically superior to the other way.[92] Consider genius. There are multiple ways of meeting the standard of genius, but none of them is categorically superior to the other.

Bach's musical genius is beyond question, but it is not categorically superior to Shakespeare's literary genius. Each exhibited genius in the way appropriate to his own genre, which were quite different from each other. Neither displayed greater genius than the other, nor can we say that they were roughly the same in genius. But suppose that Shakespeare had developed the novel as well as written plays and sonnets. This imagined Shakespeare would be better than the real one, but would we say that he exhibited greater genius than Bach? This would make no sense. The situation exhibits what Raz calls intransitivity: Bach does not possess more genius than does Shakespeare, nor does the opposite hold true.[93] But there is a third option—the imagined Shakespeare—and this option is better than one but not the other. Intransitivity is the mark, Raz says, of incommensurability.[94]

Just how common is the phenomenon of incommensurability of values? It depends.

Values are guides for decisions or reasons for action. In this respect, values implicate the question of human agency.[95] There are, broadly speaking, two schools of thought about human agency. The crucial differences between the two are: First, the rationalist considers the agent's preferences as a reason for decision or action, whereas the classical school regards preference as an independent factor rather than a reason; second, the rationalist holds that incommensurabilities are relatively rare anomalies, whereas classicists consider value incommensurabilities far more common.[96]

The rationalist's move of regarding preferences as reasons is highly problematic.

92. Anderson, Value in Ethics and Economics, *supra* note 46, at 55.

93. *See* Raz, The Morality of Freedom, *supra* note 5, at 325–26.

94. *See id.*

95. *See* Joseph Raz, *Incommensurability and Agency, in* Incommensurability, Incomparability, and Practical Reason, *supra* note 82, at 110, 111.

96. *Id.*

Preferences are motivations, but they are not, at least not necessarily, reasons. Reasons require both information and reflection, qualities that preferences may or may not exhibit. My preference for vanilla ice cream over chocolate is not the result of information (at least not much) or reflection but instinctive reaction to taste. By considering preferences as reasons, rationalists cover the universe of motivations, thereby rendering the category of nonchoice among incommensurate goods an empty category. A nifty move, but unconvincing. Unconvincing and unnecessary. There is another way to approach the problem of rational choice among incommensurate goods that does not require treating preferences as reasons. I turn to that approach in the discussion below.

One final point about preferences needs to be added. Welfarists and other consequentialists sometimes try to avoid the problem of incommensurable goods by arguing that all preferences are complete, and that being the case, any two available options to someone who faces a choice between them are commensurable. The preferences are complete, the argument goes, because in a given situation the chooser may always be forced to choose, hence revealing her preference.[97] This argument succeeds by reducing preferences to choices, but that is surely a mistake. Choices are sometimes forced in situations in which it would be absurd to call the chosen option a "preference."[98] Sometimes choices reflect preferences, but at other times, choices are just choices. They certainly tell us nothing about values. The fact that a person's choices are complete is no reliable indicator of the person's value rankings. Hence, the preference maximizer cannot sidestep the problem of incommensurability.

THE OBJECTIVITY OF VALUES

The second defining characteristic of the human flourishing concept is the claim that moral values are objective. As Richard Arneson states, an objective "theory of what makes someone's life go best . . . is a complex animal."[99] Many analysts will deeply contest the claim that there are objectively valuable patterns of living. The question of whether and how an objective conception of moral values is possible is, of course, a central topic in moral philosophy. This is not the appropriate occasion for detailed discussion of the matter, but I do need to clarify what I mean by "objectivity" when speaking of moral values.

97. *See* Anderson, Value in Ethics and Economics, *supra* note 46, at 58.

98. Consider, for example, the eponymous choice posed in the novel *Sophie's Choice*. *See* William Styron, Sophie's Choice (1979).

99. Richard J. Arneson, *Human Flourishing versus Desire Satisfaction*, 16 Social Phil. & Pol'y 113, 117 (1999).

By "objective," I mean the notion that the truth of claims about what patterns of living are valuable is not strictly dependent on the subjective states of mind of the affected agents, or what Matthew Adler and Eric Posner call "mental-state views." Nor do they depend on personal preferences ("preference-based accounts" in Adler's and Posner's parlance).[100] Adler and Posner oddly distinguish between "welfare" and "value," arguing that "the nub of the difference" between the two is that welfare is "essentially responsive to the welfare subject's point of view," whereas value is not.[101] Their characterization of the welfare agent's subjective point of view as "the nub of the difference" is infelicitous. Just as many versions of "welfare" or "well-being" compete, so too do multiple conceptions of "value" compete. Indeed, because of the strong similarities between some counterpart conceptions of each, one can understand "welfare" and "value" as virtually synonymous. For example, one can understand value in preference satisfaction or even mental state terms. "Value" is a verb as well as a noun; hence, the value that inheres in something is, at least in part if not entirely, a function of someone actually valuing it. On this understanding, value is a matter of that person's mental state, rather than, as Adler and Posner have it, an objective matter in the sense that value is independent of mental states or preferences.

The objectivity of moral values is not necessarily inconsistent with taking subjectivity and subjective judgments into account. Sen points out that the fact that moral evaluation is "position-relative" does not imply that moral values are relative. Sen states, "Moral valuation can be position-relative in the same way that statements such as '[t]he sun is setting.' The truth of that statement varies with the position of the person, but it cannot vary from person to person among those standing in the same position."[102]

Although I shall not provide a detailed account of the arguments in favor of value objectivity, I will note quickly three lines of reasoning that seem especially persuasive in the protracted debate on the issue. First, when we deliberate or when we act, we always assume that there are genuine reasons for such deliberation or action (that is, unless we act arbitrarily or capriciously). We might discover that our deliberation has been erroneous or that we have taken the wrong action, but that is just the point. Such a discovery bears out the truth of the assumption we made—that there are correct or genuine reasons. As Allen Wood states it, "To be an inquirer or an agent at all is to presuppose that there are some reasons for

100. *See* Matthew D. Adler & Eric A. Posner, New Foundations of Cost-Benefit Analysis 29–32 (2006).

101. *Id.*

102. Amartya Sen, *Well-Being, Agency and Freedom: The Dewey Lectures 1984*, 82 J. Phil. 169, 184 (1985).

believing and for acting—whether or not we have found them, or ever will find them. In this way, to be an inquirer or an agent at all is to presuppose that some values are *real*."[103]

Second, and along related lines, we ourselves confirm the objectivity of values as we live our ordinary lives. Ronald Dworkin points out that our practices of arguing on behalf of values commits us to the proposition that some truth of the matter exists in the realm of moral values.[104] The common human practice of making normative arguments and assertions—"What she did was wrong!"—is unintelligible in the absence of a commitment to normative objectivity.[105]

The third line of reasoning emerges from the argument sometimes made that fundamental differences about moral values proves that values are strictly subjective, or matters of taste. That argument rests on a gross non sequitur. To be sure, fundamental moral differences do exist. But from the existence of disagreement between two individuals or two communities about the moral correctness of some action it does not necessarily follow that in principle the dispute is irresolvable or beyond genuine rational resolution. If the two parties are engaged in a dispute over the moral correctness of their respective views, then presumably they are capable of continuing their dispute to a final rational resolution of it.[106] That is, which moral values are valid can be known only at the end of dialogues between rival value systems, but those values were valid even prior to their discovery. The claim that the Earth is round rather than flat was valid even prior to its verification. Moreover, even if their validity is ever established at some final stage of moral debate, their validity still holds.

RATIONAL CHOICE AMONG INCOMMENSURATE GOODS

Are we left, then, with no alternative but to conclude that values are indeed irreducibly plural and thus that it is not (or at least may not be) possible to make a rational choice between two moral values? Can we make nonarbitrary (though contestable) decisions in such situations in the absence of an available metric?

103. Allen Wood, *The Objectivity of Value*, NEW LITERARY HISTORY, vol. 32, at 859, 867 (2001).

104. *See* Ronald Dworkin, *Objectivity and Truth: You'd Better Believe It*, 25 PHIL. & PUB. AFF. 87, 88–89 (1996).

105. *See id.* at 96. For other general defenses of moral objectivity, *see* JAMES GRIFFIN, VALUE JUDGMENT: IMPROVING OUR ETHICAL BELIEFS (1996); Philippa Foot, *Does Moral Subjectivism Rest on a Mistake?*, 15 O.J.L.S. 1 (1995). In addition, Daphna Lewinsohn-Zamir has developed an objective conception of well-being, which she applies to property law. *See* Daphna Lewinsohn-Zamir, *The Objectivity of Well-Being and the Objectives of Property Law*, 78 N.Y.U. L. REV. 1669, 1672–73 (2003).

106. *See* Eric Matthews, *Objectivity, Values, and History*, AM. PHIL. Q., vol. 10, at 213, 220 (1973).

I think there is an alternative, and it is one that resonates with suggestions that a number of other moral theorists have raised. To introduce it, let me quote a passage from Aristotle's *Nicomachean Ethics* in which he discusses *epieikeia,* or equity:

> [A]ll law is universal [generally], but there are some things about which it is not possible to speak correctly in universal terms. Now, in [those] situations where it is necessary to speak in universal terms but impossible to do so correctly, the law takes the majority of cases, fully realizing in what respect it misses the mark. The law itself is none the less correct. For the mistake lies neither in the law nor in the lawgiver, but in the nature of the case. For such is the material of which actions are made. So in a situation in which the law speaks universally, but the case at issue happens to fall outside the universal formula, it is correct to rectify the shortcoming, in other words, the omission and mistake of the lawgiver due to the generality of his statement. . . . There are some things about which it is impossible to enact a law, so that a special decree is required. For where a thing is indefinite, the rule by which it is measured is also indefinite, as is, for example, the leaden rule used in Lesbian construction work. Just as this rule is not rigid but shifts with the contour of the stone, so a decree is adapted to a given situation.[107]

As usual, Aristotle is highly instructive, not only about the problem of rules and standards but more generally about making practical decisions and the nature of the practical.[108] In this passage, of course, Aristotle is discussing practical reason, and practical reason is not solely concerned with means but with ends as well.[109] Aristotle reminds us that in living their lives, individuals are able to deliberate about seemingly intractable choices and to evaluate what ends are important to

107. Aristotle, Nicomachean Ethics bk. V., ch. 10, at 1137b–1138a (Martin Ostwald trans., 1962). The reference to Lesbian construction work is to its molding, which had an undulating curve. The Lesbian rule was "a flexible piece of lead which was first accommodated to the irregular surface of a stone already laid in position, and then applied to other stones with the view of selecting one of them with irregularities which would fit most closely into those of the stone already laid." 1 John Alexander Stewart, Notes on the Nicomachean Ethics of Aristotle 531 (1973).

108. The following discussion draws inspiration from essays by Charles Taylor and David Wiggins. *See* Charles Taylor, *Leading a Life, in* Incommensurability, Incomparability, and Practical Reason, *supra* note 82, at 170; David Wiggins, *Incommensurability: Four Proposals, in* Incommensurability, Incomparability, and Practical Reason, *supra* note 82, at 52.

109. *See* David Wiggins, *Deliberation and Practical Reason, in* Essays on Aristotle's Ethics 221 (Amélie Oksenberg Rorty ed., 1980).

them and why. They do not do so merely by relying on their personal preferences, which they treat as some sort of unexamined black box. Rather, they look inside the box and closely examine its contents. Nor do they do so by engaging in some sort of maximizing calculation but by reflecting, oft times in a kind of semiconscious way, on what really matters in their lives, where "what matters" pertains to considerations such as how they find personal fulfillment or what provides meaning for their lives.

In referring to "what really matters," I mean those actions, modes of behavior, personal characteristics, virtues, ways of life that deeply and honestly express and embody the kind of life that the individual regards as satisfying, worthwhile, and fulfilling—in short, good.[110] What may really matter to some people is kindness to others, best experienced by easing their suffering or discomfort. For others, what really matters may be something quite different—the esteem of one's peers, perhaps, or unshakeable courage, and so on. If those who consider kindness to be the most important good in life, or at least among the most important goods, reflect on what accounts for their valuation of kindness, they will come to a deeper level of understanding of their moral constitution. They will realize that the view they hold regarding kindness as fundamental to the good life relates closely to certain background understandings they have, such as basic views of the relationship between the individual and society, the nature of humanity, and so on.[111] In deliberating about the seemingly intractable choices between two or more irreducible but incommensurable options, individuals move, often (probably usually) unconsciously, between these different levels of reflection about what really matters. In doing so, they begin to break down what really matters, whatever it may be for them individually, into more finely grained essentials, elements, threads, and dispositions.

What emerges from this process, although usually not in any clearly articulated form, are evaluative criteria through which individuals are able to avoid impasses in their reflections about what really is worthwhile in life. They develop these criteria contextually, not in the abstract, in an all-things-considered method where all the things that they consider are the concrete elements immediately at hand. The criteria, then, may lack sufficient generality to permit a general ordinal ranking, let alone a cardinal ranking, yet the criteria are sufficiently definite and substantive to enable choices to be made among available options. As the excerpt from Aristotle quoted above indicates, this is what it means to be "practical" and

110. Charles Taylor refers to such actions, ways of being, and so on, as "life goods." *See* CHARLES TAYLOR, SOURCES OF THE SELF, *supra* note 5, at 93.

111. Taylor refers to these basic understandings as "constitutive good[s]." *Id.* at 92. They are constitutive insofar as they constitute the life goods themselves. *See id.* at 92–95.

to engage in practical reasoning. It cannot be distilled into any process that we can remotely characterize as maximization, for what really matters is not a unitary supervalue in the end. What really matters is complex, irreducibly so, and part of the point of the process of reflecting on it is to come to grips with its irreducible complexity.

As Aristotle emphasizes, the nature of practical reasoning is such that no blanket general (or "universal," to use the Aristotelian term) rule will be of use in the kind of cases we are discussing. "There are some things about which it is impossible to enact a law," he urges us to acknowledge. Our decisions, our choices between multiple incommensurable goods, are intensely and inevitably fact dependent. We ourselves don't rely on general rules that abstractly rank-order our values when confronted with such dilemmas, for such rules would fail us in these cases. They would fail us for exactly the reason Aristotle identifies—because "there are some things about which it is not possible to speak in universal terms."[112] In such cases we cannot use a "rule [that] is . . . rigid but [rather one that] shifts with the contour of the stone."[113]

To continue Aristotle's metaphor, the stone is what really matters, and the contour of that stone is not always clear. The process of reflecting on what really matters may reveal that it is not morally unambiguous, and in fact it is not even a single value when viewed in a particular context. Suppose that Jill is a graduate botany student doing fieldwork on local flora in Africa. She accidentally discovers that an indigenous flower, previously known only to the indigenous tribe, has properties that allow it to be developed into an anti-HIV vaccine. A significant portion of the local tribe is infected with HIV or suffers from full-blown AIDS. She also learns that the local tribe considers the flower to be sacred and uses it in one of its most important religious rituals. Jill faces a dilemma. On the one hand, she could disclose (possibly for consideration, which she then might donate or at least share with the local tribe) the existence of the flower to a pharmaceutical firm already engaged in manufacturing anti-HIV vaccines, or she could keep the flower's existence a secret, thereby protecting the sacred ritual of the indigenous tribe. Jill consults the elders of the tribe, presenting them with the facts of her situation and asking for advice. What course of action would be in the tribe's best interest, she asks? The elders conduct an informal plebiscite among the members of the tribe, who vote in favor of negotiating with a pharmaceutical firm. But the elders reject the results of the plebiscite and tell Jill that she should keep the flower's existence a secret. Jill worries about the fact that the elders have rejected the apparent wishes of the tribe. She is also troubled by the possibility

112. Aristotle, Nicomachean Ethics, *supra* note 107.

113. *Id.*

that the elders, none of whom has AIDS or is infected with the HIV virus, have not fully taken into account the interests of those who are suffering from AIDS or are HIV-positive.

What should she do? Reflecting on her choice, Jill realizes that what she values most highly in her life is being kind to others. Jill does not consider herself to be any sort of saint, but she does share Aristotle's view that humans are social animals. Further, she believes that interdependency is an inevitable aspect of the human condition. A little further reflection about what exactly kindness to others means leads Jill to realize that what kindness to others requires is not clear in this situation. She sees that it implicates at least two quite different goods, both of which matter a great deal to her. The first is respect for the tribe's autonomy and their dignity, as individuals and as a group. An important aspect of this good is nondomination—doing what she can to protect the tribe from being exposed to forms of outside encroachment on their autonomy that risk domination and loss of their way of life. At the same time, Jill is in a position to help the tribe, to reduce their suffering, by giving the pharmaceutical firm access to the flower so that it can produce the anti-HIV vaccine, which can then be made available to members of the indigenous tribe, per Jill's demand, either free or heavily subsidized by Jill and the firm. Both options involve acts of kindness to the tribe but in very different ways. Two different goods are at stake here, and they are very hard, if not impossible, to compare. If asked to rank-order them according to their importance to her in the abstract, she could not possibly do so. How can she possibly choose in this situation?

Charles Taylor's discussion of such situations is especially insightful.[114] Taylor suggests that the crucial aspect of Jill's reasoning will not be her weighting of the different goods but will instead be what Taylor calls "complementarity."[115] Rather than balancing the different goods—dignity-non-domination and improvement in health care—in the sense of weighing them against each other, Jill will consider how both goods fit together as pieces of a whole life that she is creating.[116] We are always in the process of becoming a certain kind of human being, and we must evaluate each choice that confronts us as a part of that ongoing process rather than as an isolated decision. Precisely because our lives are an ongoing process that is inconstant, unpredictable, and surprising, we would perhaps not fit the same pieces together the same way at different points in our lives. But at any given point in our lives, a point when we face the

114. *See* Charles Taylor, *Leading a Life*, *in* INCOMMENSURABILITY, INCOMPARABILITY, AND PRACTICAL REASON, *supra* note 82, at 170, 178–82.

115. *See id.* at 181.

116. *Id.* at 179.

need to choose between two fundamentally different goods, we do have some sense of our lives, where we are leading our lives, and what kind of persons we aim to become. It is that sense that enables us to see how the pieces fit together and then to decide.

Complementarity reasoning in Jill's case is agent-relative in nature. That is, it moves away from asking what is the right choice in terms of the competing values in general or in the abstract to asking what is the right choice for the person making it (in this case, Jill). At the same time, however, complementarity reasoning does not necessarily ignore the interests that others may have in the agent's choice. The agent's own vision of how she wishes her life to unfold and what kind of person she sees herself as becoming may well lead her to take the interests of at least some others into account. This is especially likely if she is responsible (and sees herself as such) for the well-being of certain others, ranging from close family members to individuals who are members of various communities or groups that nurture her own well-being in some clear way. The range of persons whose interests the agent takes into account may be broad or narrow, depending upon a wide variety of factors. The important point is that the agent-relative character of complementarity reasoning need not lead to total exclusion of others' interests.

There is no reason to suppose that when someone in Jill's position is able to make a rational choice between incommensurable values through complementarity reasoning she implicitly relies upon some sort of super-value that allows ranking of otherwise incommensurable values. That is not the character of Jill's reasoning when she considers how the multiple values fit together. She does not view the values in binary or zero-sum terms, a situation in which she chooses one and discards the other that has been trumped. Rather, they constitute pieces of the ongoing jigsaw puzzle that is her life—her self—and she values both pieces but must imagine how they can fit with the rest of the puzzle. There is no rejection of values, no trumping. There is instead fitting and refitting until a sense of complementarity—an understanding of the relative contributions the various values make in creating the kind of person she wishes to become—is achieved. Jill evaluates the contributions of each value by looking at them in their relationships with the others, not in a sense of weighing them against each other or ranking them (ordinally or cardinally), but in the sense of investigating how each value fits with the others.

COMPLEMENTARITY ANALYSIS APPLIED TO JUDICIAL REASONING

Jill's story is an example of practical reasoning in the context of personal morality, but does it have any relevance to political morality and to legal decision making? I think it does, and the key is Aristotle's discussion of equity and its relationship to

legal rules that I quoted earlier.[117] In that passage Aristotle intends to describe the equitable judge, but he also intends to describe the lawful judge, the judge who realizes that legality means supporting the legal framework as a whole. Acting equitably, Aristotle tells us, is not acting outside of or against the law. Much to the contrary, equity actually promotes the law by making it operate better. As a noted Aristotelian scholar, paraphrasing Aristotle, puts it, "The legal system works best when legislators know that defects in their products will not necessarily result in injustice, because equitable [judges] will be on hand to recognize the exceptions that were overlooked when the laws were adopted."[118] This is not a matter of rules versus standards or ad hoc decision making, for Aristotle favors "universal law," that is, rules. Aristotle recognizes, however, that rules, precisely because of their generality, will be deficient because they are too general. Lawmakers cannot possibly anticipate every conceivable circumstance, and even if they could, the rules that would emerge would be needlessly complex. Hence, there are gaps, some intended, some not.

The role of equity, Aristotle argues, is to enable legal decision makers to correct these deficiencies in legal rules, not as a matter of refusing to enforce the law in order to do justice as they personally see fit but as a matter of attempting to sustain the lawmakers' overall vision of justice, according to the decision maker's best interpretation of that vision.

The judge's role is to examine the vision animating the relevant legal rule, identifying all of the moral values underlying the rule. When multiple and incommensurate values are involved, the judge must engage in the kind of practical reasoning I described earlier, what I called complementarity analysis. But there is an important difference between complementarity analysis in Jill's case and as it is deployed in judicial analysis. I said earlier that in Jill's case complementarity analysis is agent-relative. Jill asks, among the competing values, what is the right choice for her, in terms of her personal vision of the kind of person she wishes to become, rather than what is the right choice in the abstract. A judge has a different responsibility than an individual like Jill. As Aristotle stresses, even when doing equity, a judge must remain faithful to the law. Specifically, the judge is obligated to develop the best interpretation of the lawmakers' vision of justice animating the rule in question, to identify the vision of what really matters from the lawmakers' point of view, and then to see how the competing and incommensurate moral values best fit together to advance that vision. The reasoning is still agent-relative insofar as the analyst is not asking what the right choice is in the abstract but with respect to some agent. The relevant agent, however, is no

117. *See supra* note 107.

118. Richard Kraut, Aristotle: Political Philosophy 110 (2002).

longer the analyst. Rather, it is a collective agent whose collective vision of what really matters the judge must do her best to identify. The judge strives to develop an objective understanding of the lawmakers' vision, but the reasoning process is inevitably interpretive and contestable. In Aristotle's metaphor, the contour of the stone sometimes is not clear, and reasonable people may reasonably discern its shape differently.

It is easy to see the attraction of monist theories such as preference-satisfaction welfarism for property scholars (and judges). They hold out the promise of providing a single correct solution to cases in which seemingly difficult choices must be made by drawing upon the fundamental value at work in their theory. But the promise is illusory. In property disputes, as elsewhere in the law, the apparent value conflicts are real. As I have argued here, no fundamental value is available to mediate these conflicts. The plurality of values that inhere in our legal property system—and other areas of the law—is irreducible.

Property scholars—and legal scholars generally—when confronted with the familiar dilemma of competing values facilely state that a solution can be found only through a balancing process. But exactly, analytically, what does this balancing process involve? Does it mean, for example, that we face a zero-sum situation in which we must choose one value and discard the other? I have argued that this need not—and should not—be the case.

The moral pluralist accepts the possibility that there are multiple ways to choose well between or among competing incommensurable moral values. In the context of both personal morality and law there are situations where more than one right option is available, and it is rational to choose among these options. This view puts pluralists at odds with monists, who consider it a failure of pluralists that they cannot unequivocally endorse one uniquely correct course of action. But this is not a weakness of pluralism. Buridan's ass can rationally choose one pile of oats over the other. The ass is not really choosing one pile over the other but rather choosing one of them over starvation.

PART TWO

Ownership

2

Ownership and Obligations

Private property ordinarily triggers notions of individual rights, not social obligations. After all, the core function of private property, at least according to conventional lore, is to insulate individuals from the demands of society both in its organized political form and its nonpolitical collective form. Of course, the common law has long recognized limits on the exercise of property rights, limits that grow out of the needs of others in cases of conflicting land uses.

The obvious example is the common law of nuisance, which courts developed using the ancient maxim *sic utere tuo ut alienum non laedas* ("use your land in such a way as not to injure the land of others") as their guiding principle. But such limits on property rights are the exception, not the rule, the periphery rather than the core. The core image of property rights, on this view, is that the owner has a right to exclude others and owes no further obligation to them.[1]

1. *See, e.g.*, Thomas W. Merrill, *Property and the Right to Exclude*, 77 NEB. L. REV. 730 (1998). For an insightful discussion of how the right to exclude has changed over time in American property law, *see* Eric T. Freyfogle, *The Enclosure of America* (Ill. Pub. Law and Legal Theory Research Paper Series, Research Paper No. 07-10, 2007), *available at* http://ssrn.com/abstract=1024846. Larissa Katz has recently drawn an illuminating distinction between ownership as an *exclusive right* and

Property and Human Flourishing. Gregory S. Alexander.

That image is highly misleading. The right to exclude itself, thought by many to be the most important twig in the so-called bundle of rights,[2] is subject to many exceptions, both at common law and by virtue of statutory or constitutional provisions. For example, the common law requires landowners to permit police to enter privately owned land to prevent a crime from being committed or to make an arrest.[3]

More generally, property owners owe far more responsibilities to others, both owners and non-owners, than the conventional imagery of property rights suggests. Property rights are inherently relational,[4] and because of this characteristic, owners necessarily owe obligations to others. But the responsibility dimension of private ownership has been sorely undertheorized in American law. Property theory has relegated the social obligations of owners to the margins, while individual rights, such as the right to exclude, have occupied the center stage.

OWNERSHIP AND OBLIGATIONS IN SOCIAL WELFARE THEORY

Among the contemporary theoretical work on the obligations of owners that has been done, two approaches stand out. The first of these is based on welfarist

the *right to exclude*. Arguing that exclusivity, not the right to exclude, is the core of the concept of ownership, she states:

> [O]wnership, like sovereignty, is an exclusive position that does *not* depend for its exclusivity on the right to exclude others from the object of the right. What it means for ownership to be exclusive is just that owners are in a special position *to set the agenda for a resource.*

Larissa Katz, *Exclusion and Exclusivity in Property Law*, 58 U. Toronto L.J. 275, 277–78 (2008) (second emphasis added).

2. *See, e.g.*, J.W. Harris, Property and Justice 154–64 (1996); J.E. Penner, The Idea of Property in Law 68–104 (1997); Felix S. Cohen, *Dialogue on Private Property*, 9 Rutgers L. Rev. 357, 370–71 (1954); Morris R. Cohen, *Property and Sovereignty*, 13 Cornell L.Q. 8, 12 (1927).

3. *See* Restatement (Second) of Torts § 204 (1965).

4. Some of the important writings on the relational aspect of property include the following: Joseph William Singer, Entitlement: The Paradoxes of Property (2000); Laura S. Underkuffler, The Idea of Property: Its Meaning and Power (2003); Jennifer Nedelsky, *Reconceiving Rights as Relationship*, 1 Rev. Const. Stud. 1, 16 (1993); Eduardo M. Peñalver, *Property as Entrance*, 91 Va. L. Rev. 1889 (2005); Jedediah Purdy, *A Freedom-Promoting Approach to Property: A Renewed Tradition for New Debates*, 72 U. Chi. L. Rev. 1237 (2005).

theory[5] and is best articulated by such important law-and-economics scholars as Robert Ellickson, Thomas Merrill, and Henry Smith. I will use their work as exemplars of the welfarist approach to the matter of property owners' obligations.

Welfare-focused analysts explain which affirmative obligations owners owe to their communities on the basis of transaction and information costs. A clear example is a paper by Robert Ellickson discussing the affirmative duties of owners.[6] Ellickson identifies three general reasons why lawmakers tend to be reluctant to impose affirmative duties on property owners. First, he claims that such duties impinge on a property owner's "freedom and self-actualization" more than negative duties do. Second, affirmative duties have a "disproportionate tendency," Ellickson asserts, to add complexity to property law. Finally, legally imposed affirmative obligations "diminish intrinsic motivations to act in the same manner."[7] When law does impose affirmative obligations on property owners, it does so because of welfare considerations, such as minimizing information costs. Lawmakers may impose such duties, for example, because owners possess special information that makes them the cheapest service provider. Similarly, Ellickson explains the obligation of animal owners not to abuse their animals and the obligations of parents to care for their children on the basis of minimizing transaction costs.[8] Moreover, certain affirmative obligations that law sometimes imposes on owners toward their neighbors are due to various transaction costs, according to Ellickson. Hence, municipalities sometimes obligate owners to shovel snow from abutting sidewalks. Such a law takes advantage, Ellickson argues, of "local knowledge."[9] The lot owner knows better than others which shrubs can withstand accumulated snow, and because the owner uses the abutting sidewalk more than others do, the owner has greater incentives to do the job well.

Thomas Merrill and Henry Smith do not discuss the affirmative obligations of owners at great length. Nevertheless, their approach is very compatible with

5. I take as unexceptional Amartya Sen's definition of welfarism as "the view that the only things of intrinsic value for ethical calculation and evaluation of states of affairs are individual utilities." AMARTYA SEN, ON ETHICS & ECONOMICS 40 (1988).

6. Robert C. Ellickson, *The Affirmative Duties of Property Owners*, 3 BRIGHAM-KANNER PROP. RTS. CONF. J. 43 (2014).

7. *Id.* at [51].

8. *Id.* at [53–54].

9. *Id.* at [56] (Ellickson borrows the term "local knowledge" from Thomas Merrill; *see* Thomas W. Merrill, *The Property Strategy*, 160 U. PA. L. REV. 2061, 2081 (2012). The phrase famously dates to CLIFFORD GEERTZ, LOCAL KNOWLEDGE (19)).

that of Ellickson. Indeed, Ellickson's work on affirmative obligations draws from Merrill's[10] and Smith's[11] work, authored both individually and together.[12] Like Ellickson, Merrill and Smith focus on transaction costs and, more particularly, information costs. They emphasize the information cost advantages of a system that delegates to owners the function of gathering information about uses of property.[13] This strategy, they argue, is cost-effective because it gives protection for a wide range of use about which government officials know less than owners.[14] The information-cost account of the structure of property focuses, then, on how powers regarding the uses of property are concentrated in the hands of owners. Analysts of this structure have very little, if anything, to say about the obligations these owners have to others.

OWNERSHIP AND OBLIGATIONS AS BASED ON RECIPROCITY

The welfarist approach to defining owners' obligation is premised on a social vision that, in the words of Hanoch Dagan, "underplays the significance of belonging to a community, perceives our membership therein in purely instrumental terms, and insists that our mutual obligations as members of such a community should be derived either from our consent or from their being to our advantage."[15] The second approach picks up where the welfarist approach leaves off, by taking the idea of belonging in a community seriously and building on that idea to develop a social-obligation theory that is liberal even while it focuses on community. In recent years, Dagan has most fully developed this contractarian version of the community-based conception of social obligation.[16] Dagan is committed to the project of normatively developing the social dimension of property

10. *See, e.g.*, Thomas W. Merrill, *The Property Strategy*, *supra* note 9; Thomas W. Merrill, *Property and the Right to Exclude II*, 3 Brigham-Kanner Prop. Rts. Conf. J. 1 (2014).

11. *See, e.g.*, Henry E. Smith, *Mind the Gap: The Indirect Relation Between Ends and Means in American Property Law*, 94 Cornell L. Rev. 959 (2009); Henry E. Smith, *Self-Help and the Nature of Property*, 1 J. L. Econ. & Pol'y 69 (2005); Henry E. Smith, *Property and Property Rules*, 79 NYU L. Rev. 1719 (2004).

12. *See, e.g.*, Thomas W. Merrill & Henry E. Smith, *Optimal Standardization in the Law of Property: The* Numerus Clausus *Principle*, 111 Yale L.J. 1 (2000); Thomas W. Merrill & Henry E. Smith, *The Property/Contract Interface*, 101 Colum. L. Rev. 773 (2001).

13. *See* Henry E. Smith, *Property and Property Rules*, 79 N.Y.U. L. Rev. 1719, 1755 (2004).

14. *See id.* at 1760.

15. Hanoch Dagan, *Takings and Distributive Justice*, 85 Va. L. Rev. 741, 771–72 (1999).

16. Hanoch Dagan, *Property: Values and Institutions* (2011).

law, both in the private and public legal spheres. A community-based conception of the ownership's obligations must be based upon a vision of justice that allows a nontrivial capacity for wealth redistribution. Such a conception seems to underlie the approach to property that Dagan has developed. His approach appears to be based on a theory of justice that is clearly liberal, but not *classically* so. The fact that it remains firmly tethered to the liberal political tradition is indicated clearly by his understanding of community.

Dagan's conception of community shares with the earlier versions of community a commitment to methodological individualism. That is, it assumes that the basic unit of social organization is an individual, understood as fully autonomous from one's very beginning.[17] From this perspective, communities are agglomerations of autonomous individuals, drawn together to act volitionally for the realization of certain shared ends. Community is valuable only insofar as it contributes to the satisfaction of some individual preference.[18] Community is never an end in itself. On this view, the relationship between the self and communities is both contractual and welfarist.[19] The self and communities are bound together by mutual agreement, sometimes express but commonly implied, to associate with each other to pursue some shared end.[20]

According to this contractarian theory of community, what motivates the self to act as a member of one or more communities is preference maximization. Individuals associate with each other in groups in order to maximize their own personal welfare. Individuals choose to act with others, to participate as members, if they hold what Charles Taylor calls "convergent" goods, which he distinguishes from "shared" goods."[21] Convergent goods are those in which individuals have a

17. *See* Dagan, *Takings and Distributive Justice, supra* note 15, at 771–74.

18. *See id.* at 791–92.

19. Dagan contends that his theory of community is not contractual but constitutive. *See* Hanoch Dagan, *Re-Imagining Takings Law, in Property and Community* 39 (Gregory S. Alexander & Eduardo M. Peñalver eds., 2009). However, he also rejects an ethics of sacrificing, arguing that owners should not be under any obligation that involves sacrifice on their part, but that owners should only be obligated to forego their preferred uses if a good reason exists to believe that an owner will gain some short- or long-term benefit in return for what the owner gave up. *See* Dagan, *Takings and Distributive Justice, supra* note 15, at 769–70. This connection between some foregone preference and reciprocal gain, however, is exactly what makes his theory contractual. To be sure, Dagan's theory does not require any immediate or direct tit-for-tat exchange, but it does limit the owner's obligation to forego preferred uses to situations in which the owner experiences some sort of state-enabled gain in connection with her property. The human flourishing theory is noncontractual precisely because it requires no showing of a likely gain, short- or long-term, to justify nonenforcement of some use that the owner prefers.

20. *See* Dagan, *Takings and Distributive Justice, supra* note 15, at 772–74.

21. Charles Taylor, *Social Theory as Practice, in* 2 Charles Taylor, Philosophical Papers: Philosophy and the Human Sciences 96 (1985).

common interest; for example, the common interest of tenants in preventing a fire in their building. By contrast, goods are shared when "part of what makes it a good is precisely that is it shared, that is, sought after and cherished in common."[22] The good is not mine—it is ours. With convergent goods, individuals interact in pursuit of individually defined ends that happen to overlap with the ends pursued by others.[23] The goods are not constitutive of the group or community.

From a contractarian perspective such as this, communities can only make demands of their members if those demands are likely to pay back each individual in the community in the long, if not the short, run.[24] That is, membership in a community, political or otherwise, does not ever warrant sacrifices by its members that are highly unlikely to remain uncompensated, even in the long run.[25] Uncompensated involuntary sacrifices violate the basic commitment to personal autonomy and the protection of legitimate individual expectations.[26] To expect individuals to make personal sacrifices for the common good is legitimate just insofar as accounts will even up in the long run, that is, so long as reasonable grounds exist to believe that the total long-term burdens that the individual bears will balance out the total long-term benefits she receives.[27]

What both welfarist theories and the contractarian approach to community have in common is a commitment to the primacy of individual preferences. In this respect both theories are descendants of the social contract theories that we associate with the names of Hobbes and Locke. They trade on "a vision of society as in some sense constituted by individuals for the fulfillment of ends which [a]re primarily individual."[28] As Fergus Kerr points out, "Such theorists insist so strongly on the primacy of individual interests that they encourage us to overlook our obligations to sustain the community to which we belong and owe our identity."[29] So asserting the primacy of individual interests, both welfare and

22. *Id.*

23. *See id.* (noting that shared goods are "essentially of a community," whereas convergent goods involve simply common interests of individuals, "irrespective of whether they have some common understanding of [them]").

24. *See, e.g.,* Hanoch Dagan, *The Social Responsibility of Ownership*, 92 Cornell L. Rev. 1255, 1266–67 (2007).

25. *See id.*

26. *See* Dagan, *Takings and Distributive Justice, supra* note 15, at 758.

27. *See id.* at 776.

28. *See* Taylor, 187.

29. Fergus Kerr, *The Self and the Good: Taylor's Moral Ontology*, in Charles Taylor 84, 88 (Ruth Abbey ed., 2004).

contractarian theorists have in common an understanding of humanness that attaches the highest importance to the individual's freedom to choose how to live one's own life. That understanding of what it is to be human leads these theorists to be highly skeptical of any account of individual rights or goods that involves an acknowledgement of dependence, for such an acknowledgement risks sliding into acknowledgement of obligations which might undermine the primacy of individual preferences. It is as though these theorists are concerned that any recognition of obligations, beyond the minimal obligations implied by the conventional understanding of the harm principle, would open the door to a wide array of social obligations and eventually lead to broad and radical redistribution of wealth.[30] Such an outcome, in their view, is fundamentally at odds with individual rights and personal autonomy.

This feared domino effect has little foundation, however. Unlike taxes, the obligations of property owners are specific, not general, obligations. They apply only to certain individuals or relatively small classes of individuals the ownership of whose specific assets triggers defined obligations to members of the communities to which they belong, that is, the communities on which they depend for the development of their very autonomy and well-being. The fulfillment of these obligations may involve a transfer of wealth in the sense that the owner has now made available to other members of his communities resources previously unavailable to them and valued by them. In such circumstances only transfers of discrete entitlements occur. No wholesale or systemic transfers of wealth are involved. The obligations may be relatively substantial for some property owners, but the important fact remains that the obligations are discrete rather than systemic or general. They apply by virtue of the specific asset which the owner holds.

More basically, acknowledgement of the inherently human condition of dependency and of its consequent obligations to others is entirely consistent with both the idea of individual rights and personal autonomy. Indeed, as I shall argue, personal autonomy is possible only in the context of dependence upon communities of others who facilitate the development of the capabilities which together are necessary for autonomy.

COMMUNITY, DEPENDENCY, AND OWNERSHIP'S OBLIGATIONS

An alternative conception of community exists that is more robust and, in that sense, more demanding than Dagan's contractarian theory. This alternative conception of community builds on the Aristotelian conception of the self as social

30. *See, e.g.*, Ellickson, *The Affirmative Duties of Property Owners*, *supra* note 6.

and dependent on others, rather than self-sufficient. This second conception of community might be called "holistic," in contrast with the first, which can be called "atomistic." The terms "atomism" and holism are borrowed from Charles Taylor,[31] and other scholars commonly apply the term to his theory.[32] Both terms point to the ontological character of Taylor's theory.[33] As Taylor wrote in an essay concerning his differences with Rawls, "the deep disagreements about justice can only be clarified if we formulate and confront the underlying notions of man and society."[34]

By "atomism," Taylor means the conception of human beings as individuals who are able to think, act, and even exist independently of social connections and dependencies. Taylor defines the term as one that applies to contemporary doctrines that grew out of the seventh-century social contact theory and that "inherited a vision of society as in some sense constituted by individuals for the fulfillment of ends which [are] primarily individual."[35] He says that it "represents a view about human nature and the human condition which . . . makes a doctrine of the primary of rights plausible. . . ."[36] He rejects such an ontology in favor of holism, by which he means that the human being is a social animal, a thesis the most famous articulation of which was that of Aristotle.[37] "Man is a social animal," Taylor states, "because he is not self-sufficient alone. . . ."[38] They are not self-sufficient in a particular sense—"that they only develop their characteristically human capacities in society."[39] This sense of non-self-sufficiency leads Taylor to emphasize dependence. He stresses the fact that although human beings value and strive for autonomy, dependency is an inherent aspect of the human condition. From this observation, he develops what he terms the "social thesis." I shall

31. *See* Taylor, *Atomism, supra* note 28, *passim*; Charles Taylor, *Cross Purposes: The Liberal-Communitarian Debate*, in CHARLES TAYLOR, PHILOSOPHICAL ARGUMENTS 181 (1995).

32. *See, e.g.*, Naomi Choi, *Practice-Dependence: Social Explanation as Normative Justification* 12–15 (unpub. paper); Arto Laitinen, *A Critique of Charles Taylor's Notions of "Moral Sources" and "Constitutive* Goods", *in* MORAL REALISM 73–104 (Acta Philosophica Fennica vol.76) (Jussi Kotkavirta & Michael Quante eds., 2004).

33. *See* Choi, *Practice-Dependence, supra* note 32, at 13.

34. Charles Taylor, *The Nature and Scope of Distributive Justice*, in TAYLOR, PHILOSOPHICAL PAPERS, vol. 2, *supra* note 21, at 289–317.

35. Taylor, *Atomism, supra* note 28, at 187.

36. *Id.* at 189.

37. *See id.*

38. Taylor, *Atomism, supra* note 28, at 189.

39. *Id.* at 190–91.

discuss that thesis at some length because it is foundational to the property theory that will be developed later.

THE ONTOLOGICAL FOUNDATION: THE SOCIAL THESIS

Taylor articulates his social thesis this way:

> The claim is that living in a society is a necessary condition of the development of rationality, in some sense of this property, or of becoming a moral agent in the full sense of this term, or of becoming a fully responsible, autonomous being. These variations and other similar ones represent the different forms in which a thesis about man as a social animal have been or could be couched. What they have in common is the view that outside society, or in some variants outside certain kinds of society, our distinctively human capacities could not develop.[40]

It is important at the outset to understand the kind of thesis this is. It is, first and foremost, a moral thesis. In developing an ontology, Taylor maintains that human beings are morally required to live in ways that are in keeping with their nature. Moreover, as we will see, his ontology rests on assumptions of what the good life entails. In this respect, the right and the good fuse because humans are obligated to live the good life. This does not mean that the good life is narrowly circumscribed. But, as we shall see, it does mean that a moral conception of the right necessarily rests on a conception of the good.

In addition to being a moral thesis, the social thesis expresses an ontological vision that is an alternative to individualism, or what he calls "atomism." It is the core of his critique of atomism. His alternative ontology (what Taylor has called a "philosophical anthropology"[41]) is a version of a holist ontology.

The critique of atomism is essential to much of Taylor's work, especially his moral, social, and political philosophy. As he points out, atomism is the ontological foundation for social contract political theories in all their garb that assert the primary of individual rights and preferences above all else and the role of society to protect those rights. What Taylor wants to do is to establish the inadequacy of atomism as the understanding of the self that underlies these doctrines by establishing a conception of the self in which sociality is understood as an inherent aspect of the human condition. As Naomi Choi states, "Taylor's social thesis

40. *Id.* at 191.

41. *See* Charles Taylor, The Explanation of Behavior 4 (1964). Taylor defines this term as "the study of the basic categories in which man and his behaviour is to be explained." *Id.*

advanced the explanatory importance of intersubjectivity as conditions for social life, for individual identity, and even for the affirmation of individual goods, since he believed selves to always be interpretively situated in meaningful social, historical, and cultural contexts."[42]

According to the social thesis, a thesis whose roots in Aristotle, among others, are apparent, the self is not and cannot be autonomous or self-sufficient in any deep foundational sense, for it is impossible for a person to become a rational, self-conscious agent without interaction with others and without the resources internalized from one's culture. Each person's orientation in life, her identity, and her sense of what really matters in life are formed by a process which is socially and culturally mediated. This is not to deny that there is such a thing as an autonomous, self-determining individual—Taylor is a liberal in the most basic sense of the term—but the identity of that individual requires a social matrix, he states.[43]

Taylor's conception of the self includes another important characteristic.[44] Humans are "self-interpreting animals."[45] Humans have a capacity for interpretation, and the exercise of that capacity is what gives meaning to things. As Nicholas Smith puts it, "Who I am, as a subject or person, depends on what is meaningful or what is an issue for me,"[46] and meaningfulness depends upon how I interpret issues or concerns. The process of interpretation can never be done from a disengaged perspective, for the self's agency is always embodied and engaged. The self always operates within a world and must cope with that world, including people. Hence, self-knowledge and self-interpretation are also embodied and engaged.[47] In the process of interpreting and understanding ourselves, we draw, usually unconsciously, upon many of the social and material resources within which we exist, our family and friends, our culture, and so on.

42. Choi, *Practice-Dependence, supra* note 32, at 13.

43. Taylor, *Atomism, supra* note 28, at 209.

44. Taylor's conception of selfhood has been immensely controversial and subject to differing interpretations. Some scholars have seen his work as caught in a conflict between an essentialist aspect and an historicist dimension. *See, e.g.*, Frederick A. Olafson, *Comments on* Sources of the Self *by Charles Taylor*, 54 PHILOSOPHY AND PHENOMENOLOGICAL RESEARCH 191 (1994). However, as Ruth Abbey argues, these are best seen as two different but complementary aspects. *See* ABBEY, TAYLOR, *supra*, p. 56.

45. CHARLES TAYLOR, HUMAN AGENCY AND LANGUAGE: PHILOSOPHICAL PAPERS I, 45 (1985).

46. Nicholas H. Smith, *Taylor and the Hermeneutic Tradition, in* CHARLES TAYLOR 24, 31 (Ruth Abbey ed., 2004).

47. *See* RUTH ABBEY, CHARLES TAYLOR 181 (2000).

People's interpretations of themselves are not arbitrary; rather, they are purposive. That is, self-interpretations always make reference to their purposes.[48] For Taylor, having purposes is an ontology feature of selfhood.[49] Humans are creatures with objectives, desires, preferences, wishes, and the like. Crucially for Taylor, however, people do not regard these objectives, desires, and preferences equally. They are not all on the same footing. Humans are what Taylor calls "strong evaluators," and as such they evaluate their own objectives and desires, ranking them, as it were. People have preferences about their preferences. Their evaluations, moreover, reflect how they see themselves in relation to others.[50] Strong evaluation is, for Taylor, a necessary part of identity,[51] and, like other aspects of identity, it is not something that we develop on our own. It reflects our inherent intersubjectivity.

The social thesis rejects the theory of procedural liberals that society is simply an aggregation of individuals each having a conception of the good and that the role of the polity is simply to effectuate those conceptions of the good as much as possible with the state remaining a neutral arbiter. His rejection includes even sophisticated procedural liberals like the later Rawls, who recognized that his conception of the liberal society requires a societally agreed-upon common understanding of what matters in the political community.[52] Importantly, however, that common understanding is one of the right, not the good. Even sophisticated procedural liberalism continues to spurn the idea of common understandings of the good as instantiated in political institutions and practices.

One reason why Taylor rejects even this more sophisticated version of procedural liberalism is that it is self-defeating. It cannot remain true to its own principles. As Taylor points out, procedural liberals must acknowledge that their vision of a free society is viable partly because the members of such a society give their allegiance to the procedural liberals' conception of respect for the right. They are willing to defend it against forces that would cause its collapse. Such allegiance, however, is more than merely convergent respect for the right. It is "a common allegiance to a particular historical community and its institutions, a willingness to cherish the particular achievements, institutions, and individuals that made this

48. *See* Charles Taylor, *The Person*, *in* THE CATEGORY OF THE PERSON: ANTHROPOLOGY, PHILOSOPHY, HISTORY 257, 259 (M. Carrithers, S. Collins, & S. Lukes eds., 1985).

49. *See* ABBEY, TAYLOR, *supra*, at 62.

50. *See* Naomi Choi, *Liberalism and the Interpretive Turn: Rival Approaches or Cross Purposes?* 77 The Review of Politics 243, 259 (2015).

51. *See* ABBEY, TAYLOR, *supra*, at 66.

52. *See* JOHN RAWLS, POLITICAL LIBERALISM, ch. V (1993).

political community what it is now."[53] But as Stephen Mulhall points out, "[I]f a procedural republic's very survival depends on its capacity to elicit such patriotism, then its avowed neutrality between competing conceptions of the good cannot extend to antipatriots—to those who lack or reject that allegiance to the community's history and heroes, whilst being ready to abide by the rules of the republic."[54]

The more fundamental point for Taylor is that it is fruitless to attempt to establish a political theory from some supposedly neutral vantage point. The political principles and values that we affirm, such as the neutrality of the state, the priority of the right over the good, and the freedom of individuals to pursue whatever vision of the good life they hold, necessarily rest upon "background conditions necessary to affirm those goods—such as the social institutions, cultural ethos, intersubjective meanings about the good, and ideas about selfhood—that make something of value in the first place."[55]

The social thesis is not opposed to the notions of individual rights and individual preferences *tout court.* To the contrary, it affirms the moral importance of natural individual rights, but it recognizes that to do so it is necessary first to acknowledge that humans develop those capacities that make them rational, responsible, autonomous beings only in society and that these capacities shape individual rights. Hence, these capacities have special moral status and command our respect.[56] This leads Taylor to take an important step in his argument. Because certain capacities command our respect, Taylor argues, it follows that we should acknowledge a "commitment to further and foster them."[57] Such a commitment means not only that we not interfere with others' exercise of their capacities but further that under certain conditions we ought to foster their development. Moreover, and crucially, Taylor argues, proof that these capacities can only develop within societies (really, only societies of a certain kind) is a kind of proof that we ought to belong to (that kind of) society—that we have an obligation to belong.[58] The capacity for maturation as a free moral agent requires such an obligation.

As some critics have pointed out, there are problems with Taylor's notion of an obligation to belong. For example, why does acknowledgment of the conditions of

53. Stephen Mulhall, *Articulating the Horizons of Liberalism: Taylor's Political Philosophy, in* Charles Taylor, Abbey (ed.), *supra,* 105, 115.

54. *Id.*

55. Choi, *Liberalism and the Interpretive Turn, supra* note 50, at 260.

56. *See* Abbey, Taylor, *supra,* at 193–94.

57. *See id.* at 194.

58. *See id.* at 197–98.

self-formation involve an obligation?[59] If belonging, being a member of a society and a culture, are natural conditions for humans, inherent in the process of formation of a concrete self, then how can it be a matter of obligation? There is no choice about the matter. We cannot be but members of particular societies and particular cultures. Second, even if we assume that belonging involves some sort of obligation, to whom or what exactly is that obligation owed? What exactly is the communal or social entity to which the obligation is owed?[60] And if we are obligated to belong, then what are we to say of the person who has chosen to be a recluse?

The idea of an obligation to belong requires some unpacking. First, what is the source of the duty? Is the obligation to belong imposed by society, or is it part of what it means to be an autonomous person? The idea of flourishing is that an individual has an obligation to define what flourishing means in her own life. That is, what it means to be human is to take on an obligation to oneself to live well. Ronald Dworkin usefully distinguishes between living well and having a good life. Each person, by virtue of her humanity, has a responsibility to live well but not necessarily to have a good life.[61] A person may live well but still have a bad life. She may have been the victim of bad luck or other people's actions. Or because, as Dworkin put it, "he dared greatly and failed."[62] I cannot always control whether I have a good life, but I can control whether I live well. At the same time, the good life is not independent of living well. I cannot create a good life for myself without appreciating the value of living well.[63]

Each person has a life to live, and that life is valuable. She has a responsibility to live it well just as she would take care of anything else that is valuable. Further, this responsibility is indefeasible; she cannot release or waive it. The obligation is intrinsic to her humanity. To be human as a rational, autonomous self-conscious being is to be obligated to live well.

Why, then, do we have an obligation to belong? The problem stems from Taylor's perhaps infelicitous choice of the term "belong." What he really has in mind is not simply the experience of belonging, but rather participating and supporting. The social object of the obligation to participate and support is not well-defined, but it is clearly more than the family or even the neighborhood. It is an entity that is quite broad. At one point, when discussing the context within which

59. *See* Nicholas H. Smith, Charles Taylor: Meaning, Morals and Modernity 148–49 (2002).

60. *See id.*

61. *See* Ronald Dworkin, Justice for Hedgehogs 195–200 (2011).

62. *Id.* at 200.

63. *See id.* at 196.

one develops the capacity for the kind of freedom by which people are capable of conceiving of alternative choices for themselves and defining what they really want, Taylor refers to it as "an entire civilization."[64] At another point, Taylor points out that "the free individual or autonomous moral agent can only achieve his identity in a certain type of culture . . ."[65] He emphasizes how special such a culture is and how fragile it is. Such a culture, he argues, must be supported.

Here the meaning of the obligation to belong comes into sharper focus. What it means to have an obligation to belong is that we are obligated to support the institutions, associations, and infrastructure that in turn support the special sort of culture in which we live (assuming that we are fortunate enough to live within such a culture), the type of culture within which each person is able to experience life-defining freedom and to create their own personal identities. The responsibility that we owe to ourselves to live well gives each of us an obligation to support the kind of culture that makes it possible for us to live well. This obligation applies to the recluse as well as to the joiner. Even a person who chooses to use her property to live as a recluse (if that is living well for her) must support the culture that makes a reclusive life possible. That culture must include some degree of social interaction and interdependence, even for the recluse, to provide the rudimentary necessities of life if nothing else.

Recall that the basis of this obligation is ontological. At an ontological level (an important qualifier) Taylor replaces the primacy of the individual with the primacy of the community.[66] As I stated earlier, however, this is not to say that Taylor writes the individual out of the equation. It is rather to say that what makes the ideal of individual's autonomous stance from society possible is the very fact that the individual is situated within the kind of culture that enables autonomy in the first place. As Ruth Abbey states, for Taylor, "a fundamental individual identity . . . comes from the fact of belonging to a community."[67]

Membership in a community is the logical basis for Taylor's social thesis. The logical argument, as Abbey aptly frames it, runs as follows:

> If I affirm *A* (individual autonomy), and
> If *B* (my membership in a community) is a necessary condition of *A*, then
> In affirming *A* I should affirm *B*.[68]

64. Taylor, *Atomism, supra* note 28, at 204.

65. *Id.* at 205.

66. *See* Abbey, Taylor, *supra*, at105.

67. *Id.*

68. *Id.*

The gist of the argument is a logical entailment: My affirming something that is good for me as an individual entails an obligation to members of the society to which I belong, for it is that society that enables such an individual good.[69] Stated a little differently, if I value some good, then I must maintain the conditions that make that good possible, that is, the community to which I belong and without which the good would not exist.

It is important to bear in mind that affirmation of something as a good is not a subjective matter. When I affirm something as a *good*, as a matter of strong evaluation, I affirm not only that it is good for me but that it is good in and of itself. Goods are goods because they have independent value, not because individuals want or prefer them. Their value lies in reasons that go beyond subjective preferences. Rights, for example, are good not simply because people claim them but because they are good in themselves. So, if I, as an autonomous moral agent, value the right to make free choices about how my life should go, I do so not as a matter of personal preference but because the right to make free choices about my life plan is good in and of itself. Insofar as people experience goods, such as the right to make free choices about my life, as valuable in themselves, such goods should be made available throughout the society that makes them available to me. The right to make free choices about one's life plan is as good for you as it is for me. Hence, the obligation arises.

AUGMENTING THE SOCIAL THESIS

Taylor's social thesis, although powerful (if controversial), supports a social obligation that is still somewhat sketchy and a little thin. To make it do more work in the context of a theory of property that is grounded in human flourishing, we need to add more details to it and to thicken its substance.

Let us call the original version of Taylor's social thesis the ST. We saw earlier that the ST must be refined so that "belonging" takes on a more carefully specified meaning. So refined, the obligation to belong really means that we are obligated to support the institutions, associations, and infrastructure that in turn support the special sort of culture in which we live, the type of culture within which each person is able to experience life-defining freedom and to create their own personal identities.

69. Ruth Abbey interestingly points out the similarity between Taylor's argument that affirming goods entails the affirmation of the conditions of their existence and Hegel's concept of *Sittlichkeit*. *Id.* at 106. In Hegel's theory what makes a society worthy of such affirmation and support is that it is founded on the "Idea," but Taylor prunes this aspect of Hegelian thinking, retaining only the core point that individuals owe an obligation to support the ongoing maintenance of the goods they enjoy, goods that their membership in the community makes possible.

This refinement is premised on an important point: The obligation to belong does not apply to just any society or culture. It applies only to a culture and a society that make available to us the goods that we value and that are valuable objectively. What this specifically means is that the free and autonomous moral agent owes this obligation to the culture and society of which she is a member only on the assumption that the culture and society are of the sort that value and foster individual autonomy and other capacities that we value (and that are objectively valuable). One does not owe the obligation to belong—in this thicker sense of belonging—to a society and culture that deny their members goods such as the right to determine one's own life plan. Insofar as they deny their subjects autonomy to determine their own life plans, dictatorships are morally entitled to no obligation of their subjects to support them.

Certain capacities are not conditioned in the way described. One does not need socially cultivated capacities to enjoy the benefits of the right to life, for example. So, at least for that right the ST is irrelevant.[70] The other core goods valued in liberal theory, however, do depend on a social background—a certain kind (i.e., liberal) of social background—for fostering and development.[71]

As a first step in augmenting the ST, we may draw upon Amartya Sen's capabilities theory, which we considered briefly in Chapter One. Although Taylor refers to "capacities" that humans need, he does not specify what these capacities are. Moreover, Taylor's capacities constitute the background of a person's moral status;[72] they are necessary for the exercise of the person's individual rights. Sen's capabilities overlap with Taylor's capacities. They include capacities such as rationality and self-determination, but they are broader and include human capital endowments such as health, education, and sociability. The aim of Sen's capabilities, moreover, is human flourishing. Capabilities such as health are necessary because without them, a person cannot live a well-lived life. Finally, recall that what matters in the human flourishing account is not whether a person exercises the necessary capabilities but whether she possesses them, that is, whether she is positioned to exercise them if she chooses to do so. This is the gist of Sen's distinction between "capabilities" and "functionings," and by focusing on capabilities Sen maximizes respect for personal autonomy. The concept of capabilities is more robust than Taylor's capacities, then, and it better fits a theory of property founded on human flourishing.

70. *See* SMITH, TAYLOR, *supra* note 59, at 145.

71. *See id.*

72. *See* David P. Schweikard, *On and Beyond Taylor's Moral Realism* (Book Review), 8 REDESCRIPTIONS: POLITICAL THOUGHT, CONCEPTUAL HISTORY, AND FEMINIST THEORY 254 (2004).

Drawing upon the capabilities theory, let us first revise and restate the ST in the following terms:

> *In order for me to be a certain kind of person—a free person with the basic capabilities necessary for human flourishing—I must be in, belong to, and support a certain kind of society—a society that supports a certain kind of political, social, and moral culture and that maintains a decent background material structure.*

Call this revised version the ST′. The ST′ not only substitutes capabilities for capacities, but it expressly focuses on the underlying goal—promoting human flourishing. Moreover, it explicitly acknowledges the need to maintain certain material conditions in addition to those social, political, and cultural conditions that are the requisite conditions for a humane liberal order.

These revisions both sharpen the focus of the thesis and hone its relevance for a theory of property grounded in human flourishing.

Having revised the social thesis in these ways, we are now in a position to ask, what obligations exactly does the ST′ involve? By detailing the content of the ST′, specifically what particular obligations we may reasonably ascribe to it, we will augment the ST in ways that will both thicken it considerably and render it the source point for identifying the obligations of property owners.

CATEGORIZING OBLIGATIONS

Initially, it will help to divide the obligations that fall under the ST′ into different categories, for there are several sorts of them. The obligations may be divided along two axes. One axis represents the distinction between those obligations that are negative in nature, restricting what we may do, and those obligations that are affirmative, requiring us to perform certain acts.

The second axis represents the distinction between what I will call general and specific obligations. A general obligation (GO) requires a person to assist in various ways in providing others with the basic material background conditions that are necessary for them to live to flourishing lives. It is general in the sense it is the obligation that any decent liberal society owes to its own members, that is, an infragenerational obligation concerning goods that such a society ought to save rather than consume. A specific obligation (SO) exists by virtue of a position that the obligation-holder has in society. The term "position in society" has a broad meaning, ranging from government officeholder to parent. Such positions carry certain specific obligations, which themselves range broadly. Some of these obligations are formal and originate from laws or contract; others are informal and are implied, either in fact or law. The key point is that each such position carries with it a variety of obligations that are peculiar to that position.

General Obligations

A general obligation (GO) is an obligation to assist in providing members of the various communities to which one belongs the basic material conditions that a humane liberal society needs for its members to flourish. It is an infragenerational obligation concerning goods that such a society ought to save rather than consume. These goods are constitutive of the requisite material background for flourishing. No one can flourish without certain basic resources that provide the background for existence.

Which resources properly belong on such a list of basic goods that provide the background conditions that are necessary for human flourishing is the subject of endless debate. Certain goods seem unarguably on such a list, however. These include a well-functioning public security system and an adequate defense regime. Both a well-functioning police force and national security system are indispensable for personal security, without which no one can live a well-lived life.

The background infrastructure would also include a clean (or reasonably so) environment—air, water, and so on—that future generational communities will inhabit and in which they will work. No reasonable conception of a well-lived life can encompass living in an environment in which people choke daily on air that is so fouled with man-made pollutants that the sky is literally colored copper. (I am thinking of present-day Beijing, but any number of other cities around the world would serve equally well to illustrate the point.)

The background conditions must also include a reasonably well-functioning government (including legal) system, one that is free (or relatively so) of corruption and is responsive to the greater community's needs. The requisite background infrastructure will also include well-functioning transportation and communication networks.[73] It will further include a health-care system that provides decent and affordable health care.

Who—which members of society—have obligations to provide resources to maintain these background conditions, and how may they fulfill their obligations?

73. Concerning transportation, consider our own current predicament. We inherited from the generations that preceded us a transportation system that once rivaled the rest of the world. Airlines ran on time; train service was extensive, relatively cheap, and convenient; highways, local and interstate, were well-maintained; bridges were safe and in good repair; and so on. As anyone who has flown or who drives knows, the picture has changed. Airline service unreliability is a topic of late-night comedians; train service has dried up in many parts of the country (including my home town of Ithaca, New York); highways are pitted with endlessly unfilled potholes; bridges are rusting to unsafe conditions in familiar important crossings. Some politicians periodically urge public investment in at least some aspects of this infrastructure, but little action is taken in an environment of declining public investment in collective goods. The transportation infrastructure has become an inherited capital endowment that the current generation is milking.

Most although not all of these GO obligations are met by paying taxes. The armed forces that preserve our national security are funded by federal taxes that we all pay. The police forces that protect our personal security are funded through local taxes that we pay. The legal system that resolves disputes, public and private, and that even makes the notion of a private right of property meaningful is supported by general taxes. The public infrastructure on which we all depend, including public transportation systems, highways, and so on, is funded by taxes or fees. The list goes on. This is part of the point that Stephen Holmes and Cass Sunstein made in their book *The Cost of Rights*.[74] All the rights that members of a decent liberal society enjoy, including both negative and positive rights, depend upon payment of taxes for their enablement. This is part of the grand "social contract" of classical liberal lore. The community, acting through the government, protects all of us and provides certain basic background material conditions in return for our payment of taxes. Of course, the reality is more complicated than that, and the systems by which GO obligations are met are much messier and more flawed than I have depicted, but the general outline of the arrangement is nevertheless accurate.

Specific Obligations

Specific obligations (SO) are more complicated. They are specific rather than general in three senses. First, an SO is peculiar to a specific person or group of persons similarly situated in a relevant sense; they are not shared by the community or society as a whole. Second, unlike GO obligations, which generally are satisfied in cash, different SO obligations are satisfied in different ways. Some are paid in cash; some in kind. Some require positive action (affirmative obligations); others involve restrictions on some type of action of behavior (negative obligations). Third, and perhaps most important, they are specific in the sense that individuals do not owe them to society in general but to specific members of the various communities to which they belong. Parents owe obligations to their children; members of churches, synagogues, or mosques owe obligations to other members of their religious communities; police officers owe duties to residents of the communities they serve; and so on. In each case, and many others, some specific obligation (or set of obligations) exists on the basis of a position that the obligation-holder has in society, and it exists with respect to members of the specific community of which the obligation-holder is a member and within which she holds the relevant position. As I discuss in the next chapter, these

74. Stephen Holmes & Cass Sunstein, The Cost of Rights: Why Liberty Depends on Taxes (1999).

	GO	SO
NEGATIVE	NO SPEEDING	NO TAKING BRIBES
AFFIRMATIVE	TAXES	SHOVEL SIDEWALK

Figure 2.1 Some Examples of General and Specific Obligations.

communities may be quite small (e.g., the nuclear family) or quite large (e.g., a city). The important point is that beneficiaries of the relevant obligation are the members of the specific community rather than society as a whole.

Specific, like general, obligations may be either negative (restrictive) or positive (affirmative). Criminal laws establish a set of general negative obligations for all members of the society to refrain from a variety of harmful acts to others. Tort law expands the set of negative obligations in a variety of ways. More controversial are positive obligations, duties that require us to perform certain affirmative tasks, ranging from shoveling snow off the sidewalk to pruning overhanging tree branches. Some of the affirmative obligations are rather trivial, others may be rather more onerous. Because the affirmative obligations require individuals to take some positive action, the tendency throughout law, including property law, has been to be more reluctant to impose such obligations than negative obligations.

Relating these distinctions to each other, we can create the grid, as seen in Figure 2.1.

Property Owners and Their SOs

All of this is well known and relatively uncontroversial, of course. What is more controversial is the specific role of property owners. To lay the groundwork for the special role that property owners play in the intricate network of obligations, GO and SO, positive and negative, we need first to return to the matter of revising the ST′ for the purposes of thickening it and tailoring its relevance to property.

Recall that ST′, as we last revised it, states:

> *In order for me to be a certain kind of person—a free person with the basic capabilities necessary for human flourishing—I must be in, belong to, and support a certain kind of society—a society that maintains a decent background material structure and that supports a certain kind of culture.*

We can extend ST′ in this way:

In order for me to be this kind of person—a free person with the basic essential capabilities—I must have, I must *own*, certain resources.

Ownership of resources is directed at development of those capabilities that enable me to live a flourishing life. Human flourishing requires not only virtues but also resources. Each of us requires resources to enable development of the capabilities that are essential for human beings.

The dilemma is that my ownership of resources deprives others of their opportunity to own and use the same resources.[75] My ownership of those resources, then, has consequences for others' opportunity to develop the same capabilities that enable them to live flourishing lives.

This contradicts my social obligation, that is, my obligation to support and sustain the very society that makes my flourishing possible.

This apparent conflict can be resolved the following way. In order for me to be this kind of person—a free person with the basic essential capabilities—I must *own* resources that enable the development of my necessary capabilities. However, in recognition of my obligation to support and sustain the very society that makes my flourishing possible, my ownership is inherently limited by that same obligation. My obligation to support and sustain the society that makes my flourishing possible requires that I promote the capabilities essential for members of my society to live flourishing lives. This obligation to support their capabilities at times includes the obligation to provide them with the material resources that are necessary for their capabilities to develop or at least not to deny them access to such resources. So, whenever my ownership of some resource denies another person access to the same resource and when access to that resource is necessary to develop some essential capability for that person, my social obligation requires that I, as the owner, permit that person to have access to the resource to the extent and in a way demanded by the capability (or capabilities) at stake. This obligation restricts my freedom as a property owner as a limitation that is inherent in the ownership interest itself.

One question that I need to address before proceeding is why ownership rather than a more limited property interest, such as use or possession, is necessary. The first point to notice is that ownership is not always necessary to satisfy the reason why individuals require access to resources under this revision of the ST′. That reason, recall, is to enable individuals to develop their necessary capabilities. The type of property interest the individual requires, then, depends upon which capability (or capabilities) is at stake. Not all of the capabilities require full ownership of the resource in question. As we will see in Chapter Five, for example,

75. In speaking of resources here, I refer only to private goods. This analysis does not apply, of course, to public goods.

sociability at least at times requires only a use interest in affected resources. On the other hand, personal security and privacy, especially with respect to one's home, commonly requires a more robust interest, either a possessory interest such as a tenancy or full ownership. Different types of property interests fit different capabilities.

It is important to bear in mind that this obligation to support commonly is not unrestricted. It is not a blanket one-size-fits-all obligation. The obligation to promote the capabilities essential for members of the various communities to which I belong is tailored to my particular position. That is, I am obligated to provide resources to others only in ways that are appropriate to me, given my position, that is, what I own, the needs regarding my own capabilities, and so forth. My particular position may be such that my obligation is narrower than what it would be if I were wealthier or younger or healthier or whatever. Hence, the social obligation does not require that I sacrifice my own essential capabilities for the sake of promoting the capabilities of others.

The bottom line is that under the ST′

> *the social obligation may require the owner to provide resources, in ways that are appropriate to that owner, to others in the owner's community (or communities) where necessary to support the development of their requisite capabilities.*

Recall the logical entailment that we saw previously: My affirming something that is good for me as an individual entails an obligation to members of the society to which I belong, for it is that society that enables such an individual good. Moreover, we noted that affirmation of something as a good is not a subjective matter. When I affirm something as a good, as a matter of strong evaluation, I affirm not only that it is good for me but that it is good in and of itself. It is not a matter of subjective preference or desire. My affirming resources as a good that enables my flourishing entails an obligation to members of my communities, the communities that support my flourishing means that I am obligated to provide them with requisite resources, *insofar as I am able and in ways that are appropriate to me,* so that they develop the capabilities necessary for flourishing as well.[76]

Where subjectivists, or atomists as Taylor calls them, go wrong is at the outset, by supposing that my flourishing, or doing well, is up to me, a matter that I control in the exercise of my personal autonomy. So, with respect to capabilities necessary for leading a well-lived life, it is up to me whether I lead a healthy life, whether I am educated, whether I am well-socialized, whether I can reason

76. *See* James Gordley, Foundations of Private Law: Property, Tort, Contract, Unjust Enrichment 8 (2006).

effectively about the choices I make, and so on. But the acquisition of none of these capabilities really is up to me, in a robust sense. I do not autonomously control throughout my life all the capabilities that are prerequisites for leading a well-lived life. I am dependent on other members of my various communities to develop these capabilities. Once we affirm that these capabilities are something that we value as good for us and once we acknowledge that we cannot develop these capabilities on our own but are dependent on others to enable their development, then we must acknowledge that we cannot but affirm the development of the capabilities in members of our communities as goods that we value without contradicting ourselves. Unless those communities and their members flourish, we cannot ourselves do so, part of which is to say that we cannot become the autonomous agents that subjectivists take us to be. This is why our obligations are so closely tied to, indeed originate from, our identity.

From this perspective we can begin to see why the obligations that we owe to members of our multiple communities cannot be premised, as some minimalist liberals do, on the harm principle—act in such a way so as to avoid doing harm to others. Even if that principle, as it is commonly understood, were not question-begging (which it is), it would not be an adequate foundation for our social obligations, that is, the obligations to assure the continued flourishing of our communities and their members. The harm principle rests upon a conception of the self, an ontological view, that is untenable. It is as though we are born into pods of self-sufficiency, instant and complete, and within that pod each person's obligation is strictly confined to avoiding colliding with others' pods. Beyond that obligation we owe others nothing, for they are strictly self-sufficient. Society is constituted by a network of contracts into which individuals enter for the purpose of satisfying subjective preferences.

That is a false image, both of the self and of society, however. No one is born self-sufficient, and no one lives a strictly self-sufficient life. Society is not strictly a matter of contractual agreements for mutual preference satisfaction. We are born dependent on others, and we continue to be dependent on others throughout our lives. We do not enter into pods of self-sufficiency but rather complexes of social relations that we call communities, the totality of which is society. Societies, in turn, develop particular cultures that express certain values, that is, conceptions about what is good. These societies and their communities, the communities that support us, that is, enable us to develop as free autonomous persons with certain necessary capabilities, require support, and that support must come from us, their constituent members. Hence, our obligations to others cannot be stated so weakly as the harm principle, as it is conventionally understood, does. They must encompass both affirmative as well as negative obligations. Moreover, they must include certain general obligations (GO) that apply to all community members regardless of the positions those members hold in their communities and certain

specific obligations (SO) that grow out of the positions the various members hold in their societies. The source of these obligations, again, is not contract, at least not strictly, but identity, that is, who we are as persons and as members of various communities.

These obligations certainly extend beyond the ordinary support obligations of all members of political communities, such as the obligation to pay taxes. Unlike GO obligations, these ownership obligations are specific to owners of property. Moreover, unlike the relatively thin obligations that most legal regimes of private ownership recognize, these ownership obligations have the potential to be quite thick, at least when compared with the thin obligations that emerge from the harm principle.

"WHY ME?"

Skeptics of a more robust conception of ownership obligation are apt to ask why the burden of such obligations should rest upon owners rather than being shared by all members of the community.[77] They take seriously the owner's indignant demand, "Why me?" After all, the benefits of the obligations are shared throughout the community, so it seems only fair that those who benefit from the obligation should carry their share of the load. This is a serious objection, and it deserves a detailed response.

The "why me?" objection rests upon a view of private law that emphasizes its autonomy from public law and public values. According to this autonomy theory of private law, the defendant's liability or obligations must correlate with the plaintiff's entitlements.[78] As Hanoch Dagan explains, this injunction of correlativity demands "both that the reasons underlying the plaintiff's right be the same as the reasons that justify the defendant's duty [] and that these very reasons also explain the specific remedy inflicted on the defendant."[79] Moreover, the stringency of these demands leaves no room for recognition of any social or public value.[80]

As Dagan insightfully points out, the "canonical [but often implicit] strategy for deriving the thesis of [strong] private law autonomy from correlativity is to rely on the idea of property." He explains that property is the benchmark of private law's isolation from social or public values: "[W]hile voluntary changes in

77. *See, e.g.*, Smith, *Mind the Gap*, *supra* note 11, at 959, 961.

78. *See* Hanoch Dagan, *The Limited Autonomy of Private Law*, 56 Am. J. Comp. L. 809, 812 (2014).

79. *Id.*

80. *Id.*

the distribution of property obviously cannot generate any legitimate grievance, involuntary changes both justify owners' complaints and specify the appropriate remedial response."[81]

This strategy cannot succeed. The concept of property, far from being the benchmark of private law's isolation from social or public values, exemplifies the inextricable relationship between private law's values and social values. Property's social and private law values are bound up with each other in two ways. The first results from property's status as an essentially contested concept.[82] Multiple theories compete with each regarding property's content, what its core meaning is, and whether it has such a core at all, and there is no objective basis for arbitrating these contests to a final resolution. A decision favoring one theory over another is not mathematical; that is, there is no Archimedean point from which a single uncontestably correct choice is available. All of this is obvious. What is less well known, or at least expressly acknowledged, is that the upshot is that a choice among the several competing theories of property unavoidably implicates and reflects social values. If I choose a theory that emphasizes the role that property plays in securing individual freedom against state coercion, for example, my choice reflects a normative vision that stresses certain social values above others. This will be the case for the choice of any particular property theory. There is no escaping the shaping force of social values in the choice among competing property theories.

Property's social and private values are bound up with each other in another way as well. Property, both as a concept and as an institution, has its own constitution. There are, of course, multiple sources of that constitution, but they notably include social as well as legal values.

Moreover, the legal values themselves derive from multiple sources, both private and public, including the common law and the federal and state constitutions. Property's private values relate to and interact with its public or social values, so that the two dimensions of property's value constitution cohere rather than conflict.[83] Moreover, not only are the values that inhere in public law norms compatible with the values that comprise property's constitution but further that such public values may at times be necessary for realization of private property's ends.

The upshot of this symbiotic relationship is that many nominally public values are internal to private law and are constitutive of its ends.[84] Because of our overlapping social spheres, which implicate both the public and private, values

81. *See id.* at 814.

82. This point and its implications for property's relationship to social values are made in Dagan, *Limited Autonomy of Private Law*, *supra* note 78, at 814–15.

83. *See* Gregory S. Alexander, *Property's Ends: The Publicness of Private Law Values*, 99 Iowa L. Rev. 1257 (2014).

84. Dagan, *Limited Autonomy of Private Law*, *supra* note 78, at 809.

such as equality and community have a Janus-faced character. They operate in both realms, being neither exclusively public nor private. When they work in tandem with more strictly private values, such as personal autonomy, they properly belong among private law's ends. When courts draw upon these values in adjudicating disputes between private parties, they draw upon private law's internal resources rather than impose values that are exogenous to private law.

At the same time, values that are usually considered to be public in character do not always function in this way. Values such as equality and community are internal to private law and are among property's ends just insofar as they are necessary to enable other, conventional private law values to be realized. To the extent that conventional public values are not needed to enable fulfillment of one or more traditional private law ends, then those values remain exogenous to private law.

Just what does it mean to say that fulfillment of a traditional private law end requires one or more conventional public values? Consider personal security, a private value commonly given prominent place in property theory. One reason why the right to exclude looms so large in discussions of what private ownership involves is the intuition that private ownership of property protects people insofar as they have the right to exclude others out from their personal dwelling. "A man's [*sic*] home is his castle" expresses an aspiration of security, among other values. The connection between property and personal security applies not only to land, but to money and intangible forms of property as well. For personal security includes financial security as well as physical security.

Personal security cannot be fully realized in isolation from other values, including public values. Consider the relationship between personal security and equality. Though hardly apparent at first glance, the relationship between the two values is in fact mutually dependent. If we understand equality in terms of nondomination or nonsubordination, then the relationship between personal security and equality is perhaps more readily perceived. In personal relationships, especially those that are highly personal, such as marriage, security sometimes requires equality among the parties to the relationship. It may also require equality in a financial sense as well, depending upon the relationship.

Consider marriage again. Hanoch Dagan insightfully analyzes marriage as an "egalitarian liberal community" that brings together three values—community, autonomy, and equality.[85] Dagan's conception of equality reflects the same notion of nonsubordination that I have used here,[86] but he also uses an equality-of-goods conception when he analyzes marital property law. Regarding that law, he argues, "[t]he core of the[] background rules [should be] the rule of equal sharing of the

85. Dagan, Property, *supra* note 16, at 200.

86. *See id.* at 206.

marital estate broadly defined."[87] The reason he gives for this core rule reveals the connection between equality-of-resources and security. Dagan states, "This rule aims to ameliorate the inevitable vulnerability that is an inextricable part of long-term relationships of trust and cooperation."[88] What Dagan refers to as "the inevitable vulnerability" is what I have been discussing in terms of personal insecurity. Dagan seems correct in arguing that vulnerability goes with the territory in any relationship of trust and cooperation. But vulnerability—personal insecurity—is a matter of degree, and in relationships of inequality, in the sense of power subordination or resource imbalance (or both), there is a good deal more vulnerability than where the parties deal with each other as equals operating at arm's-length from each other, as in a long-term contract between two merchants. Vulnerability and inequality go together, hand-in-glove. This is why equality, a public value, is necessary for the realization of personal security, one of property's important private ends.

The dependency of security on equality is empirical, not conceptual. It is conceivable that there are or have been unequal relationships in which the subordinated party enjoys personal security. Hierarchical social relationships do inherently create vulnerability, but the dominant party may not exploit that vulnerability. If it is not, personal security is possible. To be sure, this is a somewhat tenuous form of personal security insofar as there remains a risk that the dominant party will take advantage of the opportunity to exploit. But some degree of vulnerability is always uneliminable, even under conditions of equality. I may become the victim of a bad person or a tragic accident. A standard of no vulnerability for personal security is too demanding to be realistic or workable. As an empirical matter, however, it seems plausible to suppose that the degree of vulnerability increases substantially for subordinated or dominated persons.

Facilitation between security and equality works the other way around as well. That is, personal security promotes equality (again, as nondomination). Equality between persons in which one party is subject to ongoing harm or degradation of some sort (or the threat thereof), such as through physical or emotional abuse or massive financial loss, seems false. A relationship between two equals is one that is between two individuals each of whom can, speaking metaphorically, stand on her own two feet.[89]

87. *Id.* at 208.

88. *Id.*

89. One might imagine a relationship between two individuals who both are insecure in some relevant sense, say, between two battered women who seek each other's company for solace. Wouldn't such a relationship be one between equals, one might ask. This is a false sense of equality, it seems to me. It is a relationship between comparables, but not between equals.

Human flourishing is not strictly a private matter, a matter of becoming an autonomous agent who enjoys personal security and is self-determining in isolation from particular communities and from society more broadly. Flourishing, affected as it is by the social character of human beings, must itself be a social as well as an individual matter. Moreover, human flourishing is not a matter of simply the two dimensions—the social and the individual—together; rather, it is a matter of those two dimensions inevitably working together in mutually supportive ways. This is why the public values, which are the value that attend the social dimension, must be part of property's ends along with the private values.

At the same time, it is important to add that this view of the integral relationship between private and social, or public, values does not collapse the distinction between them. Dagan states, "The implausibility of isolating private law from social values does not render correlativity vacuous. . . ."[90] He suggests that in cases posing the "why me?" challenge, plaintiffs should be required to explain "why people in her predicament should be entitled to extract from people in the defendant's category the kind of remedy she now requires."[91] This seems unobjectionable as far as it goes. The problem is that, although Dagan intends this requirement to be an additional hurdle, it does not seem to distinguish one category of case from any other. In all instances in which private plaintiffs seek remedies from private defendants we expect the complainant to give reasons establishing why *this* remedy is appropriate vis-à-vis *this* defendant.

A more analytically rigorous way of handling the "why me?" challenge is to establish a "but for" requirement. Where a private defendant-owner feels that a remedy that a private plaintiff seeks against her would unfairly single her out and that the burden that the plaintiff seeks to place on her ought to be spread among the community as a whole, the plaintiff should be required to establish that but for the public, social, values that underlie the remedy which the plaintiff seeks, the private values that underlie the plaintiff's complaint could not be realized or protected. This "but for" approach requires the plaintiff to specify the social (public) and private values at stake and then establish not simply an instrumental fit between them but a fit of dependency of one—the private—upon the other—the social, such that one or more of the very aims of having a regime of private ownership of property would be sacrificed were the plaintiff's complaint against the defendant not granted.

This approach has several virtues. It acknowledges that public and private values, although at times closely interrelated, *are* separate. Further, it establishes a de facto primacy of private over public values in the context of disputes between

90. Dagan, *The Limited Autonomy of Private Law*, *supra* note 78, at 815.

91. *Id.*

private parties, particularly "why me?" cases, insofar as it imposes a requirement that the plaintiff demonstrate that the role of public values is to support private values, rather than the other way around. It is primarily the private values at stake with which we are concerned. The public values play a supportive or facilitative role. Finally, it moves far down the road toward answering the question "why me?" by putting into issue whether what the defendant-owner's use of her property has placed in jeopardy are private values, the very values that the legal regime of property is designed to protect and promote.

OWNERSHIP OBLIGATIONS AND WEALTH REDISTRIBUTION

Under the human flourishing theory, owners have various responsibilities, some general, others specific. To what extent do any of these obligations involve redistribution of wealth? Put differently, to what extent is the human flourishing a theory of wealth redistribution? It is important to be clear about this because the human flourishing is not primarily a redistributive theory. I say "primarily" in the sense that it is not motivated by justice notions of fairness such as that developed in John Rawls' *Theory of Justice*.[92] More important, it is not primarily redistributive in the sense that most of the specifically ownership-related obligations it recognizes are not premised on a redistribution of entitlements from owners to members of their community, although some of these do involve that. Most of the obligations that property owners owe under the human flourishing theory result from ownership of property itself. That is, they are inherent in what it means to own property and what ownership involves in a modern society. As to these obligations, what the theory does is simply to articulate them expressly, to unpack ownership, as it were. Other obligations, however, are not inherent in ownership, and as to these, the theory is redistributive. Which, then, is which?

For the most part, the distinction between the redistributive and nonredistributive obligations under the human flourishing theory tracks the distinction between general and specific obligations. Specific obligations generally are not redistributive; they are incidents of ownership. I am obligated not to commit nuisance on my neighbors, not as a matter of distributive justice but as a matter of what private ownership involves. So also with the other specific obligations I shall discuss in later chapters. General obligations are different. Consider a system of progressive taxation, which the human flourishing endorses. Such a system is property-related in the sense that it is tied to income or wealth, but as I indicated earlier, its basis is the background political arrangement by which all

92. *See* JOHN RAWLS, A THEORY OF JUSTICE (1971).

citizens reap the benefits of the polity's provisions of various goods and service in exchange for the payment of taxes. The progressive aspect of such a tax system is redistributive, but the underlying obligation is not.

SEARCHING FOR THE RIGHT METAPHOR

Metaphors matter. They are powerful ways of expressing our understanding of phenomena of the world we inhabit. The right metaphor often can crystallize understanding of ideas in a way that no other form of discourse can.

Property theory has witnessed its own search for the right metaphor. The ownership-as-castle trope has been with us for a very long time and has become a bit shopworn it seems.

Property scholars have expressed dissatisfaction with it[93] and have looked for alternative ways of figuratively capturing a recognizable articulation of ownership. A recent proposal has been a gatekeeper—the owner as gatekeeper who "who can decide who gets to do what" with respect to his property.[94] The image has much in its favor. It is simple, clear, and immediately recognizable. With it, it seems, we can immediately associate the owner with any of several commonplace experiences—a farmer controlling access to his land via a gate, the attendant at a private club who limits access to members and invited guests from his gatehouse, or the guard at the entrance to a (literally) gated community. Metaphorically, the term serves to capture the image of a secretary who screens visitors and calls from an employer, to a bartender.

Gatekeeping's figurative references now include all manner of modern experiences, ranging from agenda-setting to credentialing to software. Its popularity and breadth of usages indicate how easily we identify it.

For some property theorists, the appeal of the gatekeeper metaphor lies in its suggestion of a nearly absolute power to control access. This appeal is particularly strong for those theorists who regard the right to exclude as the essence of ownership. The gatekeeper metaphor emphasizes the owner's control over his property while minimizing his obligations.

Another metaphor that has gained currency within the past few decades, particularly with respect to land, is stewardship.[95] The owner-as-steward is attractive in some respects. Unlike the gatekeeper metaphor, it emphasizes the owner's obligations. A steward is responsible for shepherding and safeguarding the valuables of others. Some scholars and environmental activists have found the concept

93. *See, e.g.*, Joseph William Singer, Entitlement (2000).

94. Eric T. Freyfogle, *Goodbye to the Public-Private Divide*, 36 Envtl. L. 101, 114 (2006). Eduardo M. Peñalver, *The Illusory Right to Abandon*, 109 Mich. L. Rev. 191, 2015 (2010).

95. *See* Eric T. Freyfogle, *Ethic, Community, and Private Land*, 23 Ecology L.Q. 631 (1996).

attractive as a metaphor for a position of responsibility and caretaking of land and resources more generally. For example, Eric Freyfogle explains private ownership of land in terms of stewardship: "The virtue of private ownership is that it designates particular people as land stewards, charged with looking after the land and putting it to good use."[96]

Some scholars trace the inspiration for the stewardship conception of land ownership to the influential early twentieth-century conservationist Aldo Leopold and his famous "land ethic."[97] In his well-known 1949 essay by the same name, Leopold articulated the ethic in these terms: "A thing is right when it tends to preserve the integrity, stability, and beauty of the biotic community."[98] The idea was to expand the concept of community to include land and its resources so that obligations to one's community included preservation of and care for land and natural resources. In this respect, the stewardship metaphor is potentially appealing, for its source, the land ethic, would seem to place a premium on relationship. That potential remained unfulfilled, both in Leopold's own work and in ownership-as-stewardship work. While Leopold and his followers intensely focus on the relationship between owner and land, they tend to neglect the social dimension of the relational mise en scène. The relationships between and among affected persons and the obligations that owners owe to humans who are members of the owners' various social communities remain largely unexamined. This is a signal weakness in the stewardship metaphor.

As an alternative metaphor that highlights the relational aspect of ownership and that corrects the imbalance between the owner's control and his responsibilities, we might consider the owner as good neighbor.[99] It is easy to lapse into sentimentality or unrealistic preachiness when speaking of neighborliness, so we need to be clear-eyed in discussing what this metaphor involves. At a minimum, good neighborliness is a matter of respecting one's neighbor's legal rights. A good neighbor respects boundaries; encumbrances on his land benefiting his neighbor, such as easements; and laws prohibiting excessive noise and other rules restricting behavior in certain ways. Good neighborliness runs more deeply than this minimal requirement of complying with legal restrictions. Suppose that I do a lot of yard work. If I am a good neighbor, I will consider my neighbor's lifestyle

96. Eric Freyfogle, Agrarianism and the Good Society: Land, Culture, Conflict, and Hope 99 (2007).

97. Aldo Leopold, A Sand County Almanac 224–25 (1949).

98. *Id.*

99. Joseph Singer also mentions the good neighbor metaphor as an alternative conception of ownership. *See* Joseph William Singer, *How Property Norms Construct the Externalities of Ownership*, *in* Property and Community 57, 59 (Gregory S. Alexander & Eduardo M. Peñalver eds., 2010).

in planning my work. After learning that my neighbor works a night shift, I will delay running the power mower and using other loud equipment until the afternoon. Or suppose I have moved into a condominium that has a shared wall with a neighbor. When deciding where to position the speakers for my music system, I will avoid placing them against the shared wall. If my property has a lawn and garden, as a good neighbor I will mow my lawn and weed the garden regularly. This is not only a matter of keeping the neighborhood attractive but also preventing weeds from spreading. As a good neighbor, I keep a watchful eye on my neighbor's property, especially during their absence, even if I am not on an official neighborhood watch committee. If I see anything suspicious going on in or around my neighbor's home, I report the matter to the appropriate authorities. Finally, good neighborliness suggests that I communicate with my neighbors regularly, keeping them in the loop, and informing them in advance if I am planning to do anything that might disturb them (e.g., host a party).

The distinguished political theorist Nancy Rosenblum recently has insightfully written about good neighbors.[100] She analyzes that a "general ethic of neighborliness" entails. Minimally, it involves matters of decency—"warning of danger, acting in emergencies, avoiding arrant cruelty and wanton disruption."[101] "Beyond that," Rosenblum writes, "a general ethic of neighborliness might be defined by attentiveness and helpfulness."[102] Rosenblum argues that the "good neighbor" has a political dimension and that the experience of neighboring in America is not completely captured by the notion of a general ethic of neighborliness. She suggests the more robust regulative ideal that she calls the "democracy of everyday life."[103] Such an ideal, in Rosenblum's account, has three facets: "reciprocity among 'decent folk,'" "speaking out," and "live and let live."[104] In her nuanced account Rosenblum points out that "reciprocity among 'decent folk'" is a delicate matter, for there is such a thing as doing too much as well as doing too little. Terms, conditions, and time frames are seldom spelled out, so reciprocity requires considerable attention.

The phrase "decent folk," she suggests, designates equality, although in just one respect, that is, as neighbor.[105] "Reciprocity among decent folk entails the

100. *See* Nancy L. Rosenblum, *Good Neighbors: The Democracy of Everyday Life in America* (unpub. ms. July 24, 2015).

101. *Id.* at 7.

102. *Id.*

103. *Id.* at 9.

104. *Id.* at 10.

105. *Id.* at 13.

deliberate disregard for our neighbor's position in the wider society," Rosenblum argues, "and for the adversarial categories that shape our perceptions of the larger social world and that give politics its business. As neighbors we regard those living nearby personally and individually, and decline to approach them as representatives or symbols. Or we try."[106]

In "speaking out" we are on our own. We selectively, and hopefully judiciously, decide when to enter into engagement and when to let well enough alone. Speaking out against a noisy neighbor who bullies others is analogous to collective self-defense against domination, Rosenblum contends. Yet she quickly adds that the analogy is imperfect, as there is no action here against abuse of authority. Injustice in a political sense is not the issue.

"Live and let live," on Rosenblum's account, is an active rather than passive notion.

Rather than working against reciprocity, it involves attention to our neighbors' business. However, that attention is "infused with self-discipline."[107] Attention in this sense requires, for example, that we share with others information about our neighbors, upon which we invariably stumble, only when necessary. "Reticence is deliberate," Rosenblum writes, "rooted in appreciation of the value, the essential human necessity, and the fragility of control over personal life at home."[108]

Rosenblum's analysis of good neighborliness provides a valuable guide for adding content to the meaning of the same concept in the context of ownership. Its most important contribution in this respect is its emphasis on the highly social character of neighborliness. Neighbors are socially embedded, of course, but good neighbors take that fact seriously and act upon it. At the same time, as Rosenblum's careful dissection of the "ethic of everyday democracy" indicates, it remains private and respects privacy and autonomy. Although Rosenblum's account of good neighborliness differs in certain important respects from the theory of ownership's social obligations developed here—notably, in my rejection of reciprocity as the basis for those obligations—it points in the general direction of attention, care, sociality, and respect as hallmarks of good neighborliness.

More broadly, the owner-as-neighbor metaphor has several virtues that recommend it over its competitors. To begin with, it captures much of what is attractive about the gatekeeper metaphor. Hence, it retains the insight that the owner works within the private realm and, further, that he has a wide margin of control over his property. Unlike the gatekeeper metaphor, however, the good neighbor image captures the critical insight that ownership is relational. More specifically,

106. *Id.*

107. *Id.* at 22.

108. *Id.* at 24.

it focuses attention on the relationship between the owner and the communities within which he dwells. Good neighbors *are* good neighbors because they attend to the relationships they have with those who live around them. The relationship need not rise to the level of friendship to satisfy the conditions of good neighborliness. It is enough to respect one's neighbors, to maintain communication with them, to offer help when help is needed.

To the extent that the actions of good neighborliness that go beyond legal injunctions are a matter of moral obligation, the basis of the obligation to behave in a neighborly way can be explained in several different ways. Reciprocity is perhaps the most obvious explanation at hand. If I want my neighbor to treat me and my property in a certain way—with respect—I need to behave the same way toward him and his property. It is in my own self-interest to nurture the relationships with my neighbors, for the odds are that doing so will reap rewards from them down the road. (The converse is also the case: If I behave like a jerk toward them, they will likely behave that way toward me. Tit for tat.)

The moral obligation to be a good neighbor may also be justified in terms of the social thesis, which we discussed previously. As we restated it, that thesis holds that we are obligated to support the institutions, associations, and infrastructure that in turn support the special sort of culture in which we live, the type of culture within which each person is able to experience life-defining freedom and to create their own personal identities. We revised this thesis in the following way: "In order for me to be a certain kind of person—a free person with the basic capabilities necessary for human flourishing—I must be in, belong to, and support a certain kind of society—a society that supports a certain kind of political, social, and moral culture and that maintains a decent background material structure." This is the ST′.

The ST′ includes an obligation to behave neighborly. My obligation to support the institutions and associations that in turn support a culture within which I am able to experience autonomy and dignity implies that in my roles both as a property owner and a citizen more generally, I act in ways that enable the development in my neighbors of the same capabilities necessary for them to experience autonomy and dignity. My neighborly behavior enables my neighbors' capabilities to experience autonomy and dignity, and by doing so, it supports the cultural environment that enables my own autonomy and dignity. Culture here has a deeper meaning than the arts, literature, and the like. In this deeper sense culture refers to the customary ways in which individuals interact with each other in routine daily or occasional transactions. It includes the social norms that guide the behavior of most people in such interactions. A society whose members take the ST′ seriously is characterized by a culture in which neighborliness is sufficiently ingrained that it is both a moral obligation and a social norm. Such a society need not be utopian. It is sufficient if a substantial portion of the society's members

behave in neighborly ways—treating others with respect and dignity—most of the time. Such societies do exist, and in general they are characterized by cultures that enable individuals to experience autonomy and dignity.

The most important advantage of the owner-as-good-neighbor metaphor over the gatekeeper metaphor is that it better fits with property's foundation—promoting human flourishing. It does so by drawing attention to the connection between ownership and development of the capabilities necessary for human flourishing, including personal autonomy, dignity, sociability, and other capabilities. It highlights the facts that owners are members of communities and that those communities foster the development of the owners' necessary capabilities. The gatekeeper metaphor creates an illusion of isolation; the neighbor metaphor stresses the socially embedded condition of property owners.

OWNERSHIP, OBLIGATIONS, AND COMMUNITY

Owners owe obligations, then. First, as rational human beings, they owe to themselves the responsibility to live well, to take care of the life that has been given to them. Next, this obligation that each person owes to herself yields a further obligation to support a certain kind of social life. Such a social environment is one that makes it possible to provide the kind of culture that enables development of her essential capabilities.[109] The obligation to support the social environment that makes it possible for me to develop the capabilities that are essential for my flourishing specifically means that I am obligated to the various communities that support me and enable me to develop those capabilities. My affirming resources as a good that enables my flourishing entails an obligation to members of my communities, the communities that support my flourishing means that I am obligated to provide them with requisite resources, *insofar as I am able and in ways that are appropriate to me,* so that they develop the capabilities necessary for flourishing as well.

Because of the important role that communities play in the development of our capabilities, I need to make clear just what I mean by communities. After all, it is communities that are the center of the kind of social life that I said is fundamental to our leading flourishing lives. The next chapter explains in some detail exactly to what sorts of social units the term community refers under the human flourishing theory.

109. This bears some resemblance to the idea of being obligated to act on one's "relationship-dependent reasons" made in Samuel Scheffler, *Membership and Political Obligation*, 25 J. Pol. Phil. (2017).

3

Community and Communities

Community is a notoriously slippery concept.[1] Both as a social institution and as a value, community has many diverse forms. Yet its diversity does not render it meaningless or useless, for the fact is that we, all of us, live our lives as members of communities, usually several of them simultaneously. In Chapter One, I noted that communities are the mediating vehicles through which we acquire the capabilities necessary for a flourishing life. In Chapter Two, I argued that each of us is obligated to belong to and support the various communities that nurture the development of our necessary capabilities. These arguments suggest that community and communities play a key role in the human flourishing theory

1. A 1955 study found ninety-four definitions of "community" in the scholarly literature, and there was little that these definitions shared among themselves. *See* George Hillery, *Definitions of Community: Areas of Agreement*, 20 Rural Soc. 111 (1955). Some analysts have been so skeptical of the term that they have dismissed it as basically useless. *See* Colin Bell & Howard Newby, Community Studies: An Introduction to the Sociology of the Local Community 49 (1973). But as Philip Selznick points out, the same lack of consensus as to their meaning applies to such terms as "morality," "the political," and "culture," yet in each case a working definition may serve the intended. In any case, it seems futile to attempt to do without such terms, including "community," altogether. *See* Philip Selznick, The Moral Commonwealth: Social Theory and the Promise of Community 357 (1992).

Property and Human Flourishing. Gregory S. Alexander.

of property. Community defines the parameters of the obligations that property owners owe.

The high degree of analytical work that community plays in this theory requires a clear understanding of just what that term means in this context. Exactly what sorts of institutions perform this nurturing function? Given that individuals typically belong to multiple communities, both over time and at any given time, how broadly do those communities range—what is their scale in terms in size and time? Are the communities exclusively territorial or geographic, or are there also nonphysical types of communities that perform the nurturing functions? Should we take seriously, at least in this context, talk about "the global community," which would effectively mean that there are no limits on the range of persons to whom property owners owe duties? What about social network communities, including virtual communities?

This chapter considers these and other questions.

Community, as a concept, is used both in a social and a normative sense. In a social sense it refers, broadly speaking, to groups of people who have something in common, such as their place of residence, their race or ethnicity (communities of identity), or even an activity such as a sport (communities of interest). A somewhat more demanding formulation provides: "'A group is a community to the extent that it encompasses a broad range of activities and interests, and to the extent that participation implicates whole persons rather than segmental interests or activities.'"[2] Philip Selznick suggests *comprehensiveness* as a threshold criterion of community in the social sense.[3] Elaborating on that term, he argues that communities are variable, meaning that they range widely among varied groups and activities. Importantly, he argues, such an approach avoids limiting communities to conventional criteria, notably, territory and size.[4]

Although community may be defined neutrally in this social sense, it also carries normative weight. One commentator has remarked that community is a word that "seems never to be used unfavourably."[5] That is surely incorrect, for community has its share of detractors, particularly among some liberals who worry about its potential for oppression of the individual.[6] Community is both a normative and a conceptual language to talk about who is within my sphere. In

2. *Id.* at 358.

3. *See id.* at 58–59.

4. *See id.* at 59.

5. Raymond Williams, Keywords: A Vocabulary of Culture and Society 66 (1976).

6. *See, e.g.*, Jeremy Waldron, *Community and Property—For Those Who Have Neither*, 10 Theoretical Inq. in Law 161, 188–92 (2009).

this regard, its meaning is more than the layperson's common usage referring to just those persons who are within my immediate circle. One can be a member of a community in different senses, some more closely fitting the more familiar usage of the term than others. I may be a member of the community of my family in a way that I am not the community of my town. As I will discuss in Chapter Nine on race and community, we may use the language of community in the normative sense to evaluate the obligations that I owe members of races other than my own, where those persons and I have special relationships that carry responsibilities under the human flourishing theory. Although the primary focus of this chapter is on communities as a social institution, I need to devote some attention to this normative concern.

THE DARK SIDE OF COMMUNITY

Community is not inherently benign. There is a dark side to community. As a political ideal, community historically has had two basic strands, both of which have been problematic, sometimes intensely so.[7] One is the corporativist strand, which is a hierarchical form of community that historically has lent itself to notorious episodes of domination and oppression (e.g., National Socialism). The other is an anarchist strand of community, utopian in inspiration, dominating and even genocidal in practice (e.g., communism).

As social institutions, communities exclude, depending on how we conceive of them. Under a conception of a community as those social groups whose members are bound together by shared values communities by their very nature exclude.[8] Precisely because they are constituted by shared commitments to specific goods they must, in symbolic effect if not in conscious intention, exclude some members of society, precluding those individuals from participating in the group's internal life. Therein lies the dilemma for communities, for by excluding others communitarian groups radically limit their capacity to develop sympathy for others, thereby contradicting a universal communitarian ideal itself.

A related problem concerns a community's internal relations. Restrictions are important for maintaining, symbolically and instrumentally, the community's identity not only in its public face but also within itself. Restrictions on specific forms of behavior—what religious or sexual practices are acceptable, what range of books may be read, or even more seemingly innocuous behavioral restrictions, like restrictions on the consumption of tobacco or alcohol—create the

7. *See* Roberto Mangabeira Unger, Knowledge and Politics 249–53 (1975).

8. *See* Gregory S. Alexander, *Dilemmas of Group Autonomy: Residential Associations and Community*, 75 Cornell L. Rev. 1, 52 (1989).

community's boundary in its own internal consciousness. Although members may give restrictions different meanings, the community cannot permit its members freely to opt out of all of its restrictions while remaining members of the community. What Roberto Unger calls the "paradox of group cohesion"[9] exists because of the community-as-ideal's commitment to protect rather than subordinate the individual self. As Unger observes, "By its very nature, community is always on the verge of becoming oppression."[10]

Jeremy Waldron has been particularly forceful in articulating concerns about community's potential for oppression. He states, "'True community' in the sense of 'actually-existing community—a real community structured by a communitarian—is not always as nice as it looks."[11] He continues, "Actually-existing communities are often exclusionary and inauthentic. . . ."[12] Moreover, "In the real world, the word 'community' is found more commonly in the company of terms like 'gated.'"[13]

Waldron's anxiety is that community as an ideal is perverted when it is converted into a social institution. He focuses specifically on homeless persons, people who lack any private property from which they are not subject to eviction. The homeless lack community as well as property, Waldron notes, and some commentators have suggested that the solution for homelessness is a greater sense of community.[14] Waldron thinks this answer to the problem of homelessness is wrongheaded. "Too often the problem for those are poor and marginalized is not that there has been insufficient assertion of claims of community in the face of (say) market individualism. The problem is, rather, one of exclusion or expulsion *from community*."[15]

Waldron's diagnosis is wrong. The problem for the homeless is not with community (although, as I have already indicated, I agree with his view that community inherently has a dark side), but with property. Specifically, it is with the view that ownership inherently and invariably carries with it a strong right to exclude the rest of the world, a view that Waldron apparently endorses.[16] To paraphrase

9. Unger, Knowledge and Politics, *supra* note 7, at 266.

10. *Id.*

11. Waldron, *Community and Property, supra* note 6, at 166, 188.

12. *Id.*

13. Jeremy Waldron, *Secularism and the Limits of Community* 8 (unpub. paper Dec. 2010).

14. *See, e.g.*, George Rupp, Globalization Challenged: Conviction, Conflict, Community (2000).

15. Waldron, *Community and Property, supra* note 6, at 190 (emphasis in original).

16. *See id.* at 188–89.

the quote from Waldron, the problem is, rather, one of assuming that the owner always has the right to exclude. It is precisely that view that I wish to show in this book is wrongheaded. Once we realize that the right to exclude is far more limited than Waldron supposes, and, moreover, that owners owe members of their manifold communities obligations to support development of the capabilities that are necessary for their flourishing, then we see that property owners, at least in some situations, are morally obligated, and should be legally obligated, to be part of the solution to homelessness. I shall discuss further how they might do so, consistently with being private owners, in Chapter Eight. For present purposes it is enough to note that Waldron's anxiety about exclusion ought to focus on ownership at least as much as on communities.

Elsewhere, Waldron recognizes an attractive side of communitarianism. This is the side, he states, that "encourages us to look at the conditions of viability of *actual* communities, and it predicts that those communities will sometimes surprise us, which means that actually existing communities have the potential to teach us something about social and political ideals."[17] Waldron states that there is a certain "sociological *given*-ness about community" in this sense of the term. It contrasts, he finds, with utopian ideals, on the one hands, and with "club, cult, and commune," on the other. In this community-as-actually-lived sense, people simply find themselves within communities not by choice but "by understanding who it *is* that that one is 'unavoidably side-by-side' with, and who it *is* that the impact of one's actions and decisions is going to be felt by, whether one chooses this or not."[18] In this sense the sharing that matters is not values but the very fact that all of the members are together, in the same space, the same predicament. Hence, "[t]he fellow members of one's community are not necessarily people like oneself: they are, rather, those with whom 'one cannot avoid acting.'"[19]

This is indeed an attractive sense of community. It is attractive both normatively and positively. Its positive attraction derives from the fact that it accurately captures how we in fact live our lives. So, I am part of the community that is Cornell Law School and, within that, the smaller communities that are the classes I teach. I have not chosen the members of these communities (at least not all of them), rather I find myself simply with them, every day. I must learn how to get along with them, and they with me, in all my many oddities and foibles. This is how we live our lives.

17. Jeremy Waldron, *Homelessness and Community*, 50 U. Tor. L.J. 371, 404 (2000) (emphasis in original).

18. *Id.* at 121–24 (*quoting* Immanuel Kant, The Metaphysics of Morals, trans. M. Gregor (1991).

19. *Id.*

This sense of community is normatively attractive because it is not exclusionary. As Waldron states, "It [community in this sense] provides a basis on which human concerns are felt, values pursued, and commitments entered into, among relatively large numbers of people who accept that, since they are living more or less permanently in one another's company, they have a responsibility to orient their actions and relations to the shared environment—moral as well as physical—in which all of them must live."[20]

Waldron's account of community-as-actually-lived closely resembles a moral value that captures much of what I take to be the meaning of community as a moral value itself—sociability. By "sociability" I mean the ability to identify with others and to see them as concrete human beings like oneself rather than as the other. It further means regarding oneself as connected with others in myriad ways, including the sharing of the quotidian details of ordinary life. In some cases the connections are thicker, such as the sharing of values. But as a normative matter what community strives for is the gradual development within each person of attitudes of sympathy, understanding, concern, openness, patience, and care. Community as a good includes an other-regarding perspective. This is not to say that such an outlook is a reality. Community in this sense is a moral value, not an account of human behavior. Reality sometimes, often perhaps, falls far short of what people consider to be the good, and such is more than likely the case with regard to the way in which most of us view other people, especially those who do not know us well or at all, some, if not a great deal of the time. Nevertheless the good remains what it is.

The problem of exclusion remains also. It remains for communities as social institutions because it is still the case that communities in any robust sense of the term exclude. Certainly many of the communities with which the human flourishing theory is concerning, communities that nurture the development of their members' essential capabilities, exclude. This exclusionary characteristic should cause us to give serious thought about the moral legitimacy of extending obligations to property owners to support members of exclusionary communities. This is a challenge to the human flourishing theory that I need to address, but not until I have first surveyed which institutions I mean to consider as candidates for recipients of obligations.

COMMUNITIES AS INSTITUTIONS

The primary focus of this chapter is on that phenomenon—social groups, in their remarkable varieties, bound together in some relevant way that we shall have to

20. *Id.*

explore, however incompletely. The central task here is to define the range of social groups that can coherently and justifiably be called communities within a theory of ownership that sees the role of communities as enablers of individual flourishing by helping people to develop those human capabilities that are essential to live a flourishing life. It is the members of these enabling communities to whom property owners owe, *qua* property owners, such obligations as we may justly conclude they are beholden, both legally and morally.

Any attempt to define community or to draw boundaries around the concept must acknowledge at the outset that the enterprise will be based on shifting sands. Community is hardly a binary concept but is instead enormously fluid. Communities arrange themselves along a rather complex continuum of types,[21] and the poles of that continuum are maddeningly difficult to identify. Despite these difficulties, the enterprise of community boundary-drawing is worth the effort.

What sorts of groups are subsumed by the capacious term "community," both in general and specifically with respect to identifying social networks that nurture essential capabilities? In what ways do those groups perform their nurturing function?

Communities and Associations

As a first cut, let us distinguish between two sort of groups, communities and associations. Communities are based upon shared characteristics that members consider important, even vital, in their lives. The shared characteristics, which may include deeply held values, ancestry, race or ethnicity, affective relationships, and other ties, are sources of identity for members of each community.[22] Members of associations, by contrast, are tied together only by contract, implied or express.[23] The ties are not constitutive of members' personal identities.

Individuals enter into these contracts for instrumental purposes. The sense of detachment among members of associations makes it appropriate to characterize these groups as aggregations of self-seeking individuals. By contrast, members of

21. *See* Amnon Lehavi, *How Property Can Create, Maintain, or Destroy Community*, 10 Theoretical Inq. in Law 43, 48 (2009).

22. This definition of "community" is close to that offered by Anthony Mason: "[A] community . . . is constituted by a group of people who share a range of values, a way of life, identify with the group and its practices and recognize each other as members of that group." Anthony Mason, Community, Solidarity and Belonging: Levels of Community and Their Normative Significance 21 (2000).

23. This distinction, of course, approximates Tönnies' famous distinction between *Gemeinschaft* and *Gesellschaft*. *See* Ferdinand Tönnies, Community and Society 63, 64, 65 (1963).

communities are united by some deeper experience of sharing that constitutes, for each of them, an important aspect of their personal identity. Within communities individuals experience group life with a sense of belonging.

The distinction between associations and communities is not strictly categorical. In practice, groups sometimes combine characteristics of both. Similarly, a group's character can change over time, beginning as a voluntary association but evolving into a community, and vice versa. The crucial question is whether social relationships within the group are based on more than an instrumental convergence of individual ends—on reciprocal sharing of some constitutive characteristic. We need not specify the degree of sharing that is necessary for a group to be a community in my sense of the term. Indeed, any effort to do so would be futile. Again, communities occupy various positions along a continuum, so perhaps we can say that different groups have differing degrees of community-ness. Our approach to defining community and to specifying the boundaries of communities, then, will have to be somewhat loose because that is the nature of the beast with which we are dealing.

Moreover, whether we term a group "community" or not depends on the reason why we ask the question whether that group is a community. There are different reasons why it may (or may not) matter whether we consider a group a community (or even a group, for that matter), and these different reasons may lead us to different conclusions regarding the proper characterization of the group. Different reasons for asking the question may lead us to require different degrees of sharing of values or of some distinct way of life. Any given group may exhibit some aspects of community without fully exemplifying all of the possible characteristics of community.[24] So, here again, the continuum metaphor is appropriate.

IDENTIFYING THE BOUNDARIES OF COMMUNITIES IN TERRITORIAL TERMS

As an initial step in providing definition to the limits of the conceivable communities that might be swept within a property owner's scope of obligations, let us first distinguish between territorial and nonterritorial communities. This distinction is useful only so far and is by no means categorical. Here again, the continuum metaphor applies. There is nothing neat about the distinction because while we can organize territorial communities as concentric circles around the individual, overlapping of course, at some point along the outer parameters of the circles that we consider communities, the relationships among the individual, the group, and

24. *See* Mason, Community, Solidarity and Belonging, *supra* note 22, at 26.

territory become so attenuated that we seem to be edging toward nonterritoriality. At that point nonterritorial communities, perhaps including so-called virtual communities, may appear as equally important to the nurturing of the necessary capabilities, if not more so, as those territorial communities located on the outer edges of a person's experiential domain. There is no good reason for demanding, either a priori or empirically, that communities involve face-to face contact.[25] It is certainly possible for members of a group to derive a sense of belonging from the group and to identify personally with the group despite the fact that they seldom or even never physically meet. Nevertheless, however incompletely it captures that domain, the distinction between territorial and nonterritorial communities is useful enough for our purposes.

The boundaries of the self's communities, territorial and nonterritorial, are set, among other factors, by the character of interpersonal relationships. More to the point from the perspective of human flourishing, they are also set by whether and how those relationships contribute to the self's flourishing through the acquisition of certain fundamental capabilities. When relationships within a group are so attenuated that one cannot say with any degree of confidence that members of the groups nurture the individual's flourishing by helping the individual to develop those capabilities without which she cannot live an objectively fruitful life, then the character of the group is such that the basis for obligations of the sort considered here is lacking. Whatever obligations the individual owes to other members of the group must be based on agreement of some sort.

The Circles of the Self's Territorial Communities

It is difficult to imagine a person who is not a member of any community. Indeed, nearly all of us belong to multiple communities, both at any given time and over time. To some extent those communities may overlap with each other; nevertheless, we usually identify them as discrete groups of people.

If we look at these communities from the vantage point of how we experience them in ordinary life, they appear as concentric circles around us. The distances between not only them and us but also between each other increase with each new ring, rather like the circles that form in a pool of water into which a stone has been tossed. With each ring, the ways in which members of the community contribute to the individual's well-being not only change. These changes are likely to be increasingly remote, but not always. Although the ties between an individual and a given community may appear remote, what connects them may

25. *See* Mason, Community, Solidarity and Belonging, *supra* note 22, at 39.

be sufficiently important to warrant a thick obligation for the individual who is also an owner of property within that community.

Families

Certainly the community that most obviously contributes to the individual's development of the necessary capabilities is her family. Putting aside for the moment important questions concerning the scope of the relevant family—Does it include all living persons related by blood or by law to the individual? Does it include past family members, future family members?—no one contributes more immediately to the development of an individual's health, security, socialization, and other capabilities than her family. From the time we are born and well into our adulthood we depend upon family members—parents most obviously, but also grandparents, siblings, aunts, and uncles—not only for obvious forms of support, such as food and shelter, but also for lessons about planning and evaluation, causes and consequences, self-restraint and discipline: These are the raw materials from which the capability of practical reasoning emerges. We inevitably depend upon these persons not only for survival but, less obviously, for our ability to function as free and rational agents.

What counts as a family is a highly contested matter in our society. Kinship based on blood is, of course, no longer the sole foundation for the functional family. State-sanctioned institutions such as adoption now augment blood ties to create families. Moreover, for some children foster care fills in familial gaps when neither blood-based nor adoption-based relationships are available or acceptable. In still other cases the functioning family may be little more than a non-state-sanctioned arrangement of persons who live together with the self-perception that they constitute a family. Whatever the basis for the family's constitution, family is a central type of community for the development of the individual's essential capabilities.

The assertion that property owners owe obligations to family members to use their assets in ways that enable the family member to flourish through capability-development is likely to encounter debate. There may be less disagreement with the assertion as a moral proposition, but as a legal claim it will encounter some resistance. At least with respect to family members who are adults, skeptics will consider such obligations unnecessary or intrusive, or both. Critics may argue that adult family members are responsible for their own well-being, and any attempt to impose a legal obligation to facilitate their flourishing on other family members directly interferes with capability-related values weighing in the owner's interest, including autonomy. This line of objection overlooks two important and related points: First, the statement that property owners owe legal obligations, *qua* owners, to adult family members to facilitate the development and protection of those persons' capabilities states only a prima facie claim, not

a final conclusion. The claim is subject to qualifications and competing considerations, notably concerns with the owners' capability interests. These competing concerns may lead us finally to conclude that an owner's prima facie obligation should not be legally enforced under the given circumstances. However, we are still left with the starting point that property owners do have duties as owners to members of their families, including adults, to help, in ways that are appropriate to the particular owner and her property, to develop the family members' essential capabilities.

Neighborhood

Most of the literature on community agrees that neighborhoods meet whatever relevant criteria have been established to identify a community as such. At least this is true of many neighborhoods, although it perhaps less true today than fifty years ago. In considering neighborhood as community, it helps to keep in mind that the community is not a binary concept. There are degrees of "community-ness," so that communities occupy different positions along a continuum.[26] Groups can be more or less communities. What matters are such factors as whether the group encompasses a reasonably broad range of activities and/or interests, whether involvement in the group is strictly strategic and goal-oriented or implicates the individual most completely, and the extent to which and the manner in which the individual identifies with the group (on a purely instrumental basis or as an aspect of self-identification).

One scholar has suggested that "the notion of neighborhood is rarely free of connotations of connection that inhere in the term community."[27] Neighborhoods are at least the potential sites of identity and involvement. Responding to the well-known, albeit contested, "death-of-community" thesis, some social scientists, however, have preferred to speak of neighborhood networks instead of neighborhoods, but the concepts overlap substantially.[28] The characteristics of neighborhood networks vary widely. Empirical work suggests that their size and character depends heavily on the extent to which an individual is socially integrated within the larger society.[29] Those who are most highly integrated tend to have larger neighborhood networks. The relationships within these networks, however, tend not to be especially intense. Individuals who are less integrated within larger society, by contrast, have smaller networks that are characterized by

26. *See* Selznick, The Moral Commonwealth, *supra* note 1, at 359 (community as a "variable").

27. Robert J. Chaskin, *Perspectives on Neighborhood and Community: A Review of the Literature*, 71 Soc. Service Rev. 521, 523 (1997).

28. *See id.* at 530–31.

29. *See id.* at 537.

more intense personal relationships. Various factors play roles in the constitution of these networks, including socioeconomic status, race, age, and the length of residence.

Neighborhood members contribute to the development of each other's essential capabilities in various ways. Sometimes, they assist each other in childrearing,[30] babysitting for their children, feeding them, reading to them, tending to minor first-aid needs. They carpool neighborhood children to school or to children's activities. They take each other to the hospital in emergencies or call for emergency care. They discuss problems with each other, sometimes deeply personal ones. They learn and practice important socialization skills among their neighbors, learning how to "live and let live," to practice generosity, to express sympathy, or simply to say hello.

Sociability is a basic capability to which neighbors contribute in multiple ways. An obvious way, of course, is by setting a good example of what it means to be a good neighbor. There are less obvious ways in which neighbors teach each other aspects of sociability. One is parenting. Social science research indicates that communities make important contributions to parenting skills.[31]

Neighbors help each other to develop important aspects of practical reasoning. This is especially so in better organized neighborhoods where some sort of governance structure exists. In such settings, neighbors, as members of local organizations, plan, set agendas, establish goals, listen to each other, reason with each other, and, finally, vote. No one possesses any of the capabilities upon birth; they must be taught. One place where people learn practical-reasoning skills is in organizations, especially in smaller organizations. Neighborhood organizations, or at least some of them, are effective vehicles for teaching these skills because they are more fluid and less threatening than larger, more hierarchically structured organizations.

Not all neighborhoods have all or any of these characteristics. Many do not.

Neighborhoods vary widely in the degree to which they exhibit characteristics of community. In some neighborhoods residents simply coexist, barely acknowledging each other. There is no sharing in such places, no sense of identity derived from the place where one lives or the group among which one resides. There is an utter lack of the normative infrastructure that defines the meaning of community.

More common, perhaps, are residential places that exhibit some but not all such normative signs of community. An important and interesting form of modern

30. *See* Judith Rich Harris, *Where Is the Child's Environment? A Group Socialization Theory of Development*, 102 Psych. Rev. 458, 467 (1995).

31. *See, e.g.*, J. Garbarion & K. Kastelny, *Neighborhood and Community Influences on Parenting, in* Tom Luster & Lynn Okagaki, Parenting: An Ecological Perspective (2nd ed. 2005).

residential life in which some sense of community exists, but to varying degrees, is the common interest community (CIC). Some commentators have questioned whether CICs are properly considered communities at all,[32] but they are too diverse to permit any sort of generalization in this regard. Some residents of CICs experience little or no sense of shared identity with fellow members of their group. They choose to live in a CIC for strictly instrumental reasons, especially property values. Others have a different experience that tracks the characteristics of community life much more. They meet their neighbors at local events, ranging from knitting societies to musical concerts. They invite their neighbors over for coffee and have dinner with friends from the CIC. They play golf together, sometimes at the CIC's own facilities. The more comprehensive such social activities are a part of the residents' lives, the closer the arrangement moves toward community.[33]

Local Institutions

A good deal of nurturing of capabilities occurs in local institutions. That term includes a wide array of small institutions, ranging from churches, synagogues, and mosques to Elks Clubs, V.F.W. halls, literary groups, AAUW chapters, and many other organized local organizations. They also include an extraordinary variety of unorganized groups which act in many respects like some of the organized institutions just named. Such groups and local institutions are communities in a strong sense of the term. They provide a sense of identity for their members and a supportive structure of activities and relationships. Members derive a sense of belonging there.

Local institutions such as these are important sources of nurturing the capabilities necessary for human flourishing. An obvious example is sociability. Institutions such as these typically meet for social events on a regular basis, and those occasions are important opportunities for members to develop socialization skills, including listening, respecting differences of opinion, expressing one's one opinion, learning and expressing sympathy and empathy with others. These skills are all constituent aspects of sociability, and they contribute directly to a well-lived life. Indeed, it is precisely those sociability experiences that lead people to join and participate in local organizations.

In recent years there has been a robust debate over the question whether social capital has declined since 1950. This debate was triggered by the influential book by Robert Putnam, *Bowling Alone*.[34] Based on evidence he collected over several

32. *See* Lehavi, *How Property Can Create, Maintain, or Destroy Community, supra* note 21, at 58.

33. *See* Selznick, The Moral Commonwealth, *supra* note 1, at 358–59.

34. Robert D. Putnam, Bowling Alone: The Collapse and Revival of American Community (2000).

years, Putnam concluded that membership in a wide variety of civic and social organizations, ranging from the PTA to the League of Women Voters to the Elks has substantially declined, and he argued that this decline is problematic for democracy.

Putnam's thesis, if correct, would be problematic for the contribution of local organizations for capability development. However, his study has been challenged by several social scientists on different grounds. Everett Carll Ladd in his book, *The Ladd Report*, challenged Putnam's data, pointing out that while some civic and fraternal organizations have declined in the past few decades, others have expanded considerably.[35] Other researchers showed that it is only in the United States that a decline in civic participation has occurred.[36] Still others suggested that rather than declining the locus of socializing has shifted. Parents may no longer bowl together, but they do contribute to social capital through their active participation in their children's soccer leagues.[37] In view of this work, there is good reason to question Putnam's thesis.

Cities/"Urban Communities"

The types of communities surveyed so far have all been relatively small and geographically local groups of people. As we begin to move toward more remote concentric circles surrounding the individual, the question of community becomes more problematic. There is a perspective, however, from which cities may legitimately be characterized as communities, albeit a special type of community.[38] If we adopt a different approach to community, one that defines it in terms of functions rather than feelings or relationships, then the city can properly be considered as a community. One suggested functional definitional of community is that a community is "a group of social units and systems organized on a residential basis to carry out the functions of the residential area."[39]

In modern American society communities perform several functions. The most essential of these are, first, providing essential goods and services to community members. For cities, such goods and services span the entire array of basic material needs—food, housing, clothing, medical care, employment, and

35. Everett Carll Ladd, The Ladd Report (1999).

36. *See* Robert Andersen, Edward Grabb, & James Curtis, *Trends in Civic Association Activity in Four Democracies: The Special Case of Women in the United States*, 71 Am. Soc. Rev. 376 (2006).

37. *See* Nicholas Lemann, *Kicking in Groups*, The Atlantic Online, Apr. 1996.

38. *See* Alan S. Berger: The City: Urban Communities and Their Problems (1978).

39. *Id.* at 8.

other similar goods and services. Cities themselves directly provide some of these goods to some residents, but other needs are met by smaller communities within the city. For cities, including all of their individual neighborhoods, to thrive, certain types of both commercial and public establishments and services must be readily available for residents. These include grocery stores, drugstores, gas stations, public transportation stations, and garbage disposal. Decent roads must exist as well as access to well-functioning communication networks.

Second, communities create and maintain normative cohesion among their members. This means that they establish norms that guide the behavior and values of its members, and members must agree upon those norms. Without such behavioral regulatory guidelines, the community quickly disintegrates into confusion, disagreement, and perhaps even chaos. In the context of cities, of course, the result would be sheer disaster. The community must educate newcomers about these norms, for they may not always be self-evident or obvious. This kind of socialization takes place in all sorts of settings, from clubhouses to schools, from churches to private homes. In all of these settings fellow community members instruct, sometimes formally but more commonly informally, new members in the behavioral ways, norms, and values of the group. This is as true of cities as it is of soccer leagues. Jaywalking may be perfectly fine in New York City but in other parts of the country it simply isn't done. The newcomer quickly learns such norms from fellow residents.

The third function is generating a shared sense of identity among the residents.

Communities give their members a common identity, and cities are no different. Even in the largest American cities residents share a way of understanding themselves that includes their residence in "their" city. Ask a New Yorker who and what he is and in some way he will answer, "I'm a New Yorker." The Big Apple is not unique in this respect. The phenomenon is just as true of residents of San Francisco, Omaha, and Birmingham. This sense of identification becomes especially apparent when two residents of the same city encounter each while traveling. Two Chicagoans meeting each other in China are apt to ask each other in what part of the city they live ("Northside or Southside?"). If they are both longtime residents of the same city, they will exchange information ranging from favorite restaurants to high schools attended.

A fourth function is providing spaces for socialization among community members.

Clubs and other socially oriented voluntary associations do so by holding regular meetings and other events in clubhouses and similar venues. Groups affiliated with churches, synagogues, and mosques meet in their places of worship for various social activities as well as worship. It is not only socialization that occurs

in these venues but mutual support as well.[40] Cities provide support through welfare agencies. Private agencies supplement this supportive work.[41]

Although cities perform these community functions, they—entire cities—are communities only in a limited sense. They are not communities in the second, more robust respect that we discussed earlier, the dimension that defines community according to feelings and relationships. No sense of solidarity binds all city residents together. Anonymity is pervasive in cities, and some city residents live lives of isolation. Nevertheless, cities do nurture their residents' human capabilities and by doing so contribute in important ways to their opportunity to flourish. For purposes of identifying the range of subjects to which owners owe duties, then, it is legitimate to consider cities as communities.

Nation-States as Communities

Several political scientists, political geographers, and sociologists have debated the questions whether modern nation-states can or should be considered as communities and if so, in what sense. A prior question is whether nations can even be considered as groups. Like cities, nations are groups in a sense that is quite different from families or even neighborhoods. As several analysts have noted, the group construction of nations is social, not organic.[42] The defining features of a nationalist discourse, a rhetoric that constructs a group as a nation, relate to boundaries, indivisibility, sovereignty, legitimacy, culture, territoriality, and temporal depth.[43] In this respect nations might be defined as "communities of people that are imagined through a series of nationalist discourses."[44]

The construction of nations as communities is functional as well as discursive. Nation-states perform many of the same functions as cities. Like cities, nations provide essential goods and services to their residents. Among these are security, both military and material. Nations differ, of course, in their approaches to various basic material services, including, notably, health care. Some provide generous health care through universal coverage while others, such as the United States, are considerably less generous and less extensive in coverage. Well-working national service plans can be a source of national pride and identity for residents.

40. *Id.* at 31.

41. *Id.*

42. *See* Craig Calhoun, Nationalism 98 (1997); Helen Ting, *Social Construction of Nations—A Theoretical Exploration*, 14 Nationalism & Ethnic Pol. 453 (2008).

43. *See id.* at 4–5.

44. Martin Jones et al., An Introduction to Political Geography 76 (2nd ed. 2015) (*citing* Benedict Anderson, Imagined Communities (1983)).

Nations give their citizens a common identity, which is, for many, a source of pride. Shared national identities become especially apparent to citizens as they travel abroad. They readily identify themselves as "Americans," "French citizens," or "Chinese." True, citizens of some nations are reluctant to reveal their national identity outside their borders, but that reluctance does not minimize the internal pride they may feel. True also that some citizens in many countries feel embarrassed, even ashamed of their national identity. Still, the vast majority of their fellow citizens take pride in being who and what they are and feel a bond with their fellow citizens.

Nations provide spaces for socialization among fellow citizens and other residents. They provide parks and other physical locations for socialization. In some nations they form sports teams that represent the nation in international competitions. These teams often are the source of great pride to their citizen-fans and unite them in their cheering.

Most citizens of nation-states feel a sense of belonging to the nations. One scholar has defined a sense of belonging to a polity this way: "a person has a sense of belonging to a polity if and only if she identifies with most of its major institutions and some of its central practices, and feels at home in them."[45] This is a fairly undemanding standard, one that would seem to fit most citizens, though perhaps not all residents. On this view one may feel a sense of belonging with their polity even if they disagree, perhaps radically, with policies of the government. Many Americans have strongly disagreed with policies of past administrations of the government, yet they still identify with the country's institutions, as such, and with core practices such as singing the national anthem. However alienated they may feel from a current administration, Americans feel that they belong here. They would no more live elsewhere than they would deliberately crash their car. As they experience things, they are Americans, and this is home.

Mason aptly points out, however, that it is one thing to feel a sense of belonging to a polity but another to feel a sense of belonging together.[46] It is conceivable that one could feel a sense of belonging to the nation but not belonging together with one's fellow citizens. Although such a scenario is conceivable, it is implausible. As Mason notes, it is not easy to find nations where the citizens hold a sense of belonging to that polity but do not hold a sense of belonging together.[47] For one thing, it is possible to say that one is derivative of the other—a sense of belonging together follows from a shared sense of belonging to a polity. On this view Americans share an identity by virtue of identifying with the nation's core

45. Mason, Community, Solidarity and Belonging, *supra* note 22, at 127.

46. *See id.* at 127.

47. *See id.* at 128.

institutions and practices, or at least some of them, such as "the flag, the Pledge, the Fourth, the Constitution."[48] They share the understanding that whatever other differences they may have, it is appropriate that they associate with each other because they all identify with these core practices and institutions.

There may be a second, stronger respect in which Americans hold a sense of belonging together. David Miller argues that for citizens to share a national identity, "there must be a sense that the people belong together by virtue of the characteristics they share."[49] Miller than explains the idea of common characteristics in terms of a public culture that "may be seen as a set of understandings about how a group of people is to conduct its life together."[50] This set of understandings includes basic political principles such as the rule of law but also social norms such as queuing for the movies.[51]

One might question whether there are any shared principles or norms that are distinctive to Americans.[52] There are reasons to think that there are, however. We need not engage in the discourse of American exceptionalism to believe that there are widely (though not universally) shared norms and principles that bind Americans together. One often hears visitors from other nations, including a wide variety of nations, comment on how different the United States is from anywhere else in the world they have traveled. Something about the United States and its people sets us apart. One observation that visitors often make is that individual risk-taking is far more common here than elsewhere. We rely on ourselves and private action rather than the government to an extent that is perhaps unique among nations. More than 150 years ago Ralph Waldo Emerson wrote a famous essay extolling the virtues of self-reliance.[53] Still today, self-reliance is a social norm and principle that is widely shared among Americans and that is distinctive to the United States. This is a difference between American society and other societies that Americans are apt to notice as they travel abroad. Self-reliance and other shared practices and norms connect Americans together in ways that enable self-identification as an American. This is an adequate basis for community.

48. *See* Michael Walzer, *What Does It Mean to Be an "American"?*, 57 Soc. Research 602 (1990).

49. David Miller, On Nationality 25 (1995).

50. *Id.* at 26.

51. *Id.*

52. Andrew Mason, for one, is skeptical that there are such distinctive shared principles or norms. *See* Mason, Community, Solidarity and Belonging, *supra* note 22, at 130.

53. Ralph Waldo Emerson, Self-Reliance and Other Essays (1993) (1841).

Global Community?

Moving outward one further step, the final concentric circle among possible territorial candidates is a global community. The notion of a global community suggests the closely related phenomenon of globalization, and we need to consider briefly globalization for its possible consequences on local communities. There exists something of a modern myth that globalization has squeezed out all that is distinctive about local communities, leaving only on a standardized mode ofliving in the contemporary world.[54] On this rendering, globalization stands for homogenizing global corporations that have overpowered the local, which are characterized by tradition, authenticity, and diversity.[55] Some analysts have challenged this view. One has pointed out that some local communities have contested globalization processes, such as big-box spread, and occasionally succeeded. There is evidence, then, that local actors can influence the outcomes of global processes and that the rumor of the death of local communities is premature.[56]

Still, there is no doubting the spread and force of globalization processes and their effects on social relations. The world has gotten smaller, and this change places in bold relief the question whether the concept of a global community is coherent.

If we apply the same criteria that we have used up to this point, there are good reasons to conclude that at least for our purposes, the global community is an incoherent concept. Recall that we said earlier that when relationships within a group are so attenuated that one cannot say with any degree of confidence that members of the groups nurture the individual's flourishing by helping the individual to develop those capabilities without which she cannot live an objectively fruitful life, then the character of the group is such that the basis for obligations of the sort considered here is lacking. This is just the condition that exists among members of the "group" that would constitute the global community. The vast majority of the world's inhabitants—the members of the supposed group—are total strangers to each other. Of course, it is still possible that they might contribute to the development of each other's capabilities in some meaningful way, but this possibility seems remote. Without some sort of contact or communication between them, inhabitants of the world who are complete strangers to each other have no opportunity to contribute to the development or nurturing of each other's human capabilities.

We also saw that community, to be meaningful in this context, requires that members of the group identify with the group and derive a sense of belonging

54. *See* Jones et al., Political Geography, *supra* note 44, at 159.

55. *Id.*

56. *See* Doreen B. Massey, For Space 83 (2005).

from participation in the group. The "global village" is an attractive term, but it does not match how people actually experience their membership in this supposed village. Perhaps some people regard themselves as citizens of the world and derive a sense of belonging and identify from that self-conception, but even that connection is highly abstract, lacking any personal dimension or identification.

Of course, even if we reject the idea of a global community, as I do, that does not foreclose the possibility that property owners might still owe moral obligations of support to people around the world, even total strangers. But the basis of whatever obligations we may find owners hold toward such unknown others must be something other than membership in a community of persons who have nurtured and supported the development of the owner's essential human capabilities. Some scholars and other commentators refer to the obligations that attend "global citizenship,"[57] but that phrase merely substitutes one metaphor for another. Other candidates to serve as the foundation for such a moral duty exist, to be sure, and I do not mean to reject all or any of them necessarily. For reasons that I have already indicated, however, I do think that the approach to human flourishing that I detailed in Chapter Two is the most normatively attractive such candidate.

One further complication with the question of a global community remains. Thus far, I have assumed a particular sort of person—an individual human being. Not all legal persons are this simple, however. More to the point, in the modern world—the globalized modern world—property owners often are highly complex, multinational organizations. The existence of these organizations pose two important questions relating to the human flourishing account of ownership: First, should we treat such organizations, taking them as entities unto themselves, as owners? Second, assuming that the answer to the first question is affirmative and given the far-flung operations of such enterprises and their deep involvement in many countries around the world, is the notion of a global community more coherent as applied to them? Before turning to those questions, I need to consider two other possible candidates.

Nonterritorial Communities

Not all communities are territorial. Families, including extended families, are an obvious example of communities that are not identified, at least not necessarily, with any particular place. In ordinary language we often refer to many such nonterritorial communities, including racial communities (e.g., "the African American community"), ethnic communities (e.g., "the Italian community"), professional or occupational communities (e.g., "the legal community"), and so

57. *See, e.g.*, Jones et al., Political Geography, *supra* note 44, at 169.

on. Are these speech practices only appropriations of the community concept as a trope, or do they refer to groups that bear enough of the characteristics of community outlined earlier that they, or at least some of them, may be added to the list of communities to which property owners owe obligations?

Philip Selznick has stated that it is not "slipshod" to speak of the Catholic community or the police community.[58] What makes such talk coherent in his view is his important observation that community is a variable. What he means by that is that there is no single litmus test, including territoriality, for qualification as a community. What matters is that the group is connected by bonds that provide personal identity, a sense of belonging, and supportive relationships.[59]

In addition to being a variable, community is a matter of degree. It is not a binary category, an on/off matter that either is or isn't. In this respect territoriality looms large. Whether a group is territorially based is not decisive to its existence as a community, but it does figure very importantly into the calculus of how strongly knit together a given community is and where, along the spectrum of community robustness, a community lies. Territory matters. Nonterritorial communities resemble extended families in a sense. The more attenuated the relationship becomes, the weaker the bonds and the sense of identity. This is important for all types of communities, but especially nonterritorial communities, because, as we shall see, the obligations that property owners owe to other members of their communities vary according to the strength of the community connection. Hence, although there may be obligations owed to members of nonterritorial communities, they are apt to be weaker than to fellow members of those community with whom the owner lives and works.

Virtual Communities?

The final possibility I shall consider among the list of candidates is the virtual community. By that term I mean social networks that communicate and interact via social media. The term itself is usually attributed to the book with the eponymous title by Howard Rheingold.[60] Members interact through a variety of social networking forms, including chat rooms, social network websites, and virtual worlds. Millions of people around the world now participate, albeit to varying degree, in these social networks, and their growth has been nothing short of spectacular. Is it appropriate to include these virtual communities as communities for our purposes, that is, mediating vehicles for enabling individuals to develop

58. *See* Selznick, The Moral Commonwealth, *supra* note 1, at 358.

59. *See id.* at 358–59.

60. *See* Howard Rheingold, The Virtual Community: Homesteading on the Electronic Frontier (2000).

the capabilities necessary for their flourishing and the groups to whose members property owners owe obligations, *qua* owners, of support?

As the discussion of nonterritorial communities suggested, the connection between place and community has become attenuated, if not quite cut, in modern Western societies.

Responding to these changes, analysts now conceptualize communities in terms of social networks rather than physical propinquity.[61] This conceptual shift would appear to make it easier to treat online networks as communities, and some scholars have done so.[62] To some extent this conclusion seems warranted. After all, even territorial communities today are, by and large, not all-encompassing but partial.[63] That is, unlike the traditional village-like communities, the ties with modern territorial communities are specialized and provide only partial support.

Community members usually turn to different fellow community members for different kinds of help.[64]

However tempting it may be to compare virtual groups with other groups that seem fairly comfortably to fit within the category of community, such comparisons are dangerous. Part of the reason why we should hesitate to draw such comparisons is that relatively little is known about social relationships within virtual groups. We lack systematic evidence about whether such relationships are broadly or narrowly focused.[65] Moreover, it is very difficult to generalize about virtual groups because there are so many of them (and increasing) and because they are so widely diverse. Some groups simply provide information or are outlets for exchanging opinions. Others, however, do provide support and a form of companionship.[66] In this respect virtual groups resemble and perform certain functions of more traditional communities.

Is the resemblance strong enough to warrant considering them as communities under the human flourishing theory of property? As we have discussed, according to that theory what matters most are whether an individual's membership in a group is constitutive of his identity, at least to a nontrivial extent, and whether an individual derives a sense of belonging from it. It is difficult to see how virtual

61. *See, e.g.*, Peter Kollock & Marc A. Smith, *Communities in Cyberspace, in* COMMUNITIES IN CYBERSPACE 3, 17 (Marc A. Smith & Peter Kollock eds., 1999); Barry Wellman & Milena Gulia, *Virtual Communities as Communities: Net Surfers Don't Ride Alone, in id.* at 167, 169.

62. *See* Wellman & Gulia, *Virtual Communities as Communities, supra* note 61, at 170.

63. *See id.* at 171.

64. *See id.*

65. *See id.*

66. *See id.* at 172–74.

groups could be constitutive of personal identity or provide a sense of belonging in any robust sense of the term. The available evidence regarding the nature of relationships within these groups indicates that the social ties among members are weak and superficial.[67] This is probably true also of some traditional communities, especially those that are nonterritorial, but the difference is that even as to nonterritorial communities the opportunity for face-to-face contact within them enhances the likelihood that the ties among their members will strengthen.

Another way of looking at the question is to ask whether virtual groups nurture the capabilities that people need to live well-lived lives. In the case of face-to-face communities it is easy to see how such nurturing occurs, but can such nurturing occur virtually? And does it?

Certainly such nurturing is possible. Members of online groups can receive a wide array of help from fellow group members, especially if they are regular and long-term participants in groups.[68] Moreover, there is evidence that group members do give each other help, mostly in the form of emotional support, companionship, and advice.[69]

Still, it is an open question whether the quality of that help, the nurturing within online communities, matches that of traditional communities. Scholars like the distinguished MIT social scientist Sherry Turkle have raised concerns about the effects that uses of online technology, uses that increasingly replace face-to-face conversation, have on both personal relationships and individual capacities. She argues, for example, that online technologies "have not only changed what we do; they have changed who we are."[70] The change, she continues, is most profoundly seen in our capacity for empathy. She argues that empathy is not about proving someone with information or helping them find a support group but "convincing another person that you are there for the duration."[71] In this respect she is skeptical. She contends that a subtle but very important shift has occurred in our society regarding communities. In her view we no longer live in actual communities; rather, we have settled for having a sense of community. So, she questions whether a similar shift has occurred with respect to empathy: "Have we moved from empathy to a *sense* of empathy?"[72] In an interview she states, "You

67. *See id.* at 175–76.

68. *See id.* at 177.

69. *See id.* at 173–75.

70. Sherry Turkle, Reclaiming Conversation: The Power of Talk in the Digital Age 172 (2015).

71. *Id.* at 173.

72. *Id.* (emphasis in original).

need to suppress your empathy 'gene' in order to participate fully in the mobile revolution."[73]

This is not the proper occasion for evaluating Turkle's thesis or her overall, long-term project, but some observations about the debate she has sparked are relevant to the question of virtual communities for my purpose. Some of Turkle's critics have attacked her for implicitly relying on what they have called "digital dualism"—a separation of physical and virtual selves, with a privileging of the former over the latter. These critics attack this dualism as theoretically contradictory and empirically unsubstantiated.[74] They claim that empirical work from several countries "show a rich and heterogeneous relationship between humans and their communication devices."[75] They further argue that although Turkle is correct in pointing out that our society has experienced a decline in relationships that are characterized by their depth, she is wrong about the cause of the decline. It is not technology, or at least not technology alone, they contend, that has led to this decline. Rather, it is the totality of our technologies, digital and no-digital, that has transformed the way we communicate and interact with each other.

Critiques of digital forms of socialization such as Turkle's risk exaggerating both the "loss" of "real" communities and the thinness of social relationships online. Although such critiques are doubtless accurate to some degree, they tend to rely on anecdotal evidence, upon which generalizations are unreliable. There is, moreover, a certain nostalgia to such critiques, looking back to a golden past that in reality never existed and staring at a present that perhaps is not as different from the past as the critics would have one believe. Breakthrough technologies have always aroused anxieties about their negative impact on social ties and communication, but just as children's soccer teams have replaced bowling leagues, new forms of social ties develop in place of the old.

The bottom line is that we lack enough reliable evidence about the character of relationships within digital groups for us to be confident that they can properly be treated as communities under the human flourishing theory. Communities constitute the boundary marker for the range of persons to whom owners owe obligations to contribute toward capability development, and under these circumstances it is especially important to be cautious about the reach of communities under this theory.

73. Lauren Cassani Davis, *The Flight from Conversation*, The Atlantic, Oct. 7, 2015, *available at* http://www.theatlantic.com/technology/archive/2015/10/reclaiming-conversation-sherry-turkle/409273 (last visited Oct. 22, 2015).

74. *See, e.g.*, David Banks, *Sherry Turkle's Chronic Digital Dualism Problem*, The Society Pages, Cyborgology, Apr. 23, 2012, *available at* http://thesocietypages.org/cyborgology/2012/04/23/sherry-turkles-chronic-digital-dualism-problem.

75. *Id.*

CORPORATE OWNERS

So far, I have said nothing about the type of owner who may be subject to obligations. Specifically, do the obligations to support the capabilities of fellow community members apply to corporate owners as well as to individuals? The short answer is that there is nothing unique about the human flourishing theory in this respect. Corporate entity-owners have always been subject to obligations, some inherent, some contractual, and the same holds true under the human flourishing theory. The question of corporate personhood poses no great problem here.

Corporations, even very large multinational ones, are members of various communities. They belong to professional organizations; they have ties with the local communities where they have their headquarters and where they do business; and they are members of their national communities. These ties create interdependent relationships that enable the firms to support these communities' capability needs in multiple ways, and the communities support the firms' capability development as well. General Motors, headquartered in Detroit, has close ties with the state of Michigan and the city of Detroit, providing various benefits to those communities, and they to it. The federal government's bailout of General Motors in 2009[76] is only the starkest and most extreme such capability-building contribution to a corporate member. For smaller firms, the community ties that enable capability development are even stronger.

If corporations, including large multinational firms, are owners for purposes of the human flourishing theory, this raises the further question whether the communities to which they owe obligations include the global community. Firms such as General Motors, Apple, and McDonald's do business around the world, and they own property around the world. They pride themselves on their global status. Every day, their activities beyond the boundaries of the United States touch the lives of millions of people in very direct ways. Should we, then, treat the idea of the global community as coherent as applied to multinational corporations? I don't think we need to answer this question because I don't think it is the relevant question to ask. The proper question is, when a firm-owner does business in another country, affecting that country's inhabitants, what obligations does the firm-owner owe to *those* people. The coherence of the global community concept is really beside the point here. True, some activities of corporations cause harms that have a global impact—carbon emissions is an obvious example—the same is true for individuals. All of us engage in activities that have global impacts, so there is no particular reason to single out corporations for special treatment in

76. *General Motors Chapter 11 Reorganization*, Wikipedia, *available at* https://en.wikipedia.org/wiki/General_Motors_Chapter_11_reorganization (last visited July 21, 2017).

this respect. Nor is there any good reason to consider the idea of a global community useful for purposes of the human flourishing theory.

THE DARK SIDE OF COMMUNITY—REVISITED

Finally, we must confront the remaining problem of community's dark side—the inherent tendency of communities to exclude persons who do not meet the requirements for membership. We cannot evade or sidestep the issue by simply pointing to Jeremy Waldron's comments about the attractive aspects of community-as-actually-lived, for Waldron himself goes on to note that what are sometimes called "community norms" in fact represent "the imposition of a particular a priori vision by a few persons (often outsiders) on a community that has traditionally organized itself on quite another basis."[77]

Waldron is certainly right to be concerned about this dark side of community. I am talking about a different side of community, however, a side that we all need. We all need to feel that we belong somewhere, to be comfortable with a group of people with whom we share some experience that is deeply important in our lives.

I have friends who have problems with overeating. Suppose that I am one of them.

Suppose that I have issues with self-image that lead me to eat excessively, then purge. Someone says something to me that devastates my sense of self-worth. I eat a quart of ice cream to relieve this pain, but finding that it doesn't help but indeed contributes to the problem, I purge. So, I join a twelve-step support group, Overeaters Anonymous (OA), and experience a sense of belonging.

These are the only folks who really understand how I feel and what I experience, and for the first time, I feel comfortable with them. OA does have a requirement for membership. Closed meetings are open only to persons who "have a desire" to stop overeating. This requirement does act as a form of exclusion, but it is not at all like the exclusion practiced by people who form closed armed encampments in remote places in Montana or Idaho. It is a benign form of exclusion, not contributing to further subordination of traditionally oppressed groups. This is not community's dark side but instead the type of community that humans need to experience a fruitful life.

Community is both a social fact and a norm. In both respects, there is reason to be mindful of community's capacity to contribute to forms of exclusion that are simply unacceptable. But our cautiousness about this dark side of community should not lead us to overlook or undervalue what it contributes to our lives or how it enables humans to flourish.

77. Waldron, *Homelessness and Community, supra* note 17, at 406.

PART THREE

Obligations

4

Intergenerational Communities

Do the communities to which property owners owe obligations include future and/or past generations? Stated otherwise, do property owners owe obligations to members of future and/or past generations? Although the question can be reframed in rights-terms so that it faces rights-oriented theories of property, it seems to pose a greater challenge to those theories of property that directly focus on the obligations that property owners owe to others rather than (or, better, along with the rights of owner). The challenge is compounded where such theories emphasize the relationships between individual property owners[1] and the various communities to which they belong. Do those communities include members of future generations? This chapter addresses these questions as they apply to the human flourishing theory of property.

So far, I have argued that our dependence creates for us an obligation to participate in and support the social networks and structures that enable us to develop those human capabilities that make it possible for living members of the various communities to which we belong to flourish. My concerns in this chapter are whether such an obligation extends to nonliving members of our communities,

1. Although I do discuss collective obligations to past and future generations to some extent in this chapter, my main focus is on the obligations of individuals. More specifically, I focus on individual obligations as they pertain to property concretely.

past and future, as well, and if so, what is the scope of such an obligation and whether the fulfillment of the obligation is always a strictly private matter or is at least collective in some contexts. I argue that we do indeed owe obligations to nonliving members of our generational communities. I argue further that with respect to members of future generational communities there are two types of obligations, one general, the other specific.

The general obligation (GO) is to provide future generations with the basic material background conditions that are necessary for them to be able to carry out what I call life-transcending projects that their forebears have transmitted to them. This obligation is general insofar as it is not project-specific; rather, its purpose is to enable future generations to flourish. It is general, moreover, in the sense it is the obligation that any decent liberal society owes to its own members, an infragenerational obligation concerning goods that such a society ought to save rather than consume. Such goods will then remain available for future generations.

Although many other theorists have discussed the GO, what I add to the literature is a discussion of the specific obligation (SO). The SO is project-specific; that is, its purpose is to enable successive generational community members to whom particular life-transcending projects have been forwarded to be carried out in their way. The future generational members to whom the project is transferred must also be given whatever resources or goods are necessary to carry the project forward in its intended way.

I argue further that each generational community owes its predecessors the obligation to accept life-transcending projects transmitted to them by their forebears and to make reasonable efforts to carry those projects forward into the future. The obligation is based on the past generational community members' dependency on their successors for the projects to continue into the future, a matter that is constitutive of the project creators' flourishing. This obligation is defeasible, rather than absolute, however. Persons to whom life-transcending projects have been forwarded for caretaking and fulfillment must be free to reject the projects that are themselves immoral or that otherwise unreasonably burden them. Concomitantly, creators of life-transcending projects, in transmitting such projects to successive generational members, are under the moral obligation not to impose immoral, unreasonable, or foolish projects on their successors.

The scope of both the GO and the SO are more restricted than some rights theorists, such as Jeremy Waldron, have claimed.[2] Unlike Waldron, I argue that

2. *See* Jeremy Waldron, The Right to Private Property 115–17, 423, 425–27, 430–39, 444–45 (1988) (developing a general-rights theory of property with broadly distributive implications).

the obligations that property owners owe to past and future generations are grounded on dependence. Specifically, I argue that in the intergenerational context dependency involves reciprocity (and vice versa) and that there are two distinct, although related, senses of reciprocity at work here. One is a form of serial reciprocity, a "pay it forward" version of reciprocity that exists between one generation and its successors. The second version is a more direct form of reciprocity, what we might call a "quid pro quo" reciprocity. This form of reciprocity exists between the persons transferring life-transcending projects and their future generational counterparts who receive the projects. The idea is that members of future generational communities continue the life-transcending projects of their predecessors in return for the transferors' obligation to provide the project recipients with goods that are necessary to continue and, where possible, improve the project. The two versions of reciprocity, pay it forward and quid pro quo, although reinforcing, are distinct from each other because each is more closely associated with one or the other obligation, the GO or SO. Specifically, quid pro quo reciprocity does the most work with respect to those assets that are the subject of the SO, which is project-specific. Serial reciprocity fits better with the GO, which is not asset-specific and not peculiar (although relevant) to life-transcending projects.

As the distance between the living and the future increases, the obligations between generational communities gradually weaken. Time generally mitigates or dilutes the moral obligations that generations owe to the past.[3] After an extended period of years the possessor of the asset that began as a life-transcending project is apt to regard that asset as her own, free to use it as she wishes, and the asset loses its identity as life-transcending. No fixed period of time can be given for such a loss of identity. The matter is highly context-dependent, varying according to such factors as the type of asset (a modest personal hobby or collection versus a family farm or business), changes that may be needed to maintain or improve the project over time, the level of personal skill necessary to carry the project forward, and so forth.

The primary focus of this chapter is on the obligations that individuals *qua* property owners owe to members of future generations. However, I also certainly recognize that collective obligations to members of future generations exist, especially with respect to GO. Both types of obligations, individual and collective, may, and as I argue, do coexist, but it is important to keep them separate, for both their scope and respective bases may differ.

3. *See* Jeremy Waldron, *Superseding Historic Injustice*, 103 Ethics 4 (1992).

ARE THERE INTERGENERATIONAL COMMUNITIES?

The idea that there are communities that cross generational boundaries has been widely contested. Without reviewing all the objections and questions that theorists have raised regarding this concept, we must at least consider some of these doubts. For example, given that individuals do not regularly interact with members of future generations, how are intergenerational communities even possible? Second, how can such communities be said to exist when some individuals do not identify with any generation other than their own? Third, if communities are constitutive of individual identities insofar as its members share notions of the good or at least participate in open debates about shared goods, how are transgenerational constitutive communities possible where members of future generations do not directly participate in such debates?

The first problem is familiar in the literature on intergenerational justice. The notion of intergenerational communities seems implausible given the fact that members of the present generation do not interact with future generations.[4] In the absence of such interaction, there is no reciprocity between present and future generations.[5] There must be, one scholar argues, "the exchange of ideas and conceptions of purposes that must be available to persons before they can be considered to stand as joint participants in a common project."[6]

This objection trades on a narrow conception of interaction. It supposes that social interaction must be face to face, direct, or synchronic. But interactions among groups often are diachronic. The transmission of cultural memories, shared political histories, and traditions,[7] for example, are diachronic, yet are forms of group interaction. In the process of such transmissions, past generations speak, as it were, to the present and future generations. Those generations, in turn, speak back to the past by interpreting these histories and traditions from their own point of view. What results is a hermeneutic conversation that is certainly an "exchange of ideas and conceptions of purposes." Indeed, this hermeneutic intergenerational conversation is sometimes more robust than that among generational contemporaries.

4. *See, e.g.*, Ernest Partridge, *Future Generations, in* A Companion to Environmental Ethics 377 (Dale Jamieson ed., 2001).

5. *See* Norman S. Care, *Future Generations, Public Policy and the Motivation Problem,* 4 Envtl. Ethics 195 (1982).

6. Norman S. Care, Decent People 112 (2000).

7. In the United States, for example, a clear example is the history and tradition of the U.S. Constitution, a cultural memory that has been the subject of extraordinarily lively debates.

Related to the question of interaction is another objection that is sometimes raised. Because present and future people are not positioned so as to be able to reciprocate with each other, they cannot develop a sense of identity with each other, a feeling of being on the same side.[8] This objection fails to take account of the multiple ways in which people can and do identify with each other. It is not fruitful to ask whether members of one group identify in the abstract with members of another group. The more helpful question is whether there is some specific level or respect in which members of the different groups identify with each other. For example, as a practicing Roman Catholic, I identify with Catholics around the world on the various issues that concern the Church despite the fact that I am not in a position to reciprocate with many of them. Identification for purposes of community existence does not require complete or 100 percent identity of interests or views. Such a requirement would disqualify many groups that otherwise plainly are communities, including families. What is required is that members of the two groups experience a sense of common membership with respect to some value that is important to them both.

A third objection concerns shared purposes. Presumably, members of communities hold shared purposes or norms. Such sharing is indispensable to the existence of communities because of their constitutive nature. According to this constitutive conception of communities,[9] a "community [is] . . . constitutive of the shared self-understandings of the participants and embodied in their institutional arrangements. . . ."[10] That is, what binds members of the community together is not sentiment but identity.[11] Community members share understandings of whom and what they are, and these understandings are sufficiently fundamental that they constitute part of the members' self-identities.

Avner de-Shalit refers to the experience of sharing that is necessary for constitutive communities by the term "moral similarity."[12] He distinguishes that term from cultural homogeneity that may characterize groups that may lack shared ideas or purposes.[13] Nor does moral similarity require unanimity. Communities experience debate about the ideas and norms they share, sometimes quite robustly. Old ideas may be re-examined; new one proposed and either adopted

8. *See* Care, *Future Generations, Public Policy and the Motivation Problem, supra* note 5, at 208–09.

9. *See* Michael Sandel, Liberalism and the Limits of Justice (1982); Avner de-Shalit, Why Posterity Matters: Environmental Policies and Future Generations (1995).

10. Sandel, Liberalism and the Limits of Justice, *supra* note 9, at 173.

11. *See* de-Shalit, Why Posterity Matters, *supra* note 9, at 33.

12. *Id.* at 25–31 and *passim.*

13. *Id.* at 27.

or rejected. As the community's normative constitution shifts, some members may become disaffected, losing their moral similarity, and drop out. The shift may attract new members in turn. The point is that debate is very much a part of, indeed even necessary for, the experience of moral similarity.

If debate is necessary for the moral similarity that characterizes communities, how is such a debate possible between members of present and future generations? Here de-Shalit introduces another concept that is useful—cultural interaction. De-Shalit points out that every community has its own history of cultural interaction, which includes political, social, and cultural experiences that they share as well as shared traditions, symbols, practices, and codes.[14] Cultural interaction is not confined within the same generation, of course, for children interact in various ways with their parents and grandparents about the meanings and even legitimacy of their traditions and beliefs. These interactions are face to face, but others are not. For example, religious communities whose shared traditions include historical texts read, interpret, reinterpret, and debate those texts over many generations, sometimes centuries, in an ongoing debate about the meaning and legitimacy of various textual meanings. These debates are between present and past generations as well as within single generations. This example is what Alasdair C. MacIntyre has in mind when he writes "[L]iving tradition then is an historically extended, socially embodied argument, and an argument precisely in part about the goods which constitute that tradition. Within a tradition the pursuit of goods extends through generations, sometimes through many generations."[15]

The contested meaning and even legitimacy of the religious group's core texts are the topics of an ongoing argument as to the religion's very identity. In this respect, as MacIntyre points out, "Traditions . . . embody continuities of conflict."[16]

These continuities are forward-looking as well as backward-looking. Cultural practices commonly speak to the future, even the distant future. When originators of core religious texts (or glosses upon those texts) write, they address not only their contemporaries but followers (including future converts) who will listen to their texts and reply, as it were, throughout the generations ahead. The conversation is not face to face, but it is very real nonetheless. It is as real as when an American citizen writes a letter to her president, knowing that there will be no reply. The letter writer does not think she is speaking to herself, for there is some

14. *Id.* at 23.

15. Alasdair MacIntyre, After Virtue 222 (1981).

16. *Id.*

possibility that her letter will influence the president in some way, however indirectly or slightly.

Future community members to whom the group's cultural values, traditions, and practices are addressed receive the message. Their cultural and normative starting point is what they inherited from their forebears. But they are not merely passive receptors. They answer back by reviewing, critiquing, and sometimes revising the cultural traditions and normative material that they inherited. Revision is sometimes necessary because of changes in the community's circumstances and economic, social, technological, or other types of changes.[17] Eventually, the degree of moral similarity will diminish to the point that it is no longer meaningful to consider the intergenerational community as still existing. De-Shalit explains:

> When it comes about that the values of the members of the community change drastically, many members will find themselves in a state of growing alienation from the community of their ancestors. This will continue until the question arises as to whether they still regard it as the same transgenerational community, a community which defines the "self[”] of its members. A time will come when it becomes questionable whether future generations will still speak of the same transgenerational community.[18]

Intergenerational constitutive communities, then, are both dynamic and contingent. They change, and their duration is limited, dependent as they are upon external factors that affect their members' identification with them and their shared normative orientation.

CAN OBLIGATIONS EXIST WITHIN INTERGENERATIONAL COMMUNITIES?

The human flourishing theory grounds obligation on dependence. As we have seen, it locates the source of property owners' obligations to their communities on the fact that all human beings are dependent throughout their lives on others to provide them in various ways with the means necessary to enable the development of certain indispensable capabilities. Even if one agrees, following the previous analysis, that communities are not confined to presently living persons, one may argue that, on the theory's own premises, property owners cannot owe obligations to members of future generations because the living are not

17. *See* DE-SHALIT, WHY POSTERITY MATTERS, *supra* note 9, at 46–49.

18. *Id.* at 47.

dependent upon unborn persons. This is a powerful objection, and it requires careful consideration.

Looking Back: Obligations to Past Generations—Dependence and Life-Transcending Projects

Before looking forward, we must first look back. That is, we need first to discuss obligations that the present generation owes to past generations and the basis for such obligations. Much has already been written on this topic,[19] but what matters for my purposes is the role of dependence in establishing obligations between members of different generations. The basis for skepticism that such an obligation exists is the very fact that members of past generations are dead. Because they are gone, the skeptic argues, nothing that we do or do not do today can possibly make their lives go any better or worse. The response to this objection that I shall make will pave the way for the case for obligations that we owe to future generations.

LIFE-TRANSCENDING PROJECTS

The skeptic's argument that living persons can do nothing to affect the lives of those who are dead ultimately rests on the assumption that obligations must be based on avoidance of harm.[20] Whether the dead can be harmed is a matter of considerable debate in the philosophical literature,[21] but we need not resolve that debate to conclude that the present generation does owe obligations to the past. There is another basis for such obligations, an alternative to the harm principle. That basis is what we can call *life-transcending projects*. People have interests in having life-transcending projects carried through and realized after their deaths, sometimes many years after their deaths, but obviously they cannot do so themselves. They are dependent upon the living to honor the interest that the dead have in seeing their life-transcending projects continued and realized beyond the death of their creators.

19. *See, e.g.*, Thomas Scanlon, What We Owe to Each Other (1998); George Pitcher, *The Misfortunes of the Dead*, 21 Am. Phil. Q. 183 (1984).

20. *See* Janna Thompson, Intergenerational Justice: Rights and Responsibilities in an Intergenerational Polity 56 (2009).

21. *See, e.g.*, Joan C. Callahan, *On Harming the Dead*, 97 Ethics 341 (1987); Pitcher, *The Misfortunes of the Dead*, *supra* note 19; Joel Feinberg, *The Rights of Animals and Unborn Generations*, *in* Philosophy and Environmental Crisis 4 (William T. Blackstone ed., 1974).

Life-transcending projects are those projects the personal value or importance of which transcend creators or originators of the projects personally and so to transcend their lifetimes. Such projects vary widely. They range from moneymaking personal projects, such as businesses that people have created, to public-minded projects, such as charitable foundations. Nor are life-transcending projects limited to material affairs of these sorts. They may be as abstract as ideas or theories that a person has developed and to which she has devoted a great deal of effort and time. There are many obvious examples of life-transcending projects, including important private institutions including universities (e.g., Stanford, Cornell, the University of Chicago), museums (e.g., the Barnes Museum, the Guggenheim Museum); foundations (e.g., the Ford Foundation, the Carnegie Foundation); private hospitals, and so on.

Wealthy individuals commonly create charitable trusts in their wills, and these charitable trusts typically involve life-transcending projects. Charitable trust donors usually impose restrictions on what the trustees can do with the trust funds, and these restrictions represent attempts to assure that future trustees fulfill the donor's life-transcending project. Sometimes these restrictions become impossible or impracticable to implement, and the law must modify the terms of the trust instrument so that the trust can operate on terms as close as possible to the donor's original intent.[22] At other times, however, the donor's restrictions are so extreme or become irreconcilable with evolving public policy that courts are no longer willing to carry out the donor's project as originally intended. (A racially discriminatory trust is an example.[23]) When that occurs, the court must decide whether the donor's project was so intimately tied to the offensive feature that he would not want to go forward without it. If that is the case, then the court must refuse to carry out the trust. But if the court concludes that in its judgment the offensive feature was not indispensable to the donor's project, then the court will revise the terms of the project to remove the offending feature and go forward with it.

Wealthy persons are not the only ones who have life-transcending projects the fulfillment of which require the help of future generations. Owners of small businesses and family farms usually hope that the enterprises to which they have devoted the better portion of their lives will continue to thrive after their deaths, and they depend on future generations to carry out their hopes and dreams. Inventors hope that their creations will continue to be used many years after their

22. This is known as the *cy pres* doctrine (*cy pres* is short for *cy pres comme possible*, a phrase taken from old Law French, meaning "as nearly as possible"). It is well established in the common law. *See, e.g.*, UNIFORM TRUST CODE §413 (2010); RESTATEMENT (THIRD) OF TRUSTS §67 (2003–12).

23. *See, e.g.*, Home for Incurables of Baltimore City v. University of Maryland Medical System Corp., 797 A.2d 746 (Md. 2002) (trust for "white patients who need physical rehabilitation").

deaths. Authors hope that their works will continue to attract readers for decades, even centuries to come. Scholars hope that future scholars will use their work, and so on.

Other examples are less obvious. For example, personal activities such as artwork (painting, sculpture, etc.), crafts (pottery, knitting, needlework, etc.), and even gardening develop into life-transcending projects for many people. So, too, do collections ranging from coins and stamps to artwork. Collectors commonly are passionate about their collections, and they pass them on to others at their death in the hope that future owners will recognize the project's significance. Such collectors hope that their projects will survive rather than simply being tossed away as if it were nothing more than yesterday's newspapers. Such activities and collections are not life-transcending for everyone, of course. Some are just hobbies or amusements that people use to pass the time. But for many people, wealthy and poor alike, activities and collections, often quite modest, are indeed life-transcending. They enable their creators in important ways to flourish. The results of these activities often are weighted with self-expression and personal identity. It would be surprising if even the most modestly talented amateur artist or woodworker is indifferent to the destiny of her or his creation. Creators care about the future of their creations. Creators of all sorts do not value their creations solely for the enjoyment that they give the creators during their lifetimes.

Creations have deeper value than that. In a very real sense, such creations, even those limited in achievement or talent, represent a form of immortality for their creators. What such projects transcend, then, is not self-interest but time.

Even those whose lives have seemingly not been devoted to creative enterprises have their own life-transcending projects. The protection and care of family heirlooms, even though with modest or slight market value, is often a matter of great concern to ordinary people, including people of limited wealth. They pass on to their children and grandchildren objects that they themselves received from their ancestors as tokens of memory, family continuity, and love, and they depend on their children and grandchildren to care for these emotionally weighted objects and to pass them on when their turn comes.

LIFE-TRANSCENDING PROJECTS AND DEPENDENCE

The creators of life-transcending projects cannot realize the time-transcendent value of their projects by themselves; they are dependent on others—future generations—to do so. The immorality that the creators of such projects seek for their creations requires the cooperation of future generations. The dependency of past generational members upon their living counterparts may take multiple forms, ranging from recognition of the project as something worth pursuing to execution and ongoing management of the project.

Project creators sometimes attempt to reduce the discretion of their successors to recognize and implement life-transcending projects through the same techniques discussed previously, notably legal arrangements that impose duties on the donees to comply with specified restrictions. Arrangements like trusts are especially common among wealthier creators, whose life-transcending projects often are an important part of their estate portfolio. Such arrangements often pose serious problems, both legal and moral, that we need to consider.

The Dead Hand Problem

Restrictions that now-deceased creators of life-transcending projects sometimes impose on later generation beneficiaries of these projects may pose difficult questions concerning the obligations of the living generation when asked to implement the terms of the project. For example, when creators of life-transcending projects transfer their projects to later generation beneficiaries in trusts, they sometimes do so through family trusts that extend the duration of trusts for very long periods of time, over many generations of future beneficiaries who are given only limited property interests in the projects. The creator's objective is to control the project for many generations after his death. This creates a problem known to common-law lawyers as the "dead-hand" problem.[24] Anglo-American law places limits on these dead-hand trusts, albeit indirectly, through various rules, including the infamous Rule Against Perpetuities.[25] Other problematic creator-imposed restrictions in trusts include prohibitions on the sale of an asset that the creator originally transferred into the trust and which later declines in value, thereby threatening the interests of the beneficiaries. Commonly, the assets in question are life-transcending projects, such as a business that the creator personally started and developed.

A good example of this problem is the case of Joseph Pulitzer's will.[26] Pulitzer, after whom the top American annual prizes for journalism is named,[27] left a will that gave to his trustees the large majority of shares of stock in a publishing company that he owned and created, the Press Publishing Company. This firm published several newspapers, including the now-defunct *New York World*,

24. *See* Lewis Simes, Public Policy and the Dead Hand *passim* (1955).

25. The common-law version of the rule, first set out in the famous case of Duke of Norfolk's Case, 22 Eng. Rep. 931 (Ch. 1681), provides that "[n]o interest is good unless it must vest, if at all, not later than twenty-one years after some life in being at the creation of the interest." John Chipman Gray, The Rule Against Perpetuities §201 (4th ed. 1942).

26. Matter of Pulitzer, 249 N.Y.S. 87 (Sur. Ct. 1931), aff'd mem., 260 N.Y.S. 975 (App. Div. 1932).

27. *See* Columbia Journalism School, *The Pulitzer Prizes*, http://www.journalism.columbia.edu/page/164-pulitzer (last visited Dec. 14, 2013).

to which Pulitzer was particularly devoted. The trust was for the benefit of his sons. Pulitzer's will expressly withheld from the trustees the power to sell the Press Publishing Company stock "under any circumstances whatever. . . ."[28] The will went on to give Pulitzer's reasons, reflecting the fact that the Press Publishing Company was his life-transcending project:

> I particularly enjoin upon my sons and descendants the duty of preserving, perfecting and perpetuation "The World" newspaper (to the maintenance and upbuilding of which I have sacrificed my health and strength) in the same spirit in which I have striven to create conduct it as a public institution, from motives higher than mere gain, it having been my desire that it should at all times be conducted in a spirit of independence and with a view to inculcating high standards and public spirit among the people and their official representatives, and it is my earnest wish that said newspaper shall hereafter be conducted upon the same principles.[29]

Some years after Pulitzer's death, readership of the *World* newspaper steadily eroded, causing the value of the Press Publishing Company stock to substantially decline. The trustees sought judicial approval to sell the stock on the ground that the unanticipated changes of circumstances threatened to defeat the purpose of the trust, which, they argued, was the benefit of Pulitzer's sons. The court agreed, holding that it had the inherent power to respond to emergency circumstances that threatened total destruction of the trust itself. Regarding the will's language that the stock not be sold under any circumstances, the court stated, "A man of his [Pulitzer's] sagacity and business ability could not have intended that from mere vanity, the publication of the newspapers, with which his name and efforts had been associated, should be persisted in until the entire trust asset was destroyed or wrecked by bankruptcy or dissolution."[30]

John Langbein has posed the challenging question, "Suppose . . . that the settlor in *Pulitzer* had foreseen and recited in the trust instrument the danger that the newspaper might become unprofitable, and he directed the trustees to continue operating it anyhow." Langbein points out, "Such a restriction would not have been enforceable."[31] He goes on the explain, "Attempting to prevent the court from

28. *Id.* at 92.

29. *Id.*

30. *Id.* at 95.

31. John H. Langbein, *Mandatory Rule in the Law of Trusts*, 98 Nw. U. L. Rev. 1105, 1118 (2004) (footnote omitted).

modifying the trust in response to such materially worsened circumstances would offend the anti–dead hand principle embodied in the rule that the trust must be for the benefit of the beneficiaries."[32] The "benefit-the-beneficiaries" rule to which Langbein refers expresses the public policy that once a person has placed property in trust for the benefit of third parties, their benefit must override any personal motive that the creator may have had regarding the continuing use of the property that is fundamentally incompatible with the beneficiaries' interests.[33]

The *New York World* newspaper was a life-transcending project of Joseph Pulitzer, as his restriction so vividly manifests. The case is a good illustration of both the fact that there must be limits on the obligations, especially legal obligations, that the living owe to the dead to implement life-transcending projects of the dead, however fundamental they may have been, and some of the reasons why such limits must exist.

The dead hand problem creates a risk of undermining the communal character of intergenerational relations. Past generations may not only impose restrictions of the sort I have just described, but they may refuse to transfer important assets to future generations of family members altogether. For example, Joseph Pulitzer may have chosen to leave his newspaper businesses to a business associate rather than to his sons. This undermines the dependency between generations and inhibits future generations from working within the framework necessary for communal relations between the generations. The role of future generations is, after all, to participate in the life-transcending projects of past generations, enhance them, and enable them to be carried forward into the future. If members of past generations exercise their control over those projects by refusing to transmit them within the family, broadly defined, then this role will be frustrated.

There is no obvious or easy way to avoid this risk. It is a consequence of a legal system that prefers the freedom of past owners over the interests of the living. American law imposes no restrictions upon the ability of testators to leave their property at death to whomever they wish, disinheriting any members of their family except the surviving spouse.[34] We must work within whatever limits the existing legal system creates. Nevertheless, reasons of self-interest suggest that this risk is not great. Creators of life-transcending projects usually trust their

32. *Id.* at 1118–19 (footnote omitted).

33. *See* Uniform Trust Code §404, 105(b)(3); Restatement (Third) of Trusts §27(2) (2003–12).

34. American states have statutes, called elective share statutes, that protect a surviving spouse from disinheritance. The statutes vary in their details, but typically give the surviving spouse a nonbarrable share of one-third of the decedent's estate. *See* Thomas P. Gallanis, Family Property Law: Cases and Materials on Wills, Trusts, and Future Interests 349–53 (5th ed. 2011).

children and grandchildren more than non–family members to carry through with their projects. After all, in most cases the creator's children have been with the project since its inception and are more aware than most people of its importance to their parent. The parent may even have groomed the children or grandchildren to take over care and management of the project at the appropriate time in the future. This is by no means an invariable scenario. Parents sometimes do disinherit their children, but the incidence of this is sufficiently small that the risk of this aspect of the dead hand problem is not great.

Are Intended Transferees Obligated to Accept Life-Transcending Projects?

Do the transferees of life-transcending projects owe obligations to past-generation creators to accept the projects and carry through with them, or are they free to refuse to accept the projects? Normally, of course, the law of gifts provides that intended donees are free to refuse gifts—acceptance is a requirement for completion of a donative transfer.[35] But is there a moral obligation here? There may, after all, be different considerations when asking whether a legal or moral obligation exists to the past generation.

There really are two separate questions here: first, whether the intended transferee is free to refuse the transfer entirely or instead must accept the life-transcending project; second, whether, if the transferee accepts the project, she is free to possess, use, or enjoy that project in whatever way she sees fit, regardless of the creator's original purpose or intent. With respect to the first question, autonomy considerations loom here, but they do so as to both sides, donor and donee. Inevitably, someone's autonomy interest must be sacrificed—that is precisely the rub of the dead hand dilemma.

I have suggested earlier that human dependence upon members of communities to which we belong, communities that enable us to flourish, creates for us a moral obligation to support, in ways that are appropriate to us, their flourishing. Does this general principle mean that intended recipients of life-transcending projects are morally obligated to accept transfers of those projects? I think it does, although the obligation that it creates must be one that is defeasible, for reasons that I shall explain. In transmitting life-transcending projects to their future counterparts, members of each generational community become dependent upon those successors to accept and carry forward the project in order to fulfill the project's life-transcending purpose. The fulfillment of that purpose is constitutive of the creator's life as one that is as well-lived as possible. Creators transmit

35. *See* Richard Hyland, Gifts: A Study in Comparative Law 484, 493 (2009).

their projects to their future counterparts with the expectation that the designated recipients will accept the projects and exercise reasonable efforts to carry the projects forward in the best possible way. If creators knew that their projects would die with them, their lives would be significantly diminished.

At the same time, this obligation is defeasible, rather than absolute. Persons to whom life-transcending projects have been forwarded for caretaking and fulfillment must be free to reject the projects that are themselves immoral or that otherwise unreasonably burden them.[36] The reason is the recipient's individual autonomy. Although autonomy is not the paramount value in the human flourishing theory, it is nevertheless relevant to that theory.

This leads to the second question, whether the recipient of a life-transcending project should be free to possess, use, or enjoy that project in whatever way she sees fit, regardless of the creator's original purpose or intent. I said earlier that intended recipients are under a morally defeasible duty to accept such projects and to make reasonable efforts to carry those projects forward and promote them in their intended way. Just what does this duty of "reasonable efforts" entail? The question eludes any precise answer. Certainly, transferees are not entirely free to possess, use, or enjoy projects they possess in any way they seem fit. Nor is the duty absolute in the opposite sense: It makes no moral sense to say that, having accepted the project, the transferee is strictly and unconditionally bound to whatever terms the creator may have imposed. The matter is inevitably context-dependent, as the very term "reasonable" suggests. Among the variables that we should consider is, how much of a burden the project imposes upon the possessor. The greater the burden and the more the project disrupts the recipient's life, the greater amount of freedom she should have. Displaying a painting created by the transferor is a far simpler matter than continuing, with the possible need for substantial future improvements, a family farm. Conversely, we should consider how much of a benefit the possessor is obtaining from the project. A possessor should be required to make greater efforts to promote a project from which she obtains substantial benefits.[37] Another factor that will carry weight in the reasonableness calculus is time. The further removed in time the recipient is

36. Concomitantly, creators of life-transcending projects, in transmitting such projects to successive generational members, are under the moral obligation not to impose immoral, unreasonable, or foolish projects on their successors.

37. For example, suppose a project is a rental building that is aging and beginning to require greater maintenance if its life is to be extended. If the building's net income-stream would continue to be high enough to provide the current owner a comfortable level of support even after paying expenses necessary for the building's upkeep, the owner should be required to make improvements necessary to extend the building's lifetime, rather than "milking" the building to derive a higher rental level.

from the creator, the weaker the obligation becomes. This is not only because it becomes more difficult to determine exactly what the creator's wishes were but also because circumstances are likely to change as more time passes, creating the need to weaken the recipient's obligations to the dead. American trust law, even while requiring that the original donor's intent be respected, recognizes the need to build flexibility into the trust arrangement to accommodate future changes in circumstances.

For charitable trusts, the *cy-pres* ("as near as possible") doctrine permits courts to revise the terms of trusts where changed circumstances have made it impossible or impracticable to fulfill the donor's original plans.[38] For private trusts, the deviation doctrine permits courts to modify the terms of a trust where unanticipated changes of circumstances put the trust's well-being in jeopardy.[39] Similar considerations apply with respect to moral obligations owed to past generations.

Looking Forward: Obligations to Future Generations and Forms of Reciprocity

Let us now reverse direction and look forward. Having concluded that members of the living generation owe duties, moral and at times legal, to honor and carry out certain life-transcending projects of the dead, does it necessarily follow that the same holds true of the relationship between those who are now living and the unborn? After all, the relationship between present and future generations can be seen as just the mirror image of that between the present and the past: Living people are the future dead, and unborns are the future living.

Earlier, I suggested that the basis of obligations that community members owe to each other, inter- as well as intragenerationally, is dependence. I suggested further that dependence can be understood in terms of reciprocity between intergenerational community members.

Finally, I have distinguished between two different sorts of reciprocity, "quid pro quo" reciprocity and "pay it forward" reciprocity, and suggested that although the two forms of reciprocity overlap with and indeed reinforce each other, each has greater valence with respect to past or future generational communities, as the case may be. Quid pro quo, a more direct form of reciprocity, has greater salience in the context of the relationship between present and past generational communities. As I discuss in greater detail in the next section, quid pro quo

38. *See* Uniform Trust Code §413 (2010).

39. See Uniform Trust Code §412 (2010).

reciprocity is more particularly relevant to specific obligation, which generally involves specific assets ("in return for honoring my deceased father's desire that I take care of the family farm he passed on the me, he endowed me with the capital and other material means necessary to make it succeed").

A dependency relationship also exists between present and future generations, and this dependency relationship, too, creates reciprocity. But the nature of the reciprocity is more serial than direct, more "pay it forward" than "give back for what you get." Serial reciprocity has a kind of asymmetrical character. We pay on to the next generations what we have received from the past—clean environment, basic infrastructure, a workable public system of government, that is, the goods that are the substance of the general obligation. Future generations generally depend on their ancestors to leave them with such goods as their starting point.

Of course, it is possible for future generations to create these conditions themselves in the absence of such an endowment, but that seems neither realistic nor morally sound. Successive generations have forwarded material endowments to their forebears for millennia, and there are good moral reasons why they should. Just as the past has endowed us with the material background goods required for us to have the kind of lives that enable us to carry on their life-transcending projects, so we should endow the future for the same reason. Future generations are dependent upon us to provide such endowments to that end. That is the point of serial reciprocity.[40]

Serial reciprocity imposes an obligation not to consume the capital endowment that we have received from past generations, the capital endowment that enabled us. We are morally obligated to conserve it, maintain it, and improve it, where necessary. We cannot simply "milk" such capital endowments for our own

40. This view of serial reciprocity places considerable distance between my approach and that of John Rawls. According to Rawls (A Theory of Justice 287 ff. (1999)), the obligation between generations is best solved on the basis of a "just savings principle." That principle requires each generation, acting under the veil of ignorance, to adopt a rate of capital accumulation that is appropriate to each stage of advance. Rawls says that eventually, once just institutions have been established, the required accumulation rate will be zero, and all that the society need do is to maintain just institutions and preserve their material base. Rawls, A Theory of Justice, *supra*, at 287. Rawls contends that every generation gains a reasonable rate of accumulation if maintained. "The process of accumulation, once it is begun and carried through, is to the good of all subsequent generations," he argues. "Each passes on to the next a fair equivalent in real capital as defined by a just savings principle." *Id.* at 288. This form of reciprocity is "peculiar," Rawls recognizes, because rather than paying back to the generation from which it received accumulated capital, each generation pays its accumulated capital on to the succeeding generation—hence, the term "serial reciprocity." *Id.* at 290. Unlike my theory, Rawls' view of serial reciprocity between takes no account of the role of dependency.

benefit, consuming them with no investment for the future. "Milking" is a practice that effectively dissipates and ends the endowment.[41]

Consider our transportation infrastructure, which, as I will discuss in the next section, is part of the substantive content of the GO. We inherited from the generations that preceded us a transportation system that once rivaled the rest of the world. Airlines ran on time; train service was extensive, relatively cheap, and convenient; highways, local and interstate, were well-maintained; bridges were safe and in good repair; and so on. As anyone who has flown or who drives knows, the picture has changed. Airline service unreliability is a topic of late-night comedians; train service has dried up in many parts of the country (including the town of Ithaca, New York, where I work); highways are pitted with endlessly unfilled potholes; bridges are rusting to unsafe conditions in familiar and important crossings. Some politicians periodically urge public investment in at least some aspects of this infrastructure, but little action is taken in an environment of declining public investment in collective goods. The transportation infrastructure has become an inherited capital endowment that the current generation is milking. The current generation is seriously at risk of breaching its moral obligation, based on serial reciprocity, to pass on to future generations the same necessary capital endowment that it received from its forebears.

This example also suggests why it is a mistake to appeal to market-based discount rates in analyzing the present generation's moral obligations to future generations.[42] Discount rates value the costs and benefit accruing to future generations less than those of the current generation.[43] It is "a numerical way of expressing the value judgment that beyond a certain point the future is not worth anything to presently living people."[44] There seems little room for doubt that individuals do engage in discounting in making decisions in their own lives, and their rates of discounting are, it appears, high.[45] But it is a very different question whether discounting is appropriate, or even relevant, as to the question whether the current generation owes obligations to the future.[46] As John O'Neill observes, "It is not

41. *Cf. supra* note 37.

42. The literature on this topic is vast. A few sources that I have found especially helpful include Derek Parfit, Reasons and Persons 480–86 (1984); Douglas A. Kysar, *Discounting . . . on Stilts*, 74 U. Chi. L. Rev. 119 (2007); Eduardo M. Peñalver, *Land's Virtues*, 94 Cornell L. Rev. 821, 853–56 (2009).

43. *See* John O'Neill, Ecology, Policy and Politics 48–49 (1993).

44. Herman E. Daly, Beyond Growth: The Economics of Sustainable Development 35–36 (1996).

45. *See* Shane Frederick et al., *Time Discounting and Time Preference: A Critical Review*, 40 J. Econ. Lit. 351, 393–94 (2002).

46. *See* O'Neill, Ecology, Policy and Politics, *supra* note 43, at 49–59.

that discount rates should be zeros, negative or positive, but that they are on the whole irrelevant to the discussion of the policy one should adopt to the future."[47] He goes on to note, "There are good principles that govern our dealings with the future—that we minimize resource depletion, that we avoid irreversible changes that we engage in sustainable economic activity and so on."[48]

THE SUBSTANTIVE CONTENT OF OBLIGATIONS TO FUTURE AND PAST GENERATIONAL COMMUNITIES

Assuming, at least provisionally, that intergenerational communities exist (i.e., that such a concept is meaningful) and that members of such communities owe each other duties, just what are those duties, and, equally important, what are the limits of those duties? These duties are moral duties, although conceivably they might have legal implications. My main concern here is with the moral duties, although I have some comments regarding possible legal aspects.

More important for my purposes than the distinction between moral and legal duties is the distinction between, on the one hand, the GO, the obligation to pass on to successor generational community members the basic material conditions that any decent liberal society owes to its own members, that is, an infra-generational obligation concerning goods that such a society ought to save rather than consume, and on the other hand, the SO, the obligation that creators of life-transcending projects owe to their recipients of such projects to provide such particular goods are necessary to carry the project forward in its intended way. As I have already indicated, the GO and SO, although overlapping and reinforcing, are distinct from each other and involve different forms of reciprocity that involve different sets of goods. After describing the substance of two types of obligations, I then discuss the extent to which each is collective rather than individual.

Paying It Forward: The GO and Necessary Background Conditions

What members of future generational communities minimally require in order to further the life-transcending projects transferred to them are certain essential material conditions. We cannot reasonably expect our future generational members to continue the projects that we have begun unless they live in circumstances within which they can live decent lives. No one can flourish without certain basic

47. *Id.* at 59 (emphasis in original). Rawls also rejects discounting from the moral point of view. *See* Rawls, A Theory of Justice, *supra* note 40, at 253.

48. O'Neill, Ecology, Policy and Politics, *supra* note 43, at 57.

resources that provide a background for existence. They are the goods that any decent society owes to members of its own generation, that is, they are infragenerational, and there is nothing uniquely intergenerational about them. At the same time, they constitute the substance of intergenerational obligations—the obligation owed to future generations—insofar as future generations must be enabled to flourishing generally in order to fulfill projects, their own as well as those transmitted to them by their predecessor. These goods are constitutive of the requisite material background for flourishing. From this perspective, they are the substance of the living generation's general obligation to the future, discussed in the preceding section, to pass on to future generations the material endowments that past generations have forwarded to us.

Which resources properly belong on such a list of basic goods that provide the background conditions that are necessary for human flourishing is the subject of endless debate. Certain goods seem inarguably on such a list, however. These include a well-functioning public security system and an adequate defense regime. Both a well-functioning police force and national security system are indispensable for personal security, without which no one can live a well-lived life. The background infrastructure would also include a clean (or reasonably so) environment—air, water, and so on—that future generational communities will inhabit and in which they will work. Lacking such an environment, they simply will be unable to carry through with any life-transcending projects, including their own. As Joel Feinberg remarked, "Surely we owe it to future generations to pass on a world that is not a used up garbage heap."[49] The background conditions must also include a reasonably well-functioning government (including legal system), one that is free (or relatively so) of corruption and is responsive to the greater community's needs. The requisite background infrastructure will also include well-functioning transportation and communication networks. It will further include a health-care system that provides decent and affordable health care.

This is a list of what we minimally owe, as a moral matter, to unborn members of the various communities. The resources on this list are those goods that nurture the capabilities necessary for their flourishing. The list, as I have already indicated, is not exclusive. I have kept it minimal in order to attract a broad range of agreement regarding what must be provided. Far less agreement will be reached on the questions of who bears the obligations to provide these goods and what the bases of those obligations are.

49. Joel Feinberg, *The Rights of Animals and Unborn Generations*, *in* Philosophy and Environmental Crisis 64–65 (William T. Blackstone ed., 1975).

BASES OF COLLECTIVE OBLIGATIONS

I consider three possible bases for obligations owed to future generational communities: collective action problems; contract, including implied understandings; and dependency.

Although it is possible that they will overlap in particular cases, it is important to treat them separately, for the scope and content of moral obligations that each may justify is likely to differ.

Collective Active Problems and Other Economic Rationales

From a strictly cost-minimizing perspective, the obligation to provide some but not all of the goods on the list of resources necessary for adequate background conditions is public. Other goods should be privately provided. Several of these resources are classic public goods, insofar as they meet the two usual characteristics of such goods, that is, nonrivalry and nonexcludability. These resources include a clean environment, a well-functioning public security (police), and an adequate defense regime. Due to well-known collective action problems, we cannot rely on individual preferences or market forces effectively to provide such resources. The obligation to do so, both now and into the future, must be collective, carried out by the state, through taxation and regulatory programs.

Other resources that make up a necessary background for flourishing are not classic public goods but are goods whose characteristics are such that their social provision is nevertheless most efficiently provided through public rather than private means, both now and for future generations. These resources include at least some aspects of the health-care system that generate substantial externalities (e.g., vaccination and care for communicable diseases; arguably, prenatal care[50]—in both cases, there are substantial externalities that make these goods public goods–like). However, there is much of health care that may not implicate externality concerns of this nature.[51] If we move beyond public goods analysis, we can note the many private market failures that may plague the health-care marketplace, justifying public involvement quite apart from public goods considerations. Basically, private provision of health insurance has proven itself to be plagued by high administrative costs which derive from many forces. Public

50. Thanks to George Hay for these examples.

51. If we start with the presumption that our society as a baseline will guarantee some forms of care—for example, emergency care (legislatively mandated in the United States)—and acknowledge that some individuals cannot pay for such care, then we can see that the U.S. system and its many forms of cross-subsidization imposes externalities of other sorts. I am grateful to Mike Frakes for pointing this out to me.

provision is simply cheaper. Employment-based plans heavily subsidized by the tax code has been one good middle ground.[52]

Contract-Based Obligations

A second possible basis for the obligation to future generational members is contract.

Where an agreement, explicit or implicit, existed between the transferor of the life-transcending project and the recipients, the presumption should be that the agreement, assuming that it can be satisfactorily proved, creates an obligation, both moral and legal, in the recipients. This is simply a matter of basic contract principles. The real question is whether there ought to be any limits on the scope of that moral obligation. Plainly, there are some limits, both as a matter of law and morality, to freedom of contract. Terms, conditions, or restrictions that creator-donors place on transfers that violate public policy do not and should not create obligations, moral or legal, on beneficiaries of such transfers. Transfers subject to racially restrictive conditions, to pick an obvious example, impose no enforceable obligations on beneficiaries even where the beneficiaries had previously agreed to such terms. The autonomy interests of the donor and the beneficiaries should not trump the larger stakes that society has in assuring that no group of its citizen is subordinated, dominated, or rendered unable to fully participate in the society's ongoing affairs, private as well as public.

Beyond terms or conditions of that sort, the question becomes more difficult to evaluate. Suppose, for example, that a testator bequeaths her business to her children with the understanding that the children continue to operate the business in exactly the way that the testator had; that is, for precisely the same business functions, with no expansion or other change in scope of business, no diversification of type of business, place of doing business, and so forth. Suppose further that some years later, the business's future is in jeopardy because the market for the firm's product had all but disappeared. The firm's current owners, the beneficiaries of the bequest of the firm's creator, want to save the business by diversifying its product line, but doing would clearly contradict the terms of the bequest. Would diversifying the firm's product line to save the family business breach an obligation, legal or moral, that the current owners owe to the past owner (all of whom are members of the same generational community)? From a legal perspective, it is unclear whether such an obligation exists. Normally, the law of donative transfers gives maximum effect to the transferor's wishes, but this is only the baseline. There is an exception for public policy, of course, just as

52. *See* Jonathan Gruber, *Covering the Uninsured in the United States*, 46 J. ECON. LIT. 571 (2008).

there is a public policy exception for the enforceability of agreements. For example, restraints that testators impose on a beneficiary's personal conduct may be unenforceable on public policy grounds. Here, the restriction is on business conduct rather than personal conduct. Different policy considerations are involved where the restriction is on business conduct rather than on personal affairs such as the beneficiary's right to marry, especially here where an agreement between the transferor and the beneficiaries apparently exists. No personal rights of the beneficiaries are at stake, only the well-being of the business firm. Given the law's reluctance to interfere with freedom of disposition, it is quite possible, indeed likely, that the answer to the legal question is a legal obligation on the beneficiaries to comply with the transferor's conditions exists, even at the risk of the firm dissolving into bankruptcy in the future.

As a moral matter, there is little reason to reach a different conclusion. Although somewhat different considerations come to bear when we move from the legal to the moral sphere, the matter does not change fundamentally. The principles of freedom of disposition and freedom of contract have a moral as well as a legal dimension, and there are no overriding moral considerations that weigh in favor of relieving the beneficiaries of an obligation that they voluntarily assumed, even at the expense of the firm's future. Perhaps they regret doing so now (as in all likelihood they do), but regret alone surely is not adequate moral grounds for relieving someone of a moral obligation that they voluntarily assumed.

Dependency

The third, and strongest, basis for the moral obligations we owe to future generational communities is the very factor that is the foundation for the general claim that past, present, and future generational communities may owe each other obligations—dependency. What we minimally owe, as a moral matter, to both deceased and unborn members of the various communities that nurture the capabilities necessary for our flourishing, derives from our and their dependency on each other. Specifically, the content of our and their obligations must relate to their and our life-transcending projects and the fact that the fulfillment of those projects is dependent upon the cooperation of others who come after us.

Those life-transcending projects and our dependency of future generations for the realization of such projects provide the reference point for our moral obligations to future generational communities. But that reference point is beguilingly robust. It means, or might be taken to mean, that our obligations include providing the entire background infrastructure that is necessary for any such project's continuation or realization, that is, all the goods described above.

All these background conditions—a reasonably clean environment, well-functioning transportation and communication networks, a minimally acceptable (both in terms of quality and distribution of health-care services) health-care system—are circumstances that those in present-day generation communities take for granted. If, then, those present-day community members expect, or at least hope, that their fellow community members in future generations will continue the life-transcending projects that the living members began, it is incumbent on them to provide the same background conditions that they enjoyed to those future community members to whom they transfer the responsibility of continuing or fulfilling their life-transcending projects. That obligation should apply to the extent that such background conditions are reasonably necessary or facilitative for the implementation of the relevant projects. This is a basis upon which we can explain Brian Barry's equal-opportunity maxim: "[T]he overall range of opportunities open to successor generations should not be narrowed."[53]

The obligation to provide the same background conditions that living community members enjoy to those future community members to whom they transfer the responsibility of continuing or fulfilling their life-transcending projects is foundational and general. It serves as a broad basis upon which the pursuit of life-transcending projects can be conducted, a necessary but not always sufficient condition for such projects to continue beyond the lives of their creators.

Beyond this minimal obligation,[54] what further obligations living community members owe to future generational members will depend on the project that living members pass on to their future co-members. Additional obligations must

53. Brian Barry, *Circumstances of Justice and Future Generations*, *in* OBLIGATIONS TO FUTURE GENERATIONS 204, 243 (R.I. Sikora & Brian Barry eds., 1978).

54. Regarding the legal dimension of this minimal general obligation, the question is: Should members of future generational communities have positive legal rights to such background conditions? If they do have such rights, against whom would those rights be enforceable, at what time(s), and by whom? The question of the timing of enforcement comes up because if the rights are enforced only when the future generational members come into existence, then it is possible that the duty-bearers may no longer be available. The timing issue relates to the question of the identity of the duty-bearer, or at least the identity of the party against whom the right is enforceable. Specifically, are such positive rights enforceable against the state, acting as the agent or representative of community members who are the real duty-holder? Further questions exist. These positive rights, like all positive rights, pose problems concerning the exact scope of the right: May the rights-holders demand that the duty-holder(s) take any and all steps necessary to provide a clean environment, and so forth, or is it sufficient if the duty-holder puts into place a reasonable policy or program designed to achieve a clean environment, and so forth, given the financial and other constraints under which the duty-holder is acting? It is worth noting that the latter is the approach that countries like the Republic of South Africa have taken in interpreting the positive socioeconomic rights provisions of their constitutions. *See Government of the Republic of South Africa v. Grootboom*, 2001 (1) SA 46 (CC).

be reasonably connected to the particular life-transcending projects in the sense that the obligations are reasonably necessary for the project's continued existence or fulfillment. We may think of these specific obligations as endowments that support the life-transcending projects.

What might such endowments include? It depends, of course. Suppose, for example, that the life-transcending project that a current generation community member wishes her future community members to continue and advance to the extent possible is a business that the current member created. She legally transfers the business to her descendants at death, enjoining them to continue and grow the business. Should the business creator be morally obligated to transfer to the recipients of the business with any additional resources by way of an endowment to carry out that project? Of course, it is possible that there has been some agreement or understanding between the transferor and the recipients, as we will see, and in that case the agreement should normally control the parties' obligations.

But suppose there is no such understanding. Does the transferor owe the transferees of her business an obligation to provide any sort of endowment to support that business? This is not an easy question to answer, especially given the transferor's explicit injunction to the transferees to continue and advance the business to the extent possible. Initially, we have to suppose that the transferees accept the transfer, for donees are free, at least legally, to reject attempted gratuitous transfers, both during a lifetime and at death.[55] Assuming that the transferees accept the bequest and assuming further that the testator's injunction is merely precatory and creates no legal obligation, it may nevertheless create a moral obligation on the transferees, who, after all, accepted the business knowing of the testator's injunction to them and its likely importance to her. If such a moral obligation exists, a strong argument can be made that the testator should provide the transferees with some sort of additional endowment to the extent that additional resources are necessary to enable the transferees to fulfill their moral obligation to the testator. If additional resources are needed to allow the transferee to carry out the testator's injunction and the testator provides no further support, the transferees must deplete their own resources to do so. Of course, they could simply reject the bequest, but that would present them with a Hobson's choice: either accept the bequest with the consequence that they must deplete their own resources to fulfill their moral obligation to the testator, or reject the bequest entirely (which has the undesirable side effect of frustrating the testator's life-transcending interest). Fairness seems to suggest reciprocity of moral obligations here. The moral obligation on the transferees to fulfill, to the extent

55. *See* Jesse Dukeminier, Robert Sitkoff, & James Lindgren, Wills, Trusts, and Estates 152 (2009).

reasonably possible, the testator's injunction should they choose to accept the bequest should be matched by a moral obligation on the testator to provide such resources as are reasonably necessary to allow the transferees to fulfill their obligation to the transferee, should they choose to accept the bequest. This approach maximizes the likelihood that the testator's wishes, particularly the continuation of her life-transcending project, will be carried out and at the same time achieves fairness between the testator and the transferees.

THE OBLIGATIONS OWED TO MORE REMOTE FUTURE GENERATIONAL COMMUNITIES

Thus far, the future generational communities that I have considered have all been foreseeable descendant generations—the generations of children and grandchildren of creators of life-transcending projects. The more difficult aspect of the general problem of future generational communities involves more remote generations. Such generations pose more difficult questions because project creators cannot expect to share a common life with such persons, at least not in any literal sense.[56] The problem is not simply that project creators will not know persons who are more than three generations removed from them (or vice versa), but, more fundamentally, that little connects living persons to such remote future generations other than the most basic sorts of commonalities, notably genetic ties and perhaps family names. Even those ties become more attenuated with each generation removed.

Given such more attenuated connections, one may question whether such remote future generations are members of the same generational communities as the living at all. I previously indicated that community members share understandings of whom and what they are, and one might suppose that the attenuation of ties between present and remotely future generations means that such shared understandings will be lacking. At the same time, I indicated, echoing Avner de-Shalit,[57] that part of what constitutes communities is cultural interaction[58] and that cultural interaction includes shared traditions, which may involve "historically extended, socially embodied argument[s]. . . ."[59] As Alasdair MacIntyre observed, such arguments and such traditions may extend through many generations.[60]

56. *See* Martin P. Golding, *Obligation to Future Generations*, *in* RESPONSIBILITIES TO FUTURE GENERATIONS 61, 61–62 (Ernest Partridge ed., 1981).

57. *See* DE-SHALIT, WHY POSTERITY MATTERS, *supra* note 9.

58. *See* Partridge, *Future Generations*, *supra* note 4.

59. MACINTYRE, AFTER VIRTUE, *supra* note 15, at 222.

60. *Id.*

Assuming that the creator's generational community includes remote future generations, the question then becomes whether the same obligations that are owed to relatively near generations also are owed to remote future generations. Some years ago, Martin Golding argued that our obligations to future generations ought to be confined to our "immediate posterity"[61] because we cannot know what is good for future generations beyond them. We do not know what the condition of their lives will be or even whether they will share with us the same conception of the good life for human beings.[62] We would be well-advised, then, Golding concluded, simply not to plan for remote future generations.

Conceding Golding's points regarding the lack of information about the specific condition of the lives of remote future generational members and their conception of the good life, it does not follow that the living owe them no moral obligations whatsoever. The same problem may exist for some living persons who are members of cultures that are far removed from and quite alien to ours, but that fact does not warrant the conclusion that we owe no moral obligations to them. We owe such persons moral obligations by virtue of their humanity.

Regardless of the specific conditions of their existence, members of remote future generations share with us certain basic features that are inherent in the human condition—the abilities to love and to enjoy; vulnerability to pain, suffering, and ultimately, death; self-consciousness; and so on.[63] Given these fundamental commonalities, the moral norms of equality and human dignity suggest that, although differences may exist between the moral obligations that we owe members of immediate future generational communities and their remote counterparts, we owe members of our remote future generational communities at least minimal moral obligations.

Nevertheless, our lack of information about remote future generational communities and their attenuated relationship to the living do have a bearing upon the content of our obligations to them. Golding's point that we cannot plan for such persons seems correct as far as it goes. It bears upon the basis of both types of obligations I have described, the GO and the SO, that is, dependency. Although some degree of dependency may still exist between the living and the fellow community members three or more generations into the future, the extent of that dependency is likely to be substantially more attenuated than it is between living community members and their counterparts one generation ahead. At any

61. *See* Golding, *Obligation to Future Generations, supra* note 56, at 70.

62. *Id.*

63. *See* Gregory Kavka, *The Futurity Problem, in* Responsibilities to Future Generations, *supra* note 56, at 109, 112–13.

rate, we cannot possibly predict just how much dependency will exist or what its character will be as we move three or more generations into the future. For this reason, the obligations that living creators of life-transcending projects owe to remote future generational community members must be of a more basic sort. The obligations should be aimed at constituting a framework within which members of remote future generational communities who wish to continue life-transcending projects transmitted to them may do so, a background that enables such individuals to pursue these projects, if they so choose. This background condition consists of certain of the fundamental capabilities discussed in Chapter One, among these the capabilities of health, personal security, and freedom.

A more concrete statement this background must take into account is the possible effects, allocative but especially distributive, of norms that would affirmatively seek to assure that resources are available to remote future generations. This is, of course, a familiar problem in discussions on intergenerational justice.[64] The problem is complex, for it involves two uncertain variables: first, increasing scarcity of resources over the future, and second, the contingency of future generational communities. This is not the proper occasion for anything like a full analysis of the distributive problem, but a few comments on these two variables will indicate why caution is appropriate in mapping out a specific account of the background condition.

With regard to future scarcity, the dilemma posed by uncertainty is this: Whether economic growth can be sustained in a finite natural world is one of the most persistent questions in economic literature. The unprecedented rate of consumption of natural resources and the concomitant effects have given rise to acute concern with sustainability, a term that has come to be closely associated with intergenerational justice in the relevant literatures. Because the growth in the rate of consumption has been exponential, the fear is that relevant consumption rates at some future point will swamp production rates, leading to potentially catastrophic results.

But this scenario is far from certain. We cannot categorically exclude the possibility that human creativity will ameliorate increased scarcity. After all, in the past, humans have proved to be quite adept at finding solutions to the problem of scarce natural resources. Repeatedly, they have developed new technologies that economize on scarce natural resources or that allow the use of resources that were previously uneconomical. There is no obvious reason to think that this pattern will not continue, allowing us not merely to avoid passing on to remote future generations a greatly degraded and depleted environment but to transmit

64. *See, e.g., id.*; Daniel Callahan, *What Obligations Do We Have to Future Generations? in* Responsibilities to Future Generations, *supra* note 56, at 73.

a set of conditions that is at least as good as what we currently enjoy (thereby satisfying a future generational counterpart to the Lockean proviso[65]).

Which scenario will transpire? We cannot know, of course, and that is precisely the problem. For if we are to develop anything like a concrete account of the background condition that we owe to members of our remote future generational communities, we must have some idea of what the probable state of resources available to such future persons is. In the absence of that basic information, we simply cannot specify our obligation in any sort of detail.

The second variable of uncertainty is the contingency of future generations. This contingency is not simply a matter of *when* but of *whether*—members of our future generational communities may not exist at all. Their existence depends, to a considerable extent, upon decisions that living members make. How does this existential uncertainty affect the moral obligations that living community members owe to potential members in the future? Gregory Kavka poses a useful analogy.[66] Imagine, he suggests, a poor couple that has some children and is contemplating have more. The question is whether they should treat the prospective children as being on a par with their living children with respect to the consumption of their resources, that is, by conserving resources for unborn children. Kavka's answer is that they should not if doing so would cause the living children to suffer serious deprivation.[67] This answer seems to me to be the right one. The living have moral obligations to living members of their communities, and those obligations must be met first. This is not to say that the living owe no obligations to conserve resources for future generational members, including remote future generations. The point is one of priority—under conditions of scarcity, priority in the distribution of resources must be given to existing resource consumers. Moreover, the more remotely in the future the generational members are, the weaker the moral obligation that the living owe to them.

The Contingency of Our Obligations to Unborn Communities

Grounding our obligations to future generational communities on dependency between generations, that is, the dependency of the living generation upon their future generational counterparts to carry on life-transcending projects, seemingly makes those obligations contingent in a way that other bases for such obligations

65. *See* John Locke, Two Treatises of Government (Peter Laslett ed., 1988).

66. Kavka, *The Futurity Problem, in* Responsibilities to Future Generations, *supra* note 56, at 114.

67. *Id.*

do not.[68] The apparent vulnerability of the obligations to future generations on this account results from an implied advance deal between the generational communities: The living will provide the future counterparts with a clean environment, a well-functioning infrastructure, a reasonable efficient economy, and a minimally acceptable health-care system in exchange for future generations' reasonable efforts to carry out the life-transcending projects of their forebears. This may be a troubling conclusion to some who think that our obligations to transfer such a material foundation to future generations should be unconditional and unconstrained. From one perspective, the dependency theory looks like a hold-up. More fundamentally, the theory seemingly encroaches upon future generations' autonomy interest in creating their own lives and the conditions of those lives.

This concern, although understandable, does not, I think, fundamentally undermine the dependency theory. The reason is that it misconstrues the character of the obligation to provide the background material conditions necessary to carry forward any and all life-transcending projects, that is, the GO. That obligation is general, and because it is general it applies unconditionally, that is, to all members of all members of foreseeable future generations. That is what distinguishes the GO from the SO.

To be sure, the GO is still more limited than the broadly redistributive account offered by some rights theorists.[69] Its principle aim is not redistribution as such, and even as to the GO (certainly as to the SO) contingency still exists. But contingency is an inescapable aspect of the human condition. No one can guarantee future conditions of the world. There are too many variables over which we have little or no control. Weather conditions may change catastrophically for non-man-made reasons (as best as science can presently tell), globalization of financial markets may produce long-term economic depressions over which any single nation has little control, global changes in population and immigration (legal and illegal)—all of these possible future scenarios may seriously affect the ability of any generation to transmit to future generations stable and decent material conditions and structures. All that the living can commit themselves to do for future generations is to make reasonable efforts, under whatever circumstances happen to prevail at the given time, to transmit decent minimal material conditions. Admittedly, that commitment is limited, and it leaves future generations with risks.

But that is the most the living can, or at least should, promise the unborn.

68. I am grateful to Hanoch Dagan for raising this point.

69. *See supra* note 2.

The living do owe moral obligations to unborn members of their communities, but those obligations are limited. They are limited in multiple ways, including the basis, or source, of the obligations, and the distance between the presently living members and unborn members. The basis of the obligations is rooted in the idea of what I have called life-transcending projects: the desire that living persons have in seeing that certain projects or interests of theirs be carried on after their deaths. This basis of the obligation helps define the range of persons, resources, and precise nature of the obligations. Moreover, the obligations that the living owe to future generational communities generally weaken as the distance between the living and the unborn increases. In an environment of uncertainty and of scarce resources, our first and greatest moral obligation regarding the distribution of resources is to those members of our communities who are living with us and who continue to nurture the capabilities necessary for us to flourish. The second priority should be given to the future generational communities who come immediately after us, for the relevant ties between those generations usually will be relatively strong. The further out the generational line stretches, the weaker our obligations become.

5

The Complexities of Land Reparations

The last chapter examined the obligations that property owners owe to members of past and future generations, devoting particular attention to future generations. We saw that those obligations are important but confined. This chapter turns to the obligations owed to past generations and their present-day descendants, focusing on the special case of land and reparations for historic injustices committed regarding land.

When an injustice to a property right has been perpetrated by a wrongful appropriation, it is perhaps natural to think that justice requires that the object in question be returned to its original owner. Justice is not done, at least not completely, our intuitions run, solely by requiring the wrongdoer to pay money damages and certainly not by an apology alone. Only a full restoration of the thing itself to the rightful owner will do, we are perhaps apt to say. The common law often reflects precisely that intuition. I take a ring that has been in my family for generations to a jeweler to have it appraised. When I return, the jeweler, discovering that the ring would command an enormous sum on the market, refuses to give it back but offers me a price that is far greater than the value that I expected the ring to be worth yet far less than what it could fetch at an auction at Sotheby's. I refuse and demand return of the ring itself, which the jeweler refuses. I then sue the jeweler for return of the ring. Assuming that I can prove ownership, clearly I will win, as I should.

But suppose that when I return to collect my ring, I learn that the jeweler no longer has it, but has sold it to an innocent buyer who paid a fair price for the ring. If I sue the buyer for return of the ring, will I still prevail? This is a harder case because now the possessor of the ring is not the original wrongdoer. Not only that, but the possessor is an innocent party whose own *bona fides* are apt to draw our sympathies. As between two innocent parties, who is entitled to the ring? The law is more complicated here. The general rule is that a thief cannot transfer good title. This is but an application of the ancient rule *nemo dat quod non habet* ("you cannot give what you do not have"). Under this simple rule the original owner was permitted to recover the purloined object. Under a limited exception known as the doctrine of market overt, however, a bona fide purchaser may acquire good title from a thief if the sale takes place in an open market.[1] Civil law expands the exception. German law, for example, provides that the buyer in good faith who acquired a good under normal circumstances gains good title if he bought it on the market or from a trader and from someone to whom the good was voluntarily entrusted.[2] The law's more complicated responses to this situation reflects the fact that where we are dealing with two innocent parties our intuitions fail us. At least, they are not nearly so strong as in the simple case with which I began.[3]

And so it is with respect to the topic that I shall address here—the return of land to dispossessed peoples from whom it was unjustly appropriated. The question whether unjust dispossessions of land perpetrated on whole peoples in the past should be corrected by restitution in kind, that is, granting reparations in the form of returning land to the dispossessed former owners or their present-day successors is substantially more complex than the problem of claims to an object by two innocent parties. In the remainder of this chapter I shall outline the sources of this greater complexity and shall suggest why our intuitions about the proper resolution of such claims are apt to be ambivalent. I shall argue that the complexities involved in all the situations where claims for land reparations are made to correct historic injustices give us good reasons to be hesitant about granting such claims. At the same time, we should not dismiss such claims out of hand: As Jeremy Waldron has pointed out, "[R]eparations may symbolize a society's undertaking not to forget or deny that a particular injustice took place,

1. English law recognizes the doctrine of market overt for centuries until it was statutorily abolished in 1995. In the United States, the doctrine was rejected in colonial times. *See* Peter M. Smith, *Valediction to Market Overt*, 41 AM. J. LEG. HIST. 225 (1997).

2. German Civil Code (BGB) §932(1). Compare UCC §2-403(2).

3. On legal problems of this type, *see* HANOCH DAGAN, PROPERTY: VALUES AND INSTITUTIONS 18–20 (2011); Menachem Mautner, *"The Eternal Triangles of the Law": Toward a Theory of Priorities in Conflicts Involving Remote Parties*, 90 MICH. L. REV. 95 (1991).

and to respect and help sustain a dignified sense of identity-in-memory for the people affected."[4] Reparations which take a form other than restitution of dispossessed land may be both necessary and sufficient to establish a public marker of acknowledgment.

There is a very large literature on reparations, and it is not my intention in this chapter to review all or even much of that literature. I discuss, albeit in a selected fashion, literature that is relevant only to the points under discussion. My goal is to avoid being digressive while acknowledging other points of view and points similar to mine that others have made.

This chapter makes three contributions to that literature. First, it surveys and summarizes the major problems facing claims for reparations of land specifically as distinguished from all other forms of reparations for historic injustices. Second, it argues that although there is considerable overlap between the problems facing reparations of land and problems with reparations generally, land reparations raise unique problems that are usually not appreciated[5] and therefore should be analyzed separately. Third, its strongest normative aim is for pragmatic, conceptual, and moral reasons, a skeptical attitude toward specific reparations, that is, return of unjustly appropriated land to original occupants and/or their successors, is generally appropriate. There are, however, limited circumstances in which specific reparations are pragmatically and morally warranted, arguably even required.

Few commentators focus on property reparations alone; fewer still on reparations of land. Posner and Vermeule distinguish between cash and in-kind reparations, but they include as in-kind reparations affirmative action and special voting rights.[6] They do mention reparations of land briefly, but state that such reparations "are of limited interest for the theory and policy surrounding reparations."[7] This is a surprising statement, given the recent experience in South Africa and what may yet occur in Israel and the occupied territories. At any rate, one of the principle burdens of this chapter is to show why reparations of land should be treated separately.

4. *See* Jeremy Waldron, *Superseding Historic Injustice*, 103 Ethics 4, 6 (1992).

5. Eric Posner and Adrian Vermeule point out that most reparations discussions focus on the choice among three forms of reparations: cash, affirmative action, and apologies. *See* Eric A. Posner & Adrian Vermeule, *Reparations for Slavery and Other Historical Injustices*, 103 Colum. L. Rev. 689, 725 (2003).

6. *Id.* at 724.

7. *Id.* at 733.

THREE SOURCES OF COMPLEXITY

Claims to reparations of land unjustly appropriated from entire peoples in the past are fraught with many complexities. Some of these can be worked out, of course, through flexible administrative mechanisms. I want to focus here, however, on three sources of complexity that are not simply a matter of administrative difficulty but that raise normative challenges to the claims. They can go under the headings of *time, land,* and *peoples.*

Time

The passage of long periods of time following unjustified appropriations of property can have negative effects, both legally and morally, on the force of claims for return of the property in question. This is true in the simple cases of wrongful dispossessions, such as my ring example, as well as more complex situations of historic injustices. In simple cases like the purloined ring, the original owner, even if she was initially entitled to recover the object from the present possessor, may lose her title through the working of limitation statutes that bar causes of action upon which the plaintiff has not acted within a stated period of time (say, ten years). Hence, through the operation of these limitation statutes the present possessor of an object or parcel of land may acquire good legal title even though she may have acquired it from a thief.

The law gives considerable weight to the effect of time on the legitimacy of property titles in this situation, and it does so for four reasons. The first is the difficulty of proof when claims have grown stale. Evidence disappears, records are lost, memories fade, and in general proof of title becomes less reliable the further removed we get from the original dispossession. The second reason is repose—we need to quiet titles, especially to land, in order to keep land records reliable. An efficient and well-functioning market in land depends upon reliable records to title. The third reason is to create incentives for owners periodically to give notice to the world that they are the owner by penalizing them for "sleeping on their rights," as is sometimes said. The fourth reason is Hegelian[8] but is also explainable in terms of modern cognitive psychology.

Justice Holmes provided a good version of the reason, saying: "A thing which you have enjoyed and used as your own for a long time, whether property or an opinion, takes root in your being and cannot be torn away without your resenting the act and trying to defend yourself, however you came by it."[9] The development

8. *See* G.W.F. Hegel, The Philosophy of Right (T.M. Knox trans., 1952).

9. *See* Oliver Wendell Holmes, *The Path of the Law,* 10 Harv. L. Rev. 457, 477 (1897).

in cognitive psychology known as prospect theory holds that people consider the loss of an object that they possess as more significant than forgoing the opportunity to realize an apparently equivalent gain.[10] Inadvertently perhaps, the law acts upon this insight in property law by settling title in a current possessor who has occupied land for an extended period of time and used it in ways that one would expect of the true owner.

Interestingly, the law calls for no compensation from the new owner to the dispossessed owner.

My point in raising this legal doctrine, adverse possession, as it is called in the common law, is not to offer it as template for a solution to the more intransigent problem of claims for the return of land appropriated from entire peoples in the past and now stably settled by another people. The point rather is to establish both the fact of law's sensitivity to the effects of the passage of time on the strength of claims to land titles and the reasons for its sensitivity to time. In the context of claims for specific restitution for land appropriation time poses two different sorts of issues. The first concerns the objectives of land restitution. The second problem is based on the pragmatic need for repose.

Two Possible Objectives in Land Reparations

We need to be clear at the outset about just what the objective of land reparations is and what that objective realistically can be. There are two possible bases of claims involved in cases where entire peoples seek return of land that was unjustly seized, and they involve two quite different conceptions of what justice requires is such cases. This difference is important, but it is not always kept in mind.

The first is that reparation claims are "about ongoing injustice rooted in actions that took place in the past."[11] That is, the foundation of the argument for return of land is actually not compensation (or even reparations) for a past injustice that has gone unrectified but to correct an *ongoing* injustice whose origin lies in the past. Suppose that I am a subsidence farmer who lives in a society that lacks a legal system with genuine due process and principles of equality.

Someone wrongfully evicted me from my land a year ago, and I have not been able to recover possession of the land. Since losing my land, I have been compelled to become a day laborer, exposed to workplace hazards and oppressive management. The injustice of my circumstances does not end with the dispossession of my land. My present harm is not exhausted by that dispossession. It

10. *See* Amos Tversky & Daniel Kahneman, *Rational Choice and the Framing of Decisions*, 59 J. Bus. S251 (1986).

11. Jeremy Waldron, *Settlement, Return, and the Supersession Thesis*, 5 Theor. Inq. in L. 237, 345 n.13 (2004).

includes the consequential harms that are causally connected with the dispossession but not exhausted by it. Suppose that ten years from now, laws have changed, and I am awarded a sum of money that will enable me to purchase my own land. What does this award of money represent? Its objective is not to compensate me for an injustice that was committed in the past, a discrete past event. Rather, it is "a way of remitting an injustice that is ongoing into the present."[12] It is *present- and forward-looking*, seeking to alter my current and (presumably) future circumstances in an effort to counteract, to the extent feasible, the ongoing effects of the past act of injustice.

The second line of reasoning behind arguments for reparations is *historically focused*. It views the justification of entitlements from a historical perspective rather than on the basis of present- and future-minded arguments such as that outlined. Perhaps the most famous of such historical arguments is John Locke's theory of property. Locke justified property in the original acquisition of the basis of the historical act of mixing one's labor with some resource in a commons.[13] Robert Nozick is the clearest and most forceful modern exponent of historic entitlement theories, and his principle of justice-in-rectification bears attention because many arguments for reparations often rely, implicitly if not openly, on it. Nozick explained the principle of rectification this way:

> This principle uses historical information about previous situations and injustices done in them [including unjustified expropriations of property], and information about the current course of events that flowed from these injustices, until the present, and it yields a description (or descriptions) of [property] holdings in the society. The principle of rectification presumably will make its best estimate of subjunctive information about what would have occurred (or a probability distribution over what might have occurred, using the expected value) if the injustice had not taken place. If the actual description of holdings turns out not to be one of the descriptions yielded by the principle, then one of the descriptions must be realized.[14]

I shall have comments on both these approaches to reparation claims, suggesting that justice is best served when the question of reparations is approached from the present- and forward-looking perspective, and that from that perspective, specific reparations, that is, return of land itself is not necessarily the appropriate

12. Waldron, *Superseding, supra* note 4, at 14.

13. *See* John Locke, Two Treatises of Government 286–89 (Peter Laslett ed., 1988).

14. Robert Nozick, Anarchy, State and Utopia 152–53, 230–31 (1974).

remedy. For now, however, I wish to concentrate on the principle of rectification just described.

Several philosophers have noted problems with Nozick's principle of justice-in-rectification.[15] That principle, and the historical approach generally, requires us to go back in time, identifying discrete occasions of unjust appropriations of property, and—this is the crucial step—reverse or undo the unjust act by giving the appropriated asset back to the aggrieved owner. One difficulty is that sometimes wrongful appropriations of assets cannot be undone for the simple reason that the asset no longer exists. If that asset is a consumable object and has been consumed, for example, the aggrieved owner can be given substitutes for it but not the original. Or, suppose the asset is land—you wrongfully dispossess me of my farmland. You then proceed to degrade the land through harmful farming practices, and the degradation is irreversible.

Suppose I recover my land at a future point. Has the past injustice been rectified? Certainly not, for I will be in a worse position than I was prior to the wrongful dispossession. Perhaps you will be forced to pay me a sum of money to compensate me for the damage you have done to my land, but that will not make me whole in the sense in which the historical principle requires that I be made whole. For I have not been restored to just the state that I was in before the wrongful dispossession.

These and other difficulties plague the historical principle.[16] Taken collectively, these difficulties underscore the fundamental problem with the historically focused approach. They also clarify what a legal system's objective should and should not be when presented with claims for reparations for past injustices, in view of what that system realistically can and cannot do.

The brute fact is that we cannot undo the past. What makes specific restitution seem so appealing is that it appears to be the way to return us to the status quo ante, but specific restitution does not and cannot do that. Even if the confiscated land is returned to its original owner, so much else has changed over time. The land was possessed, used, and enjoyed by someone else in the intervening years,

15. *See* Jonathan Wolff, Property, Justice and the Minimal State (1991); Shelton Davis, Land Rights and Indigenous Peoples (1988).

16. In a very interesting and helpful paper, Theunis Roux uses the case of South Africa's 1994 land restitution scheme to test where a Nozickean approach successfully redresses the moral wrongs done to the victims of past unjust land transfers. *See* Theunis Roux, *Land Restitution and Reconciliation in South Africa, in* Justice and Reconciliation in Post-Apartheid South Africa 144–71 (François du Bois & Antié du Bois-Pedain eds., 2008). He argues that the South African land restitution scheme is an appropriate test case because it was essentially Nozickean in character. His basic finding is that South African's restitution plan, "while remarkable in many respects . . . largely failed to redress the moral harm done to victims of apartheid forced removals." *Id.* at 2.

and other people may have benefited from that person's ownership. Specific restitution does not reverse the clock—it does not return all these people to *their* original positions, that is, the situations they occupied prior to the time of the land's confiscation. These individuals may have made different choices in their lives but for the land's confiscation. We cannot know that. The clock simply cannot be turned back.

What a legal system *can* do, and what its objective should be in reparation cases, is to change the present (and presumably future) circumstances of the victims of unjust land expropriations in various ways calculated to counteract the ongoing effects of those past injustices. As I discuss below, those ways may include specific restitution in a limited set of circumstances, but in the main, the remedies will include other, multiple forms of remediation, including monetary compensation, depending upon a wide variety of factors (number of persons involved, how many years have passed, whether original victims are the claimants, etc.).

Time, Life Plans, and Selves

Several commentators have viewed the effect of time on claims for land reparations as problematic.[17] There are good reasons for these qualms. Both the common law and civil law are replete with examples of rules and doctrines reflecting the insight that at least certain property rights fade over time. The law of prescription and the cognate doctrine of adverse possession are but two examples.[18] Many legal entitlements that were fully cognizable in the past do not survive today. In considering whether reparations to land should fall into this category, we need to understand why the law often treats time as corrosive of past entitlement.

One reason refers to the principle of rectification to which I referred previously. The substantive foundation of that principle is the idea that the moral justification for protecting a person's entitlement originally lies in the role that the entitlement plays in that person's life. If I own a piece of land and use it in some way, the land becomes an important element in how I shape my life, both now and in the future. So, if someone confiscates that land, the act disrupts my life in important ways, rupturing my plans. The principle of rectification constitutes both an attempt to remedy that disruption so that my life course is restored to its original path. The difficulty with this justification is the fact that "[i]f something was taken from me decades ago, the claim that it now forms the centre of my

17. *See* Ruti G. Teitel, Transitional Justice (2000); Jennifer Nedelsky, *Should Property Be Constitutionalized? A Relational and Comparative Approach*, *in* Property Law on the Threshold of the 21st Century 417–32 (G.E. van Maanen & A.J. van der Walt eds., 1996); Waldron, *Superseding*, *supra* note 4.

18. *See generally* the essays published in the symposium entitled *Time, Property Rights, and the Common Law*, *in* 64 Wash. U. L.Q. 667 (1986).

life and that it is still indispensable to the exercise of my autonomy is much less credible."[19] If the thing has been gone from me for a long time, it can no longer, in any meaningful sense, be said to be essential to my life plans. As circumstances change, whatever the reason, people move on with their lives. They change their plans. Things that were once essential in their lives fade in significance and are replaced by other things.

Nor can it be said to be essential to my personal identity. Indeed, the changes may become so great that they have effected a fundamental change in the identities of the individuals involved. The very selfhood of the former owners may have been fundamentally altered, so altered, in fact, that they may echo the words of Dickens' Scrooge, "I am not the man I was."[20]

This is the core insight behind the multiple-selves theory, to which such otherwise disparate scholars as Derek Parfit and Richard Posner subscribe.[21] In its strong version, the multiple-selves theory posits that the differences between our selves at different stages of our lives can be so great that these selves at different stages are most fruitfully understood in terms of different persons rather than the same person at different points in time.[22] Posner points out that there is a big difference in degree between many adjacent successive selves, on the one hand, and, on the other hand, selves that are separated by so many years and experiences that they have gone through so many successive selves that there is real discontinuity. He give the illuminating example of his mother who, while still vigorous at age sixty-five, noticed a frail elderly woman in a wheelchair and said to Posner's wife, "'If I ever become like that, shoot me.'"[23] Twenty years later, his mother had become just like that woman, but, as Posner says, "[S]he did not express any desire to die."[24] The conclusion that Posner draws from this anecdote indicates how selves change over significant periods of time. He states, "Aging changed my mother so much that she acquired a totally different outlook, *becoming a stranger to her younger self*."[25]

The multiple-selves theory has important consequences for the Hegelian notion of the importance of property to the self.[26] If time and the experiences

19. Waldron, *Superseding*, *supra* note 4, at 158.

20. Charles Dickens, A Christmas Carol 78 (1907).

21. *See* Richard A. Posner, Aging and Old Age (1995); Derek Parfit, Reasons and Persons 199–351 (1984).

22. *See* Posner, Aging, *supra* note 21, at 8–9.

23. *Id.* at 87.

24. *Id.*

25. *Id.*

26. *See* Hegel, The Philosophy of Right, *supra* note 8, at 40–46.

that go with it create new identities, then it cannot be said that a thing that I once possessed years ago but lost is essential to the self I now am. Rather, my present self must be based on other things, of which I have present possession. It is those things that are truly constitutive of my present self, not things that I once owned. Those are memories, and while memories may be vivid, they do not constitute our present living selves, the selves that experience the here and now.

The Propriety of Looking Back: The Limits of Time's Effects

Time will not always have had an opportunity to do its corrosive work. In some cases reparation claims may be made within a reasonably short period of time since the initial wrongful expropriation, and under such circumstances a backward-looking approach may be more appropriate than the present- and future-looking approach generally preferred. Just how short the length of time between the expropriation and the claim should be is debatable and depends upon several circumstances, but certainly if a claim is made within, say, five years of the initial dispossession, many of the problems identified and discussed here will either not occur or be substantially minimized. There is a built-in limit to the effect of time upon the reasons for adopting a present- and future-focused approach.

To illustrate with a perhaps not entirely fanciful hypothetical from our own time, imagine that the Israeli government has adopted a radically new policy toward Hamas (and Hamas toward it), and that they are negotiating directly with each other. As a result of these negotiations, the Israeli government declares that in exchange for important concessions (for reasons of self-interest) from Hamas, it has frozen all new Jewish settlements in the occupied West Bank indefinitely. Further, it has told Hamas that it is willing, in principle, to consider a program of reparations for some Palestinians who were removed from their homes in portions of the occupied territories (or who left under threat when the Israeli government declared the area open to Jewish settlers), but precisely what form these reparations will take has not yet been resolved and if they involve specific reparations (i.e., return of land to original occupants), how broad a program of such specific reparations should be.

In developing a plan of reparations, should the government's perspective be present- and forward-looking, or is there room under these circumstances for a backward-looking approach, at least with respect to some of the former Palestinian occupants? The logic of presentist thinking itself suggests that an approach to reparations that is focused on the past may be more appropriate as to at least some of the former Palestinian occupants. Although some of the settlements in the occupied territories were quickly established after the Israeli military success in the 1967 war,[27] other settlements are quite recent, established within just within the past few years. Let us suppose, as seems likely, that Palestinians were

27. *See* Avishai Margalit, *Settling Scores*, N.Y. Review of Books, Sept. 20, 2001, 14.

the immediate past occupants of at least some of these recent settlements and were wrongfully dispossessed, either by force or under duress. For claimants in circumstances such as these, the case for a past-looking approach to reparations seems strong. The reasons for adopting a present- and future-looking approach in most cases are absent in these circumstances, and there are no other compelling reasons for denying the past occupants the right to return to occupation of their former homes.

What makes the case for looking back—for specific reparations—as to former Palestinian occupants of recently established settlements so strong is the fact that so little will have changed since the wrongful dispossession. For as Waldron emphasizes,[28] it is not the passage of time that does the work of gradually weakening the case for specific reparations, but the changes in circumstances of people's lives that accompanies the passage of time that does the work. Given the short period of time, the identities of the claimants and the original occupants are likely to be the same. Moreover, the occupants will not have made the same major changes in life plans as they would have done over a much longer time interval. Finally, there is a much higher probability that the property will be in the same condition as it was at the time of the wrongful dispossession than if several decades or even centuries have passed since the initial act of injustice. The closer the current circumstances are to those that prevailed at the time of the initial dispossession, the more compelling the case for returning the land, together with improvements on it, to the original occupants. In my hypothetical, there will surely be some former Palestinian occupants whose claims for specific restitution cannot be ignored, despite a general reluctant to grant such a form of reparations. The present- and forward-looking perspective has its limits.

Land

Land's Memory

The second source of complexity in land reparation claims is *land*. As Eduardo Peñalver has stated, "[L]and has memory."[29] Land's memory has several dimensions.[30] One is physical. As Peñalver observes, physical changes that humans make to land tend to remain in place unless they are affirmatively removed.[31]

28. *See* Waldron, *Settlement, Return, and the Supersession Theory, supra* note 11.

29. Eduardo M. Peñalver, *Land Virtues*, 94 Cornell L. Rev. 821, 829 (2009). *See also* Eduardo M. Peñalver, *Property's Memories*, 80 Fordham L. Rev. 1071 (2011).

30. *See id.* at 829–31; Peñalver, *Property's Memories, supra* note 29, at 1078–85.

31. *See* Peñalver, *Land Virtues, supra* note 29, at 830.

Sometimes these changes cannot be removed. Whether for good or ill, human activities sometimes mark land in irreversible ways.

A second dimension of land's memory is psychological. Land's psychological memory is closely related to the point made earlier about the strong psychological ties that develop between land and its users.[32] Joseph Singer has argued that such ties develop to the point that a "reliance interest" develops in the current users of land, an interest that merits legal protection.[33]

A third dimension of land's memory is social. There is a path dependency of land uses that results from their interlocking character. One use relies on another, and so on, creating a network of interdependent uses. Once in place, a given land use is difficult to undo. The stability of neighborhoods, for example, results, at least in part, from expectations, sometimes rooted in legal devices such as covenants, that the use of the neighboring land will remain strictly residential. Stability increases if this expectation is coupled with a network of thick social relationships.

Land's memory has powerful effects, a fact that has not gone unnoticed. It may explain policies that involve expropriations of contested land, for example. Nomi Stolzenberg argues that the Jewish settlements on the West Bank are an example of this.[34] In her view the settlements constitute an attempt to establish "facts on the ground" that will prove difficult to undo. Less controversial examples are provided from land invasions that result in the establishment of so-called "informal settlements." This is a familiar phenomenon in many parts of the world, including Latin America and South Africa. The politics may be different from that involved in the West Bank settlements, but the core concept is the same—land's memory.

Land's memory has obvious consequences for the problem of land reparations. But the direction of those consequences is unclear. We are perhaps inclined to say that land's memory favors existing owners. After all, if land use is path dependent, this suggests existing land uses cannot be undone or changed without incurring extremely high costs, if at all. The present users, many of whom have used their land for a very long time indeed, have already made their mark on the land. The land has been stamped, as it were, and the stamp is very durable.

Yet, no matter how much the current users have molded the character of the land in their own image, they likely have not entirely erased all prior memories of the land. Land's memories work both ways. Memories of the past lurk just beneath virtually every road we trod. Sometimes these memories push their way into our

32. *See* text accompanying notes 3 and 4 *supra*.

33. *See* Joseph William Singer, *The Reliance Interest in Property*, 40 Stan. L. Rev. 611 (1988).

34. *See* Nomi Stolzenberg, *Facts on the Ground*, *in* Property and Community 107–39 (Gregory S. Alexander & Eduardo M. Peñalver eds., 2009).

present consciousness, forcing us to take cognizance of, even to honor, former uses whose traces we cannot entirely erase. Even in a relatively young country such as the United States we must periodically—and painfully—confront the past. In many parts of the United States it is not uncommon to find vestiges of our native past not far beneath the surface. In Hawaii, confrontations between land's past and its present occur on a regular basis as land developers dig up ancient Native Hawaiian gravesites, which are legally protected under Hawaiian law.[35] Memories of less ancient past land uses are even more ubiquitous, challenging the legitimacy of current land uses. Even if we decide that current land uses must be protected, we must acknowledge the past and honor it in appropriate ways. Failing to do so creates a cloud on the legitimacy of the present.

Improvements

Land involves another problem in addition to its memory. Any land that is returned to former occupants will almost certainly include improvements, and many, perhaps most, of these will have been constructed since the time of the initial appropriation. The improvements may be privately owned, such as residences and businesses, while others will be public improvements, for example, hospitals, schools, parks, and so forth. Are present-day owners of these improvements entitled to compensation for the loss of the improvements, apart from the land? Would monetary compensation make them whole, assuming they are entitled to be made whole?

Postappropriation improvements are distinguishable from structures that existed at the time of the appropriation. Improvements that were already there when the land was unjustly appropriated are in theory indistinguishable from the land itself. They, too, were unjustly taken from their former occupants, and if justice requires returning the land to its former owner-occupant without compensation, it also requires returning the improvements without compensation. Questions regarding psychological attachments to and financial and social dependency upon improvements are, at least in theory, the same as those that occur in the context of land. Nothing fundamentally distinguishes the improvements from the land on which they sit. Postappropriation improvements are different. The former owner-occupant of the land did not construct the improvement and was not its occupant or owner. If the improvement is transferred to the former owner of the land on which it sits and no compensation is paid, the person to whom it is transferred seemingly is unjustly enriched at the expense of the former owner. But is this in fact the case? After all, the improvement was constructed on land that we have supposed was unjustly appropriated. We might draw an analogy, perhaps not too fanciful, to common-law doctrine known as

35. *See* Hawaii Rev. Stat. § 6E-1-43 (2009).

the improving trespasser.[36] Under American law, ordinarily buildings and similar structures constructed on land are fixtures attached to the land and treated as part of the land.[37] Title to the improvement follows title to the land. But where someone constructs a building or other structure entirely on land belonging to another, the matter is more complicated. Generally, American law distinguishes between mistaken and intentional improving trespassers. The mistaken improver, because he acted in good faith, is protected against unjust enrichment through one or another remedy (such as a forced sale to the new owner). However, the intentional improver is denied all relief, and, in fact, the new owner may force the improver to remove the structure regardless of the degree of hardship.[38]

Which rule would apply in cases where the land was unjustly appropriated and is now being returned? Surprisingly perhaps, the answer is not obvious. On the one hand, the bad-faith improver seems to apply. Cases of mistaken improvements that are entirely on another person's land usually involve situations such as where the improver in good faith relied on the error of a surveyor who incorrectly read a deed description and mistook one lot for the neighboring (and correct) lot.[39] No such mistake occurred here. The improvements were located exactly where they were supposed to be located. Nor is it plausible to suppose that any mistake of law occurred. The improvers surely realized and were aware of the political circumstances that led to the change in possession of the land, and we must attribute to them knowledge of the law, including international law, regarding ownership of the land that results from such an act of political occupation of land and its distribution to citizens, just as we ordinarily attribute knowledge of the law to individuals regardless of their actual ignorance. Moreover, we may be inclined to say that because the original occupation was unjust, as we have supposed it was, then that injustice continues and any material change made upon that land without the original owner's consent must itself be unjust. Unless we say that the original injustice has since been erased or ended somehow, such as under Jeremy Waldron's controversial supersession theory,[40] all subsequent acts done upon the land are tainted by that original injustice, and improvers upon that land cannot be considered innocent.

36. *See* Jesse Dukeminier et al., Property 141 (7th ed., 2010). *See generally* Kelvin H. Dickinson, *Mistaken Improvers of Real Estate*, 64 N.C. L. Rev. 37 (1985); John Henry Merryman, *Improving the Lot of the Trespassing Improver*, 11 Stan. L. Rev. 456 (1959).

37. *See* Ray A. Brown, The Law of Personal Property 514 (3rd ed., 1975).

38. *E.g.*, Hollified v. Monte Vista Biblical Gardens, 553 S.E.2d 662 (Ga. Ct. App. 2001); Goulding v. Cook, 661 N.E.2d 1322 (Mass. 1996).

39. *E.g.*, Howard v. Kunto, 477 P.2d 210 (Wash. Ct. App. 1970).

40. Waldron's supersession thesis posits that changes in circumstances may overtake a historical injustice so that a situation that was unjust when its initially occurred may later become just—the

On the other hand, the improvers were not scofflaws. They thought the land was theirs, and arguably they had good reasons for their belief. The land was acquired as the result of an act of state, and the state in turn either affirmatively transferred apparent title to the improvers or at least tolerated their acts of possession. They relied on the state's representation, implicit if not explicit, that the state had good title to transfer. These circumstances make an arguable case for good faith.

The proper resolution is not entirely clear, although I am inclined to think that it is difficult to characterize the improvers as engaging in bad faith. That is really beside the point, however. What matters for my purposes is to demonstrate why the case of land restoration, where substantial improvements are involved, is so much more complex than monetary reparations alone. All the difficult questions that I have raised go away, obviously, if we decide that the land need not be returned to its former occupants or their descendants.

Peoples

The third source of complexity for land reparations is the involvement of entire *peoples.*

Unlike ordinary restitution cases, land reparations involve whole cultures and collective identities. Scholars have written extensively on the important role that

original injustice may be superseded. *See* Waldron, *Superseding, supra* note 4. Waldron's thesis, although generally well received, has attracted its share of critics. One argument is that if any injustice has been superseded by later changes in circumstances, it is only the possible injustice in the present occupation of the land in question, not the historical injustice itself. *See* TAMAR MEISELS, TERRITORIAL RIGHTS (2nd ed., 2009); Paul Patton, *Historic Injustice and the Possibility of Supersession*, 26 J. INTERCULTURAL STUD. 255 (2005). Cara Nine has raised several objections, including the following: (1) Referring to Waldron's example of an ecological change in conditions the threatens the survival of colonists, Nine points out that there is a problem in identifying exactly for what land the colonial state is a candidate for sovereignty; history provides no basis for such identification because the colonial state had no historical connection with any land. (2) She argues that the colonial state's status as a candidate for sovereignty is not itself sufficient to create actual territorial rights. Other criteria must be considered, such as rights of self-determination of all groups and the concern for stability and peace. *See* CARA NINE, GLOBAL JUSTICE AND TERRITORY 171–72 (2012). Although I cannot respond to all (or other) of these criticisms of the supersession thesis, I will concede that at least some of them have validity. Nevertheless, it does not seem to me that they fundamentally undermine the basic insight behind the supersession thesis: the general relevance of subsequent changes of circumstances for the justice of present and continued holding of at least some land that was acquired through unjust dispossession. This leaves open the view, argued by Tamar Meisels, that supersession does occur, but what is superseded is only the possible injustice of the present and continued holding of the land in question in the particular circumstances, but not the original injustice itself. I return to this view subsequently in discussing the identity of the entitlement involved in the reparations claim.

land plays in creating and maintaining a self-conception and identity of indigenous people.[41] As one has stated, "[L]and is the most important cultural legacy that [indigenous people] inherit from their ancestors, and the foundation of their peoples' other claims to ethnic identity, cultural and political autonomy."[42] Despite their diversity, indigenous peoples and cultures derive their identities, indeed their survival, from their relationship with their lands.[43] Both the U.N. Human Rights Committee and the Inter-American Commission on Human Rights have recognized this deep connection in several cases.[44]

Land reparation claims commonly raise issues of indigeneity, culture, even language rights. Despite the diversity of the contexts in which such claims have been raised, they all are premised on the notion that land, specifically, the land of the ancestors of the current claimants, is essential to the preservation (and in some cases, a recreation) of a particular culture. No other remedy—not monetary compensation, not even substitute land—is adequate to satisfy the core premise of these claims, that particular land, the land initially appropriated, is constitutive of a peoples, a group identity.

Closely related to this premise is the further, and more controversial, premise that the land initially appropriated is indispensable to the autonomy of not only that group of people but also to each member of it such that unless possession of that land is restored to the group neither it nor any of its members will be genuinely autonomous.[45] This is why it is a mistake to view land reparation disputes as involving merely an aggregation of individual claims and, so, capable of being treated like ordinary restitution claims. In these cases, the whole is greater than the sum of the parts.

41. *See, e.g.,* Omaira Bolanos, *Redefining Identities, Redefining Landscapes: Indigenous Identity and Land Rights Struggles in the Brazilian Amazon,* 28 J. Cult. Geography 45 (2011); S. James Anaya, *International Human Rights and Indigenous Peoples: The Move Toward the Multicultural State,* 21 Ariz. J. Int'l & Comp. L. 13 (2004); Duncan Ivison, Paul Patton, & Will Sanders, *Introduction, in* Political Theory and the Rights of Indigenous Peoples (Duncan Ivison & Paul Patton eds., 2000); Garth Nettheim, *"Peoples" and "Populations"—Indigenous Peoples and Rights of Peoples, in* The Rights of Peoples 120–22 (James Crawford & Hans Kruuk eds., 1988).

42. Shelton Davis, Land Rights and Indigenous Peoples 65 (1988).

43. *See* Anaya, *International Human Rights, supra* note 41, at 35.

44. *See, e.g.,* Ominaya v. Canada, Comm. No. 267/1984, Report of the Human Rights Committee, U.N. GOAR, 45th Sess., Supp. No. 40, vol. 2, at 1, U.N. Doc. N4/40, Annex 9(A) (1990); Report of the Situation of Human Rights in Equador, Inter-Am. Comm. on Hum. Rts., O.A.S. Doc. OEA/Ser.L/V/II.96, doc 10, rev. 1, at 24, 31 (1985).

45. Nozick himself recognized the possibility of extending his libertarian theory to the group level, linking autonomy, property, and group claims. *See* Nozick, Anarchy, State and Utopia, *supra* note 14, at 178.

Commentators have noted the potential problems of identifying beneficiaries of reparation when claims are presented several, perhaps many, years after the initial act of injustice.[46] The problems are not confined to the historical problem of tracing genealogies of the original victims, however daunting that task may be, but includes a meta-ethical problem of determining which ethical theory should apply—ethical individualism or ethical collectivism.[47] As Posner and Vermeule point out,[48] under ethical individualism only actual victims or those having a proper relationship with victims are privileged to have cognizable claims. Persons having a proper relationship with victims include might include, Posner and Vermeule observe, "that between the victim and a person who can show that confiscated property would have been given or bequeathed to him by the victim if the wrongdoing had not occurred."[49] If the ethical perspective switches to ethical collectivism, this counterfactual requirement is removed or at least mitigated, for now claims for the return of land involve entire peoples and cultures. Peoples and cultures are durable; they persist over long periods of time. In the United States, some of the Indian nations that have filed claims are the same nations that existed at the time when their lands were originally dispossessed. Moreover, as

46. On the problems of the identities of the recipients of reparations, *see, e.g.*, Eric A. Posner & Adrian Vermeule, *Reparations, supra* note 5, at 689; Leif Wenar, *Reparation for the Future*, 37 J. Soc. Phil. 396, 399–401, 405 (2006); Kok-Chor Tan, *Colonialism, Reparations, and Global Justice, in* Reparations: Interdisciplinary Inquiries 280–306 (Jon Miller & Rahul Kumar eds., 2007). One particular identity problem that other commentators have noted is the "existential worry." Wenar, *Reparations for the Future*, 400. The problem is that

> for a person to have been wronged by another it has to be the case that the wronged person is worse off than they would have been had the wrongdoing not occurred. But the identity of the wronged party is not independent of the wrongful conduct. Unconceived children of the enslaved, oppressed, and expropriated would not have been born without the enslavement, oppression, and expropriation.

Id. at 400. Commentators have suggested that a solution to this existential problem is to focus on corporate entities, such as peoples, rather than individuals, as the beneficiaries of reparations. *See, e.g.*, Tan, *Colonialism, supra* note 46, at 280. But this move raises problems of its own, as I have suggested above. In addition to the problems I have identified, Leif Wenar points out that injustice itself can be an identity-fixing fact for peoples as well as for individuals. "The identity of a people," he states, "has often been formed through resistance to oppression. *See* Wenar, *Reparations for the Future, supra* note 46, at 401.

47. Ethical individualism posits that morality—moral values, rights, and obligations—are essentially individual; so, only individuals can have moral rights. *See* Steven Lukes, Individualism 99 (1973). Ethical collectivism recognizes loosely defined groups as entities capable of bearing moral rights and responsibilities.

48. *See* Posner & Vermeule, *Reparations, supra* note 5, at 739.

49. *Id.* at 739.

Posner and Vermeule point out, although members of the group come and go, a natural characteristic of groups is that they retain their legitimate identity as groups despite shifting membership.

There are limits to the duration of peoples and tribes, however. Many of the New England tribes that were the original occupants at the time when southern New England was settled no longer exist.[50] Where this occurs and the present occupants are moved to provide some sort of remedy, then the counterfactual difficulty rears its head again.

Indigeneity

The congeries of concepts that includes peoples, indigeneity, and collective identity, face their own problems of complexity, however. Take indigeneity, a term that is now very much a part of the *lingua franca* of the cultural rights movement and movements for the rights of First Peoples. Both the term and the concept are actually quite ambiguous. At least two meanings are possible, and the difference between them has important implications for the basis of the argument for the return of property associated with each.[51] One meaning refers to the original occupants of the land in question or the descendants of those occupants. We can call this meaning "absolute indigeneity," for it refers to the root inhabitants, if you will. The other meaning is relative in the sense that it refers to the original occupants of the land in question relative to a particular point in time or other group of people. In this case it is the original occupants relative to the time of the land's appropriation (or the descendants of those occupants).

The distinction between these two possible meanings matters for our purposes because the claims that the two different two groups of "indigenous people" make for return of the land will rest on two different legal principles.[52] The argument that corresponds to the claim asserted by the first group, the first human occupants of the land—let us call this group Group 1—will rest on the well-known legal principle of First Possession (or Occupancy). The argument asserted by the second group, the original inhabitants at the time of the dispossession—let us call this group Group 2—will rest on the equally well-established legal principle known as Prior Possession (or Occupancy). Let us briefly examine the

50. *See* Roberta Estes, *Where Have All the Indians Gone? Native American Eastern Seaboard Dispersal, Geneology and DNA in Relation to Sir Walter Raleigh's Lost Colony of Roanoke, available at* http://www.dnaexplain.com/Publications/PDFs/WhereHaveAlltheIndiansGone8-30-09JoggV3.2.pdf (last visited Nov. 2, 2016).

51. *See* Jeremy Waldron, *Indigeneity? First Peoples and Last Occupancy*, 1 New Zealand J. Pub. & Int'l L. 55 (2003).

52. *See id.* at 66–75.

distinction between these two principles and the arguments that they generate in this context. We will then consider some problems with both arguments.

The principle of First Occupancy provides that the first person (or people) to take possession of some resource or land acquires property rights in the thing or land possessed. The principle has a long history and is recognized by many legal systems. In the Anglo-American tradition it is perhaps most intimately identified with Locke, who used a version of it as the basis for original acquisition of individual property rights in his famous theory of property.[53] As applied to peoples, First Occupancy is not simply a matter of property rights but sovereignty: The first people who take possession of land thereby gain sovereignty over it.[54] So close is the relationship between property and sovereignty that, in fact, the two concepts are sometimes conflated.[55]

The principle of Prior Occupancy has an equally ancient and established pedigree. It holds that as between two claimants to a resource or land, the one who was the earlier possessor acquires rights superior to the other claimant. So, in the context of land return claims, the group or people whose land was appropriated has superior rights to the present possessors, at least prima facie, whether or not they were the aboriginal inhabitants.

Jeremy Waldron points out that the difference between the two principles, First Possession and Prior Possession, is not solely a matter of time and relativity.[56] The difference is more fundamental. Prior Possession is, as Waldron aptly characterizes it,[57] a conservative principle. Its purpose is to maintain stability and order by preserving the existing status quo.[58] It is unconcerned with the historical questions that First Possession poses, for it recognizes that the costs of answering those questions will often be insuperably high. At the same time, there is a very real danger in making the legitimacy of the extant order contingent upon proof of a highly contestable and murky past. The values expressed by the principle of Prior Possession are peace, order, stability, security, and certainty.[59]

53. *See* Locke, Treatise, *supra* note 13, at 287–88.

54. *See* Benjamin Ederington, *Property as a Natural Institution: The Separation of Property from Sovereignty in International Law*, 13 Am. U. Int'l L. Rev. 263 (1997).

55. *See* Morris R. Cohen, *Property and Sovereignty*, 13 Cornell L.Q. 8 (1927).

56. *See* Waldron, *Indigeneity?*, *supra* note 51, at 71–72.

57. *See id.* at 71.

58. *See* Dukeminier et al., Property, *supra* note 36, at 24.

59. *See* Pierson v. Post, 3 Cai. R. 175, 2 Am. Dec. 264 (N.Y. 1895).

Let us consider the application of Prior Possession to the land return context more closely. As indicated earlier, the apparent consequence of Prior Possession does not favor the dispossessed claimants. Prior Possession does not question their assertions that injustices were committed when they were dispossessed, but its concern is not with correcting that injustice. Its concerns are with protecting a stable order. Now, dispossessed claimants might use the very same principle to the opposite effect by pointing out that prior to their dispossession *they* had a stable order and property regime which is at least equally entitled to recognition and respect. The Prior Possession principle, they point out, is itself a double-edged sword. They might try to break the tie, as it were, by adding to this argument that on account of their indigeneity, their order was entitled to greater respect and recognition, if indigeneity is to have any role to play at all.

What are we to make of that argument? Which way does the principle of Prior Possession cut, in favor of the dispossessed former occupants or of the current possessors? Is it truly a double-edged sword? Recall that the principle is aptly characterized as conservative. Prior Possession is concerned with a form of justice, but the justice of order, stability, and security, rather than restorative justice. It opposes upsetting existing regimes, however they came about (with exceptions for extreme cases, such as slavery). It is with the peace, stability, and security of the *existing* order that the Prior Possession principle is concerned. So, it turns out Prior Possession is not a double-edged sword, after all. It favors the currently existing order, at least prima facie. As I said, the presumption can be rebutted in exceptional cases, but indigeneity is not in itself a basis for such an exception. Indigeneity involves invoking reasons of historical pedigree in the analysis, and the historical pedigrees of competing claims are precisely what the principle of Prior Possession, at its fundamental level, seeks to avoid for reasons I have already indicated.

Let us now consider what, if anything, changes if we suppose that the dispossessed claimants are all members of Group 1, first human occupants of the land—the aboriginal occupants—and their present-day descendants. Up to this point we have analyzed the effect of applying the Prior Possession principle to land return claims. Because the timing of possession under that principle is relative just to the two groups of claimants immediately involved, it is possible that the dispossessed claimants are members of either Group 1, Group 2—that is, the original inhabitants at the time of the dispossession and their present-day descendants—or both. But if the dispossessed claimants are members of Group 1 only, then the operative principle on which their claim rests may be either Prior Possession *or* First Possession.

First Possession introduces complication of its own, as any property lawyer or legal scholar can attest. Law students are taught in the Property course that

defining what acts count as First Possession is a normative, and therefore contestable, endeavor, rather than a mere datum point. Possession is, as lawyers are wont to say, both a fact and a conclusion. As Carol Rose states, "'[A]cts of possession' are a 'text,' . . . and the [] law rewards the author of that text." But, she continues, "as students of hermeneutics know, the clearest text may have ambiguous subtexts."[60] My point is not to suggest that it is impossible to determine who is the "First Possessor." Far from it—the common law does that all the time. The point rather is to underscore that the First Possession principle raises not only issues that are simple ones of fact but also contestable ones about policies and values.

A further complication with the First Possession principle concerns its normative weight.

Anglo-American law has long recognized the legitimacy of claims to property rights based on priority in time, and there are many reasons, both moral and prudential, why this is so.[61] Even Chief Justice John Marshall in *Johnson v. M'Intosh*[62] recognized the substantial moral claim that Native Americans had on the land they possessed before the arrival of the Europeans. Without question, First Possession is a powerful principle, both morally and legally.

Both in legal doctrine and in property theory, however, First Possession has always had to be qualified in some way to take account of considerations of others' needs and social welfare. In American property law, for example, First Possession, operating under the label of the Rule of Capture,[63] has proved not to be a workable principle without some qualification. Unqualified, the Rule of Capture generates perverse incentives that have led to overconsumption of natural resources and loss of social welfare—the familiar tragedy of the commons.[64] So it has been refined and qualified in ways that deny the First Possessor an absolute right to exclude all others. In property theory, too, an unqualified version of the First Occupancy principle has never been accepted, even proponents of historical entitlement theories such as Robert Nozick.[65] Something like John Locke's famous sufficiency proviso, which stipulated that the first person to appropriate some resources from the commons gained an

60. Carol M. Rose, *Possession as the Origin of Property*, 52 U. Chi. L. Rev. 73, 82–83 (1985).

61. *See id.*; Richard A. Epstein, *Possession as the Root of Title*, 13 Ga. L. Rev. 1221 (1979).

62. 21 U.S. (8 Wheat.) 543 (1823).

63. *See* Dukeminier et al., Property, *supra* note 36, at 37–38.

64. *See, e.g.*, Barnard v. Monongahela Natural Gas Co., 65 A. 801 (Pa. 1907). On the tragedy of the commons, *see* Garrett Hardin, *The Tragedy of the Commons*, 162 Science 1243 (1968).

65. *See* Nozick, Anarchy, State and Utopia, *supra* note 14, at 174–82.

exclusive property right in that resource so long as there be "enough, and as good left"[66] for others after the appropriation, has always been seen as necessary to accommodate other considerations of justice.

There is more to justice in claims for the return of dispossessed land than simply looking at the original injustice perpetrated upon the prior (or first, as the case may be) possessors and restoring them to the status quo ante. However strongly our initial instincts may lead us to think that is what justice requires, a full accounting of justice must give us pause. After all, full restoration of the status quo ante means committing a second act of radical dispossession. The current possessors, who may have been in possession of the land for generations and have come to be dependent upon that land, are now to be summarily removed without any consideration given to their needs or the substantial changes in circumstances, for both sides, that may well have occurred in the intervening years since the original act of injustice was perpetrated. And what is to happen to the newly dispossessed people? Shall the new occupant have the right to exclude them altogether? After all, the property right that the First Possession principle confers is usually understood to be a robust sort of right that includes the right to exclude. So presumably this means that the new occupants may banish their predecessors from the land entirely. Is that not an injustice as well? Can it be justified by the mere fact that one group was there first? I will not purport to answer these questions, but I suggest that it is difficult to justify failing to give adequate weight to the others' interests, particularly their needs, when assessing what justice requires. At a minimum, I insist that these questions raise very serious complications in the case for any attempt to resolve the issue of return of land solely on the basis of the fact of First Possession.

Peoples—Concept and Conceptions

Let us briefly consider the concept of peoples itself. That concept is another source of complexity in the sort of land return claims under discussion. Although it is now a term of common currency in international law,[67] "peoples" is hardly unproblematic.[68] In the context of international law it is closely associated with

66. Locke, Treatise, *supra* note 13, at 291.

67. *See* S. James Anaya, Indigenous Peoples in International Law 55–61 (2nd ed., 2004); Zelim Skurbaty, As If Peoples Mattered 55–57 (2000).

68. *See* David Makinson, *Rights of Peoples: Point of View of a Logician, in* The Rights of Peoples 69 (James Crawford ed., 1988); Ian Brownlie, *The Rights of Peoples in Modern International Law, in id.* at 1.

the concept of the right of group self-determination,[69] the meaning of which is itself deeply contested.[70]

One problem with the concept of peoples is a frequent failure to keep straight whether the term is being used as a political concept or a sociological one. This is important because differences sometimes exist between the group to whom political rights are given (or who seek such rights) and their sociological composition. This is a point that is often made with respect to postcolonial "people." Anna Michalska observes, for example, "One cannot ignore that colonial states were often artificially created: they were composed of different national, ethnic and religious groups (which sometimes remained markedly different).... Can such an exercise of the right to self-determination of colonial and dependent peoples fully satisfy [such] peoples?"[71] Moreover, a strictly sociological perspective cannot account for the fact that in some cases (e.g., Estonia) large minorities have joined in demands for national self-determination, yet in other cases (e.g., Bohemia) sociologically cohesive populations have failed to unite in self-determination movements.

A further problem with sociological definitions is that they are quickly losing traction as the world's population becomes increasingly heterogeneous. My own country may be an extreme example, but the rest of the world is catching up as the pace of migration and intermarriage quickens. Hitler once called the United States "a mongrel nation,"[72] and for once he was right. We *are* a mongrel population, and we consider it one of our strengths (at least most of us do). It will not be many more years before much of the world's population catches up with us and becomes itself mongrelized. So it seems that the sociological approach to defining the concept of people is unlikely to prove very fruitful.

This is not to say that we should abandon the concept of "peoples" or that it does no analytical work in arguments for the return of indigenous lands. To the contrary, peoples has proved to be a powerful trope in both legal and political discourse about both self-determination and return of land. Moreover, it does have value as an analytical tool. The point, rather, is that a strictly sociological approach to defining the concept is in and of itself inadequate.

69. *See* Anaya, Indigenous Peoples, *supra* note 67, at 60.

70. *See* James Summers, The Idea of the People: The Right of Self-Determination, Nationalism and Legitimacy in International Law (doctoral dissertation, University of Helsinki, 2004), *available at* http://ethesis.helsinki.fi/julkaisut/oik/julki/vk/summers/theideao.pdf (last visited July 8, 2016).

71. Anna Michalska, *Rights of Peoples to Self-Determination in International Law, in* Issues of Self-Determination 71, 82 (William Twining ed., 1991).

72. Geoffrey C. Ward, *Mongrel Nation*, Smithsonian (Nov. 2001).

How else might we define the concept of "peoples" in a way that satisfies both its descriptive and analytical purposes? One possibility is to limit the term to populations located in territories that either are or in the reasonably near past were under conditions of colonialism.[73]

Support for such a restrictive view might be taken from the very fact that the context in which "peoples" is usually employed in international law these days is precisely at the behest of the asserted right of group self-determination in post-colonial (or colonial-like) environments. But that approach seems unduly restrictive or artificial. Putting aside questions about what counts as a postcolonial environment (can the current situation of the Palestinians be so characterized?), if land reversion is the (or a) legitimate means of correcting a historic injustice, this is the case whether that injustice occurred as a result of colonial domination or some other form of oppression.

Another possibility takes its lead from the opposite instinct: to broaden rather than to restrict. Some analysts have developed capacious conceptions of peoples in their efforts to avoid the sorts of defects we have just seen with conceptions that define peoples in terms of some objective standard. James Anaya, for example, offers this definition: "The term *peoples* . . . should be understood to refer to all those spheres of community, marked by elements of identity and collective consciousness, within which people's lives unfold—independently of considerations of historical or postulated sovereignty."[74] This approach, while avoiding problems of restricting peoples by underinclusive objective standards such as ethnicity or shared colonial experience, risks being overinclusive. Shorn of historical identification or "postulated sovereignty," peoples are "spheres of community," the defining characteristics of which are "identity" and "collective consciousness." Consider which groups this conception might be interpreted as including: in some parts of the West, including the United States, skinheads and neo-Nazis would qualify as "peoples" under this definition. These groups exhibit strong feelings of identity, to such a degree in fact that they experience alienation from the mainstream of their societies.

73. Something like this seems to have been the view taken in India's reservation to article 1 of the International Covenant on Civil and Political Rights, Dec. 16, 1966, G.A. Res. 2200(XXI), art. 1(1), 999 U.N.T.S. 171 (entered into force Mar. 23, 1976), made at the time it ratified the Covenant: "[T]he Government of the Republic of India declares that the words 'the right of self-determination' appearing in this article apply only to the peoples under foreign domination and that these words do not apply to . . . a section of a . . . nation—which is the essence of national integrity."

74. Anaya, Indigenous Peoples, *supra* note 67, at 103.

And there is little doubt that they share a "collective consciousness," a consciousness that has been developed to such an extent that it may accurately be called an ideology. Yet surely we will hesitate to place skinheads alongside the Maori as groups who may justly be considered entitled to a right of self-determination, assuming for the moment that we wish to recognize such a right. Of course, Anaya might respond that even if he conceded that skinheads and neo-Nazis are peoples under his definition, it does not follow that they should be recognized as bearing all the same political and legal rights as other peoples. We may draw rational and legitimate distinctions between certain groups as peoples, recognizing that some are entitled to self-determination while others are not. The response, although sensible itself, must acknowledge two counterpoints. First, there is in the literature on human rights and international law a stubborn tendency to couple peoples with a cluster of rights, particularly self-determination. Peoples is a kind of adhesive concept—other concepts tend to stick to it, and it is difficult to pry them apart. Second, resolving the problem of the implications of labeling a group as a people by leaving open the possibility of rational distinctions among different groups simply substitutes one difficult problem for another. It pushes the problem around rather than resolves it, once and for all.

Peoples, like many other political concepts, is complex, of course. This is hardly to say that the concept of peoples is incapable of doing analytical work in the context of the land return disputes we are discussing. One way perhaps of making "peoples" analytically more tractable is to use it in a way that employs both the distinction between concept and conception[75] and Wittgenstein's familiar "family resemblance" notion.[76] The concept-conception distinction, to which Gallie first drew attention and Hart and Dworkin later developed, is simply that between an abstract notion such as justice or equality, and a particular instantiation of that notion. In the land reparation context, we would say that although "peoples" is a contested concept, one may specify or develop a coherent conception of that concept which facilitates identification of the groups to be benefited by the reparations. "Family resemblances" is a term that Wittgenstein used to explain multiple phenomena (his favorite example was games) that lack any single defining characteristic but that are connected by overlapping similarities. What is helpful about the term in the land reparations context is that it illuminates why it is wrong to throw the baby out with the bathwater. There may be no one essential characteristic that

75. *See* H.L.A. Hart, The Concept of Law (1961); Ronald Dworkin, Taking Rights Seriously (1977); W.B. Gallie, *Essentially Contested Concepts*, 56 Proceeding of the Aristotelian Society 167 (1956).

76. *See* Ludwig Wittgenstein, Philosophical Investigations (1953).

all iterations of the phenomenon of peoples share, but they are all connected by certain overlapping features that help to explain why the term has gained much currency in legal, political, and other discourses. So, with regard to land reparations claims, perhaps something like a working conception of "peoples" might be developed by looking for family resemblances among the various contexts in which the term is used. Such a conception might look something like Anaya's definition but add to it characteristics such as either a political or historical form of identification to avoid the problem of overinclusion previously noted. A conception that is useful for some purposes, such as demands for self-determination under international law, may not be useful in other contexts, including land reparations. This is not a sufficient reason for abandoning the concept of peoples altogether, however. It simply means that a different conception should be developed. Although it will be neither an uncontroversial nor easy undertaking, it can be done.

DISTRIBUTIVE JUSTICE

Thus far the conception of justice under which the analysis has proceeded is backward-looking, focused on a state of affairs that existed in the past and seeking to restore that state. But justice is not always backward-looking. In fact, most theories of justice are concerned with the here and now and with the future. This is where we live. Our decisions have consequences for the lives of real people, and this is especially so with respect to our responses to claims for the return of appropriated land. The justice considerations that those claims implicate surely include distributive concerns about the effects of returning land upon the large numbers of people who would be affected, one way or the other, by returning land unjustly appropriated many years earlier to the descendants of the original occupants.

Land restitution creates zero-sum situations or possibly something worse. Returning the land to *A* means taking it away from *B* (and possibly *C*, *D*, and *E*). Such a solution may not be what justice requires of us at all, or indeed even what it permits. What the morally appropriate conception of justice, the distributive conception that is present- and forward-looking, does permit, and indeed requires, is to change the present and future circumstances of those who were affected by a past injustice in ways that improve their lives now and in the future and by doing so, counteract the effects of the past injustice. As this part discusses, such a present- and forward-looking approach to justice is best realized through a program of distributive rather than reparatory justice. This part addresses, albeit too briefly to analyze fully all aspects, the distributive justice considerations that inevitably will weigh in to any discussion about claims to specific land restitution.

The Illusion of Reversion

Distributive considerations gain weight when we clarify what a decision to return land does and does not involve. The previous discussion noted that land return claims are sometimes argued in terms that set them apart from compensatory claims. The argument is that the return of unjustly appropriated land constitutes an act of the reversion of land rights.[77] On this view, title to land that was unjustly appropriated many years ago simply reverts now to the original possessors or their descendants, who thereby acquire jurisdiction to set the terms on the future use of the land. This is not a matter of compensation or reparation, but of restoration—a simple return to the status quo ante.

But there is nothing simple about the return of land taken decades, perhaps even hundreds, of years ago. The reversionary argument is based on a chimera, the notion that it is possible to restore matters to their original status. But there is no going back. That is the point of the quote sometimes attributed to the late H.R. (Bob) Haldeman:[78] "Once the toothpaste is out of the tube, it's hard to get it back in." There is no true reversion to the status quo ante, for irreversible changes of circumstances have occurred since the time of initial appropriation of land. The reversion argument asserts that return of appropriated land is a matter of a restoration of preexisting entitlement that continued to exist de jure even though de facto it was not enforced.[79] The error in this argument is that it supposes that the entitlement that the act of land return is meant to enforce is the *identical* entitlement to the one that existed prior to the land's appropriation. But this cannot be. Even if we suppose that *some* entitlement survives during the time since appropriation to the present, it does not necessarily follow that the present entitlement is identical to the preappropriation entitlement. In fact, unless the intervening time period is short, it seems highly unlikely that it is identical. The entitlement we are talking about is not like the abstract and formal sort of property right that property lawyers have in mind when they discuss reversions. Rather, it is highly contextual and substantive. It is subject to change as material changes in the conditions from which it takes its stance change, much in the way that the human self changes over time. Its identity is affected by changes in its holders, reliance by the new occupants and others, forms of adaptation by former

77. *See* Julie Cassady, *Sovereignty of Aboriginal Peoples*, 9 Ind. Int'l & Comp. L. Rev. 65, 117 (1998).

78. H.R. Haldeman was White House Chief of Staff under President Richard Nixon. He spent eighteen months in prison for his role in the Watergate conspiracy. *See Revisiting Watergate, available at* http://www.washingtonpost.com/wp-srv/onpolitics/watergate/haldeman.html.

79. *See* Benedict Kingsbury, *Competing Conceptual Approaches to Indigenous Group Issues in New Zealand Law*, 52 U. Tor. L.J. 101, 118 (1992).

occupation, expectations on the part of both present and former occupants. As the identities of the holders of the entitlement change, and the new occupants and those depend upon them come to rely upon the land for their livelihood and develop other forms of attachment to the land, the more the identity of the entitlement itself changes, putting to the lie any notion of a simple reversion of property.

If we accept this argument, then we need to rethink the supersession thesis, with which previous parts of this chapter had generally endorsed. The identities of the entitlements are based upon the injustices involved, past and present; hence, a change in the entitlement implies that some change has occurred in the injustice that Waldron's original version of the supersession theory does not admit or recognize. We can avoid this tension between the view that the identity of the entitlement change and that supersession thesis by adopting a version of the supersession thesis suggested by Tamar Meisels, which rejects the claim that changes of circumstances supersede the original injustice but accepts the argument that such changes supersede the injustice of the present and continued holding of the land in question in the particular circumstances.[80] If, as I have argued, entitlements are dynamic and, owing to their contextual character, change in response to changes in circumstances, we may reconcile this view with the supersession thesis by interpreting that thesis so that significant shifts in circumstances, affecting both the implicated societies as a whole and their individuals, may terminate old entitlements and create new ones. This argument remains faithful to the supersession thesis insofar as it recognizes the effects of changes of circumstances upon the justice calculus of reparation claims.

Redistributive Complications

Land return claims inevitably involve redistribution, and there are serious problems associated with this redistributive dimension. There are two concerns here: (1) Who should be the beneficiaries of the redistribution undertaken in the interest of restitution? (2) Restitution may well have second-order redistributive effects, that is, effects on persons other than those immediately involved in the claim.

Restitution to Whom? The Identity Problem

The first problem results from the fact that the current owner-possessor of the asset may not be the person or entity who expropriated the asset. Specific

80. *See* Meisels, Territorial Rights, *supra* note 40, at 81–82. *See also* Patton, *Historic Injustice*, *supra* note 40, at 260.

restitution involves literally taking asset *x*, now in *B*'s hands, and giving it to *A*, the original owner. (I am assuming here the quite substantial complication that *A* may not be the original owner but her heir or some other successor of the original owner's rights.)

This redistribution is easiest to justify, both as a matter of corrective justice and distributive justice, if *B* is the person or entity who wrongfully took the asset from *A* in the first place. Suppose, for example, that the original owner of a farm now seeks its return from a government that expropriated the land sometime in the past but later changed its policy and now permits restitution of expropriated property. Here the redistribution from *B* to *A* seems, all else being equal, seems fair.

This scenario will be rare. More commonly, the current owner-possessor of the farm or other expropriated asset will be a person or entity other than the one who perpetrated the original wrongful act. In this more typical case, where the expropriation was committed by a government, the current owner-possessor is likely to be either a successor government, one that followed a radical rupture from the preceding government, or a person or institution to whom the expropriating government transferred the asset. In either case the current owner-possessor is an innocent party, someone who had no part in the expropriation. Under these circumstances, correction of a past injustice through specific restitution is a redistribution that itself constitutes government expropriation that can reasonably be considered wrongful. This restitutionary expropriation is not inherently or categorically less wrongful than the original expropriation.

The argument that it is not wrongful rests on the contention that it undoes a past wrong.

Suppose the original expropriation was committed under the contention that its purpose is the undoing of past wrongs. The hypothetical is not intended to allude to one of Locke's justifications for the European expropriation of lands in America or to any other particular historical act of colonial expropriation. It is a hypothetical only, raised to make a theoretical point. Still, the hypothetical is, perhaps, not entirely without actual foundation. Acts of land expropriation have been committed in the past by government for the ostensible purpose of righting a wrong, specifically, redistributing land to redress an extant distribution of assets that was, in the expropriator's view (perhaps with reason), unjust. From its perspective, the expropriation was committed as an act of justice.

Putting aside the questions whether that perspective is warranted and whether the expropriator's justification is pretextual or in fact genuine, let us assume for the sake of argument that the justification given for this expropriation—the original expropriation—is genuine. Now we have two situations in which expropriatory acts are committed for the sincere (we have assumed) purpose of seeking justice. Are these two acts of expropriation theoretically equal? The difference

between the justifications for them is that one, the second, was done in the interest of *corrective* justice while the (hypothetical) original expropriatory act was committed in the interest of *distributive* justice. Any argument that seeks to legitimate one act of expropriation but not the other, then, must establish that one form of justice is morally privileged over or superior to the other. That is a far more challenging task, involving claims that are inherently and deeply contestable. My point is not that no rational choice can be made between the two forms of justice but rather that identity issues sometimes implicate fundamental problems of justice that proponents of specific restitution cannot always ignore.[81]

Second-Order Redistributive Concerns

The second concern is with second-order redistributive effects. In addition to the current owner herself, other people may well be affected by the shift in the asset's ownership and possession. Even if *B* is not innocent, other innocent people may be adversely affected by the redistribution. It is not only land itself that is subject to redistribution but buildings and other fixtures upon that land as well. What is to be done about the many homes that are subject to being lost as a result of a land return award? Even if the owners are compensated for their loss, the upheaval in the lives of many innocent people will certainly be great. Some portion of the losses inflicted cannot be compensated by any monetary payment because they are subjective in nature and defy objective measurement.

The problem is even more acute with respect to public institutions such as hospitals and schools. To see this, suppose that in return for returning land, the state, which previously owned hospitals, schools, and other public institutions upon the land, receives monetary compensation that Christopher Kutz calls "maximalist."[82] Cash compensation claims are maximalist when they represent "the total monetarized value of the loss suffered by the former property owner."[83]

81. Martha Minow argues that subsequent owners of unjustly expropriated property cannot be regarded as innocent because they have benefited from the expropriation. *See* Martha Minow, Between Vengeance and Forgiveness 108 (1998). I find this argument too quick. Why should one person's enrichment be regarded as unjust simply because it is the result of another person's unjust act?

Unless the current owner has in some way participated in the injustice (and, in my judgment, participation in the injustice requires more than the passive state of holding the fruit of the injustice), it is not at all clear why, from the moral point of view, that person should share responsibility for the injustice with the perpetrator. This is not to say that cogent arguments for responsibility cannot be made. It is to say that the case for attributing responsibility to that individual is difficult to sustain.

82. Christopher Kutz, *Justice in Reparations: The Cost of Memory and the Value of Talk*, 32 Phil. & Pub. Aff. 277, 292 (2004).

83. *Id.*

Such a claim includes at least the fair market value of the property at the time of return, plus, for any commercial assets, lost income from the property since the time of return, plus lost income on that income.[84]

How feasible is a program of maximalist compensation for the loss of public buildings? Not very, it seems. To begin with, it may be necessary to discount, perhaps steeply, the market value of the property in question to take into account any political instability surrounding the return of land and accompanying compensation.[85] Knowing just how much discounting is warranted will be quite difficult. Moreover, assessing any income on the property, and income on the income, leads us back into the counterfactual dilemma discussed earlier. We would need counterfactually to posit imagined rates of interest and levels of taxation in order to calculate the entitled amounts of income.[86]

A more fundamental problem is that the state that is obligated to pay such compensation may be fiscally unable to carry out its obligation. The state may be financially strapped, especially if it is newly established. Its resources already stretched too thin, it simply will not be able to pay monetary compensation at the levels likely to exist in most cases where large amounts of land have been redistributed.

Even if the new state's fisc is able to absorb the costs of compensation, there is a deeper normative issue to consider. Why should the victims of land redistribution be given priority over other possible claimants on public resources whose needs may well be greater than those who lose through land redistribution? Stated differently, why should restorative justice trump distributive justice? The apparently simple redistributive act of transferring title from *B* to *A*'s successors in fact has much more complex redistributive consequences. It inevitably involves trade-offs between the victims of unjust land appropriation (or, more likely, their descendants) and other persons who suffer from lack of adequate housing, medical care, education, and other basic needs. From the perspective of distributive justice these other persons may well have far stronger claims than the victims of past land appropriations. Under Rawls' maximin principle, for example, the just distribution of the state's scarce resources would favor these other persons over the victims of land appropriation if, as is quite possible, those persons are the least well-off in terms of welfare-conferring resources.[87]

84. *Id.*

85. *See id.* at 292–93

86. *See id.* at 293.

87. *See* John Rawls, A Theory of Justice 152–57 (1971).

But this analysis is too quick. It overlooks the possibility that the two perspectives, restorative justice and distributive justice, may coexist. Indeed, a simple version of Lockean theory would consider their relationship in just that way. There is no conflict between the two perspectives because they perform different tasks: Distributive justice fixes entitlements, and restorative (or corrective) justice protects those entitlements against unjustified encroachments.[88] Under ideal background conditions, in which the former occupants' holdings were all legitimate, restorative justice would take over and demand a return of holding to the status quo ante. But the Lockean scenario seldom works out that way because we live in a non-ideal world in which background holdings commonly are tainted by one or another form of injustice. Under such circumstances the land appropriations of the past do not trigger restorative justice because there is no Lockean injustice to begin with. As Christopher Kutz has observed, the difficulty that the Lockean perspective has in generating a coherent normative framework in the messy world in which we live "is one among many reasons for preferring a more robust conception of distributive justice."[89]

A robust conception of distributive justice need not demand that we ignore restorative justice considerations altogether. Broadly egalitarian theories, for example, can leave room for restorative justice claims. Despite the fact that, from the perspective of most theories of distributive justice, some people in the United States have more than their fair share of holdings, even very wealthy individuals are entitled, as a matter of justice, to some form of compensation when others injure them.[90] The reason the two forms of justice—distributive and restorative—are compatible with each other is that they involve different, although certainly related, moral topics. Distributive justice concerns questions about what distributions of economic (broadly defined) benefits and burdens across members of society are morally preferable and the political and social structures and institutions that affect such distributions. Its subject is, in Rawls' terms, the "basic structure of society."[91] Restorative, or corrective, justice, on the other hand, is concerned with righting wrongful losses, that is, losses that depart from norms of morally and/or legally legitimate modes of transfer, apart from considerations of equality or fairness, which are matters of distributive justice.

Yet, although distributive and restorative justice are distinct from each other in the way just described, they are not entirely independent of each other. The

88. *See* Kutz, *Justice in Reparations*, *supra* note 82, at 298.

89. *Id.* at 298–99.

90. *See* Jules Coleman, Risks and Wrongs 350–54 (1992).

91. Rawls, A Theory of Justice, *supra* note 87, at 7.

justness of restorative justice claims must be evaluated in light of the justness of the underlying pattern of distribution of actual holdings. Stated differently, a restorative justice scheme that we take to be just presupposes and rests upon a just and adequate distribution of holdings.[92] A society whose existing distributive scheme of basic resources is fundamentally unjust or inadequate cannot justify satisfying historically grounded claims on resources. This means, for example, that if a state that is contemplating returning land is one marked by high levels of poverty through its citizenry, then a basic precondition for restorative justice has not been satisfied. The state's first obligation is to attend to the fundamental needs, including land distribution, of its own members. The same holds true if the state's aggregate level of wealth is sufficient to meet its citizens' basic needs but land and other resources are so maldistributed that extreme levels of poverty prevail throughout a significant segment of the population. A state is justified in meeting its restorative justice obligations only if doing so will not jeopardize its ability to meet its distributive justice obligations to its own members.

Other commentators have pointed out that reparative claims can be fashioned in ways that meet the demands of distributive justice. Charles Ogletree, for example, has argued for a program of reparations for African Americans that is keenly sensitive to distributive concerns.[93] Ogletree suggests that individual payments of money to African Americans, as the descendants of the victims of slavery, is not the ideal course. Instead, he argues, successful African Americans, who are otherwise entitled to receive cash payments as reparations, should forgo their entitlements for the greater good of the African American community. The reparation resources released in this way should "be pooled, monitored, and distributed to address specific community needs and to empower specific community members."[94] To this end, he proposes creation of a trust fund to administer the pooled money and also an independent commission to distribute the trust funds to the poorest members of the African American community. The character of Ogletree's redistributive approach is reflected in his rationale. "The damage has been done to a group, African American slaves and their descendants, but it has not been done equally within the group," he writes.[95] "The reparations movement must aim at undoing the damage where it has been most severe."

92. *See* Kutz, *Justice in Reparations, supra* note 82, at 301.

93. *See* Charles Ogletree, *The Current Reparations Debate*, 36 U.C. Davis L. Rev. 1051, 1071–72 (2003).

94. *Id.* at 1071.

95. *Id.*

This is an example of an approach to reparations whose focus is on the present yet is keenly sensitive to the injustices of the past that generate the entitlements. The form of justice is primarily distributive, yet it seeks to honor the ideals of reparative justice. It is responsive to several concerns that have been raised here and, putting to one side the question of its feasibility, seeks to insert progressivity into a program of reparations by distributing them to those in greatest need. Of course, Ogletree's program is one of monetary reparations rather than specific land reparations, but there is no inherent reason why the program, or something like it, could not be adapted to specific reparations.[96]

Past, present, and future are linked in another way, suggested by Leif Wenar.[97] Reparative justice is related to distributive principles, he states, not instrumentally but transcendentally. By that, he means that reparative justice may be necessary to enable indigenous peoples and other victims of unjust land expropriations to live in the future with dominant groups in conditions of moral relations. Unless the past is acknowledged in some meaningful way and unless some sort of amends is made, Wenar argues, the two groups cannot live together in conditions of mutual respect and trust. "The past wrong is relevant because it poisons the groups' future life together."[98] What amends are required will likely be different in different context, but in some of them a program of complete specific restitution of all expropriated will likely be either necessary or justified under distributive principles.

It will not do simply to say, "What's past is past" or "Let sleeping dogs lie." The dogs may not really be sleeping, only pretending to sleep, and in any case dogs wake up eventually. The point is that an injustice was done, and it needs to be acknowledged and dealt with. Of course, how we should deal with it is precisely the question before us. My objective here has not been to provide a definitive answer to that question but rather to point out some reasons to hesitate before leaping to a solution that seems superficially appealing. Land reparations—returning land that we consider unjustly taken from peoples in the past—may appeal to our instincts for justice, but as I have tried to show, it is far from clear that this is what justice requires in order to acknowledge past injustice and to make amends. Here, as elsewhere, justice turns out to be a very complex matter.

96. I discuss the specific question of obligations of property owners to members of the African American community in Chapter Nine.

97. *See* Wenar, *Reparations for the Future, supra* note 48, at 403. *See also* Ivison, Postcolonial Liberalism, *supra* note 43, at 100–01.

98. Wenar, *Reparations for the Future, supra* note 48, at 403.

6

The Right to Exclude

The right to exclude others has been a controversial topic in property legal scholarship in recent years. This should hardly be surprising. As the distinguished English property scholars Kevin and Susan Gray have pointed out, "the 'exclusion question' throws a sharp focus upon an increasingly fierce confrontation between the social ethics of self-reliance or self-interest and a competing philosophy of co-operative or communitarian value."[1] Stated differently, the "exclusion question" exposes the main fault lines in the institution of private ownership. It inescapably confronts us with the question that is implicated in every dispute over property rights: What type of society do we wish to have? As Professor Joseph Singer states, "What is at stake is a vision of social life."[2] Resolving disputes over access rights of all manner and types concretizes in the most immediate way disagreements about the how social life should be ordered.

The right to exclude has never been absolute, of course, but judicial decisions over the past few decades have whittled away at its breadth. One of the most

1. Kevin Gray & Susan Francis Gray, *Private Property and Public Propriety*, *in* Property and the Constitution 11, 15 (Janet McLean ed., 1999).

2. Joseph William Singer, Entitlement: The Paradoxes of Property 11 (2000).

controversial contexts in which this narrowing has occurred is public access to beaches, specifically, privately owned beaches.

Although courts have provided the public access to beaches on various doctrinal grounds,[3] the most important—and controversial—of these has been the public trust doctrine.[4]

The controversy surrounding the public trust doctrine has gained steam in recent years as some courts have used it to extend public access to beaches, including privately owned dry-sand portions of beachfront property,[5] concomitantly reducing the scope of the right to exclude. As one scholar has stated:

> To some, the doctrine . . . is a check on government attempts to give away or sell [important natural] resources for short-term economic gain. To . . . others, it is a back-door mechanism for judicial taking of private property without just compensation through a clever argument that the property was never "private" in the first place.[6]

I will use the controversy over public access to private beaches as the vehicle for examining the right to exclude and its limitations from the perspective of the human flourishing theory. More basically, right-to-exclude disputes provide an opportunity to consider the method by which legal analysts would approach property disputes generally under the human flourishing theory. This chapter, then, provides methodological guidance for applying the pluralist human flourishing theory. How, exactly, do we identify which values and which capabilities are involved in any given situation? Where, as invariably is the case, competing values and capabilities are at stake on both sides, how do we choose between

3. *See, e.g.*, Gion v. City of Santa Cruz, 465 P.2d 50 (Cal. 1970) (dedication); City of Daytona Beach v. Tona-Rama, Inc., 294 So. 2d 73 (Fla. 1974) (custom); Concerned Citizens of Brunswick County Taxpayers Ass'n v. Rhodes, 404 S.E.2d 677 (N.C. 1991) (prescription); Stevens v. City of Cannon Beach, 854 P.2d 449 (Or. 1993) (custom).

4. Other expansive uses of the public trust doctrine include use of and access to all waters usable for recreational purposes, *see* Mont. Coal. for Stream Access, Inc. v. Curran, 682 P.2d 163 (Mont. 1984); preservation of inland wetlands, *see* Just v. Marinette County, 201 N.W.2d 761 (Wis. 1972); and protection of wildlife and their habitats, *see* Pullen v. Ulmer, 923 P.2d 54 (Alaska 1996). The modern revival of interest in the public trust doctrine begins, of course, with the classic article by Joseph Sax. Joseph L. Sax, *The Public Trust Doctrine in Natural Resource Law: Effective Judicial Intervention*, 68 Mich. L. Rev. 471 (1970).

5. *See, e.g.*, Glass v. Goeckel, 703 N.W.2d 58 (Mich. 2005); Raleigh Ave. Beach Ass'n v. Atlantis Beach Club, Inc., 879 A.2d 112 (N.J. 2005); Matthews v. Bay Head Improvement Ass'n, 471 A.2d 355 (N.J. 1984).

6. Alexandra B. Klass, *Modern Public Trust Principles: Recognizing Rights and Integrating Standards*, 82 Notre Dame L. Rev. 699, 699 (2006).

them? If the values underlying property are incommensurate, how can we make rational choices among them? This chapter provides an opportunity to consider these questions. The cases that I consider here are important both intrinsically and—indeed, more so—because they successfully address the methodological issues that the human flourishing theory faces.

To provide background to the recent disputes over access to beaches and other venues, we need first to trace the traditional understanding of the common-law right to exclude. This background allows us to see that the parameters of the right to exclude have changed over time.

THE GOOD OLD RIGHT TO EXCLUDE

The right to exclude is widely recognized as an important constitutive of individual ownership. Blackstone was hardly alone in associating ownership with "that sole and despotic dominion which one man claims and exercises over the external things of the world, in total exclusion of the right of any other individual in the universe."[7] On multiple occasions the U.S. Supreme Court has stated that "the right to exclude others" is "one of the most essential sticks in the bundle of rights that are [*sic*] commonly characterized as property."[8] Similarly, scholars over the years have attached considerable importance to the right to exclude as an attribute of private ownership.[9] Thomas Merrill has even argued that the right to exclude is "a necessary and sufficient condition of identifying the existence of property."[10]

The Common-Law Baseline

The traditional nineteenth-century common-law baseline regarding the right of property owners to exclude others was extraordinarily broad. Owners, courts

7. William Blackstone, Commentaries on the Laws of England, 4 vols., vol. 2, at 2 (1979).

8. Kaiser Aetna v. United States, 444 U.S. 164, 176 (1979). *See also* Dolan v. City of Tigard, 512 U.S. 374, 384 (1994); Lucas v. South Carolina Coastal Council, 505 U.S. 1003, 1044 (1992); Nollan v. California Coastal Comm'n, 483 U.S. 825, 831 (1987); Loretto v. Teleprompter Manhattan CATV Corp., 458 U.S. 419, 435 (1982).

9. *See, e.g.*, J.E. Penner, The Idea of Property in Law (1997); J.W. Harris, Property and Justice (1996); Felix S. Cohen, *Dialogue on Private Property*, 9 Rutgers L. Rev. 357 (1959); Morris Cohen, *Property and Sovereignty*, 13 Cornell L.Q. 8, 12 (1927).

10. Thomas W. Merrill, *Property and the Right to Exclude*, 77 Neb. L. Rev. 730, 731 (1998). *See also* Henry E. Smith, *Exclusion and Property Rules in the Law of Nuisance*, 90 Va. L. Rev. 965 (2004); Henry E. Smith, *Exclusion versus Governance: Two Strategies for Delineating Property Rights*, 31 J. Legal Studies S453 (2002).

repeatedly have said, have a nearly absolute right to exclude anyone and for any reason.[11] Certain privileged nonpermissive entries upon land possessed by another are recognized, but these exceptions are closely circumscribed.[12] Still, there *were* limitations. These limitations were broadest with respect to land that is open to the public and narrowest with respect to land that is closed to the public. The family home is the obvious example of property that is closed to the public. Yet even here outsiders may be privileged to enter. *A* may enter *B*'s house, for example, for the purpose of saving *B*'s life or *A*'s.[13] With respect to shared property, tenants have long been permitted to receive visitors, and unless an agreement provides otherwise, landlords are not free to exclude such visitors.[14] The classic case in American law of necessity privileging nonpermissive entry upon another's property is *Ploof v. Putnam*.[15] There the court held that it was not trespass for the owner of a boat to tie the boat to a privately owned dock without the dock owner's permission where an unexpectedly bad storm forced the boat owner to seek safe harbor.

Public policy is conventionally cited to explain another exception to the common-law rule of exclusion. The conventional wisdom is that the common law severely limited the right of access to businesses open to the public.[16] Only innkeepers and common carriers were duty-bound to serve members of the public, subject to reasonable restrictions designed to protect their legitimate business interests. As to other businesses, however, the basic common-law rule of arbitrary exclusion applies.[17] This means that in the absence of any contrary statute, virtually all businesses, meaning property to which the public is invited, are free to exclude anyone they wish and for any reason (or no reason). Of course, federal and state statutes have changed this rule to some extent, but as to property open to the public, the common-law baseline categorically limits the duty to include to innkeepers and common carriers.

11. *See* Joseph William Singer, *No Right to Exclude: Public Accommodations and Private Property*, 90 NW. U. L. REV. 1283 (1996).

12. *Id.* at 1293.

13. *See* Restatement (Second) of Torts § 197, comment *h*.

14. *E.g.*, State v. DeCoster, 653 A.2d 891 (Me. 1995); Williams v. Lubbering, 63 Atl. 90 (N.J. 1906).

15. 71 Atl. 188 (Vt. 1908). In the case the dock owner's agent unmoored the boat, resulting in injuries to the boat, its cargo, its owner, and the owner's family. The court held that to unmoor the boat was a wrongful act, entitling the boat owner to damages.

16. *See* Singer, *No Right to Exclude, supra* note 11, at 1291–92.

17. *But see* Uston v. Resorts Int'l Hotel, Inc., 445 A.2d 370 (N.J. 1982).

The Public Trust Doctrine at Common Law

At the other end of the spectrum from this robust right to exclude lies property that is subject to a right of access by the public in general, what Roman lawyers called *res publicae*,[18] or what Carol Rose has called "inherently public property."[19] At traditional common law, property subject to these public access rights included roads and highways, navigable waterways, and tidal lands.[20] Although the public's use rights with respect to such property were limited in various ways,[21] the important fact was the very existence of a property right[22] of access held by the public at large. It represented a virtual reversal of the usual Hohfeldian arrangement of rights and privileges. Ordinarily, private ownership is a regime of all rights in the individual owner and no privileges in the rest of the world. However, property that was subject to public access involved no right of any individual to exclude others, and the public held all privileges of access and use (subject to some sort of reasonableness constraints).[23] These narrowly defined public access rights were later used, as we shall soon see, as the wedge for more expansive public access rights, particularly for recreational purposes.

Historically, public access to beaches under the public trust doctrine was quite limited. Basically, the public was permitted to access only the land between the mean high- and low-tide lines, that is, wet-sand areas. The purposes for which the public was permitted to access this land were also limited—only fishing. (Navigable waters themselves were also subject to public access for navigation and commerce as well as for fishing.)

18. *See* William W. Buckland, A Textbook of Roman Law from Augustus to Justinian 183 (rev. 3d ed. 1963). *See also* Carol M. Rose, *Romans, Roads, and Romantic Creators: Traditions of Public Property in the Information Age*, 66 Law & Contemp. Probs. 89, 96–97 (2003).

19. Carol Rose, *The Comedy of the Commons: Custom, Commerce, and Inherently Public Property*, 53 U. Chi. L. Rev. 711 (1986).

20. *Id.* at 723–30.

21. For example, the use of tidal lands was originally restricted to navigation and fishing. Also, obstruction of a highway constituted trespass justifying eviction. *See, e.g.*, Regina v. Pratt (1855) 119 Eng. Rep. 319, 321–22 (hunting on highway). The right to use navigable waterways was restricted to purposes of "navigation, commerce, trade, and intercourse." Blundell v. Catterall, (1821) 106 Eng. Rep. 1190, 1199–1200.

22. The proprietary character of such public access rights is sometimes disputed. *See, e.g.*, Kanak v. Minister for Land and Water Conservation, (2000) 180 ALR 489, at [31] (NSW). For this reason some English authorities refer to these rights as "quasi-proprietary." *See* Kevin Gray & Susan Francis Gray, Elements of Land Law 315 (5th ed. 2009).

23. *See* Frank I. Michelman, *Ethics, Economics and the Law of Property*, NOMOS XXIV: Ethics, Economics & the Law 3 (J. Roland Pennock & John W. Chapman eds., 1982).

Things have been changing in the past few decades, however. Several courts have added recreation as one of the purposes for which the public is entitled to use the wet-sand portion of the beach,[24] but this is a relatively modest change that does not drastically affect the right to exclude since it is limited to the wet-sand area, where a kind of public easement has long existed anyway. It is the extension of the public right of access to the dry-sand portion of the beach that signifies a major departure from the traditional law of trespass. The development has been controversial, but it is fully consistent with the human flourishing theory. To see why, we need first briefly to look at the major cases expanding the public's right of access.

THE EXPANDING PUBLIC RIGHT OF ACCESS: NEW JERSEY AS A CASE STUDY

In no state has the public's right of access to privately owned property been expanded more than in New Jersey. It is tempting to push aside the New Jersey developments in the law of public access as aberrational, for no other state has followed the New Jersey Supreme Court's lead. It would be a mistake not to take the New Jersey example seriously, however. The New Jersey Supreme Court has decided a number of cases concerning the right to exclude over the past several decades, and these decisions have been quite influential on other courts throughout the country.[25] Some of these decisions are based on state constitutional grounds, others on state statutory or common-law grounds. The contexts range from private university campuses to private farms. To provide context for the beach access cases, I will first briefly survey these cases.

The first case to consider is *State v. Schmid.*[26] In that case a member of the United States Labor Party was convicted of criminal trespass when he distributed political literature on the campus of Princeton University without first obtaining the university's permission. University regulations made permission a prerequisite for the on-campus distribution of materials by off-campus organizations but did not do so for university-affiliated groups or Princeton students.

24. *See, e.g.,* Borough of Neptune City v. Borough of Avon-by-the-Sea, 294 A.2d 47 (N.J. 1972); State *ex rel.* Thornton v. Hay, 462 P.2d 671 (Or.1969); Hixon v. Public Service Comm'n, 146 N.W.2d 577 (Wis. 1966). *But see* Bell v. Town of Wells, 557 A.2d 168 (Me. 1989) (refusing to extend public trust doctrine to recreational uses); Opinion of the Justices, 313 N.E.2d 561 (Mass. 1974) (same).

25. *See, e.g.,* Jacobs v. Major, 132 Wis.2d 82 (Or. App. 1986) (following State v. Schmid, 423 A.2d 615 (N.J. 1980)); Batchelder v. Allied Stores Int'l, 445 N.E.2d 590 (Mass. 1983) (same).

26. 423 A.2d 615 (N.J. 1980).

Defendant Schmid acknowledged that he was aware of these regulations. On appeal from his conviction, Schmid argued that the conviction violated his rights to free speech and assembly under both the federal and state constitutions. The university argued that as a private institution it was not subject to either constitution.

The New Jersey Supreme Court found sufficient reasons to "stay its hand" in deciding that the First Amendment of the federal constitution applied to Princeton under the instant circumstances. Nevertheless, the court found alternative grounds for supporting Schmid in New Jersey's state constitution. The court concluded that the state constitution furnishes to individuals rights to free speech and assembly complementary to those under the First Amendment and that such rights are available against "unreasonably restrictive or oppressive conduct on the part of private entities that have otherwise assumed a constitutional obligation not to abridge the individual exercise of such freedoms because of the public use of their property."[27]

Seeking to balance the university's property rights against Schmid's free speech and assembly rights, the court announced a multifactored standard. The standard includes the following elements: (1) the private property's "normal" use; (2) the extent and nature of the public's invitation to use that property; and (3) the purpose of the expressional activity upon the property, in relation to both the public and private use of the property. Applying those factors, the court concluded that Princeton had violated Schmid's speech and associational rights. In particular, the court emphasized that the university's regulations that applied to Schmid had no standards for governing the exercise of expressional freedoms. "[G]iven the absence of adequate reasonable regulations," the court stated, "the required accommodation of Schmid's expressional and associational rights, otherwise reasonably exercised, would not constitute an unconstitutional abridgment of Princeton University's property rights."[28]

The New Jersey court again relied on its state constitution to decide *New Jersey Coalition Against War in the Middle East v. J.M.B. Realty Corp.*[29] In that case, a coalition of groups opposed to American military response to Iraq's invasion of Kuwait sought to distribute political leaflets to shoppers at ten large shopping malls in New Jersey. They requested permission to do so from each mall. Some of the malls agreed but only with restrictions that made it difficult for the groups to reach shoppers. Other malls refused to give any permission. The coalition went to court seeking to compel the malls to allow the protesters to distribute

27. *Id.* at 628.

28. *Id.* at 632–33.

29. 650 A.2d 757 (N.J. 1994).

their literature among shoppers. It claimed that the malls' refusal violated the coalition's free speech right under the state constitution as interpreted in *Schmid.* Relief was denied at both the trial and appellate level.

The Supreme Court applied the multifactored standard that it had developed in *Schmid.* The court found that each of the elements supported leafleting in the malls. It specifically found that the malls impliedly invited the public into the premises and that the invitation was open-ended. As the court expressed that invitation, "'Come here, that's all we ask. We hope you will buy. But you do not have to, and you need not intend to. All we ask is that you come here. You can do *whatever* you want so long as you do not interfere with other visitors.'"[30] This all-inclusive invitation has included past expressive activities, including partisan political speech such as voter registration drives organized by political candidates.

The court also applied a balancing standard, balancing the expressional rights and the property interests. The court found that the weight of the owners' private property interest had been diminished substantially by the types of uses permitted and the open-ended public invitation. The owners, the court stated, had intentionally "transformed their property into a public square or market, a public gathering place, a downtown business district, a community. . . ."[31] On the other side, the plaintiff's speech interest, the court said, is "the most substantial in our constitutional scheme." Given these respective weights, the court easily concluded that the plaintiff's speech rights prevailed over the owners' right to exclude.

Another basis on which the New Jersey court has limited the right to exclude is the state's public accommodation statute. Like many other states, New Jersey has a statute prohibiting places of public accommodation from discriminating on various grounds. In *Dale v. Boy Scouts of America,*[32] The question was whether the Boy Scouts of America (BSA) was a "place of public accommodation" within the meaning of this statute. The plaintiff was an assistant scoutmaster whom BSA had expelled after he publicly declared that he was gay. The New Jersey public accommodation statute included sexual orientation among the proscribed grounds of discrimination. The court reasoned that "[a] membership association, like the Boy Scouts, may be a 'place' of public accommodation even if the accommodation is provided at 'a moving situs.'"[33] It concluded that the Boy Scouts were a "public

30. *Id.* at 773 (emphasis in original).

31. *Id.* at 776.

32. 734 A.2d 1196 (N.J. 1999), *rev'd on other grounds sub nom.* Boy Scouts of America v. Dale, 530 U.S. 640 (2000).

33. *Id.* at 1209 (citing National Organization of Women v. Little League Baseball, Inc., 318 A.2d 33 (1974)).

accommodation" within the meaning of the state statute on the basis of three factors: (1) the Scouts engaged broadly in public solicitation; (2) the organization's close relationships with federal and state governmental bodies; and (3) the organization's similarity to other previously recognized public accommodations.

The court then rejected the Boy Scouts' argument based on its First Amendment right to intimate association. Whether a membership organization enjoys such a right depends, the court reasoned, on the organization's size, purpose, selectivity, and whether others are excluded from critical aspects of the relationship. The court found that the Boy Scouts lacked the requisite characteristics of intimate association organizations. Hence, the court concluded, the application of the New Jersey public accommodation statute violated no constitutional right of the Boy Scouts.

The New Jersey Supreme Court has limited the right to exclude on nonconstitutional grounds as well. A well-known nonconstitutional right-to-exclude decision of the New Jersey Supreme Court is *State v. Shack*.[34] In *Shack*, two individuals who worked for government-funded organizations that provided health and legal services to migrant farm worker entered a privately owned farm to provide assistance to migrant workers who worked and were housed there. Specifically, one aid worker was there to remove sutures from a farm worker, and the other, an attorney with a federally funded legal aid program, was there to discuss a legal problem that another farm worker had. When the two aid workers entered the farm, the owner, Tedesco, confronted them and demanded to know their business. After they disclosed their mission, Tedesco told the aid workers that he would allow them onto his farm for their purposes but only on condition that he was present when they met their clients, the farm workers. The two aid workers refused to agree to this condition, and Tedesco then called the police, who removed the aid workers when Tedesco filed a written complaint charging them with criminal trespass.

At trial, the two aid workers were convicted of criminal trespass under New Jersey's criminal trespass statute, and their conviction was sustained on appeal.[35] The New Jersey Supreme Court took a different view of the situation. It reversed the lower courts, holding that the two defendants had not invaded Tedesco's possessory right. Hence, the state trespass statute did not reach their conduct.

The heart of the New Jersey Supreme Court's opinion is its famous statement, "Property rights serve human values. They are recognized to that end, and are limited by it."[36] Property, in other words, is created to further social

34. 277 A.2d 369 (N.J. 1971).

35. N.J. Stat. Ann. 2A:170-31–2A:170-41, repealed by L.1978, c. 95, § 2C:98-2, eff. Sept. 1, 1979.

36. 277 A.2d at 372.

ends, or values, and by the same token, values define the limits of property rights. The court found it "unthinkable" that the farm owner could be permitted to isolated migrant workers from persons who were trying to help them under the auspices of government aid programs. The court emphasized the predicament of these workers—their rootless condition and their isolation from the rest of the community. These workers—Tedesco's employees—were dependent upon help coming to them rather than the other way around. "Hence representatives from [federal, state, or local agencies, or from recognized charitable groups seeking to assist migrant workers] may enter upon the premises to seek out the worker at his living quarters."[37] But the court then went further, adding, "So, too, the migrant worker must be allowed to receive visitors there of his own choice, so long as there is no behavior hurtful to others, and members of the press may not be denied reasonable access to workers who do not object to seeing them."[38]

A subsequent important nonconstitutional New Jersey case involved public access to a business open to the public, in this case a casino. The dispute arose over the casino's exclusion of a patron who engaged in card-counting.

When properly practiced, the card-counting method of playing blackjack can give its practitioners a slight statistical advantage over the casino. If the card counter has the resources to place large bets and overcome short-term variations in luck, she can impose significant financial losses on casinos. According to the rules of blackjack, however, card-counting is not cheating.

Nevertheless, and for obvious reasons, casinos do not want capable card counters playing high-stakes blackjack at their tables.

Kenneth Uston was a pioneer of card-counting in blackjack. Uston, who died in 1987, was so successful that casinos began to ban him from their tables. He responded by donning disguises in order to ply his trade incognito. He also sued casinos in Las Vegas and Atlantic City, arguing that it was unlawful for them to exclude him from their tables for engaging in a lawful card-playing strategy. The casinos responded that under the common law of property they could exclude any person from their premises for any reason, so long as the reason was not specifically prohibited by a civil rights statute such as Title II of the Civil Rights Act of 1964.[39]

Uston's two lawsuits yielded dramatically different results. His lawsuit against Nevada casinos was dismissed by a federal district court on the ground that a casino had no legal obligation to permit Uston to play at its tables. The court

37. *Id.* at 374.

38. *Id.*

39. 42 U.S.C. §§2000a et seq.

reasoned that, although innkeepers and common carriers historically have had some common-law duties to do business with patrons, casinos—at least in their capacity as places for gambling—are not inns and so are not similarly constrained. They can excluded a person for any reason not specifically prohibited by law, such as civil rights laws.[40]

The federal court's account of the common law is debatable. Although the historical record is not altogether clear, it suggests that prior to the Civil War, the law probably required all businesses that held themselves out as open to the public to serve anyone who requested service.[41] There is good historical reason to doubt whether a rule giving the owner the right to exclude arbitrarily ever consistently existed.[42] In the seventeenth century, Sir Matthew Hale, Chief Justice of the Court of Kings Bench, observed that private property, when "affected with a public interest, . . . ceases to be *juris private* only."[43] Even Blackstone, that supposed defender of the "sole and despotic dominion" of owners, recognized a rather generous set of exceptions in his discussion of the right to exclude.[44]

In Uston's New Jersey lawsuit, the state supreme court was more faithful to this earlier common-law tradition when it ruled in his favor. The court stated, "When property owners open their doors to the general public in pursuit of their own property interests, they have no right to exclude people unreasonably."[45] "On the contrary," the court continued, "they have a duty not to act in an arbitrary or discriminatory manner towards persons who come on their premises." According to the court, for a casino, which has opened its doors for people to come and gamble on its property, to exclude a gambler who is not acting disruptively or violating the rules of the game is to act in an arbitrary or unreasonable manner. As a consequence, the court opined, casinos in New Jersey had no right to exclude Uston for counting cards.

Under this approach to exclusion, a business owner's common-law right to exclude is more restricted than that of an ordinary private homeowner simply by virtue of the commercial nature of the property. In its subsequent decisions

40. *See* Uston v. Grand Resorts, Inc., 564 F.2d 1217, 1218 (9th Cir. 1977).

41. *See* Joseph William Singer, *No Right to Exclude, supra* note 11, at 1283, 1292.

42. *See* Kevin Gray & Susan Francis Gray, *Civil Rights, Civil Wrongs and Quasi-Public Space*, 4 Eur. Hum. Rts. L. Rev. 46 (1999).

43. Matthew Hale, *De Portibus Maris*, 1 Harg L. Tracts 78. In the famous case of *Munn v. Illinois*, Chief Justice Waite stated that Hale's observation has been "accepted without objection as an essential element of the law of property ever since." Munn v. Illinois, 94 U.S. 113, 126 (1877).

44. *See* William Blackstone, Commentaries on the Laws of England, 4 vols., II, at 2 (1766; rpt. 1979).

45. Uston v. Resorts Int'l Hotel, Inc., 445 A.2d 370, 375 (1982).

concerning the public's right of access to the beach, the New Jersey Supreme Court pointed to other aspects of the character of the property that affect the scope of the right to exclude.

EXPANDING PUBLIC ACCESS TO BEACHES

The Expanding Right of Beach Access

As we have already discussed, historically, public access to beaches under the public trust doctrine was quite limited. The public was permitted to access only the land between the mean high- and low-tide lines, and the purpose for which the public was permitted to access this land was limited to fishing.

In recent years the New Jersey Supreme Court has taken the lead in the expansion of public beach access under the public trust doctrine. In *Matthews v. Bay Head Improvement Association*,[46] the court held a private nonprofit entity which owned or leased most of the beachfront lots in the Borough of Bay Head did not have unlimited right to exclude members of the public from the dry-sand portion of its beach. "The public must be afforded reasonable access to the foreshore [i.e., wet sand area] as well as a suitable area for recreation on the dry sand," the court said.[47] In defining the contours of this right of reasonable access to privately owned dry-sand area, the court identified four factors as relevant: (1) the location of the dry-sand area in relation to the foreshore; (2) the extent and availability of publicly owned sand area; (3) the nature and extend of the public demand; and (4) the usage of the upland sand land by the owner.[48]

The holding in *Bay Head* was limited by the fact that the Bay Head Improvement Association was, in its view, a "quasi-public" entity.[49] The court subsequently expanded the scope of public access under the public trust doctrine when it held that a private beach club that was not a quasi-public entity was required under the *Matthews* reasonable access norm to provide members of the public access to the beach across its dry-sand area.

The same court subsequently expanded its holding in *Raleigh Avenue Beach Association v. Atlantis Beach Club*.[50] The club owned a waterfront parcel in Cape

46. 471 A.2d 355 (N.J.), cert. denied, 469 U.S. 821 (1984).

47. *Id.* at 366.

48. *Id.* at 365.

49. *Id.* The court concluded that the improvement association satisfied its obligation by opening up its membership to everyone rather than limiting it to Bay Head residents and by making daily passes as well as seasonal passes available for sale to nonresidents.

50. 879 A.2d 112 (N.J. 2005).

May County, New Jersey, which it made available to the general public for a substantial fee.[51] For nearly a decade before it opened up the private club in 1996, its owner made no effort to exclude the public from the beach. Consequently, nearby residents had long since become accustomed to crossing the dry-sand area of the club's beach to reach the wet-sand portion of the beach, that is, the area between the high-tide line and the water, which the state owns. In 1996, the club began to attempt barring nonmembers from crossing its property, eventually erecting a gate at its entrance. Local residents who were not club members went to court claiming that the public trust doctrine entitled them to access the beach via the club's land.

Addressing this claim, the New Jersey Supreme Court concluded that in light of the specific history of public access to the club's parcel and the lack of public beaches in the area, the club was required to make its upland sand area, though privately owned, available for use by the general public to the extent necessary to provide the public with "reasonable access" to the wet-sand beach. The obligation to provide reasonable beach access did not stop there. The court went on to say:

> [R]ecognizing the increasing demand for our State's beaches and the dynamic nature of the public trust doctrine, we find that the public must be given both access to and use of privately-owned *dry sand areas* as reasonably necessary. While the public's rights in private beaches are not coextensive with the rights enjoyed in municipal beaches, private owners may not in all instances prevent the public from exercising its rights under the public trust doctrine. The public must be afforded reasonable access to the foreshore as well as a suitable area for recreation on the dry sand.[52]

The club would, however, be permitted to charge nonmembers a reasonable fee (to be approved by the state) to cover expenses for services such as lifeguarding and trash removal.

Not only in New Jersey, but elsewhere as well, the contours of the right to exclude are both more complex and more interesting than the simple homeowner's claim of an unqualified right reflects. In the remainder of this chapter, I will discuss why developments in the right to exclude, such as those in New Jersey, are warranted, morally and legally, and why recent theories that endorse a broad, substantially unlimited right to exclude cannot be sustained.

51. *Id.* at 113, 115.

52. *Id.* at 121.

THE RIGHT TO EXCLUDE IN INFORMATION-COST THEORY

As we have already seen, a recent strain of utilitarian theory opposes the familiar bundles-of-rights conception of property on the ground that the claim-by-claim analysis undermines the core logic of property institutions, which allocate in rem rights in things.[53] Crucial to this theory is the right to exclude. Exclusion theorists such as Thomas Merrill and Henry Smith focus on the way in which property institutions employ what they describe as an architecture of boundaries. Such an architecture, they argue, economizes on information costs by delegating most decision making about the exercise of those rights to owners. By establishing boundaries and by granting to owners the broad power to control access to (and therefore uses of) an object within those boundaries, the institution of private property, they argue, rewards people who successfully gather information about the most productive use for the things they own. According to these theorists, maintaining a robust and relatively simple law of trespass is crucial to property's boundary logic and its attendant information-cost savings. Hence, Merrill and Smith argue:

> The right to exclude allows the owner to control, plan, and invest, and permits this to happen with minimum information costs to others. People generally do not need to consult lists of use-conflict resolutions (or specific right-duty pairs) when they approach a piece of property they do not own. Instead, they know that, unless special regulations or private contracts carve out some specific use rights, the bright-line rules of trespass apply.[54]

In sum, according to exclusion theorists, the legal recognition of a robust right to exclude has the effect of creating an open-ended set of in rem rights that grants owners broad freedom to deploy the information they have gathered in choosing how to exploit the object without seeking the permission of others. And, because they can exclude others from their property, those who gather the best information about the most productive uses of that property will reap the rewards of their efforts. In addition, these theorists argue, by creating a relatively simple set of duties (e.g., "keep out"), trespass law's exclusion logic makes respecting the rights of others less demanding for nonowners.[55] For the exclusion theorist, then,

53. *See* Thomas W. Merrill & Henry E. Smith, *Whatever Happened to Property in Law and Economics*, 111 Yale L.J. 357, 360–83 (2001).

54. *Id.* at 389.

55. *See* Henry E. Smith, *Property and Property Rules*, 79 N.Y.U. L. Rev. 1719, 1729–31 (2004).

the sheer importance of the power of physical exclusion and the utilitarian benefits it generates constitute a further reason for honoring the owner's exclusion claims, even in the presence of evidence of some degree of market failure.

Some decisions by owners will so obviously undermine utility that deviation from this core logic of exclusion is occasionally justified. In these circumstances—for example, when the law of nuisance limits owners' freedom to engage in actions that impose significant harm on neighboring owners—the law may opt for modes of decision making that rely more heavily on use-by-use evaluations of utility ("governance," as Smith has put it). But, although governance strategies are sometimes necessary, exclusion theorists argue that excessive reliance on them will end up being counterproductive because the governance calculation is so costly to carry out and because creating too many exceptions to the logic of exclusion undermines the open-ended reward structure it establishes. Case-by-case allocation associated with governance also generates increased information costs for nonowners.

At the outset, it is worth emphasizing that these two utilitarian camps are not as far apart in practice as this stark description suggests. Bundle theorists are indeed comfortable with case-by-case tinkering. But, at least among legal theorists, their analysis typically starts with existing property institutions, whose basic outlines they tend to take for granted, rather than with a call for wholesale stick-by-stick re-evaluation of property entitlements from the ground up. This observation does not detract from the importance of Merrill's and Smith's contribution, which helps to illuminate utilitarian implications of the modularity of existing property institutions. But it does mean that the differences between exclusion and bundle-of-rights theorists operate more at the level of emphasis and presumption.

Exclusion theorists are no doubt correct that relentless right-by-right, case-by-case allocation of property interests, with no standardization of bundles of rights, would place enormous informational demands on owners and nonowners alike.[56] But what seems insufficiently defended is the exclusion theorists' claim that there is a specific connection between information costs and the right to exclude as such. Containing information costs is arguably just as consistent with understanding property as the delegation to owners of broad, spatially defined, standardized bundles of affirmative use rights as it is with understanding property as the residuum of negative liberty created by protecting a robust right to exclude. This is particularly true if the contours of the more qualified right to exclude conform to an intelligible pattern that permits us to form generalizations and (tentative) predictions about the likely outcome of cases of first impression.

56. *See id.* at 1753.

The conceptual gap between the right to exclude and the information costs story told by exclusion theorists is most apparent with property onto which the owner has invited the general public. For these kinds of property, it is far from clear that unfettered exclusion rights make the world an easier place to navigate for nonowners. For private property that is open to the public, such as a department store, the message sent by the legal ratification of private control of property boundaries is, in practice, far more complex than "keep off." In the pre-civil-rights-era South, that message might have been: If you are white, come in and browse, shop, sit down, and eat; if you are African American, come in, shop, order food at our lunch counter, but do not sit down to eat or interact with white customers. In the modern shopping center, the message might be: Come in, browse, walk around, sit down, eat, perhaps even participate in an aerobics class or watch schoolchildren put on a show, but do not engage in political speech, no matter how orderly. Particularly in the case of land, which can sustain multiple nonconflicting uses at the same time, a system that permits owners to create intricately qualified invitations to the general public may generate higher information costs than a system in which owners of commercial property must choose from a limited menu of exclusion options.[57] Moreover, this latter regime is consistent with a coherent conception of private ownership, since, although owners would enjoy a more limited right to exclude, nonowners would still be obligated not to interfere with the use decisions that owners have made.[58]

Another complication for exclusion theories results from their uncertain fit with existing structures of property lawmaking and enforcement. We can think of exclusion accounts of property as analogous to the rule-utilitarian position within moral theory. While some utilitarians (so-called act-utilitarians) apply their calculus to individual actions or decisions, others (rule-utilitarians) argue that the utility-enhancing strategy is not to subject each decision to thoroughgoing utilitarian analysis, but instead to cabin utilitarian decision making to certain limited rule-making contexts. Outside those contexts, the best strategy is simply to follow the rules laid out in advance. A rule-utilitarian might argue, for example, that it is utility-enhancing if people always keep their promises, even in those (presumably exceptional) situations in which not to keep the promise would be utility-enhancing. The loss of utility in the exceptional case is outweighed, the argument goes, by the costs of having to constantly weigh whether keeping a promise in a particular situation would be utility-enhancing as well as by the

57. *See* Thomas W. Merrill & Henry E. Smith, *Optimal Standardization in the Law of Property*, 110 Yale L.J. 1 (2000).

58. *See* Larissa Katz, *Exclusion and Exclusivity in Property Law*, 58 U. Toronto L.J. 58 1710 (2008); Eric R. Claeys, *Exclusion and Exclusivity in Gridlock*, 53 Ariz. L. Rev. 9 (2011).

gains made possible by being able to rely on other people always keeping their promises.

The exclusion theory of property works in roughly the same way: It argues that an exclusion strategy is utility-enhancing even though in individual instances it might seem better (in the short term) to deviate from it, because adhering to the relatively simple core structure of exclusion over the long run economizes on the need to constantly engage in utilitarian calculation and avoids the costs arising from uncertainty (among owners and nonowners alike) about the scope of property rights. But exclusion theory also confronts some of the same kinds of objections that have been leveled against rule-utilitarianism. Most important among these is the difficulty of preventing rule-utilitarianism from collapsing back into act-utilitarianism. For every rule that is supposedly utility-enhancing, it would at least arguably be even more utility-enhancing to craft a rule that is nearly as simple but that also builds in an exception to the rule for certain situations in which it is clearly not utility-enhancing to follow it. The problem is that, if we make too many exceptions, the rule simply disappears and we are left with act-utilitarianism.[59]

Something similar seems true of the exclusion theories of property. As exclusion theorists recognize, in some situations exclusion is so costly that it is worth paying the price of governance. In evaluating the various exceptions to the right to exclude discussed at the beginning of this chapter, an exclusion theorist might well endorse one or more of them on this ground. The problem, from the perspective of exclusion theory, is that too many exceptions will undermine the informational efficiencies asserted on behalf of the open-ended right to exclude.

But this raises a difficult question for the exclusion theorist. Apart from being able to rule out the extremes (unlimited exclusion power without exception and universal case-by-case utilitarian [re]calculation of each and every claimed right of access), how can we know what mode of decision making to employ in any given situation? How are we to know whether the costs of considering this particular exception to the core exclusion structure of property outweigh the benefits unless we actually carry out a full utilitarian calculus? Perhaps more important, how are we to evaluate the actual substantive question whether making a new, seemingly utility-enhancing exception to the core structure is utility-enhancing (even over the long run) or, instead, "a bridge too far"? We cannot make the just-so move of simply assuming that the existing state of the common law of property (or the common law as it existed prior to the rise of the regulatory state) is the optimal one.

59. *See* David Lyons, The Forms and Limits of Utilitarianism ch. 4 (1965); R.M. Hare, Freedom and Reason 130–36 (1963).

Thus, the apparent lack of fit between the exclusion theory and the existing law concerning the right to exclude, pockmarked as it is with exceptions, is something of an embarrassment for this approach. The exclusion theory struggles to offer a genuine explanation for the many qualifications to the right to exclude already built into the law of property (and not just in New Jersey). These include (among others) Title II; the law of adverse possession and prescription, which places a time limit on owners' rights to exclude; the numerous doctrines of implied easements; the law of airplane overflights;[60] the doctrine of necessity, which requires owners to allow those in extreme situations of need onto their property; and the law governing innocent improvers. Each of these doctrines is, from the exclusion standpoint, a departure from property's core logic of exclusion that must be justified to the same extent as proposed new exceptions, such as beach access, that exclusion theorists tend to oppose.

One response to this problem of fit might be to shift our focus toward considerations of institutional competence. Legislatures, the argument might go, are well equipped to engage in a comprehensive utilitarian calculus that evaluates the costs and benefits of prospectively incorporating into property law exceptions to the right to exclude. Courts, on the other hand, have limited investigatory tools, and must approach decision making through the lens of the disputes parties bring before them. On this view, a legislatively enacted exception to property's exclusion logic, such as Title II, might be entitled to more deference than judge-made exceptions, such as the New Jersey Supreme Court's apparent solicitude for novel claims of access rights to beaches or commercial establishments.

As noted in the preceding discussion of Uston's unsuccessful claims against Las Vegas casinos, however, prior to the mid-nineteenth century, the common law of property recognized broad rights of access to commercial establishments. Judges then changed the law to narrow those access rights to inns and common carriers. This sort of judge-made change has been the rule rather than the exception in property law. If judge-made law were suspect, a great deal of existing trespass doctrine would be called into question. Since part of the exclusion theory's project is to describe how property law actually operates, this is not a result that they can accept lightly.

On the other hand, if we try to incorporate judge-made rules into the exclusion model, maintaining the stability of its two-tiered (exclusion/governance) structure becomes even more challenging. How is a court to know whether a particular case is the proper vehicle for introducing an exception to the logic of exclusion or whether instead it is an occasion merely to enforce the baseline

60. *See* Stuart Banner, Who Owns the Sky? The Struggle to Control Airspace from the Wright Brothers On (2008).

boundary principle? And if the court opts for the former, how is it to gather the vast amount of data necessary to answer the second-order question? Again, besides ruling out the corner solutions of no exclusion and an unlimited power to exclude, the empirical burden seems daunting.

A broader question for the utilitarian approach to the right to exclude, one that affects both the exclusion and bundle-of-sticks camps equally, concerns the nature of the interests at stake. These interests frequently resist the common utilitarian characterization of the value to be maximized as preference satisfaction or wealth maximization. For example, in determining the utilitarian implications of a provision like Title II, it seems morally questionable to evaluate the strength of African Americans' entitlement not to be excluded from places of public accommodation in terms of which rule would satisfy more (or more intense) preferences. It is easy to imagine situations in which the calculus would come out against rights to be free from racial discrimination—for example, where intense racist sentiment is widespread among the majority of the population and the excluded minority is small in number. But most people reject the notion that, under such conditions, legally sanctioned racial discrimination would become morally acceptable (or even obligatory). This observation about the utilitarian misconceptions of the moral foundations of civil rights, while commonplace, is still an important one. Its salience in the context of civil rights statutes is an example of a broader challenge for utilitarian theory—its willingness, in principle, to trade off on the well-being of individuals. The human flourishing theory offers a way to capture many of the benefits of utilitarian theories' contextual flexibility without losing the ability to account for the kinds of robust individual moral entitlements implicated by laws like Title II.

It is worth noting that New Jersey's sliding-scale approach to the right to exclude, much criticized by exclusion theorists for its alleged ad hoc character and indeterminacy, offers a relatively elegant explanation of the complex pattern of discrete access and exclusion rights operating within the law of property. To see this, imagine that we plot the results of the New Jersey right-to-exclude cases along two axes of a graph. The horizontal axis would represent the degree to which the owner has opened her land to the public or invited the public onto the land. According to the New Jersey Supreme Court's approach, we view this variable as inversely related to the objective weight of the owner's interest in being able to exclude persons seeking entry onto her property against her will. The vertical axis represents the objective importance of the values—not the intensity of subjective preferences—that would be furthered by granting entry of the applicant to the land. If we then located the various New Jersey Supreme Court cases on this graph we would discover a fairly clear pattern emerge, a pattern that indicates a relatively high degree of predictability, or ruleness, in the New Jersey law of trespass.

So, in the upper and opposite right and left corners are the easy cases, that is, the cases that should involve little controversy. These are, respectively, cases in which the owner is a private homeowner upon whose sole residence the defendant trespasses for no reason that implicates the values that inhere in human flourishing; and in the opposite corner, Title II cases. In between, and as one draws closer to the center, lie the hard cases, more likely to be controversial. Yet, even here, a pattern emerges from the New Jersey cases. Thus, although under the conventional doctrine of necessity the nature of the needed property does not affect or change the calculus of necessity, the gap between the claimant's need and the owner's interest in exclusion narrows as the property to which the person in need seeks access becomes more private, or less open to the public. We should expect, then, that the necessity doctrine's application will be more controversial, that is, less easily justified, the less the owner has opened her property up to the public. Conversely, the more the owner has opened her property up to the general public, the easier the case becomes for justifying the claimant's right of access.

Exclusion theorists prefer bright-line rules, that is, rules that operate in a binary fashion, and so they may still find the patterned New Jersey approach lacking. One problem with this view is that the traditional common law of trespass never has been a regime of truly bright-line rules. The common-law right to exclude is so riddled with exceptions that justifying the status quo requires a great deal of special pleading. Moreover, these exceptions are themselves subject to standards, thereby maybe the apparent ruleness of the rule illusory and misleading to actors. For information-cost theorists, this feature must be taken into account in the utilitarian calculus.

More fundamentally, one may put into question the whole logic behind bright-line rules.

For example, Seana Shiffrin has argued that "[t]he superficial opacity of standards is often a virtue."[61] She contends that opacity of standards serve moral and deliberative purposes. "Rather than applying a rule by rote, citizens must ask themselves . . . whether they are treating one another fairly, whether they are acting in good faith, whether they are taking due care, whether they are behaving reasonably, and the like. . . . [T]his sort of induced moral deliberation is important for our moral health and for an active, engaged democratic citizenry."[62] Shiffrin explains that many, perhaps most, standards incorporate moral elements, and where they do, citizens who aim to comply with the law have to grapple with the relevant moral concept.

61. Seana Valentine Shiffrin, *Inducing Moral Deliberation: On the Occasional Virtues of Fog*, 123 Harv. L. Rev. 1214, 1214 (2010).

62. *Id.* at 1217.

Shiffrin states:

> Where standards incorporating moral terms regulate conduct, citizens themselves may have to deliberate about what is morally proper and should be expected of them. They will not always have to: if like circumstances have presented themselves before, and precedent has been established to the effect that certain specific behavior falls inside or outside of the directive, the citizen may draw the simple analogy and follow suit. But when the circumstances differ or when it is unclear whether the prior case sets the ceiling or the floor, citizens will have to ask themselves more directly whether their behavior is reasonable, whether they are acting in good faith, whether the deal they propose is exploitative or merely savvy, what the other party would want or would know or would object to, or how the other party might perceive the action.[63]

Like Shiffrin, Jeremy Waldron also defends standards, but he does so on dignitarian grounds. Waldron persuasively argues that human dignity requires possession of certain human capacities. Among those capacities, he suggests, are the "ability to internalize a norm, to monitor and control one's behavior on the basis of that norm, and the ability to notice the features of one's environment and circumstances and relate those to . . . other abilities in the service of compliance with the internalized norm."[64] The capacities are not the exclusive constituent elements of the dignity of a human agent, Waldron continues. Human dignity further consists in the agent's "capacity for practical deliberation in both structured and unstructured ways." "An open-ended standard . . . invokes that capacity and relies on it. It credits the subject with the sophisticated ability to adapt his agency to his own practical thinking, and it indicates the kind of circumstance in which that ability is required of him."[65]

A rule theorist might object that Waldron's standard-based approach, unlike rules, fails to provide guidance to relevant actors. Waldron argues that, *pace* the rule theorist, laws that rely on standards such as "reasonable" do, or may, provide guidance. Consider a statute such as one providing, "Whoever operates a motor vehicle . . . on the public roads . . . at a speed greater than is reasonable . . . , having regard for width, traffic, use and the general and usual rules of such road . . . ,

63. *Id.* at 1223 (footnote omitted).

64. Jeremy Waldron, *Vagueness and the Guidance of Action* p. 6. (NYU Public Law & Legal Theory Research Paper Series Working Paper No. 10-81), *available at* http://ssrn.co,/abstract+1699963.

65. *Id.* at 10.

or so as to endanger the property, life or limb of any person, shall be fined. . . ."[66] Such a law, Waldron suggests, does indeed involve some determinate guidance. Although it does not specify to the driver precisely which acts are permitted and which are not while driving, the statute provides guidance this way: It "identifies a pair of circumstance, indicates that some adjustment of behavior is appropriate when one of these circumstances is overtaken by the other, attempts to focus [the driver's] practical reason on what that change of behavior should be, and indicates by whatever penal provisions are attached to [the statute] that [the driver] should take this whole business seriously." "That," Waldron contends, "is guidance."[67] It empowers, indeed directs, the actor's exercise of practical reasoning in the context of the circumstances set out in the statute. Moreover, it provides relevant information to affected and potentially affected persons regarding what is expected of them when they drive on public roads.

With these observations in mind, let us return to the beach access issue. Under New Jersey's *Matthews/Raleigh Avenue* standard, private beach owners are obligated to provide members of the public with "reasonable access" to the dry-sand portion of the beach. "Reasonable access" is, of course, a very open-ended norm that in the abstract seems to provide owners with little, if any, guidance about the precise scope of their duty to the public. At the same time, the full measure of the *Matthews/Raleigh Avenue* standard, as the New Jersey court enunciates it, includes more information. It identifies four factors as relevant in determining when and under what circumstances a private must open her beach to the public: (1) the location of the dry sand area in relation to the foreshore; (2) the extent and availability of publicly owned sand area; (3) the nature and extend of the public demand; and (4) the usage of the upland sand land by the owner. These factors guide not only courts in future cases but private owners who wish to know the extent to which their beach property is subject to public access. In this context the reasonableness standard is not indeterminate as rule theorists sometimes assert.[68] Although it does not let property owners know *ex ante* exactly where they stand vis-á-vis the public, it does give them ample guidance. Based on the factors that bracket the reasonable-access standard, beachfront owners should be able to predict with a reasonably high degree of accuracy whether their beach property will or will not be considered as subject to public access. For example, are there public beaches within a reasonable distance from the owner's property?

66. *See* State v. Schaeffer, 117 N.E. 220 (Ohio 1917) (quoting then-existing Ohio Gen. Code §12603).

67. Waldron, *Vagueness and the Guidance of Action*, *supra* note 64, at 11.

68. For a classic example of just this assertion, *see* FRIEDRICH HAYEK, THE ROAD TO SERFDOM (1944).

If so, it is considerably less likely that the owner's private beach will be considered open to the public. Similarly, does the owner use the beach property as his primary residence? By asking herself questions that the *Matthews/Raleigh Avenue* standard invite the owner to ask herself, the owner will be able to predict with a relatively high degree of probability the scope of her duty to the public. This kind of self-questioning is precisely an exercise in guided practical reasoning that Waldron has in mind.

THE RIGHT TO EXCLUDE AND HUMAN FLOURISHING

The qualifications on the right to exclude we discussed at the beginning of this chapter and all of the other restrictions of the right that we have seen can be readily be explained in terms of the human flourishing theory of property. The case is easiest to make for the kinds of status-based exclusions addressed by Title II. But, as we will see, structuring property law so as to facilitate the pursuit of human flourishing can justify significantly broader limitations on the right to exclude while still retaining a basis for recognizing the importance of owners' exclusion rights in many contexts.

Excluding people from places of public accommodation on the basis of morally irrelevant characteristics—particularly characteristics over which they have little control—has obvious implications for their ability to participate fully in the social life of the community.

Moreover, such social exclusion inhibits the capacity to flourish. Where legal enforcement can be effective, and where countervailing interests in the owner's right to exclude are not overriding, the human flourishing theory supports using the law to prevent private owners from exercising the right to exclude in ways that undermine the ability of others to flourish.

Moreover, while by no means always easy, antidiscrimination norms in such privately owned (but publicly accessible) spaces is relatively straightforward. Enforcement of antidiscrimination norms is facilitated, moreover, if the exercise of exclusion rights in places of public accommodation is the exception, rather than the norm. Thus, as the New Jersey Supreme Court suggested in the *Uston* case, the extension of rights of access to all users—including card counters—makes good sense as an indirect means of protecting against more morally troubling forms of exclusion.[69] Creating an open-ended right of reasonable access to places of public accommodation may also economize on information costs.

As Lior Strahilevitz has argued, even where the law deprives owners of the right to exclude (by limiting what he calls the owner's "Bouncer's Rights"),

69. 445 A.2d at 374 n.4.

owners retain a great deal of power over who will enter their premises.[70] Through the use of indirect means (what he calls "Exclusionary Vibes" and "Exclusionary Amenities"), owners can deter many people from even seeking entry. For example, after being told by the New Jersey Supreme Court that they could not exclude card counters from their tables, Atlantic City casinos employed other means to accomplish their goals. If they suspected a patron of counting cards, they might lower the bet limit at the table or slow down the game, both of which would reduce the return the card counter could hope to earn. Relatedly, owners can manipulate their use of the Bouncer's Right in ways that evade enforcement of antidiscrimination norms, through the use of such ostensibly race-neutral mechanisms as price and dress codes. One bar in New York City, for example, was investigated by the New York Human Right Commission for enforcing a "no baggy jeans, no bling" dress code that many patrons perceived to be racially coded.[71] Once in place, these indirect uses of the Bouncer's Right create their own Exclusionary Vibe.

Such indirect means of exclusion are often, as Strahilevitz observes, imperfect substitutes for the direct use of the Bouncer's Right to exclude the targeted group. Proxies for race will allow some unwanted people in while excluding some of the desired group. Lowering bet limits and slowing down the dealer cost the casino money. Because they are often more costly and less effective for owners, the possibility that owners will resort to these less direct means of excluding does not make it unreasonable for the law to focus on trespass law as a strategy for combating racial discrimination more broadly. In addition, there is a difference, from the agent-focused human flourishing perspective, between legally sanctioned racial exclusion (as in the pre–Title II South) and exclusion achieved through informal means, without the law's affirmative cooperation. The former invokes the law's agency on its behalf (e.g., when police cleared out sit-in protesters from private lunch counters at the owner's request) while the latter does not.

Moreover, punishing unwanted acts of exclusion is just one way that a legal prohibition, such as Title II, changes behavior. In addition to forcing some owners to resort to more costly means of satisfying their preference to exclude, such a legal prohibition not only penalizes those preferences but may also, over time, change owners' (and customers') preferences for the better. There is some evidence of such a cultural shift away from preferences for racially segregated places of public accommodation in response to Title II. Indeed, Richard Epstein's argument that

70. *See* Lior Jacob Strahilevitz, *Information Asymmetries and the Right to Exclude*, 104 Mich. L. Rev. 1835, 1843 (2006).

71. *See* Douglas Quenqua, *Dress Codes in New York Clubs: Will This Get Me In?*, N.Y. Times, July 27, 2011, E1.

Title II is no longer necessary depends very strongly on the notion that just such a shift has occurred.[72] His argument, however, ignores the continuing expressive (preference-forming) value of a law like Title II, even where it no longer coerces. His argument also depends on the notion that Title II is an intrusive rule that deprives owners of common-law exclusion rights that they would otherwise have—a view that in turn depends on a conception of the right to exclude that, as this chapter has demonstrated, is highly contestable as a matter of descriptive law.

The human flourishing theory recognizes, however, that the limits of legal enforcement of antidiscrimination norms do not reach the outer boundaries of owners' moral obligations not to discriminate. This is because countervailing interests of owners, such as personal security and associational freedom, are implicated by owners' ability to exclude others from property, even when they will predictably exercise that ability immorally. Certainly, when no comparable human capabilities are at stake on the other side, plainly, owners should be entitled to exclude unwanted intruders or users, even for trivial reasons.[73]

Even when there are weighty interests in favor of access, those access interests must sometimes give way if there is a powerful connection between the right to exclude and the owner's own capability for flourishing. As the New Jersey Supreme Court has repeatedly observed (and as the U.S. Supreme Court has occasionally acknowledged), owners of places of public accommodation have only attenuated associational interests in picking and choosing among those who can enter their property.[74] On the other hand, the common law has historically (and properly) attached great weight to the interests of privacy and associational autonomy by recognizing a robust right to exclude in the residential context. Tellingly, from the standpoint of human flourishing, the rights of tenants to receive visitors has traditionally trumped the rights of landlords to control access to their land.[75] Although the right to exclude, even in residential contexts, has long been subject to certain limited exceptions, such as the privilege of firefighters to enter for purposes of protecting the home, it has always been regarded as strongest with respect to the home.

72. *See* Richard A. Epstein, *Public Accommodations Under the Civil Rights Act of 1964: Why Freedom of Association Counts as a Human Right*, 66 Stan. L. Rev. 1241 (2014).

73. *Cf.* Jacque v. Steenberg Homes, Inc., 563 N.W.2d 154 (Wis. 1997).

74. *See* New Jersey Coalition Against War in the Middle East v. J.M.B. Realty Corp., 650 A.2d 757 (N.J. 1994); *see also* Amalgamated Food Employees Union Local 590 v. Logan Valley Plaza, Inc., 391 U.S. 308 (1968), overruled by Hudgens v. NLRB, 424 U.S. 507 (1976). *But see* PruneYard Shopping Center v. Robbins, 447 U.S. 74 (1980) (employing the distinction between commercial and noncommercial property within a takings challenge to a state law decision requiring access to shopping centers for certain expressive activities).

75. *See* State v. Shack, 277 A.2d 369 (N.J. 1971).

This emphasis on residential privacy of the home makes good sense from the point of view of the human flourishing theory. Developing the capability of sociability, for example, depends upon one's having a sense of security, a sense that many, perhaps most, people experience most strongly in their own homes. It also requires a degree of discretionary control over the people with whom one will intimately socialize, a sense that many, perhaps most, people experience most strongly in their homes. A willingness to protect a zone of autonomy, however, does not require a commitment to the view that the choices people make within that zone are a matter of moral indifference. It is no less immoral to refuse to invite people into your house because of their race than it is to refuse to serve them in your restaurant. But the impact for the excluded person's ability to flourish is usually greater in the public accommodation context, and, in addition, concerns with residential owners' and occupants' interests in privacy, security, and associational autonomy justify protecting the power to exclude in certain contexts even when doing so will predictably result in forms of discrimination that are nonetheless immoral. Thus, antidiscrimination law generally—not just Title II but also the Fair Housing Act and Title VII—carve out space for such private associational decisions.[76] The point is not that such intimate discrimination is morally justifiable. It is, instead, that competing dimensions of human flourishing—combined with the difficulty of enforcement—render the legal prohibition of such discrimination unworkable and inappropriate.

The human flourishing theory's ability to cope with this kind of nuance differs in an important way from the flexibility and contextual sensitivity of various versions of utilitarian property theory. It is one thing to protect a zone of private choice in order to safeguard the affirmative value of intimate association, as the human flourishing theory aims to do, but quite a different thing to carve out the same space for the purpose of maximizing the satisfaction of individual preferences.

Because the human flourishing theory's focus is on human flourishing rather than on preference-satisfaction (or solely on preference-satisfaction), it remains consistent with recognition of a strong moral entitlement to, for example, access without regard to race—regardless of preferences—even when it declines, for any

76. The same considerations would seem to explain the so-called "Mrs. Murphy" exception in the federal Fair Housing Act's ban on racial and other forms of discrimination by landlords in the selection of tenants. 42 U.S.C. §3603(b)(2), 3604(a). Although the statute bars landlords from refusing to rent to otherwise qualified applicants on the basis of race, religion, gender, national origin, and familial status, it permits them to do so when the unit in question is part of a dwelling intended for occupancy by no more than four families living separately if the owner actually occupies one of the units. This exception and other statutorily permitted forms of discrimination in housing can be understood as reflecting the same concern with protecting the associational interests of owners in the privacy of their homes. It is in that context that a robust right to exclude is most easily justified on the basis of nurturing the capabilities necessary for human flourishing.

number of reasons, to enforce that entitlement through law. Moreover, when facing strong moral entitlement, human flourishing theory can justify legal efforts to attack immoral preferences (e.g., for racial exclusion even in intimate contexts) in ways that do not impinge as heavily upon owner autonomy. In contrast, conventional forms of the utilitarian calculus take preferences as the calculus finds them, making it difficult for that calculus to explain the point in trying to shape preferences in this way.

As an illustration, the human flourishing theory offers a distinctive and illuminating view of why the federal Fair Housing Act (FHA) permits discrimination in certain private housing markets. Although the statute bars landlords from refusing to rent to otherwise qualified applicants on the basis of race, religion, gender, national origin, and familial status, it permits them to do so when the unit in question is part of a dwelling intended for occupancy by no more than four families living separately if the owner actually occupies one of the units.[77] This exception and other statutorily permitted forms of discrimination in housing can be understood as reflecting the same concern with protecting the associational interests of owners in the privacy of their homes. It is in that context that a robust right to exclude is most easily justified on the basis of nurturing the capabilities necessary for human flourishing. At the same time, the FHA prohibits even those exempted owner-landlords from advertising their (legally permissible) discriminatory preferences.[78] This explanation for the FHA's prohibition on advertisements goes beyond the standard economic/utilitarian explanations of advertising prohibitions, which explain such prohibitions solely in terms of externalities. Those externalities, while fine as far as they go, are incomplete, on utilitarian grounds. Identifying an externality is only the first step in the utilitarian determination whether to prohibit a particular behavior. That determination ultimately rests on an empirical question about the cost of the externality relative to the costs (measured in terms of frustrated preferences) of prohibiting the advertising. Unlike this utilitarian approach, the human flourishing theory assigns no weight to those racist preferences, even while it declines to prohibit some owners from acting on them.[79]

In addition to its ability to justify both legal limits on the right to exclude to combat discrimination and exceptions to those limits the human flourishing

77. This is the so-called "Mrs. Murphy" exception. *See* 42 U.S.C. §§3603(b)(2), 3604(a).

78. *See* Rigel C. Oliveri, *Discriminatory Housing Advertisements Online*, 43 Ind. L. Rev. 1125 (2010).

79. *See* note 84 and accompanying text *supra*. Some utilitarians and law-and-economics theorists would favor screening preferences and disregarding those considered objectionable, such as racial preferences. Such a move abandons their positions that preference are taken as given and that welfare is a purely subjective matter, and it brings their approach closer in line with the human flourishing theory with its objective account of well-being.

theory can accommodate the outcome in beach access cases. Recall that the human flourishing theory seeks to maximize well-being by facilitating the development of certain essential human capabilities. The theory views property as a means to enable the development of those capabilities. In the context of beach access two such capabilities seem relevant, recreation and sociability.

Recreation is not a luxury but a necessity. It is an important aspect of health, itself a vital dimension of the capability of life. Ample and growing medical evidence indicates that recreation and relaxation contribute importantly to good health, reducing the risk of diseases ranging from depression to heart disease.[80] Yet some of the very groups who need recreation the most do not, as a practical matter, have access to it. This includes the working poor, women, and especially single mothers, who are notorious self-sacrificers.

Public beaches and parks do exist, of course, but in many parts of the country, they are few and far between. In some coastal states long stretches of the beach are privately owned. For a person without a car, even a distance of mile or two between public beaches may make access practically impossible. Access to them is often difficult or impractical especially for the urban poor, the very people who in some ways need recreation the most.

Recreation also supports sociability as a good. Sociability in turn encompasses subsidiary goods such as friendship and social participation. It includes the ability "to recognize and show concern for other human beings, to engage in various forms of social interaction; [and] to be able to imagine the situation of another." Through recreation, people of varied backgrounds mingle together and learn how to treat each other civilly, with respect and courtesy. Thus, creating focal points for such indiscriminate recreational mingling may well help indirectly to combat the sorts of private associational discrimination the law wisely declines to prohibit. The opportunities for these educative experiences exist only in spaces that are open to all, or reasonably so. Strictly private spaces inhibit the process of socialization through which we learn how to be concerned for others, how to show that concern, and how to place ourselves in their shoes.

Carol Rose has eloquently explained the relationship between public places available for recreation and socialization. She states:

> [R]ecreation can be a socializing and educative influence, particularly helpful for democratic values. Thus rich and poor would mingle in parks, and learn to treat each other as neighbors. Parks would enhance public mental

80. *See, e.g.*, J.N. Morris, D.G. Clayton, M.G. Everitt, A.M. Semmence, & E.H. Burgess, *Exercise in Leisure Time: Coronary Attack and Death Rates*, 63 BRITISH HEART J. 325 (1990); G. Samitz, M. Egger, & M. Zwahlen, *Domains of Physical Activity and All-Cause Mortality: Systematic Review and Dose—Response Meta-analysis of Cohort Studies*, 40 INT'L J. OF EPIDEMIOLOGY 1382 (2011).

> health, with ultimate benefits to sociability; all could revive from the anti-social characteristics of urban life under the refining influence of the park's soothing landscape.[81]

Substitute "beach" for "park," and the point is the same. Rose goes on to point out that these socializing benefits can be maximized only if recreation is "open to all at minimal costs, or at costs borne by the general public, since all of us benefit from the greater sociability of our fellow citizens."[82] As Rose concludes, "[T]his value should not be 'held up' by private citizens."[83] Under the traditional law on beach access, sociability is indeed "held up" by private citizens.

I do not claim public access alone creates social capital or that it facilitates the creation of participatory democracy. Such a claim is implausible, given what we know from recent ethnographic work as well as our own everyday experiences. The shared space/discursive democracy thesis that historians have made in connection with eighteenth-century Britain is echoed in recent political geographic studies of urban shared spaces. Some urban geographers and political scientists have argued that urban public spaces can serve as loci of discursive democracy, places where unequals meet as equals, debate the problems of their societies, and form consensuses that influence public policy.[84]

More recent ethnographic work has challenged this thesis. For example, an important study of class relations on Rio de Janeiro's beaches finds that these public beaches are not democratic in this strong sense but that "there is a politics of class in the public space whereby the legitimacy of the social order is challenged, renegotiated, and ultimately reproduced." After studying the practices of self-location by social groups along Rio's famed beach at Ipanema, the author found that "the beach seems to be divided into many small cells of sociability that exist side by side but whose boundaries are clearly demarcated by space, time, behavior, and dress." At the same time, the author continues,

> [T]he idea of the beach as democratic space . . . resonates with lower class beach users, maybe because there is a degree of truth to it: There does seem to be a certain anonymity to the bathing suit, and to the culture of public

81. Carol Rose, *The Comedy of the Commons*, *supra* note 19, at 711, 779 (footnotes omitted).

82. *Id.* at 780.

83. *Id.*

84. *See, e.g.*, Robert D. Putnam, Making Democracy Work: Civic Traditions in Modern Italy 6 (1993); Susan Christopherson, *The Fortress City: Privatized Spaces, Consumer Citizenship*, *in* Post-Fordism: A Reader 409 (Ash Amin ed., 1994); James Freeman, *Democracy and Danger on the Beach: Class Relations in the Public Space of Rio de Janeiro*, 5 Space & Culture 9 (Feb. 2002), 10, 14.

> space more generally, that provides an opening for socializing across status groups.[85]

On the whole, however, the conclusion is that "[r]ather than being democratic in the sense of unmarked space free of power relations where every citizen is an equal participant in a conversation with nothing at stake, the beaches of Ipanema and Copacabana are the highly stratified location of an unequal conversation that has winners and losers."[86]

In ordinary modern life, especially in cosmopolitan urban areas, there are many occasions in which people of different backgrounds are in regular contact with each other at work, while shopping, or in public transportation. Despite these repeated interactions, perceived social differences persist and certain boundaries are maintained.

Shared beach space may yet promote sociability. As a capability, sociability is not the same as democracy in the strong discursive sense that some urban geographers and political scientists intend. Inequality still remains between unequals, and owners and visitors may never interact beyond some perfunctory exchanges. Yet, however perfunctory these exchanges and however casual the interactions between owners and visitors, they meet and engage with each other as concrete persons rather than as imagined others. They witness each other engaged in the same activities that the other enjoys. They come to appreciate each other as actual human beings.

METHODOLOGY

Right-to-exclude cases are valuable not only intrinsically but also methodologically. They illustrate how the human flourishing theory resolves disputes where, as we should expect will nearly always be the case, both sides have stakes that are legitimate and worthy of our recognition, at least prima facie so. Such property disputes implicate capabilities on both sides.

We cannot escape the questions of whose flourishing should prevail and what kind of community flourishing should be privileged. We can gain some insight into how decision makers determine these questions under the human flourishing theory by comparing two well-known right-to-exclude cases, *State v. Shack*[87] and *Jacque v. Steenberg Homes, Inc.*[88]

85. Freeman, *Democracy and Danger, supra* note 84, at 19.

86. *Id.*

87. 277 A.2d 369 (N.J. 1971).

88. 563 N.W.2d 154 (Wis. 1997).

In *Shack*, two defendants entered private property to aid migrant farmworkers employed and housed on the property. The defendants worked for government-funded organizations that provided health-care and legal services to migrant farmworkers. The owner-employer demanded that the defendants leave his property, and they refused. The defendants were convicted of violating the New Jersey criminal trespass statute. On appeal, the New Jersey Supreme Court held that no trespass had occurred nor had a breach of the right to exclude. The court said that title to land could not include dominion over people whom the owner allows on the land, in this case, the farm workers. The owner's property right is not absolute and must be accommodated with the interests of others.

In an oft-quoted passage, the court in *Shack* recognized this point, "Property rights serve human values. They are recognized to that end, and are limited by it."[89] Although the owner-employer in *Shack* certainly may have expected that his autonomy interest as owner entitled him to exclude whomever he wished and for whatever reason, the question was whether such an expectation would be reasonable. The court concluded that the owner's autonomy interest has limits, and in this case other values were at stake as well. The court was not entirely clear in identifying those values, but analyzing the case under the human flourishing theory allows us to identify them with some precision. It also allows us to see how, under that pluralistic theory, we identify which values matter and how they are evaluated.

Perhaps the value most obviously at stake on the defendants' side was health. As I have already indicated, health is a subsidiary of life as a capability essential for a flourishing life.

Obviously, no one can enjoy a well-lived life without life itself—that is simply a truism. But we, at least the great majority of us, want more than just to be able to breath. We want, and we objectively need, a basic measure of good health to flourish. Obviously, not all of us enjoy good health all of the time. Illnesses and injuries of various sorts can and do strike all of us at some point in our lives, and for nearly all of us more than once. What health as a capability requires, then, is not good health itself but access to health, that is, to medical care.

Access to medical care includes access to information about medical care. As the court pointed out in *Shack*, migrant farm workers are a rootless and isolated community, often unaware of the opportunities that exist for them to meet their needs to medical care.[90] Without access to the kind of information about medical care that the defendants provided, migrant farm workers might suffer unnecessarily from lack of proper care.

89. *Id.* at 372.

90. *Id.* at 372–73.

The other value is sociability. In the context of *Shack*, sociability takes on a more fundamental meaning, literally grounding the capability of life, without which it would be impossible for the lives of the migrant farm workers to flourish. Sociability includes, at a minimum, human contact, and in connection with other capabilities, that includes communication with other persons, not otherwise available, who provide information about or access to care that is essential to life and other capabilities. Living a life of isolation as the owner-employer in *Shack* wished his workers to do would have mocked any sensible meaning of human flourishing.

Of course, there are capabilities at stake on the owner's side as well. If the owner has a home on the property, these capability-related interests may be quite strong. Consider, for example, the well-known right-to-exclude case, *Jacque v. Steenberg Homes, Inc.*[91] In that case, homeowners, Lois and Harvey Jacque, sued Steenberg Homes for damages for intentional trespass to the Jacques' land.[92] Steenberg delivered a mobile home by plowing a path across the Jacques' snow-covered field despite strenuous protests from the Jacques. Although other means of accessing the delivery location were available, Steenberg used the path across the Jacques' land because that was the easiest route for him. The jury awarded the Jacques $1 in nominal damages and $100,000 in punitive damages. On appeal, the Wisconsin Supreme Court held that if a jury awards nominal damages for intentional trespass, the jury may also award punitive damages, and thus the court upheld the verdict.[93]

The Jacques had strong capability-related reasons for excluding Steenberg Homes. The most important of these interests was the Jacques' autonomy and privacy. The common law historically, and properly, attached great weight to the interests of homeowners in protecting their privacy and associational autonomy by recognizing a robust right of homeowners to exclude the public from entering their property without permission. From the perspective of the human flourishing theory, with its focus on the capabilities necessary for the well-lived life, this emphasis on privacy of the home makes sense. The home is the central locus for developing and experiencing all, or nearly all, of the capabilities necessary for human flourishing. The capability of sociability, for example, depends upon one's having a sense of security, a sense that many, perhaps most, people experience most strongly in their own homes. The more vulnerable we feel to others' power, both physically and emotionally, the less apt we are to form healthy relationships

91. 563 N.W.2d 154 (Wis. 1997).

92. *Id.* at 156–58.

93. *Id.* at 165–66.

with others. The legal right to exclude others from entering our homes, absent a compelling reason (a reason that itself is instrumentally tied to one or more of our necessary capabilities), creates an environment within which individuals experience the sense of personal security that is essential to the capacity to develop healthy social relationships. This analysis suggests that in *Jacque*, the legal interest in promoting the homeowners' capability of sociability, among other capabilities, was quite strong. Steenberg Homes' intentional trespass directly threatened the Jacques' sense of security, however small the economic damage to the Jacques' property may have been.

The owner's capability-related interests are less compelling when the house is not the owner's primary residence. This will often be the case when the house is located on beachfront property. The owner's security interest becomes more attenuated in these circumstances simply by virtue of the fact that he resides in the house less frequently than someone, like the Jacques, for whom the house is their primary, indeed their only, residence. A homeowner's security capability concern attaches primarily to her principle residence. Owners of beach houses typically spend just a few weeks per year there, and in some cases far less than that. Even in repeat-visit cases where an owner annually spends her summer vacation at the beach house with her family, the primary locus of capability interests remains the year-round residence. Still, even in cases where the beach house is not the owner's primary residence, we need to take his capability interests and their concomitant values into account.

The difference between the owner's situation in *Shack* and that of the Jacques was the presence of the migrant workers living on Tedesco's land in *Shack*. Although having workers living on his property did not mean that Tedesco had opened his property to the public, it did mean that his farm was not strictly his personal residence in the way that the Jacques' home was. There was a certain loss of privacy involved in having employees living on his property. Tedesco himself had waived to some extent his right to exclude persons who wish to enter his land for the purpose of assisting the workers he had invited to live there. Knowing of the situation of migrant workers, specifically their lack of access to the outside world, Tedesco could not have it both ways. He could not both have them live on his property and retain the same measure of exclusion over his land that someone in the situation of the Jacques enjoy.

CHOOSING BETWEEN INCOMMENSURATE GOODS

Still, Tedesco did have a right to exclude. So, how shall we choose between the owner's right to exclude and the need of others to enter the owner's property where the focus of the analysis is promoting human flourishing, itself defined in value pluralist terms? In Chapter One, I discussed why the values that constitute

human flourishing are not only multiple but incommensurate.[94] If it is the case that such values are incommensurable, how can we make a rational choice between the two interests in access cases where both sides involve values that implicate important human capabilities?

As I further discussed in Chapter One, rational choice is possible in such situations even if that choice is not always the determinate outcome or the only rational choice. It is a mistake, a common mistake but a mistake nevertheless, to suppose that to make a rational choice between two competing value options "one must choose a good better than or equal in value to any alternative."[95] Elizabeth Anderson calls this belief "the optimization principle."[96] Anderson argues that this principle is false and that it is false because practical reason itself generates the structure of values.

She explains this on the basis of the theory of pragmatism, which she defines as "say[ing] that the meaning of a statement is exhausted by its practical implications."[97] Anderson argues this theory better explains how people make deliberate, rational choices when they are faced with choices between two intrinsically valuable goods, that is, goods that a person values for themselves rather than derivatively. The basis of choice, she argues, is not a judgment about which of the two goods is more valuable but instead "a judgment telling us how best to reconcile the expressive demands of the different kinds of concern we owe to and have for them."[98] Elaborating on this claim, she draws on a hypothetical choice that Ruth Chang posed:

> Suppose the only way I can save my dying mother is by ending my friendship with Eve. It would be very odd to think, at least under normal circumstances, that it would be wrong for me to give up that friendship in order to save my mother. Clearly, I ought to trade the friendship for my mother's life. And it is just as clear that the reason I ought to trade the friendship is that my mother's life is more valuable. So my friendship with Eve *can* be compared with and properly traded off against the life of my mother.[99]

94. *See* pages 23–26 *supra*.

95. Elizabeth Anderson, *Practical Reason and Incommensurable Goods, in* Incommensurability, Incomparability, and Practical Reason 90 (Ruth Chang ed., 1997).

96. *Id.*

97. *Id.*

98. *Id.* at 103.

99. *Id.* at 101, quoting Ruth Chang, *Emphatic Comparability and Constitutive Incommensurability, or Buying and Selling Friends* (unpub. ms.), at 3.

Anderson rejects Chang's view that her friendship with Eve can be compared with and traded off against her mother's life. She regards the two goods as incommensurable but still thinks that a rational choice between them is not only possible but plausible and likely. The problem with Chang's account is that it is too thin; it lacks the texture and fine detail that make it possible for people in such situations to make meaningful choices. Anderson contends that ordinary moral thinking does not operate the way Chang describes. We don't place the mother's life and the friendship on a common scale and decide that one is more valuable than the other.

Rather, we take into account considerations of what we *owe* our mothers and our friends in different circumstances. There are different kinds of concern that we have for and that we owe to mothers and friends, and these different kinds of concerns yield different expressive demands, as Anderson calls them. The basis for choice in such situations is a judgment telling us how best to reconcile these different expressive demands.[100] Anderson illustrates the way in which different expressive demands may work in the context of Chang's mother/friend dilemma by pointing to possible considerations that may enter: Perhaps it would be a loving act not to prolong the mother's life. Perhaps she is dying of a painful illness and prolonging life would only add to her misery. Or perhaps the mother has lived a long and fruitful life and is now ready to face death.

Perhaps as the friend well knows, the choice of the mother over the friend expresses an anxious dependency on the mother, a dependency that has undermined the daughter's ability to maintain independent relationships. If this were the case, Anderson suggests, "Dropping my friendships to save my mother's life would thus express a failure to love my friends, not a failure to love my mother."[101] Hence, no contemplated means of saving the mother's life would be justified. It all depends on the particular contours of the obligations to mother and friend where those contours are shaped by "the respective expressive requirements of filial love and friendship."[102]

Charles Taylor explains the process of rational choice between incommensurate goods through the exercise of practice reasoning in terms that somewhat resemble Anderson's account. Taylor describes the process in terms of what he calls "complementarity."[103] By that term, he means how different goods fit together as different aspects of the same phenomenon at the same level of

100. *Id.* at 103.

101. *Id.* at 102.

102. *Id.* at 103.

103. *See* Charles Taylor, *Leading a Life, in* Incommensurability, Incomparability, and Practical Reason, *supra* note 95, at 181.

understanding. How do they cohere together as complementary components of a meaningful whole? Such a whole may be a person's life or a rule, a concept, or a system.[104] In the context of the beach access problem, the whole just is the concept of ownership itself, including its moral foundation. Complementarity here means examining the values underlying the competing property interests, the beach owner's exclusionary interest and the public's access interest, in a particularistic way to assess how those interests and their underlying values interact in this context with respect to the overall concern with human flourishing. It requires consideration of the respective parties' capabilities that are at stake. How do those respective capabilities fit together under the circumstances immediately posed? If members of the public are given access, under reasonable conditions, to the owner's beach, will the values that those capabilities support clash and override equaling compelling values on the owner's side? Or are the circumstances such that the values that weigh in favor of the right to exclude—personal security, privacy, and the like—not in jeopardy, at least not in any immediate sense? If this is the case, then a degree of complementarity between the values on the two sides exists to such an extent that we are warranted in concluding that choosing the public's side in these circumstances is a rational solution.

Reversing the question, if members of the public are given access, with reasonable conditions attached, to the owner's beach, will that occur only by sacrificing the capabilities that are essential to the owner's opportunity to flourish? Perhaps the owner has a house on the beach property that is not only his primary but also his sole place of residence. If that is the case, that brings us closer to the circumstances involved in *Jacque*, where, as I discussed earlier, the homeowner's capability interests in personal security, autonomy, and privacy were especially important to his ability to flourish. Perhaps it is also the case that other places for the public to access the beach are available within a reasonable distance from the owner's property such that denying the public access at this location does not practically deny the public all meaningful access to the beach. Under those circumstances the values on the two sides are complementary to the extent that enforcement of the owner's exclusion interest would not substantially undermine the values that inhere in the public's access interest.

The four factors that the New Jersey identified in *Matthews* and *Raleigh Avenue* approximate this sort of complementarity analysis. Their contextual focus requires the court to consider, as complementarity analysis does, the immediate circumstances involved in the dispute. There are important differences between New Jersey's four-factor approach and complementarity analysis. Most obviously and importantly, the latter is concerned with the respective parties' capabilities

104. *See id.* at 183.

and the relationship between the immediate circumstances and those capabilities. The New Jersey factors have nothing to do with human capabilities as such. To the extent that the New Jersey factors bear upon the capabilities that are essential for human flourishing, they do so only inadvertently and elliptically. The reason reflects a more basic difference between the two approaches. The New Jersey approach is premised on the view of the values under the competing interests—exclusion and access—as commensurable and, hence, subject to be weighed against each other. The New Jersey approach is essentially a balancing approach, and balancing assumes that the two matters being weighed with respect to each other are subject to commensuration via an assumed though unidentified common scale.

Complementarity analysis rests on the view that the goods that are constitutive of human flourishing and that underlie the competing property interests are both plural and incommensurable for reasons that I discussed earlier.

This is why it is important to understand that complementarity analysis is not a matter of balancing. Rather, it is a matter of analyzing how the pieces of a whole, albeit not a unitary whole, fit together. Less metaphorically, it is not a matter of pitting one value against another and deciding that one is more valuable than the other but instead evaluating differences of importance between the goods. Here an important point that Charles Taylor makes is particularly salient: "Now there are differences of importance not only between goods, but also between occasions when what we are calling the same good is invoked."[105] As Taylor goes on to recognize, this is why no systemic priority can be given to the same good whenever it is involved.[106] In one context, under some particular set of circumstances autonomy should be given priority, but under another, very different circumstance it should be sacrificed for the sake of, say, another's health.

Perhaps this sort of analysis will appear to some as act-utilitarianism in another guise. It is not. To see why, consider an example that Taylor gives. According to the account in the Gospel of John, while Jesus was at the home of Martha and Mary, Mary took a pound of ointment and anointed his feet, wiping them with her hair. A speaker identified as Judas Iscariot grumbles, "Why was not this ointment sold for three hundred pence, and given to the poor?" (John 12:5). Taylor asks, "An act of devotion, meant to foreshadow the imminent death of Jesus . . . ; what price?" His answer? "In a sense, none."[107] The reason is that "it is not in the same register as calculations about what can be given to the poor. . . ."[108] Still,

105. Taylor, *Leading a Life, supra* note 103, at 176.

106. *Id.*

107. *Id.* at 178.

108. *Id.*

Mary's act of devotion did have something to do with weights, else why would she have used ointment, which we are to understand has some considerable money value? As Taylor observes, "The act of devotion here could find expression only through something of value." At the same time, however, "something whose use would condemn to poverty masses of people would be obviously wrong to use here."[109] So, there is a sense in which weighting is involved, but the evaluation is nothing like the straightforward act-utilitarian maximization that Judas proposes. The good that is Mary's act of devotion is so different from three hundred pence that to have foregone that act and sold the ointment for money would have utterly missed the point. There simply was no cash-nexus here, nor any straightforward welfare-maximizing strategy. Yet although faced with such different kinds of goods, Mary was able to make a rational choice between them, choosing the good that, given this context, best articulates its relative importance in her life as a whole. That is, Mary has an understanding or a vision of herself and the kind of person she aims to become in relation to the world, and that vision of herself and the kind of life she is living and wants to live helps her understand how the different goods in her life fit together in such a way that she can make rational, meaningful decisions about how to proceed in the face of conflicting goods.

This idea of complementarity is not unlike Elizabeth Anderson's theory of choosing between incommensurable goods as a matter of "judgment telling us how best to reconcile the expressive demands of the different kinds of concern we owe to and have for them"[110] It is this notion of reconciling conflicting expressive demands that is salient for our purposes, for what both Anderson and Taylor have in common is not only a rejection of balancing competing goods but a shared insight that ordinary moral judgments and choices follow from careful consideration of how the goods relate to each other in particular contexts, leading to discernment that their fit in this set of circumstances is such that one good demands more here than others. In other contexts it may not. As Anderson stresses, the decision, and the evaluative process that leads up to it, has nothing to do with optimization. Rather, it has everything to do with evaluating the relative demands of intrinsic goods within a particular set of circumstances.

The right to exclude is important, but it is not everything. As Felix Cohen observed, although every property right involves some power to exclude others from doing something, this is a "rather modest truism," one that lacks any real practical implications.[111] There are occasions when the owner properly lacks the

109. *Id.*

110. Anderson, *Practical Reason and Incommensurable Goods, supra* note 95, at 103.

111. Felix S. Cohen, *Dialogue on Private Property*, 9 Rutgers L. Rev. 357, 362, 370–74. 379 (1954).

power to exclude everyone in the world. The common law has long recognized that this is the case. The real questions today include: (1) whether the exclusionary interest's scope should be defined by narrow and noncontextual rules or by contextualized norms; (2) whether the scope of exclusionary interest should be defined on the basis of some sort of utilitarian calculus or instead on the basis of an understanding of property's fundamental purpose as realizing human flourishing, itself understood as pluralistic and objective; and (3) if the scope of the right of exclusion is defined in terms of multiple and incommensurate values or goods, whether and how rational choices between or among those goods is possible. This chapter has addressed all of these questions. Doubtless there is more to be said about each of them, but the important point to make here is that these are the vital question now facing property theorists regarding the right to exclude.

7

Expropriations and Eminent Domain

Governmental power to expropriate land for the common good is ancient. It dates at least back to Roman law. Indeed, Susan Reynolds argues that "in any settled society in which individuals or groups have acknowledged rights in particular pieces of land there may be some occasions, like the digging of drainage or irrigation channels, or the building of roads or fortifications, on which such rights may come into conflict with the needs of the community as a whole, however it is defined and ruled."[1] Expropriation for the common good is found in most, although not all of such societies.[2]

The existence of expropriation is one thing; its justification is another. Several rationales for the power to expropriate land have been suggested. In the United States, the dominant explanation is economic: what justifies the power of the state to force the sale of private property is economic efficiency.[3] Expropriation is necessary to overcome monopolies that occur when desirable government projects are site-specific. To pick a familiar example, say a city plans to build a new

1. Susan Reynold, Before Eminent Doman: Toward a History of Expropriation of Land for the Common Good 3 (2010).

2. *Id.* at 4.

3. *See* Richard A. Posner, Economic Analysis of Law 55–56 (6th ed. 2003).

Property and Human Flourishing. Gregory S. Alexander.

airport on land that is privately owned by several owners. No other site is feasible, so the city must acquire each of these parcels. As economists have long pointed out, this means that each owner has a monopoly on an asset critical to the government's plan, and each is in a position to extract monopoly rents from the government in exchange for selling her parcel.

Expropriation allows the government to achieve the benefit of building the airport at a lower cost to taxpayers than would be the case if the government had to acquire each parcel through market transactions.[4]

The power to expropriate land for the common good can be understood in quite different terms, however, terms that derive from a conception of property's underlying purpose as promoting human flourishing. Like utilitarianism, the human flourishing theory explains the government's power of eminent domain in terms of the common good, but it understands the common good as more complex than aggregate utility or preference satisfaction.

At its most general level, the power of expropriation represents the polity's collective judgment that the state is justified in demanding transfer of title to our land to the members of the political and society community that nurtures us as flourishing individuals—that under certain conditions landowners may have to sacrifice title to their land in exchange for just compensation. This forced sale of land is necessary to create and maintain the material conditions that are necessary prerequisites for all members of the society to lived well-lived lives. Specifically, these material conditions include a certain physical infrastructure that is necessary for individuals to develop human capabilities.

To develop the capabilities necessary to flourish as autonomous moral agents, individuals depend upon the existence of social networks within which they can carry out the activities that enable them to experience freedom. This includes what Charles Taylor calls "the mundane elements of infrastructure without which we could not carry on these higher activities. . . ."[5] These elements of infrastructure include just the sorts of public projects for which the power of eminent domain is routinely exercised: roads, airports, utility lines, public buildings, communication systems, and the like. Each of us depends upon the continued effectiveness of this infrastructure for maintaining it, even at some personal cost that is not equally shared with others.

Eminent domain is a legal and political process for determining just what that responsibility is. Although eminent domain has a component of shared sacrifice, it also includes an element of irreducible individual loss. Its effects are

4. *See* Thomas W. Merrill, *The Economics of Eminent Domain*, 72 Cornell. L. Rev. 61, 81–82 (1986).

5. Charles Taylor, *Atomism*, *in* Charles Taylor, Philosophy and the Human Sciences: Philosophical Papers, vol. 2, 205 (1985).

necessarily concentrated on those whose property is expropriated. Because just compensation is, under current American judicial doctrine, fair market value, those who lose their property through eminent domain really do lose something that the rest of us (who are paying our taxes in part to fund their compensation) do not.

Not every social structure or political institution and not every social activity is necessary to foster the goods that are required for a well-lived life. From the perspective of developing these essential goods, some social structures and activities are more important than others. A tighter nexus between the institution whose activity is under challenge and the goods necessary to a well-lived life is required before the political community can legitimately demand that an owner sacrifice property entitlement. This is especially true when the affected property interest is the owner's personal residence. The Supreme Court's controversial decision in *Kelo v. City of New London*[6] illustrates the point.

THE PUBLIC USE REQUIREMENT

In *Kelo*, the city of New London, Connecticut, approved a development plan that was intended to revitalize this economically distressed but not blighted city. The plan involved acquisition of land by purchase or expropriation for a large multi-purpose project that was stimulated by the announcement that a large pharmaceutical firm (Pfizer) intended to build a research facility in the area. Much of the acquired land was to be used for residential and commercial purposes rather than more familiar public use purposes such as public parks, roads, and the like. When some property owners refused to sell, the public development agency began expropriation proceedings. The petitioners brought a lawsuit that the expropriation would violate the constitutional public use requirement. A narrowly divided Supreme Court held that an expropriation for economic development purposes meets the public use requirement.

In his opinion for the Court, Justice Stevens pointed out that some parameters of the public use requirement are clear. On the one hand, the government may not simply expropriate land from a private owner solely to transfer it to another private party, even if compensation is paid. On the other hand, the government clearly may expropriate land if actual use by the public is intended, as in instances of expropriation for railroad rights-of-way or parks. But is "public use" confined to situations where the public actually uses or has a right to use the expropriated land? Such a view would greatly limit the state's expropriation power, and American courts have not so narrowly construed the requirement, at least not

6. 545 U.S. 460 (2005).

since the nineteenth century.[7] A far more relaxed view equates "public use" with "public benefit." On this view, so long as the public enjoys any benefit from the intended use of the expropriated land, the requirement is met. A much narrower view holds that public use must involve provision of "public goods" in the technical economic sense. That is a very limited category of use because true public goods are rare. They have two defining characteristics: (1) Once the good is provided, it is impossible to prevent anyone from consuming it; (2) consumption by one person does not diminish or otherwise affect the ability of others to consume it as well.

Justice Stevens chose none of these. Rather, he stated that the test is whether the project in mind serves a "public purpose," such as a plan to clear and reclaim an urban area in which some parts are blighted but others are not.[8] Plans such as this are legitimate and traditional functions of the state.

Stevens' opinion made a second point. The Court will not try to second-guess the judgments of legislative bodies regarding the need or importance of public projects that are the basis for expropriation. Rather, the Court will apply a deferential standard of judicial review that gives legislatures "broad latitude in determining what public needs justify the use of the [expropriation] power."[9] In the instant case, the city of New London had, Justice Stevens said, "carefully formulated an economic development plan that it believe[d] w[ould] bring appreciable benefits to the community, including—but by no means limited to—new jobs and increased tax revenue."[10] In view of the plan's comprehensive character and the "thorough deliberation" leading up to the plan's formulation, the Court deemed it appropriate to resolve challenge to the plan in its entirety rather than piecemeal by looking at each owner's land in isolation.[11]

Justice Stevens was hardly the only voice on the Court to express an opinion in *Kelo*.

Justice O'Connor wrote a dissenting opinion expressing the view that any expropriation for the purpose of economic development is not a public use. The public benefits from economic development, she contended, are incidental only and insufficient to constitute a public use.[12] In her view the Court's approach to

7. *See* Lawrence Berger, *The Public Use Requirement in Eminent Domain*, 57 Or. L. Rev. 203, 205, 209 (1978).

8. *See* Berman v. Parker, 348 U.S. 26 (1954).

9. 545 U.S. at 483.

10. *Id.*

11. *Id.*

12. *Id.* at 494.

the public use requirement is far too broad. She read the majority opinion to hold that "the sovereign may take private property currently put to ordinary private use, and give it over for new, ordinary private use, so long as the new use is predicted to generate some secondary benefit for the public—such as increased tax revenue, more jobs, maybe even esthetic pleasure."[13] The danger posed by that holding, she asserted, is that "nearly any lawful use of real private property can be said to generate some incidental benefit to the public."[14] The result, in her view, is that "[t]he specter of [expropriation] hangs over all property." She suggests several possible scenarios: "Nothing is to prevent the State from replacing any Motel 6 [a chain of cheap American motels] with a Ritz-Carlton, any home with a shopping mall, or any farm with a factory."[15]

Kelo is an excellent vehicle for discussing how eminent domain disputes are analyzed under the human flourishing theory. The Supreme Court's public use analysis is deficient, both analytically and morally, and the human flourishing theory provides a more satisfying method of identifying and assessing the multiple values and capabilities that state expropriations of land implicate. It also clarifies how choices among those competing values can be made in a rational way.

KELO AND HUMAN FLOURISHING

The *Kelo* decision aroused considerable public outrage.[16] From the perspective of the human flourishing theory the reaction is understandable. The plaintiff had strong flourishing-related reasons for resisting the forced sale. The common law historically, and properly, has attached great weight to protecting the privacy and autonomy interests of homeowners by recognizing and enforcing a strong right to exclude the public from entering their property without permission. As we saw in Chapter Five, although the right to exclude has long been subject to certain limited exceptions, it generally has been strongest with respect to the home. From the perspective of the human flourishing theory, with its focus on human capabilities necessary for the well-lived life, this emphasis on privacy within the home makes sense. The home is a central locus for developing and experiencing many of the capabilities necessary for human flourishing. Moreover, the home is example par excellence of an asset to which most owners have significant

13. *Id.* at 501.

14. *Id.*

15. *Id.* at 503

16. *See* Janice Nadler & Sheri Seidman Diamond, *Government Takings of Private Property:* Kelo *and the Perfect Storm, in* Public Opinion and Constitutional Controversy 287 (Nathaniel Persily et al. eds., (2008).

nonfungible attachments.[17] As Margaret Jane Radin states, the home "is the scene of one's history and future, one's life and growth . . . [O]ne embodies or constitutes oneself there."[18] The home is a place where, above all other places, most people experience a sense of belonging. This sense of belonging grows stronger for most people as they remain in the same place longer. This is one reason why moving, even if just to a new house or a different apartment in the same city or town, is an emotionally challenging experience for many individuals. Homes are not fungible: Most of us do not discard one and acquire a new one lightly, like an article of clothing. We invest much more of our personality in them. The human flourishing theory gives considerable weight to that sense of attachment and the reasons behind it. In the context of *Kelo*, it might have led the Court to be far more sensitive to the concerns that the *Kelo* plaintiffs raised.

On the other side of the ledger, the importance of jobs to members of the New London community is not to be underestimated from the standpoint of human flourishing. But the linkage between the jobs the city hoped to produce through its redevelopment project and the land acquired from the *Kelo* plaintiffs was more attenuated than the impact the use of eminent domain had on the plaintiffs' sense of security and personal autonomy. Taking into account all the relevant values at stake rather than just aggregate utility, human flourishing seems best advanced by protecting the homeowners' interests here. For this reason, as a first-order question, the exercise of eminent domain in *Kelo* was probably inconsistent with the human flourishing theory.

To say that the exercise of eminent domain was not wise, however, is not the same as saying that the Supreme Court was necessarily wrong to avoid intervening on behalf of the *Kelo* plaintiffs. Although it views property as a morally laden institution, the Aristotelian-based property theory does not reduce questions of property doctrine to a simple moralistic analysis.

Rather, it distinguishes between the first-order moral question and the second-order question of how best to respond to the demands of morality through law and legal institutions. The Court's opinion in *Kelo* focused a great deal on these sorts of second-order questions, such as federalism and institutional competence. The moral complexity and contextual sensitivity of the implications of any particular exercise of eminent domain may counsel in favor of delegating decisions about its propriety to local officials, who are closest to the situation, reserving (federal) judicial intervention for situations in which those officials appear to

17. For some contrary evidence, *see* Stephanie M. Stern, *Residential Protectionism and the Legal Mythology of the Home*, 107 Mich. L. Rev. 1093 (2009). *But see* Lorna Fox, Conceptualizing Home: Theories, Law, and Policies (2007).

18. Margaret Jane Radin, *Property and Personhood*, 34 Stan. L. Rev. 957, 992 (1982).

have abdicated their responsibility to act on behalf of the public welfare. That did not appear to have been the case in New London, as the Supreme Court noted in emphasizing that the use of eminent domain in *Kelo* was the product of a lengthy and comprehensive planning process. And so it is possible to affirm from within the human flourishing theory both that the use of eminent domain in New London was likely wrong and that *Kelo* was nevertheless correctly decided.

KELO IN COMPARATIVE PERSPECTIVE

Kelo is an appropriate case to use as a vehicle for considering how the human flourishing theory would address the public use requirement for two reasons. First, it poses a particularly difficult set of circumstances for the public use test: It is a case in which the state plans to expropriate land from one private owner and give it to another private owner, or, in short, to take from *A* and give to *B*. Second, the Court's legal analysis in *Kelo* clearly exposes the character of American judicial reasoning in expropriation cases and its defects. Those defects become most clearly evident when the *Kelo* reasoning is compared with judicial reasoning used by other nation-states, in particular, the German Constitutional Court.

The constitutions of several nation-states, including Germany[19] and South Africa,[20] include provisions in their property clauses that expressly recognize such a social obligation.

Even in the absence of such an explicit form of legal recognition, however, the obligation exists, not as an externally imposed limitation on property interests but implicit in the concept of ownership itself. Property rights and their correlative obligations are cognizable as social goods, worthy of vindication by the state, only insofar as they are consistent with community and human flourishing more generally. The social obligation norm is the legal recognition of this straightforward conceptual entailment of the way the legal system justifies the institution of private property itself. Another way of putting this point is to say that the very factor that makes the institution of private property a social good is also the very factor which renders its limits, that is, human flourishing.

Cases that involve taking from *A* and giving to *B* are especially troublesome for the public use requirement for the obvious reason that the benefit seems purely private. The German Constitutional Court has faced the question whether the public use, or public interest, requirement,[21] can be met where *B*, the ultimate

19. Basic Law of the Federal Republic of Germany art. 14(2).

20. Constitution of the Republic of South Africa sec. 25(2), (4).

21. *See* 1949 Basic Law of the Federal Republic of Germany art. 14.3.1 ("Expropriation shall only be permissible in the public interest.").

recipient, would profit from the expropriation, and its approach is illuminating. The Court has held that the fact of private profit alone does not prevent the public interest requirement from being met.[22] The case involved expropriation of land for the purpose of providing electricity. Following expropriation, the state gave the land to a private firm, which supplied electricity to its customers with whom it had a contractual relationship. This seems to be an easier case than *Kelo* because the ultimate use of the land—supplying electricity—is a function traditionally performed by public utilities. In this sense the recipient of the land, although a private firm, is a quasi-public entity. The same can hardly be said of the circumstances in *Kelo,* where the expropriated land was to be used for building hotels, apartments, stores—strictly private activities. From this perspective it becomes easier to understand why Justice O'Connor characterized the public benefits of increasing jobs and raising revenue as "strictly incidental." The question in *Kelo,* then, boils down to whether increasing jobs and taxes have a sufficiently public character to constitute a "public use." The German court has faced that question as well, reaching a different result than its American counterpart. In the *Boxberg* case,[23] the state expropriated privately owned land for the purpose of transferring it to the Daimler-Benz automobile firm that intended to use it as a testing ground for their new cars.

The court held that the expropriation was unconstitutional despite the fact that, as in *Kelo,* the intended project would have created much-needed jobs and stimulated the economy in the local region. "Condemnation for the benefit of private persons . . . that serves the public interest only indirectly and presents an enhanced danger of abuse to the detriment of the weak poses particular constitutional problems," the court said.[24]

The second, more fundamental insight to be gained from studying *Kelo* concerns the reasoning by which courts decide whether and when land expropriation is in the public interest. Here a comparison with the German Constitutional Court's mode of reasoning reveals *Kelo*'s basic flaw. Despite the Court's discussion of judicial deference to the legislature, the Court in *Kelo* relied on consequentialist reasoning to reach its decision. This is the aspect of the case that bears the greatest scrutiny, for it is the greatest weakness of the American approach to analyzing expropriation cases.

22. BVerfGE 66, 248 (1984).

23. BVerfGE 74, 264 (1987).

24. *Id.* at 287.

CONSEQUENTIALIST REASONING

That the Court relied on consequentialist reasoning in *Kelo* comes as no surprise. Not only do judicial precedents strictly employ consequentialist reasoning, but the very concept of a public use as a limitation on the scope of the state's power to expropriate land seems to compel inquiry into the intended effects of state expropriation. The problem is not with consequentialist reasoning as such but with the type or character of the Court's consequentialist analysis.

Consequentialism is not of a piece. There are different modes of consequentialism, and the characteristics that distinguish one form from another make it more or less persuasive, both analytically and normatively. We need to identify, then, these different modes of consequentialism.

Forms of Consequentialism

Stated in its most basic form, consequentialism is the theory of action which holds that in any given situation the right act for people to do is the one that will produce the best possible outcome. More precisely, this definition has two parts: (1) It provides some principle for ranking overall states of affairs from an impersonal point of view; (2) it then asserts that in any given situation the right course of action to take is the one that will produce the highest ranked state of affairs that the actor is capable of producing. The theory lends itself to as many variations as there are criteria for ranking overall states of affairs. Beyond agreement that the rightness of an act depends upon its consequences, action theorists debate about other requirements for a theory of action to be consequentialist. For example, some theorists argue that a theory of action cannot be properly considered consequentialist unless it is agent-neutral, that is, the reason for action can be fully expressed without referring back to the person for whom it is provided (if it cannot be completely stated without reference back to such a person, given the reason is "agent-relative."). Other theorists deny that agent-neutrality is a requirement for any reason for action to be consequentialist. I hold with this latter view, for, as we shall see, the theory of value that I shall endorse here is one that allows in aspects of agent-relativity.

A more fundamental distinction concerns the theory of value that underlies any consequentialist action theory, that is, what outcomes the theorist seeks obtain. The most familiar version of consequentialism is utilitarianism, which in its classical form states that the best outcome from among any set of possible outcomes is the one that maximizes the net amount of human pleasure. Classical utilitarianism has been subject to criticism from several angles, of course, including the focus on pleasure. One widely shared modern variant of classical utilitarianism substitutes preference-satisfaction for pleasure. It holds that the best

possible outcome is the one that maximizes the satisfaction of aggregate individual preferences.

In analyzing expropriation questions both courts and legal scholars commonly rely upon some version of utilitarianism, usually without acknowledging so. Although they are seldom so explicit, courts and scholars tend to assess the merits of proposed state projects with regard to the public use or public interest requirement in roughly utilitarian terms. The often-unarticulated value that underlies their evaluations is aggregate social welfare, a variation of classical utility. What I wish to suggest here is not only that this value foundation for public use evaluations is not the only available form of a consequentialist approach to public use analysis but, more boldly, that it is normatively inferior.

The human flourishing theory provides an alternative form of consequentialism. Which of two varieties of consequentialist reasoning is better suited to analysis of the public use requirement in expropriation cases? For reasons that I shall explain, the human flourishing form of consequentialist reasoning is preferable to utilitarian forms of reasoning. To do so, I need first to turn to a related matter—purposive analysis in constitutional property cases.

Purposive Analysis

Purposive analysis is a general mode of constitutional interpretation. It is a method by which an interpreter handles the task of gleaning the meaning of constitutional terms and norms. By "purposive," I mean that the analyst openly and systemically inquires what substantive value or values underlie the decision to make property a constitutionally protected right. An interpretation is purposive when the interpreter openly and systemically asks what is the core purpose (or what are the core purposes) that can most plausibly be attributed to a constitutional property clause.

Within liberal theory there are, of course, competing views about the core goal of making property a constitutional right. Securing individual autonomy is one obvious candidate, but there are others as well. Indeed, one might plausibly conclude that a purposive theory of constitutional property that is most compatible with liberalism is one that is pluralist, recognizing multiple purposes inhering in the constitutional protection of property. The constitutional courts of Germany and South Africa have both engaged openly and systemically in this sort of purposive reasoning, and their experience points the way to an illuminating approach to constitutional property issues, including the public use requirement. Before examining their experience, I need first to consider a quite different form of analysis that might also be called purposive. This form of reasoning was used by the American Supreme Court in *Kelo*, and it contrasts in important respects with that used by the German and South African courts.

Characteristically of American courts in constitutional property cases, the Supreme Court in *Kelo* (apart from its judicial deference rationale) was project-focused. That is, it examined the purposes or goals of the project in question, rather than the purposes of constitutional property itself. The Court asked whether economic development, the putative purpose of the city's project in the case, created benefits that were sufficiently "public" to satisfy the public use requirement despite incident private benefits. It then considered what those public benefits were, and then concluded that the character of the project's purpose was, on balance, public.

This is an unduly narrow approach to examining purposes. Obviously the project's purposes are relevant, but they are not dispositive. A broader, more nuanced purposive analysis of the public use requirement would begin with the basic purpose of that requirement itself—to prevent the state from forcing sales of land in circumstances which would sacrifice the values of property as a legally protected, especially as a constitutionally protected, interest. The public use requirement does work that the compensation cannot do and that is to assure that the fundamental values that property rights serve are not sacrificed for the sake of promoting private interests. The public use requirement represents a recognition that property's core values are not compensable by monetary damages but can be adequately protected only by preventing the state from acting in the first place. In the terminology coined by Calabresi and Melamed,[25] property's values can be protected against sacrifice for private benefits only through a "property rule" rather than a "liability rule."

Property's Values

The work of protecting property's core values requires close examination of just what these values are and how they relate to the property interest immediately involved. Precisely what those values are is, of course, a highly contestable matter. I argue here that the best purposive account of property is one that expresses property's values its terms of human flourishing, which, as we have seen, is itself a pluralistic concept that includes multiple values. We can identify at least five private law values that are at the core of human flourishing and that are commonly considered to be among property's main aims—autonomy, personal security/privacy, self-determination, self-expression, and personal responsibility. Although this is by no means an exhaustive list, it captures those values that I take to be central to the instrumental fit between property and human flourishing.

25. *See* Guido Calabresi & A. Douglas Melamed, *Property Rules, Liability Rules and Inalienability: One View of the Cathedral*, 85 Harv. L. Rev. 1089 (1972).

Autonomy will perhaps be the least controversial of the five values that I identify as private values that are property's ends. Many, if not most, property theorists identify individual autonomy as an important value that property serves. Among property theorists, some, notably libertarians and Kantians, place autonomy at the core of property's raison d'être. But even those who do not view autonomy as the foundational end of property still view it as an important aspect of the justification for private property rights.

Personal security is the second core goal. Property, it has long been thought, provides a person a safe haven. As Jeremy Waldron observes, "Humans need a refuge from the general society of mankind."[26] Property, especially landed property, supposedly provides that refuge to its owners.

An important aspect of the security that is thought to result from private ownership of property is privacy. The connection between privacy and property is familiar, of course. The home, for example, is perhaps the most familiar nexus between property and privacy. Indeed, the home is the *locus classicus* linking property, security, and privacy with autonomy (or freedom).

A third value underlying property is self-determination. Self-determination is "a power to act from determinate ends that are themselves coherent expressions of freedom because they are neither adopted unreflectively nor imposed by an external will." Here is another brief explanation: "When we . . . view[] our desires as material to be regulated and ordered in line with desires of a high order still (for example the desire not to be the kind of person we see ourselves being or becoming) we reach a clearer understanding of the slippery concept of self-determination."[27]

The connection between this understanding of self-determination and property comes through in the notion of ordering our desires. Because we live in communities with others, we will use our property in pursuing our considered goals, but we do so in full recognition of others' legitimate claims to respect. Ordering our desires also means that in pursuing our goals through property, we will develop and rely on a system of norms regulating the scope of property rights.

The point to emphasize about this approach to self-determination is how social it is. Self-determination cannot occur atomistically or in isolation from society. Self-determination is a process that is deeply dependent upon community for its higher and higher realization.

The fourth value of property is self-expression. By "self-expression," I mean to include a capacious range of forms and senses by which people assert who they are, what they desire, and so on. Possession is one of property's techniques

26. Jeremy Waldron, The Right to Private Property 296 (1998).

27. Dudley Knowles, *Hegel on Property and Personality*, 33 Phil. Q. 45, 54 (1983).

of self-expression. As Carol Rose reminds us, possession constitutes a mode of communication. "Possession as the basis of property ownership," Rose suggests, "seems to amount to something like yelling loudly enough for all who may be interested."[28] It is a matter of communicating a claim in a particular sort of way, a mode of expression that carries a great deal of meaning regarding the claimant's psychological attachment to the object in question.

Responsibility is the final value of property that I shall identify. The connection between property ownership and personal responsibility can be developed on the basis of diverse strands of thought. One is the tradition of positive liberty. From this perspective a person is not truly free until his desires, plans, and goals are stabilized so that there is continuity between the plans and actions of his past and those of his future. The person who acts on the basis of whim, who flits from one impulse to another, is not truly free but instead is a hostage to such unstable urges. Such a person has no real sense of enduring identity. Even his moral agency is subject to doubt. Private ownership of property, the argument goes, fosters a deeper sense of freedom by stabilizing a person in particular ways. The idea is that a regime of private ownership inculcates in individuals a sense of personal responsibility because they realize that they must effectively manage their own property if they are to satisfy their own needs. Through ownership individuals acquire not only certain skills but, more important, particular habits of thought—forward-looking, calculating, and mindful of alternatives—that free them from caprice and whim and give them an understanding of what T.H. Green called the "permanent good."[29]

Another strand of thought connecting property with responsibility focuses less on responsibility to oneself than responsibility to others. There is a very old tradition of property theory that is concerned with the responsibilities that individual owners owe to their societies. Connected with ideas of ownership (especially of land) as stewardship, the tradition dates back at least to Biblical texts.[30] The idea that owners owe responsibilities to their societies is a major theme in property theory in many jurisdictions. In some civil-law jurisdictions there is an important tradition in property legal theory emphasizing the "social function of property."[31] This tradition, whose origins are usually traced to the French legal

28. Carol M. Rose, *Possession as the Origin of Property*, 52 U. Chi. L. Rev. 73 (1985).

29. T.H. Green, Lectures on the Principles of Political Obligation 7 (1967)(1882).

30. *See* Peter W. Salsich, Jr., *Toward a Property Ethic of Stewardship: A Religious Perspective*, *in* Property and Values: Alternatives to Public and Private Ownership 21 (Charles Geisler & Gail Daneker eds., 2000).

31. *See* Symposium, *The Social Function of Property: A Comparative Perspective*, 80 Fordham L. Rev. 1003 (2011).

theorist Leòn Duguit,[32] views property not in terms of a right but rather as a social function. Not only does the owner owe responsibilities to put the property to the service of the community, but the state should protect property only to the extent that the owner fulfills this social responsibility. The connection between property and responsibility to others is the basis of the social obligation idea in American property legal theory. The major difference between that idea and the civil-law social function doctrine is that the latter is externally imposed on owners, unlike the social obligation norm, which is conceived as internal to the concept of ownership itself.[33]

Linking Property's Values with Property's Types

The next step is to discern which of the values that ground property are at stake in the disputed plan of expropriation. It might seem at first that this inquiry implies that public use analysis must proceed on an ad hoc or case-by-case basis. That is not necessarily so, however. Different values implicate different types of property so that it is reasonable to develop legal presumptions about outcomes based substantially on the type of property involved.

The human flourishing theory embodies a practice of the German Constitutional Court on this step. As mentioned previously, the property clause of the German Basic Law includes a social obligation provision.[34] A key practice that the courts have developed in applying this provision is the so-called "scaling" function (*Abstufung der Sozialpflichtigkeit*).[35] The court scales, or grades, the social-obligation norm's limitation on property according to its relation to the individual owner. As one observer explains, "the closer the specific property right is involved in providing security for the personal liberty of its holder, the narrower the restrictions which prevent the legislature from interfering with that right; and the further a specific property right is removed from the sphere within which the personal liberty of its holder is preserved, the easier it becomes for the legislature to regulate the limits of that right."[36] As part of this analysis, the

32. *See* Leòn Duguit, Las Transformaciónes del Derecho Público Y Privado (Editorial Heliasta 1975). For an introduction to Duguit's thought, *see* M.C. Mirow, *The Social-Obligation Norm of Property: Duguit, Hayem, and Others*, 22 Fla. J. Int'l. L. 191 (2010).

33. *See* Gregory S. Alexander, *Ownership and Obligations: The Human Flourishing Theory of Property*, 43 Hong Kong L.J. 451 (2013).

34. *See* Basic Law of the Federal Republic of Germany art. 14(2).

35. *See generally* H.J. Papier, *Art. 14*, *in* Grundgesetz Kommentar [253] (T. Maunz et al. eds., 28th ed. 1990).

36. Andre van der Walt, Constitutional Property Clauses 135 (1999).

court inquires whether and to what extent other persons are dependent on the use of the owner's property. The greater the degree of dependency, the greater the social function and, consequently, the greater the degree of legislative freedom to define the individual owner's zone of autonomy more narrowly.

As a result of this scaling function, the German court has created a hierarchy of types of property interests, granting stronger protection to some, relatively weaker protection to others, depending upon the social functions they serve. Property interests whose function is primarily or even exclusively economic, that is, private wealth-creating, receive minimal protection under German constitutional law.[37] Such interests are viewed as not immediately implicating the fundamental values of personal autonomy and self-realization. Other interests, those that immediately implicate the owner's autonomy and self-realization interests and her opportunity to practice self-governance receive stronger protection. So, for example, the interest of a landlord who does not personally reside on the premises is given lesser weight than that of her tenant, whose opportunity to remain in possession is considered essential to autonomy, security, and self-governance values.[38]

Does this mean that commercial interests always receive weaker protection than noncommercial or personal property interests? Not necessarily. Some commercial interests may implicate many of the same values embedded in personal interests. Small, family-owned businesses, for example, involve autonomy, security, and self-realization interests much in the way that residential property does, and they should receive relatively strong protection.

Purposive Analysis Is Dynamic

Another aspect of the German Court's purposive approach that is instructive is its recognition that purposes change over time. The Court's scaling analysis is functionally dynamic. It is functionally dynamic in the sense that the courts consider social and economic changes that have affected the purposes that particular resources serve over time. An influential treatise on German constitutional law aptly captures this focus on the functional change of property and its relevance to constitutional protection:

> As a basis for the individual existence and individual conduct of life as well as a principle of social order the individual ownership of property has lost its importance. Modern life is based only to a limited extent on the individual power of disposition as the basis for individual existence, with respect,

37. *See id.* at 135–36.

38. *See* 89 BVerfGE 1 (*Besitzrecht des Mieters*) (1993).

> for example, to the peasant farm or the family enterprise. The basis for individual existence is usually no longer private property as determined by private law, but the product of one's own work and participation in the benefits of the welfare state.[39]

The relevance of functional changes of property to constitutional protection is illustrated by the Small Garden Plot Case (*Kleingartenentscheidung*).[40] In that case the Court struck down a federal statute that severely limited the right of landowners to terminate garden leases. The historical background of the statute and changes in social conditions are crucial to understanding the decision. At one time in German history it was common for large landowners, particularly on the outskirts of cities, to lease to people who owned little or no land small plots for the purpose of small gardens. These garden plots were an important method of feeding the German public.

As the dominant means of agricultural production shifted to large-scale commercial productions, these individual garden plots lost their original social purpose and indeed became something of an anachronism. The individual landowners in the case wanted to change the use of their land from agricultural purposes to commercial development because the amount of annual rent from the leasehold had become insubstantial. They applied for a permit to terminate the garden lease on their land, but the regulatory agency refused to grant the permit because the federal statute did not recognize this sort of change of circumstances as a permissible basis for terminating leases.

The Court held that the statute was unconstitutional because the magnitude of the restriction on the owner's freedom of use was disproportionate to the public purpose to be served. While the original function of these garden allotments was to provide a source of food in times of social emergency, the purpose had by modern times become no more than to be a source of recreation, a social function that the court regarded as decidedly less weighty than its original purpose.

Comparing the weakness of the new function with the severity of the restriction on the owners' use, the court had little difficulty in concluding that the statute was unconstitutional.

Purposive Analysis Is Comprehensive

There is one final aspect of the purposive approach that needs to be mentioned. Purposive reasoning requires consideration of the implicated values as they apply

39. Konrad Hesse, Grundzüge des Verfassungsrecht der Bundesrepublik Deutschland 192 (20th ed. 1995).

40. 52 BVerfGE 1 (1979).

to both parties, that is, the owner whose land the state seeks to expropriate and the intended beneficiaries of the expropriation. Purposive reasoning is comprehensive, and the purposes of all affected property interests and their attendant values matter in the public use calculus. Such a comprehensive approach is necessary if the basic commitment to promoting human flourishing is to be taken seriously. Equality is itself a constituent element of human flourishing, and treating all of the affected parties as equals requires that we give each of them their due in terms of evaluating their interests at stake.

Capabilities, Values, and Resources

How do the capabilities that I discussed previously relate to this purposive analysis of property's values? Stated differently, the capabilities as the means by which the relevant values are protected and realized. As I indicated previously, human flourishing is constituted by multiple values which cannot reduced to any single foundational value. These values are themselves realized through certain human capabilities. Different values depend upon different, and sometimes multiple, capabilities, in order to be realized.

Capabilities themselves sometimes require particular resources for their nurturing and development. The capabilities of life and freedom, for example, are virtually meaningless if someone does not have a place they are entitled to be.[41] An abode, a home, is essential for the development of these capabilities, their attendant values, such as personal autonomy, and ultimately a well-lived life. A homeless person does not live a well-lived life even if it is his preference to be homeless. Such a person, accustomed to receiving little more than abuse or neglect, may come to expect little more out of life. As Amartya Sen points out, "A person who is ill-fed, undernourished, unsheltered and ill can still be high up in the scale of happiness or desire-fulfillment if he or she has learned to have 'realistic' desires and to take pleasure in small mercies."[42] Certain basic resources, then, are essential for human flourishing, and, given property law's commitment to human flourishing, those essential resources warrant legal protection.

KELO REVISITED

With the theoretical foundation laid, we can now return to *Kelo* and revisit the public use question in that case. The human flourishing theory shifts the focus

41. *See* Jeremy Waldron, *Homelessness and the Issue of Freedom*, 39 UCLA L. Rev. 295 (1991).

42. Amartya Sen, Commodities and Capabilities 21 (1999).

away from the government project involved, which was the Court's sole concern, to the values of property as a legally protected, especially as a constitutionally protected, interest. The theory asks which of property's ends are implicated in the planned expropriation and what are the human capabilities that attend those values? In *Kelo*, the asset that the city intended to expropriate had a particular and special function; it was the petitioner's personal residence, her home. As the German Constitutional Court recognizes, the home merits relatively strong legal protection because of its core purposes, individual autonomy and personal security. No one can live a well-lived life lacking security or under continual conditions of subordination in one's personal sphere.

The home involves other values as well. Consider self-expression. People express themselves in many ways, of course, nonverbally as well as verbally. Dress and conduct are obvious nonverbal expressions of oneself. So also are possessions, including the home. Indeed, for many people, one's home is a primary mode of self-expression. Others can frequently grasp an immediate sense of a person's identity by looking at his home, what type it is, where it is located, how it is decorated, and so on.

Responsibility is another of property's ends that the home involves. Whether owned or rented, the home requires the individual to acquire skills and forward-looking and deliberative habits of thought that free him from caprice and whim and give him an understanding of the long-term, stable good. At the same time, I indicated earlier that responsibility also involves responsibility to others and that the state should protect property only to the extent that the owner fulfills this social responsibility. The basic question in *Kelo*, of course, concerned the scope of Suzette Kelo's social responsibility—whether it implied subordination to the community's need for economic development. We shall return to that question shortly, but first we need to consider the values and attendant capabilities at stake on the other side, the city and the ultimate beneficiaries of the intended expropriation.

This is the stage at which the Court's focus on economic development gains salience.

Still, the Court's analysis of the community's interest in economic development seems unilluminating. Recall that the Court mentioned only jobs and taxes as the aggregate social benefits that the city hoped to reap from the development project. That tells us little or nothing about the property values at stake in the city's planned project or the human capabilities necessary to realize those values. What, then, are those values and capabilities?

The capabilities necessary for individuals to flourish as autonomous moral agents require the existence not only of social networks within which individuals carry out the activities that enable them to experience individual freedom but also what Charles Taylor calls "the mundane elements of infrastructure

without which we could not carry on these higher activities. . . ."[43] These elements of infrastructure include just the sorts of public projects for which the power of eminent domain is typically exercised: roads, airports, utility lines, public buildings, parks, communication systems, and the like. This infrastructure is literally the foundation upon which our society, our culture, and our polity rest. It is no exaggeration to say that without this infrastructure, our society, the very society that nurtures those qualities through which we experience ourselves as free individuals capable of making choices among alternatives and defining for ourselves our wants, needs, and values, would not exist. Each of us as a member of a particular political community, then, depends upon the continued effectiveness of this infrastructure, and that dependence requires that we bear some responsibility for maintaining it. That is the purpose of and justification for expropriation.

The problem now is how to resolve this conflict of property values, that is, between Suzette Kelo, the property owner, and the city and its intended beneficiaries. The German scaling approach is useful at this point. As we previously discussed, in applying the social obligation term, the Constitutional Court scales, or grades, the social-obligation norm's limitation on property according to its relation to the individual owner. The closer the specific property interest is involved in providing security and autonomy of its holder, the greater the degree of constitutional protection the interest is given.[44] So, for example, the interest of a landlord who does not personally reside on the premises is given lesser weight than that of her tenant, whose opportunity to remain in possession is considered essential to personal security, autonomy, and self-governance values.[45] The home, the Court has said, is critical to these ends.

By contrast, the city's planned project did not directly implicate property's core values. Jobs and taxes are important to society's well-being, to be sure, but are they sufficient reasons to overcome the strong property values attached to one's home? The home is not sacrosanct. There are occasions when and reasons why it may and must be sacrificed. In terms of human flourishing, the home may and at times must be sacrificed when this is essential for creating and maintaining the requisite background conditions that are necessary for the development of those human capabilities that are constitutive of a flourishing life. The intended aims of the New London, Connecticut, project would maintain those conditions only indirectly by expanding the city's tax base and creating new jobs, which in

43. Charles Taylor, *Atomism*, *in* Charles Taylor, Philosophy and the Human Sciences: Philosophical Papers, vol. II, 205 (1985).

44. *See* van der Walt, Constitutional Property Clauses, *supra* note 36, at 135.

45. *See, e.g.*, 89 BVerfGE 1 (*Besitzrecht des Mieters*, 1993).

turn would generate more taxes. Compare a more typical example of use of the expropriation power—an expropriation for purposes of a road.

Public projects such as roads are essential components of the background material infrastructure that supports society and its culture. Here the public benefit gained from the expropriation is direct, and it is vital to enabling the capabilities that are necessary for a well-lived life. A project of this sort[46] may require that even a personal residence, a home, be sacrificed, in spite of the great importance attached to that interest's values.

In situations where there are two competing property interests each supported by strong property values, it is useful again to follow the lead of the German courts. In applying the public interest requirement the German courts have said that the requirement means that expropriation is the only possible means of meeting a particular public need. Moreover, the proportionality principle requires that expropriation must be strictly necessary to accomplish that need.[47] This less-invasive-means test might be used to resolve cases where the property interests on both sides involve strong property values, particularly values associated with the personal residence.

Sacrifice of the personal residence would then be required only when no other means of achieving the public goal is available. That will be true in cases of expropriation for public projects like roads and airports. Projects such as these are not only essential, they are site-specific, meaning that there is usually no readily available alternative location for them. This is why such projects nearly always satisfy the least-restrictive-alternative test.

Can the same be said of the development project in *Kelo*? Assuming for the sake of argument that the project was the only means by which the city could increase taxes and create more jobs, it is not clear that the project required the exercise of the expropriation power. The development area was ninety acres in size, comprised of 115 parcels.[48] The planners originally had prepared six alternative plans for the project.[49] The final development plan divided the total area into seven parcels, each having a different use purpose (residential, retail store, hotel, etc.).

Pfizer, the large pharmaceutical firm that was the driving force behind the development project, had never made any demands regarding the location of any of the particular uses within the development plan.[50] The trial court found that

46. There are other examples, of course. Airports and public utility easements are obvious ones.

47. *See* Andre van der Walt, Constitutional Property Law 499–500 (3d ed. 2011).

48. Kelo v. City of New London, 268 A.2d 500, 509 (Conn. 2004).

49. *Id.*

50. *Id.* at 539.

one of the seven parcels was not essential to the project.[51] At least one of the expert witnesses testified that the disputed expropriations were not necessary to the project's success, and some of the alternative plans would have permitted the petitioners' homes to remain undisturbed.[52] Given this evidence, there is reason to doubt that the least-restrictive-alternative test would have been met in *Kelo*. The human flourishing theory, however, would not have used the least-restrictive test to reach this result. Instead, it would have relied on the methodological predicates outlined earlier—the special claim of homeowners, given the importance of the capabilities of personal security and privacy, the idea of scaling, the evaluation of the relationship between the new use of land and the community, and the choice between incommensurate values.

This is not to say that attempted expropriations of a home would never succeed under this approach. To illustrate the human flourishing theory's analysis of the values underlying ownership of the home, suppose that the home in question is a second home, a vacation home where the owner lives only for limited periods of time each year. Under these circumstances the values associated with the primary residence are not in jeopardy to nearly the same extent as they are where the owner's sole or main abode is threatened, and so they do not weigh as strongly in the calculus of human flourishing and attendant capabilities. Depending upon the nature of the interest on the other side, it is entirely possible that the property values associated with that interest will be sufficiently important to prevail.

The public use requirement need not be the anemic doctrine that currently is in the United States. The consequentialist mode of reasoning described here, one informed by the experiences of courts of other countries, particularly the German Constitutional Court, permits a more structured and more principled application of that doctrine, one that requires the court to attend to underlying property values at stake in the disputed expropriation matter. The ultimate strength of this approach is that it promotes human flourishing, the real foundation of property.

51. *Id.* at 552–55.

52. *Id.*

8

Of Buildings, Art, and Sperm

The Right to Destroy and the Duty to Preserve

The right to destroy is one of the least discussed twigs in the proverbial bundle of rights constituting ownership. Aside from two articles, by Lior Strahilevitz, the other by Edward McCaffery,[1] and Joseph Sax's 1999 book *Playing Darts with a Rembrandt*,[2] virtually no modern legal scholarship exists on the right to destroy. Yet if we take the right in its broader sense, to include not simply the Hohfeldian privilege to destroy but also the privilege to use and its correlative duty to preserve and maintain, the right implicates some of the most contentious and difficult issues in property law and cognate areas today, including historic preservation, the right of artists to alter or even destroy their work, and the right to destroy frozen sperm, embryos, and other human tissue. This is reason enough to discuss how the right to destroy fits within a human flourishing theory of ownership.

Another reason to discuss the right to destroy is the centrality of the right's role in mapping the terrain of ownership. It defines the outer boundaries of the right

1. Lior Jacob Strahilevitz, *The Right to Destroy*, 114 Yale L.J. 781 (2005); Edward J. McCaffery, *Must We Have the Right to Waste?*, *in* New Essay in the Legal and Political Theory of Property 76 (Stephen R. Munzer ed., 2001).

2. Joseph L. Sax, Playing Darts with a Rembrandt: Public and Private Rights in Cultural Treasures (1999).

to use, marking the point at which the useful life of an asset ends. Its exercise represents a form of asset-euthanasia. Hence, it should come as no surprise that, as one distinguished scholar observed, "A discourse on this extreme property right quickly implicates some of the most interesting, fundamental, and contentious questions in property law."[3]

A third reason is that the little recent scholarship that does exist on the right to exclude has made it a topic of some controversy among property theorists. McCaffery's essay takes the position that most courts have adopted,[4] rejecting the claim that owners have the right to destroy that which they own. McCaffery regards such a right as "an embarrassment in Anglo-American law."[5] This appears to be the conventional wisdom, with the recent edition of *Black's Law Dictionary* excluding the right to destroy from the incidents of ownership included in its definition of ownership.[6]

More recently, however, Lior Strahilevitz has provided a powerful defense of the right to destroy. Strahilevitz bases his argument substantially on expressive values implicated in an owner's preference to destroy an object that is his. The focus on expressive values provides an opportunity to analyze the human capability of personal autonomy more deeply that I have done so far, for the expressive values that Strahilevitz identifies are very much part of what personal autonomy means. At the same time, Sax's book, which opposes a right to destroy with respect to works that have cultural significance, provides an opportunity to explore in greater depth the meaning and limits of the human capabilities that arguments like Sax's implicate.

In this chapter I will discuss three controversies in relation to the questions of whether owners have a right to destroy what they own and whether they have obligations to preserve their property. The settings that I will examine, albeit briefly, are historic preservation, destruction of artwork, and destruction of frozen sperm. My aim is to show how the human flourishing theory provides an illuminating framework for analyzing what is at stake in disputes over an owner's asserted right to destroy something that he owns. Hopefully, this framework will provide a more satisfying, analytically and morally, means of resolving such disputes. To set the stage for these case studies, I begin with a brief summary of Lior Strahilevitz's argument in support of the right to destroy.

3. Strahilevitz, *The Right to Destroy*, *supra* note 1, at 795.

4. *See, e.g.*, J.C. & Assocs. v. D.C. Bd. of Appeals & Review, 778 A.2d 296 (D.S. 2001); Eyerman v. Mercantile Trust Co., 524 S.W.2d 210 (Mo. Ct. App. 1975); Meksras Estate, 63 Pa. D.C.2d 371 (C.P. Phila. Co. 1974).

5. McCaffery, *Must We Have*, *supra* note 1, at 785.

6. Black's Law Dictionary 1130 (7th ed. 1999).

THE CASE FOR THE RIGHT TO DESTROY

As Professor Strahilevitz correctly observes, the right to destroy, which in past years had been widely assumed to be among the features of ownership,[7] today no longer enjoys much recognition. Under Roman law the *jus abutendi*—the right to destroy—was as important as marking the outermost boundary of an owner's rights. If an owner could destroy his own property, he could do almost anything short of that extreme action that he pleased. So also Blackstone, though hostile to wasteful destruction,[8] seemed to think that under the common law it was permissible for a property owner to burn down his own house.[9]

Things have changed. Lior Strahilevitz states that "[b]ased on a reading of recent judicial opinions, it appears that the conventional wisdom has turned against permitting a property owner to destroy valuable property."[10] An illustrative case that he discusses is *Eyerman v. Mercantile Trust Co.*[11] In that case, Louise Woodruff Johnston's will directed her executor to have the testator's house destroyed, the land sold, and the proceeds distributed to the residue of her estate. The beneficiaries of Johnston's apparently had no objection, but the neighbors did. The house was attractive, and shortly after Johnston's death, they sought to enjoin the estate from carrying out Johnston's will, arguing that razing the house would hurt their own property values.

The court held that the will provision directing destruction of Johnston's house was unenforceable on public policy grounds. The court stated, "Destruction of the house harms the neighbors, detrimentally affects the community, causes monetary loss in excess of $39,000.00 to the estate and is without benefit to the dead woman."[12] The court regarded such destruction intolerable in a "well-ordered society."[13] It saw no justification for carrying out the testator's directions: "No reason, good or bad, is suggested by the will or record for the eccentric

7. *See* Strahilevitz, *The Right to Destroy*, *supra* note 1, at 783, 787–91. Strahilevitz points out that between the sixth and seventh editions of *Black's Law Dictionary*, the editors of that well-known volume dropped the right to destroy from their listing of the rights associated with ownership.

8. *See* William Blackstone, Commentaries on the Law of England, 4 vols., IV, 220 (facsimile of 1st ed., 1979).

9. *See id.* at 221.

10. Strahilevitz, *The Right to Destroy*, *supra* note 1, at 796.

11. 524 S.W.2d 210 (Mo. Ct. App. 1975). *Eyerman* is also discussed in Adam J. Hirsch, *Bequests for Purposes: A Unified Approach*, 56 Wash. & Lee L. Rev. 33, 69–84 (1999).

12. 524 S.W.2d at 214.

13. *Id.* at 217.

condition. . . . To allow an executor to exercise such power stemming from apparent whim and caprice of the testatrix contravenes public policy."[14]

Strahilevitz suggests that *Eyerman* contains within it "many of the threads in the right-to-destroy debate."[15] It begins to open up, he further suggests, the question of institutional competence that is the core of the matter. Ordinarily, American property law leaves to the property owner decisions about how best to use her property, but there are two exceptions. The first is negative externalities: We remove the owner's right to control when the uses she desires create negative externalities. Second, we do not permit owners who lack the capacity to make rational choices to decide how her land should be used. There is a whiff of the second factor in the *Eyerman* court's discussion of the testator's will as "eccentric," but the court's main focus is on the first factor, negative externalities. This is true for most of the home-destruction cases as well.[16] Courts focus on considerations of neighborhood property value, local tax base, and harm to estate beneficiaries, all of which weigh, in the courts' view, against destruction.[17]

Strahilevitz argues that protecting the right to destroy provides both tangible and intangible benefits. The tangible benefits are that destruction can enhance social welfare in several ways, such as protecting privacy, creating open spaces, and encouraging innovation and creativity. He argues that historic preservation laws risk locking in place land uses that are economically inefficient.[18] He further argues that such laws may create incentives that are, from a social welfare perspective, perverse: "Requiring the preservation of great buildings may ensure that some beautiful and potentially influential designs never get built."[19] We will consider arguments for the right to destroy that track efficiency and social welfare lines such as these a little later.

It is the intangible benefits that Strahilevitz identifies that are particularly original. He makes a case for the right to destroy that is based on expressive values. From the American colonists' act of dumping tea into Boston Harbor to the Taliban's destruction of the Buddhas of Bamiyan, for example, acts of destruction

14. *Id.* at 214.

15. Strahilevitz, *The Right to Destroy, supra* note 1, at 797.

16. *See id.*

17. *See id.* at 798.

18. *Id.* at 853.

19. *Id.* at 820. Strahilevitz gives as an example Daniel Burnham's famous "Great White City" designed and constructed for the 1893 Chicago World's Columbian Exposition. Of course, it was well understood at the time that Burnham's model buildings, which were made out of plaster of Paris, were never intended to be permanent.

sometimes express deeply felt values, and in some cases such acts trigger First Amendment interests.[20] Moving from these obvious examples to examples of a more quotidian stripe, such as Lady Churchill's desire to destroy the portrait painted of her husband, Winston Churchill,[21] Strahilevitz contends "that expressive motivations help explain otherwise puzzling destructive acts and situates the right to destroy within First Amendment law."[22]

Elaborating on this First Amendment connection, Strahilevitz distinguishes between two readings of the First Amendment, a "collectivist" reading and an "individual-autonomy" reading.[23] A collectivist reading permits regulation of destructive acts. Strahilevitz observes that destroying a unique piece of property is akin to heckling a speaker in the sense that neither contributes to a healthy public discussion or points toward the truth.[24] The individual-autonomy view has difficulties justifying restrictions on property-destructive acts that have expressive content. So, Strahilevitz notes, from this perspective, the destruction of the Buddhas of Bamiyan is completely uncontroversial.[25] Strahilevitz finds the individual-autonomy perspective more persuasive. He concludes that "[r]ational people usually do not destroy valuable property intentionally. So where the government witnesses a rational person destroying her valuable property, it should presume that the destructive act furthers expressive objectives."[26] Strahilevitz acknowledges that this presumption is not absolute and that expressive interests must be balanced against substantial economic and social welfare interests, but from his point of view deference to the owner's desire to destroy should be the starting point.

Returning to destruction of historic buildings, as in cases like *Eyerman*, Strahilevitz considers the case for the right to destroy to be strong for both expressive and social welfare reasons. The right is not absolute, however, largely because of social welfare considerations.[27] We need to investigate these social

20. *See, e.g.*, R.A.V. v. City of St. Paul, 505 U.S. 707 (1992) (invalidating on First Amendment grounds local ordinance barring display of a burning cross "which one knows or has reasonable grounds to know arouses anger, alarm, or resentment on the basis, color, creed, religion, or gender.").

21. Strahilevitz, *The Right to Destroy*, *supra* note 1, at 826.

22. *Id.* at 823.

23. *See* Strahilevitz, *The Right to Destroy*, *supra* note 1, at 827–30.

24. *See id.* at 827.

25. *See id.* at 829.

26. *Id.* at 853.

27. *See, e.g.*, *id.* at 822.

welfare concerns in greater detail because they dominate the debate over historic preservation. What I want to suggest is that social welfare, although clearly relevant and important to evaluating petitions to preserve buildings claimed to have significant historic value, does not capture all of the relevant values at stake. Strahilevitz, as we have seen, has pointed out another important value involved, namely, the expressive content of assertions of the right to destroy some artifact. But even that value does not exhaust what is really involved in such disputes. Social welfare, expressive interests, and other values are all aspects of human flourishing, the real foundation of such claims. The following section discusses the connection between historic preservation and human flourishing in further detail. This discussion will help set the stage for our later discussion of other aspects of the right to destroy.

HISTORIC PRESERVATION AND HUMAN FLOURISHING

Historic preservation is a contentious topic, and it nicely frames the right-to-destroy problem. Opponents of historic preservation sometimes appeal directly to the need for what they perceive as creative destruction and, with it, the owner's right to destroy. A notable example is Edward Glaeser's 2011 book *Triumph of the City*.[28] Glaeser argues that dense collections of creative people stimulate breakthrough innovations in various endeavors, particularly in advanced economies based on information technology.[29] He expresses concern that such creative possibilities are lost or minimized by land use regulations. His basic argument is that historic preservation protects too many buildings and gives too much power to neighbors to prevent vertical development, the construction of which could provide more affordable housing.[30]

In a coauthored paper, Glaeser refined his views following an empirical study of the economic impact of New York City's historic preservation districts.[31] The study found that construction activity fell in historic districts following designation. Moreover, properties just outside the boundaries of such districts increased in value after designation. This apparently was due to the positive spillover effects of historic designation. The authors further found that designation raised

28. Edward Glaeser, Triumph of the City: How Our Greatest Invention Makes Us Richer, Smarter, Greener, Healthier, and Happier (2011).

29. *Id.* at 47–49.

30. *Id.* at 260–64.

31. Vicki Been, Ingrid Gould, Michael Gedal, Edward Glaeser, & Brian McCabe, *Preserving History or Restricting Development? The Heterogeneous Effects of Historic Districts on Local Housing Markets in New York City*, 92 J. Urb. Econ. 16 (2016).

property values within historic districts, but only in the lower-valued boroughs outside of Manhattan. The broader effects of designation on property values were increases occurring only in districts where the foregone option to redevelop was relatively low. The impacts were also more positive in districts that were more aesthetically appealing.[32]

These data importantly tell us that the effects of historic districting in densely populated urban areas such as New York City are, precisely as the study's subtitle indicates, heterogeneous and that broad generalization are impossible. This means that were we to adopt a welfarist perspective on historic preservation, we would not be warranted in making any assertions about the welfare effects of historic districting in urban areas except about specific housing markets given specific housing conditions. This hesitancy also seems warranted by the conclusions of earlier research and surveys of the economic effects of preservation. One survey concludes, for example, that the field is not thoroughly studied, "nor is there much agreement on answers to basic pragmatic and policy questions."[33] Welfarism, it seems, sheds some but not enough light on historic preservation.

We are able to see why social welfare alone does not entirely illuminate the values that inhere demands to preserve certain buildings as special in ways that affect the integrity and health of their culture and the contrary assertions those who view such preservation as inhibiting innovation and creativity within the same culture. The nature of these claims is such that their animus extends beyond social welfare, at least if we define that term in strictly economic or market terms. One obvious good that proponents commonly associate with historic preservation is historical memory. Buildings such as the Fraunces Tavern in lower Manhattan and Monticello are tangible reminders to members of our political community of what our history has been and where. They express (drawing here on Strahilevitz's expressive values theme) certain fundamental values that underlie our political community. Peter Byrne tells us that "[h]istoric districts . . . offer a narrative connection with the past."[34] Such buildings, he suggests, convey meaning about the past and "exemplify or embody a historical narrative that people in the present value."

Critics have challenged this historical justification for preservation of historically significant structures and places. Again, Lior Strahilevitz has taken the

32. *Id.* at 17.

33. Randall Mason, *Economics and Historic Preservation: A Guide and Review of the Literature*, Brookings Institution, 1, *available at* https://www.brookings.edu/wp-content/uploads/2016/06/20050926_preservation.pdf.

34. J. Peter Byrne, *Historic Preservation and Its Cultured Despisers: Reflections on the Contemporary Role of Preservation Law in Urban Development*, 19 Geo. Mason L. Rev. (2012).

lead.[35] He argues that the value of authentic history over fake history is only marginal. He points to the so-called "River of Blood" monument located at the Trump National Golf Club as an example of fake history. The monument states that during the Civil War a battle occurred on that spot, and that "[m]any great American soldiers, both of the North and South, died and [that] spot. . . . The casualties were so great that the river would turn red and thus became known as 'The River of Blood.'"[36] The problem with the monument is that its claim is completely bogus. The nearest battle during the war occurred some eleven miles away, and the River of Blood story was contrived.[37] Strahilevitz uses this example to ask whether authentic history is superior, or adds anything to such fake history, and his answer is "not by much."[38] As he states, "When society presents authentic historic facts to present generations, especially in a manner tied to historic markers in physical space, it often does so in a manner that is so selective, so simplified, or so beholden to contemporary preferences that its value over contrived history appears to be marginal." The upshot, the cash value, if you will, of this claim is that, for Strahilevitz, it is questionable whether, as is now generally accepted, there is a strong state interest to compel the preservation of historic property.[39]

There are several points to make about this line of questioning of the benefits of historic preservation. The first concerns the value comparison between authentic and fake history. This is a false comparison, and at best, unhelpful. Whether the preservation of authentic historic structures is worth the candle is one matter that we can surely debate, but it adds little to the discussion to draw a comparison between such history and contrived history and ask whether one is superior to the other and, if so, by how much. There may be a false trade-off here because some examples of fake history may play a legitimate and valuable role in reminding a society and a polity of important moments in its past. The fact that they do so, if indeed they do, does not necessary mean, however, that structures or places associated with fake history merit preservation should the owner later wish to change or destroy the site. Authenticity matters to historic preservation, but it is hardly the only important criterion in the preservation calculus.

The more fundamental reason why the comparison is unhelpful is that it really does not address the underlying objections that critics like Strahilevitz have

35. *See* Lior Jacob Strahilevitz, *Historic Preservation and Its Even Less Authentic Alternative* (unpub. ms. Sept. 2016).

36. *Id.*

37. *Id.*

38. *Id.*

39. *Id.*

against historic preservation. One of those objections is a claim of arbitrariness about the selection of what gets preserved. The arbitrariness of the historic preservation process results from several factors. One factor is the subjectivity of societal judgments that are the basis of political choices between what gets preserved and what gets destroyed.[40] Strahilevitz states the argument this way: "To preservationists, soaring and expensive structures that are used and beloved by elites ought to be preserved, even if they become economically obsolete in their present form. But modest structures in overwhelmingly minority neighborhoods ought to be bulldozed in the name of progress."[41] Working here is a concern that the choices between what gets preserved and what doesn't both reflect and deeply implicate issues of class, race, and ethnicity. Historic preservation decisions are made through a political process, and political choices are often skewed in favored of the wealthy and privileged members of the community. Another factor contributing to arbitrariness, closely related, is that what gets selected for preservation reflects only contemporary preferences rather than timeless and objective considerations.[42] Those preferences then bind later generations the members of which may have very different preferences. The irreducibly subjective nature of the endeavor means that the value of preserved structures will inevitably vary both from group to group and from generation to generation.

There is, in the view of such critics, simply no stability in the matter. Strahilevitz raises another concern that needs to be taken very seriously. He worries about the exclusionary effects of historic preservation, especially among minority communities. There is surely something to this concern. Strahilevitz refers to a study by Professor Stephen Clowney of Lexington, Kentucky. Clowney's study shows how municipal and powerful private participants in that city created monuments and public parks that glorified historic white figures and ignored the role played by prominent African Americans.[43] It is the broader claims about the causal relation between historic preservation and racial exclusion that are questionable. Strahilevitz compares historic preservation with fake history projects such as The Villages, a retirement and nearly all-white residential community in Florida,[44] and argues that historic preservation, no less than the fake history perpetrated in places like The Villages, has racially exclusionary effects: "Both

40. *Id.* at 18.

41. *Id.*

42. *Id.* at 2.

43. *See* Stephen Clowney, *Landscape Fairness: Removing Discrimination from the Built Environment*, 2013 Utah L. Rev. 1.

44. *See* Strahilevitz, *Historic Preservation*, *supra* note 35, at 2–9.

historic preservation and the kind of uniformly scripted narrative on display in The Villages aim for an aesthetic homogeneity that may engender demographic homogeneity by design. When the buildings all look alike the people living in those buildings tend to look alike too."[45] Is this true? Is it the case that the racial and ethnic composition of architecturally homogenous or similar neighborhoods are or tend to be uniform? I have no data one way or the other on this question, but one can surely think of anecdotal evidence to the contrary. Queens, New York, for example, is one of the most racially and ethnically diverse regions on Earth, but there are neighborhoods in Queens, as there are throughout New York City, in which the residential structures are highly homogenous. Yet, Strahilevitz and others are right to be concerned about the gentrification effects that can and sometimes do result from preservation, especially after designation of wholesale historic zones. Gentrification has often had deeply troubling exclusionary consequences, and preservation policymakers need to be highly sensitive to the possibility of such effects.

More generally, it surely is the case that there are flaws in the preservation process. There is perhaps an excessive amount of preservation of structures in our cities, although it is hard to know objectively what is the optimal amount. And doubtless some preservation decisions are the result of well-funded and well-organized groups acting out of self-interest rather than in the public interest. But I reject the notion that there is simply no neutral or objective basis for judgments about historic or aesthetic choices. The New York City Landmark Preservation Commission had ample objective grounds for landmarking Grand Central Terminal, and it was, objectively speaking, a travesty that the original Penn Central Station was torn down in the interest of a small and unrepresentative group of powerbrokers.

We have still to consider historic preservation from the perspective of human flourishing. More specifically, what obligations, if any, to preserve historic or otherwise culturally significant structures do private owners of such places owe to members of their communities, given that the basis of such obligations is to contribute, in ways appropriate to the owners, to the flourishing of such community members' lives and to their own?

An initial, and very important, point to make in approaching these questions is one to which I alluded in Chapter Two,[46] that each of us owes an obligation to our communities to support the institutions, associations, and infrastructure that in turn support the special sort of culture in which we live, the type of culture within which each person is able to experience life-defining freedom and to create their

45. *Id.* at 20.

46. *See* pp. 52–53, 56–57 *supra*.

own personal identities. This is part of the obligation to support the social networks and structures that enable us to develop those human capabilities that make human flourishing possible. Some practical applications of this obligation are easy to identify. They are obligations that we usually associate with citizenship, for example, payment of taxes used to build roads, bridges, airports, and other common aspects of public infrastructure. Other obligations are ones that we do directly tie with property ownership. An obvious example is local property taxes, which pay for public education.

At this point it is considering an objection that economists commonly make: Taxes are one thing, they say; restrictions on private ownership are another. Economists argue that as mechanisms for redistributing wealth, taxes are much more efficient than private law rules.[47] For the time being, I will remain agnostic on the merits of the objection itself, that is, the relative efficiency of taxation versus private law as a means of effecting wealth redistribution, for wealth redistribution is not what is at stake here. What is at stake is the scope of ownership—the parameters, if you will, of the concept of private ownership itself. Private law recognizes certain limits on the range of actions that owners are free to undertake with respect to their assets. The law of nuisance is the obvious example of this. These limits are not externally imposed by the state or other actors.

Rather, as I argued in Chapter Two, they are internal to the very concept of ownership. What private law does is to recognize and clarify these limits. It does so with greater or lesser precision, depending upon a variety of factors, including the character of the owner's use, the effects of the owner's use on his community and the character and extent of those effects, and so on. The limitations to freedom to use, possess, and transfer privately owned assets that private law defines are not, at their core, redistributive rules, although they may have distributive consequences. They are, rather, boundary-defining norms, sculpting norms, if you will, that is, norms that sculpt the contours of private ownership itself. Courts tease these contours out of the concept of ownership itself through a process of giving that concept the best interpretation they can based on past understandings of ownership, both judicial and lay, and their understandings of the value foundations of private ownership. This is why it is wrong to suppose that when courts announce restrictions on what an owner may do with her property, they engage in a process of importing certain external norms, which they then use as the basis for imposing restrictions on how owners use their property.

Returning to our obligation to support the institutions, associations, and infrastructure that in turn support the special sort of capability-nurturing culture in which we live, what does this mean for the owners of historic or architecturally

47. *See, e.g.*, Louis Kaplow & Steven Shavell, Fairness versus Welfare (2002).

significant buildings? To begin with, let us assume for the time being that we can agree that some privately owned building or structure is authentically historic or architecturally significant. In real preservation disputes, there sometimes are legitimate questions about whether this is the case, so let us just put that matter aside for the moment. Does the owner's obligation to support his community's infrastructure entail an obligation to preserve that structure or building, recalling that the reason for and extent of the obligation to support the community's infrastructure is just the fact that at least some elements of a community's infrastructure are necessary to maintain the sort of capability-nurturing culture in which the owner lives?

The answer to that question depends in substantial part on whether we consider historic or architecturally significant buildings necessary to preserve the kind of culture that I have been describing, that is, one that facilitates the development of the capabilities necessary for human flourishing. Stated more directly, what are the purposes of historic preservation after all? In an especially valuable article, Carol Rose grouped the public functions of historic preservation into three broad categories: inspiration, aesthetics, and community-building.[48] Of these, Rose persuasively argued, "the chief function . . . is to strengthen local community ties and community organization."[49] Rose refers to this function as community-building, but it is just as much a matter of community *identity*. The claim is that certain physical structures can directly affect a community's understanding of its own identity.

Identity here has both a cultural and a political dimension. The connection between political identity and physical structures is easy to see if we consider famous monuments such as the Lincoln Memorial in Washington, D.C., or buildings such as Independence Hall, in Philadelphia. It is also evident, however, in privately owned structures such as Ebenezer Baptist Church in Atlanta. It is no accident that repeatedly throughout history, repressive regimes have sought to erase the historical memories of past political practices that nurtured the capabilities necessary for robust free citizenship.[50] Not infrequently, part of the regime's effort at erasure has involved destruction of architectural landmarks. Hitler planned to transform Berlin, to pick only one extreme example, through a massive project involving tearing down traditional buildings associated with the Hohenzollern dynasty, which he despised, and erecting new buildings and

48. Carol M. Rose, *Preservation and Community: New Directions in the Law of Historic Preservation*, 33 STAN. L. REV. 473, 479–80 (1981).

49. *Id.* at 479.

50. Gregory S. Alexander, *The Social-Obligation Norm in American Property Law*, 94 CORNELL L. REV. 745, 795 (2009).

monuments designed by his favorite architect, Albert Speer, all of which reflected Nazi ideology. He planned to rename this newly Nazified city "Germania."[51] Rose points out that "the Parisian architects of the French Revolution understood very well that the logic of revolution meant the destruction of the cathedrals, those sirens of a loathed ecclesiasticism."[52] As Rose states, "visual surroundings work a political effect on our consciousness."[53]

The connections among structure, capabilities, and culture are strong as well. When we speak of building and maintaining a community's identity, a large part of what we have in mind is its culture. In Chapter Three, I discussed the various sorts of communities that are relevant for purposes of considering the essential capabilities that property owners require to lead fulfilling lives. Each of those various sorts of communities, despite their differences, have their distinctive cultures that form a major part of their identities. From neighborhoods to national communities, we can and do glean distinctive cultural characteristics of and differences between various geographic communities. Physical structures are very much a part of what constitutes these distinctive community cultures. Buildings are part of what defines the sense and feel of a place, whether we are talking about a street, a city, or a nation. For New Yorkers, the Upper West Side of Manhattan "feels" different from Queens. Paris "feels" different from Los Angeles. The architectures of these places are very different from each other and so are their respective cultures. Residents often come to identify with these places, and the architecture enables such self-identification. Place, including its structures, contributes to a person's sense of self. Even in a highly mobile society, it means something to a person that she lives in Tulsa, Oklahoma, rather than Boston, and it means something to her that she lives in this neighborhood rather than that. Architecture plays an important role in creating this sense of meaning.

Architecture—structures—contributes to the development of our essential capabilities in another way. In Chapter One, I argued, following Charles Taylor's lead,[54] that we can develop as free and autonomous individuals only within cultures of a certain kind. Those cultures include communities of a certain kind, the very communities upon which we are dependent for the development of our essential capabilities. Particular places and particular buildings sometimes

51. *See* Volker Ullrich, Hitler: Ascent 1889–1939, at 601–07, 690 (2016). *See generally* Robert R. Taylor, The World in Stone: The Role of Architecture in National Socialist Ideology (1974).

52. Rose, *Historic Preservation, supra* note, at 485.

53. *Id.* at 483.

54. *See* Charles Taylor, *Atomism, in* Philosophical Papers: Philosophy and the Human Sciences, vol. 2, at 207 (1985).

embody the life of such communities and are essential to its continuing ability to thrive. Such buildings are part and parcel of the cultural life of these thriving liberal communities such that the ability of these communities to enable capabilities development quite literally requires the preservation of those buildings. What, for example, would Atlanta's Sweet Auburn neighborhood be like if Ebenezer Baptist Church were destroyed and replaced by a Hilton Garden Inn? It is hard to imagine that it would remain the same rich, vibrant community.

Historic preservation exists as a matter of a community's knowledge and understanding about its own self-identity.

What should be said on the owner's behalf? What capability-related considerations might one recognize in support of an owner's right to destroy her privately owned structure, however historically or architecturally significant that structure may be? Expectations are often said to loom large here. Private owners argue that it is unfair to deny their right to destroy or to redesign a building that was not landmarked at the time they purchased it. This is an important point, one that should be taken seriously, including under a human flourishing theory. Expectations certainly figure in the evaluation of capabilities and flourishing. Security, a capability without which an individual cannot hope to live as full and rich a life as possible for her, depends to a considerable extent on the protection that expectations receive at least to some extent.

The real questions, of course, are not whether expectations are relevant, for they clearly are as a general matter, but when, under what circumstances, and how much. Private law does not protect every subjective expectation that an individual has, nor should it. To pick one example, imagine that I am the sole child of my widowed and very wealthy mother. I may expect that upon her death I will inherit her estate, either through her will or under intestate succession. Children often have such expectations, but sometimes those expectations are dashed when the parent dies with a valid will that leaves the entire estate to a charity. This is perfectly legal, however disappointing and perhaps unfair to the child. Our legal system confers a wide degree of freedom of testamentary disposition to parents, and as a matter of policy, the law does not protect the subjective expectations of expectant heirs.

The law of takings is much concerned with protection of expectations of a certain level, and there is a rich literature on just what that level should be.[55] The seminal case on protecting owner expectations under the Fifth Amendment

55. *See, e.g.*, Frank I. Michelman, *Property, Utility, and Fairness: Comments on the Ethical Foundations of "Just Compensation" Law*, 80 Harv. L. Rev. 1165 (1967); Louis Kaplow, *An Economic Analysis of Legal Transitions*, 99 Harv. L. Rev. 509 (1986); Holly Doremus, *Takings and Transitions*, 19 J. Land Use & Envtl. L. 1 (2003); Kyle D. Logue, *Legal Transitions, Rational Expectations, and Legal Progress*, 13 J. Contemp. Legal Issues 211 (2003).

takings clause is, of course, the famous *Penn Central* case.[56] In that case the New York City Landmark Commission had previously designated Grand Central Terminal, which Penn Central then owned, as a historic landmark because of the building's incomparable nineteenth-century beaux arts façade. Penn Central wanted to erect a multistory commercial structure atop Grand Central and submitted two proposed plans to the Commission, both of which it rejected. In the Commission's view, both proposed structures would have done serious damage to unique aspects of Grand Central. The owner then went to court, claiming that the Commission's denial of its plans to develop the airspace above Grand Central Terminal amounted to an unconstitutional taking of property.[57]

The Court upheld the Commission's actions. It announced a three-prong test for determining when regulatory actions "go too far."[58] Whether a governmental action that formally is a regulation is de facto a taking depends on (1) the character of the government action (was the government intrusion of the owner's property direct or indirect?); (2) the extent to which the regulation interferes with what the Court called "distinct investment-backed expectations";[59] and (3) the resulting diminution in the value of the owner's property. The combined effect of these three factors is a focus on the owner's expectations, specifically, whether and to what extent the regulation has interfered with the owner's settled and reasonable expectations. Takings law appears to protect owner expectations only to the extent that those expectations are both investment-backed and reasonable.[60]

What would this mean in the context of an owner's asserted right to destroy a structure that is historically significant or architecturally unique? In *Penn Central* itself, it meant that Penn Central's expectations were not investment-backed because it had not invested any money in the development project.[61] The Court's subsequent use of this factor has been somewhat unclear, but some considerations have emerged as highly relevant to the calculus. One such consideration is whether the governmental regulation affects one or many strands in the proverbial bundle of rights that constitutes private ownership. If it adversely affects a reasonable investment-backed expectation as to only one strand, no taking will

56. Penn Central Transportation Co. v. New York City, 438 U.S. 104 (1978).

57. *Id.* at 115–19.

58. Pennsylvania Coal Co. v. Mahon, 260 U.S. 393 (1922).

59. 438 U.S. at 124.

60. *See* Kaiser Aetna v. United States, 444 U.S. 164, 175 (1979).

61. *See* 438 U.S. at 130.

be found.[62] That was precisely the case in *Penn Central*. The owner was still able to earn a reasonable return on its investment. Moreover, the designation of the Terminal as a historic landmark may have made it an even bigger tourist draw, generating more revenue for Penn Central. Given all of these circumstances, it is hard to see any essential capabilities that were jeopardized by the agency's denial of the owner's asserted right.

Take a very different case, however. Suppose a historic preservation agency has preserved a privately owned nineteenth-century mansion that is both historically and architecturally significant but in a state of great disrepair. The mansion has been vacant for a number of years, and the owner had planned to demolish it in order to build a new apartment complex on the same site. A local preservation agency, having determined that the mansion is historically and architecturally significant, ruled it must be preserved. The owner has established that the preservation cost greatly exceeds the market value of the mansion and that he cannot afford the cost of maintaining the mansion. The building has, literally, negative value.[63] This case surely pushes a good thing too far. Historic preservation cannot justify depriving an owner of the ability to develop or maintain basic human capability needs, including economic security in a literal sense. In my hypothetical, and the case on which it was based,[64] preservation at the owner's expense risked driving the owner into bankruptcy.

An important point needs to be made here concerning the identity of the owner. The reality is that in many preservation disputes the buildings in question have corporate rather than individual ownership. Corporate ownership makes the human flourishing calculus more complicated, but it is does not render considerations of human flourishing irrelevant.

Corporations are constituted by and of individuals, and for many shareholders how well their lives go depends in no small part on the well-being of the firms in

62. *See* Keystone Bituminous Coal Ass'n v. DeBenedictis, 480 U.S. 470 (1987); Robert M. Washburn, *"Reasonable Investment-Backed Expectations" as a Factor in Defining Property Interest*, 49 Wash. U.J. Urb. & Contemp. L. 63, 68 (1996).

63. These facts are based on a famous case from the German Federal Constitutional Court. In the Rheinland-Palatinate Monument Protection case, 100 BVerfGE 226 (1999), the German Court held that the state either had to allow the owner to destroy the mansion and develop the site or to expropriate it. The local monument protection statute, which required the owner to maintain the building at his own expense in the public interest, without taking into account the owner's interest, was, under the circumstances, in violation of the German constitutional commitment to property under the Basic Law.

64. *Id.* A somewhat similar situation occurred in *People ex rel. Marbro Corp. v. Ramsey* (171 N.E.2d 246 Ill. App. 1960). The court there granted an owner a demolition permit where the costs of repairing and maintaining a historically significant building were high and the owner would still have lost money even if the building had been renovated at the public's expense. *Id.* at 247–48.

which they are invested. It would be a great mistake to ignore the capability considerations of firms simply because of their corporate identity.

The case that I posed in which preservation would seriously jeopardize important capability interests of the owner illustrates the basic point that here, as elsewhere, the owner's well-being and capability needs, no less than those of members of his various communities count.[65] Joseph Sax struck a similar note in summary fashion: "If [private] ownership alone is not self-evidently decisive [as he had argued it should not be], neither is it obviously irrelevant."[66] The human flourishing account is not one-sided. Far to the contrary, it takes into consideration the capability needs of owners, as members of various communities, as well as the needs of other community members. It does consider, however, that owners of historically significant buildings may have obligations that extend beyond those of someone who owns one of the hundreds of nearly identical 7-Elevens that are spread across the nation.

Collectively, these obligations constitute what Chief Justice Rehnquist in his dissenting opinion in *Penn Central* called "an affirmative duty to preserve."[67] Chief Justice Rehnquist regarded this duty as something that was new and unprecedented, but it was nothing of the kind. To be sure, affirmative obligations of ownership are not common, but they do exist. Tenants may owe affirmative duties to landlords to avoid waste. Cities require property owners to shovel sidewalks in front of their buildings and in some cases shovel abutting sidewalks as well.[68] From this perspective, the affirmative duty to preserve is not unprecedented.

The final point to be made here about historic preservation is that the abstract duty to preserve is one matter, but the application of that duty is something quite different. One suspects that much of the objection to historic preservation concerns the latter rather than the former.

There may be too much of a good thing here. What is historic or architecturally significant are contentious questions about which reasonable differences can exist. Given that fact and given the fact that a decision to landmark a building may result in substantial costs for an owner, it is especially important that the process

65. One of the strangest aspects of the Monument Protection Act, challenged in the decision of the German Constitutional Court, was that it specifically provided that the owner's interests do not matter and that only the public interest was to be taken into account. As the Constitutional Court recognized, such an approach to historic preservation simply cannot be reconciled with a constitutional property regime that purports to protect private property rights.

66. Sax, Playing Darts, *supra* note 2, at 52.

67. 438 U.S. at 140, 141, 146.

68. *See* Larissa Katz, *Governing Through Owners: How and Why Formal Private Property Rights Enhance State Power*, 160 U. Pa. L. Rev. 2029 (2012).

for making preservation decisions be highly democratic and that the decision makers be judicious when deciding which structures to landmark. Not every old building is worth preserving simply by dint of its age. The operative term is "significant," and the meaning of that term turns on the sorts of considerations that I explored previously, including the relationship between the structure and the community's self-identity, its cultural life, and its political memory. What does the community's future flourishing require? To what extent does the building in question contribute to the capabilities that are necessary for the community to flourish? Would a decision to preserve the building sacrifice any of the owner's essential capabilities such that his own opportunity to lead an objectively well-lived life would be serious jeopardized? These are the sorts of questions that a serious investigation into significance requires.

DESTRUCTION OF ART

Some of the most notorious controversies implicating the right to destroy have involved art. One example is the Rockefeller family decision to destroy a mural that Diego Rivera had painted for them after Rivera had refused to remove Lenin's image from the painting.[69] Another is the story of Lady Churchill's destruction of an unflattering portrait of her late husband, Sir Winston Churchill, which Parliament had commissioned and Britain's most distinguished portraitist, Graham Sutherland, had painted.[70] Art owners may wish to destroy their art for any number of reasons. The Rockefellers objected to the political message which they attached to the Rivera mural, while Lady Churchill simply thought the painting of Sir Winston downright ugly and unflattering. Are there good reasons to restrict the rights of owners such as these or others from destroying art which they own? What I wish to show here is how the human flourishing account may help elucidate the stakes involved in the decision whether to permit or restrict the art owner's right to destroy.

As cases like the Diego Rivera mural and the Churchill portrait illustrate, destruction of art in various contexts raise different considerations. Sax once observed that "the central history of art destruction is a history of iconoclasm."[71] Iconoclasm was involved in both the Diego Rivera and Churchill disputes, but with iconoclasts in different roles. In the Diego Rivera mural matter the iconoclast was Nelson Rockefeller, the patron whose family commissioned the very work they wished to destroy. Their motive was not caprice or whimsy. This was

69. *See* Sax, Playing Darts with a Rembrandt, *supra* note 2, at 13–16.

70. *See id.* at 37–42.

71. *Id.* at 16.

a clear example of what Lior Strahilevitz calls expressive values[72] motivating destruction. The Rockefellers, lifelong Republicans, were concerned that they might be associated with the political message implicit in Diego Rivera's mural, complete with its nod to V.I. Lenin. By contrast, the iconoclast Lady Churchill had no such political motive. Her objection was purely personal and aesthetic.

Here there was no risk of the patron being tainted by some odious political message of the artist. The objection was just that Lady Churchill wanted to eliminate all traces of her late husband's unflattering (in her view) portrait, rather like a person today does with an unflattering selfie on their cell phone.

The Rockefellers were accused of being "cultural vandals,"[73] but were they? Sax argued that they were only insofar as the community has concluded that its interest in preserving the work of a great artist is more important than its concern with promoting the patron's political agenda.[74] Sax traced that conclusion back to the reaction against the excesses of the French Revolution, when iconoclasts proposed destroying, as unrevolutionary, all Latin inscriptions on public monuments. In response, Abbé Henri Grégoire premised his argument that the monuments of the ancient régime should not be destroyed on the ability to see art of the work of genius over time. Sax points out that this was a thoroughly modern and secular idea, conceiving great works of art over time "as a fundamental element of the community's human capital, and as part of its collective entitlement."[75] Sax summarized his thesis this way: "Art remains long after its (unwanted) message, or the owner's political . . . sensibilities, have been relegated to history's attic. That is the essence of the case against a patron's claimed entitlement to destroy."[76]

However compelling Sax's thesis appears to be—and on its face, it does seem compelling—there is more to it than that. Let us return to the Churchill portrait. Is Sax's argument so compelling in that case? Unless we are going to see political messages in every work of art, it is hard to see how Sax's thesis has much relevance to Lady Churchill's reasons for wishing to destroy her late husband's portrait. The existence of a political or other message in which the public has a legitimate interest (aside from sheer gossip) is one factor that qualifies the force of Sax's thesis. Another is time. Sax emphasized that the genius of the art may be revealed through history rather than immediately. True enough, but that creates a quandary. How are we to know which works by which artists history will reveal

72. *See* Strahilevitz, *The Right to Destroy*, *supra* note 1, at 824.

73. *See* Sax, Playing Darts with a Rembrandt, *supra* note 2, at 13.

74. *See id.* at 17–18.

75. *Id.* at 18.

76. *Id.* at 20.

as the works of genius? As it happens, I am an amateur painter. Suppose I paint a darkly abstract painting that I name "Tweet of Trump." I give this work to one of my colleagues as a birthday gift. My colleague, not recognizing the painting as the work of genius it is, wishes to just take it to the city garbage dump without my knowing. Should my colleague be free to do so, or should he be prohibited from destroying the painting because in the fullness of time the work may come to be seen as a masterpiece? If he is not free to destroy the work, then in effect no owner of any work of art is free to destroy it. Are there compelling reasons for adopting such an extreme position?

Viewing the matter through the lens of human flourishing considerations helps clarify what is at stake. Sax spoke of "the community's human capital," but we can translate that into human capability terms. Much of what was said earlier in connection with historic preservation applies to art. I said earlier that each of us owes an obligation to our communities to support the institutions, associations, and infrastructure that in turn support the special sort of culture in which we live, the type of culture within which each person is able to experience life-defining freedom and to create their own personal identities. I also said that the obligation to support this culture enables the development, both for members of our communities and for ourselves, of those human capabilities that make human flourishing possible. The obligation to preserve historically significant buildings was one instance of this broader obligation. The obligation not to destroy art is another. Great art contributes to a rich and robust liberal cultural life, the very kind of cultural life that is a necessary background condition for a well-lived life, one of self-definition and participation in a humane social environment.

But the obligation regarding art must be nuanced and carefully limited to circumstances where necessary capabilities are genuinely at stake. Decisions about what those circumstances are will, of course, be contestable and require identifying relevant differences to discern whose capabilities are at stake and to what extent. The Rockefeller/Rivera and Churchill cases, for example, are different in respects that bear upon the capabilities involved. The most apparent factual difference is the publicness of Diego Rivera's mural compared with a very private and personal portrait of Sir Winston. That difference bears directly upon the relative contributions of the two works to the cultural life of the two communities most intimately affected. Rivera's mural was to be publicly displayed in the RCA building, as it was then called, in Rockefeller Center in New York City. Public art has become an important source of enrichment of the cultural fund of communities throughout the United States over the past few decades. Works ranging from the Chicago Picasso to wall art have added greatly to our public cultural endowment. Not only items of aesthetic appreciation, they are also icons of community self-identity and even location.

Public art has also become, not surprisingly, the locus of great contention. A situation that has become familiar in cities throughout the country is that a city or a firm commissions an artist to provide an artwork, commonly a sculpture, for a particular public space, but upon its unveiling, the public reaction is loud and negative. The public demands its removal.[77] Here the tables are turned from the Rockefeller/Rivera controversy and from what they typically are when the right to destroy is asserted. The public, not the artist or the patron, is the party demanding destruction or removal (in the artist's view, relocation *is* destruction[78]). Should a work of art be foisted on an unwilling public? A plausible argument can be made for an affirmative answer.

There have been cases in which the public's initial hostility has over time turned around and developed into acceptance and even affection for a work of public art. The Chicago Picasso is only one example.[79] The change in public perception can be understood in terms of Sax's point about the role of time in the eventual perception of pieces of art as the works of genius. But time does not always work this magic; sometimes the public continues to detest a work of public art no matter how much time has passed since its first appearance. Are there compelling capability-related reasons favoring the artist's or the patron's right to compel the piece's indefinite public display? Other than an abstract autonomy right, no capabilities, at least none that are essential to human flourishing, of the patron appear to be at stake here. The artist perhaps has greater flourishing-related concerns that are worthy of attention, notably her reputation. If the piece is removed in response to a strongly negative public reaction, the artist may worry that removal will seriously jeopardize her reputation as a successful artist both within the artistic community and the broader community. That seems to be a legitimate concern, but it misses the mark. Whether or not the piece is removed, the damage to reputation has already occurred, so that removal will have only marginal effect. The only possible response that the artist may make is that if the public reaction does change over time, á la the Chicago Picasso, the artist's reputation will be restored. So the calculus of capabilities is fraught with uncertainty as to both the artist and the public. Perhaps in the face of this uncertainty, which results from the effect of time, one prudent solution might be to leave the work in place for a

77. *See generally* Erika Doss, Spirit Poles and Flying Pigs: Public Art and Cultural Democracy in American Communities (1995).

78. *See* Sax, Playing Darts with a Rembrandt, *supra* note 2, at 27.

79. *See id.* at 31–32. I am a native Chicagoan, and I remember well the public response when the Picasso sculpture first appeared on the plaza in front of City Hall (now called Daley Plaza). The overwhelming reaction was negative and derisive and strongly so. Today, Chicagoans not only accept the piece but are proud of it. They consider it an important part of what constitutes their city's identity.

set period of time, at the end of which the relevant public body might hold a public hearing to decide whether or not the piece should remain or be removed. That would allow for a possible change of public perception without permanently foisting a work of public art on an unwilling public.[80]

What, then, about Lady Churchill's right to destroy the portrait of her late husband? Is there a significant public stake involved? Stated differently, does the community—here most immediately, the British public—have any essential capabilities at stake in the preservation or destruction of Sir Winston's portrait? Sax argued that the public did have an important interest at stake.[81] In his view, destruction diminishes the public record of an important historic figure: "Posterity is denied an opportunity to see one version of a leading figure on the world stage as he really was, or at least as he was seen by a major portrait painter."[82] He further analogized destruction of such a portrait to suppression of an unfavorable biography.[83]

Art, like writing, expresses ideas. The question is at what point have those ideas become available to relevant public communities such that the removal of those ideas or denial of their availability to the community weakens the community's essential public culture. The legal definition of publication for copyright purposes is helpful here because it illuminates what it means to make the expression of ideas available to communities. In the context of copyright law, publication is defined as the distribution of copies of a work (or offering to do so) to the public by sale, lease, rental, or lending. Notably, a display of a work does not constitute publication.

Suppose I write an unfavorable biography of Donald Trump, offer it for publication to Farrar Strauss & Giroux, and they accept. However, before the book's appearance on the market, Trump's lawyers go to court, seeking to suppress publication, arguing that it contains "fake news." If Trump succeeds, serious damage has been inflicted upon the national community's public culture, and the vital capability of its citizens to decide for themselves whether what the book contains is credible or fake, a capability that is a political manifestation of the more basic

80. This, in fact, was the solution that the city of Carlsbad, California, used to resolve a controversy involving a large work of public art by New York artist Andrea Blum. *See* SAX, PLAYING DARTS WITH A REMBRANDT, *supra* note 2, at 29–30. The city kept Blum's sculpture in place for a period of seventy-eight months, at the end of which the city held a public hearing. Carlsbad voters voted overwhelmingly in favor of complete removal, and that is just what the city did.

81. *See id.* at 36–42.

82. *Id.* at 35.

83. *Id.*

capability of self-definition, has been seriously undermined. This is precisely why such efforts at suppression rarely, if ever, succeed.

Compare that with the case of the Churchill portrait. One can certainly imagine a situation involving a work of art that is comparable to my Trump biography, but the Churchill portrait is not that case. The portraitist, Graham Sutherland, did not publish or offer to publish the portrait. Parliament commissioned Sutherland to paint it as a gift to Churchill on his eightieth birthday. There was a presentation ceremony at Westminster Hall, but in copyright terms that was not a publication, that is, did not constitute making the portrait as an expression of ideas available to the public. An expression of ideas though it may have been, nevertheless, it was never intended to be made available to the public. True, it might have become available to the public years later when both Sir Winston and Lady Churchill had died and ownership of the portrait had passed to their successors. The Churchill heirs might have decided to donate it to the National Portrait Gallery in London. Perhaps not, though. They might have regarded it exactly as their ancestors had and wished to destroy it or at least to keep it hidden from the public. If any of the Churchills destroy the painting, in what sense is there injury to the community's public culture? What, if any, specific capability of members of his communities is undermined?

Sax argued that "much would be lost if we were deprived of such works." The harm to the public that Sax sees is that it undermines the public's "strong interest in knowing as much as possible about one who played as large a role on the world stage as Churchill did."[84] The public has, to be sure, a capability interest in having full access to all relevant information about such persons as Churchill, but the operative word here is relevant. The public did not have access to President Ronald Reagan following his retirement when he was suffering from the ravages of Alzheimer's disease, and properly so. It simply wasn't relevant to us. It was a strictly private matter within the Reagan family; it wasn't any of our business. By the same token, it is difficult to see why it was relevant to the British public to see Sir Winston suffering from the ravages of age. That does not seem to be the sort of information that bears upon the very legitimate public interest in whatever aspects of his life remain connected with his role upon the world stage.

On the other side, if Churchill's right to destroy is denied, will any human capability essential to his living a full and well-lived life be undermined? The capability that seems most immediately implicated is self-definition, considered as a matter of personal autonomy. If the idea of self-definition is that it is a capacity that a person needs to develop into a fully free person, then presumably self-definition requires self-awareness and self-honesty. A person who has

84. *Id.* at 41.

fundamentally deluded himself about the kind of person he is cannot be said to be free in any rich sense of the term. He is a prisoner of his own delusions. A truly free person is one who is aware of and acknowledges his weaknesses as well as strengths. He may not like them, but he does not hide from them. From this perspective perhaps recognition of Churchill's right to destroy frustrates rather than nurtures this important capability in the sense that the portrait compels Sir Winston to face the reality of who and what he now is as an eighty-year-old man who is no longer in the prime of his life. Faced with that reality, he may come to accept it and become more truly free.

There is something to be said for that perspective. Still, it seems at best paternalistic, at worst cruel. Why not let Sir Winston choose to think of himself as he wishes? What great harm is done if he wishes to think of himself, at an advanced age, as he once was. It is telling that he would have preferred to have been painted in his robes as a Knight of the Garter, but the Parliamentary committee wanted a portrait of him as a member of the House of Commons as it had known him.[85] The art critic for the *New York Times* wrote that the portraitist, Graham Sutherland, "is a man who sets down exactly what he sees, and what he saw in this instance was an indisputably great human being, the savior of his nation, who had been struck down by illness and would never be the same again."[86] Even the portraitist himself was sympathetic to Churchill's reaction, stating that "only those totally without physical vanity, educated in painting, or with exceptionally good manners, can disguise their shock or even revulsion when confronted for the first time with a reasonable truthful painted image of themselves; there is a quilted atmosphere of silence; as when it snows."[87]

Recognition of the right to destroy a work of art in the Churchill case would not necessary commit us to conceding that all other owners of art must be granted the same right. The Churchill case is reasonably distinguishable from other situations in which we might wish to conclude that art owners have an obligation to preserve the art they own because of human flourishing–related reasons. As I have already indicated, it is distinguishable from cases like the Rockefeller/Rivera dispute where what is involved is public art. The very publicness of the art means that there are important capability-related concerns of members of the community that would be deprived of the benefits of the art were it destroyed. It is also broadly distinguishable from the vast majority of cases in which the owner of the work is not also its subject. Lest we worry that recognizing Lady Churchill's right to burn her late husband's painting will set a precedent that any eccentric

85. *See id.* at 40.

86. N.Y. Times, Jan. 16, 1978, F13.

87. Times (London), Jan. 15, 1978, at 4.

owner of a Picasso, a Chagall, or a Rubens is free to chop his painting into pieces, the Churchill case is a highly unusual one in which the subject of the painting is the owner himself and the painting was intended as a private gift to that subject.

In the more typical situation in which the right to destroy artwork is at issue—where the owner has no relationship to the work other than being the current owner—the default rule should be that *jus abutendi* is not recognized. The community's capabilities are at stake, notably the very existence of the cultural life upon which it depends and in turn individual members of the community depend for their own development as genuinely free and self-defining moral agents, fit with the owner's own capabilities in a way that the lives of community members and the owners go maximally well if the art is not destroyed, whatever the owner's expressed preference may be. Recall from the discussion in Chapter One that human flourishing, unlike welfare, is an objective concept that does not depend strictly on subjective preferences. Even taking into account Lior Strahilevitz's idea that where the owner of some work of art wishes to destroy it there are expressive values at stake, there are other considerations that we need to take seriously if we wish the owner to flourish in any sense beyond his immediately expressed desire. People sometimes act rashly and later regret their actions. People sometimes change their preferences. Circumstances sometimes change in such a way that what had seemed to be a rational action at one time no longer appears that way. All of these and more are well-known pathologies in human rationality. The human flourishing explanation of why the owner's well-being is, objectively, maximized goes beyond the now-familiar critiques of the rational actor, however. It rests on the observation that the owner, as a member of the same community whose well-being requires preservation of, say, a controversial photograph of a crucifix dipped in urine,[88] requires development of the same essential capabilities as all other members of his community. Those capabilities can only develop within the kind of society in which there is such a thing as cultural, including artistic, experimentation and controversy. This is precisely the reason behind the First Amendment's protection of artistic expression from state suppression. No individual any more than the state should have the power to suppress the cultural innovation that is required for the kind of free and liberal

88. The reference is, of course, to the highly controversial 1989 photograph known as "Piss Christ" by Andres Serrano. *See* https://www.theguardian.com/artanddesign/2012/sep/28/andres-serrano-piss-christ-new-york. Imagine that a devout Catholic owned the photograph and wished to destroy it, which he viewed as deeply offensive to his Christian values. In such a case the owner's desire certainly is not irrational, and it is unlikely that his preference would change over time. Expressive values do loom large here. This is precisely the sort of case in which it is especially important to see the owner as a member of the same broader community whose well-being depends upon preservation of important art.

society that is an indispensable foundation for the development of such essential human capabilities as self-definition and practical reasoning. The individual owner of Serrano's photograph[89] who is deeply offended for religious reasons is free to sell it, lease it, gift it, or otherwise dispose of it short of destruction. He is also free to hide it from the public should he think that no one should view the photograph. The right that he lacks is to destroy it, denying it from the community for all time.

Of course, as a practical matter, regardless of the legal rule, private owners may still destroy a work secretly. There is no feasible way to prevent a determined owner from doing so. But what if an owner bequeaths a work of art to a family member with instructions to destroy it. Must or even may the family member, who is now the owner, comply with those instructions? Or what if he does not bequeath it to anyone but simply orders its destruction upon his death. Should his testamentary instructions be followed? This is an important question because most of the litigated right-to-destroy cases occur in just this context.[90] As Lior Strahilevitz correctly points out, "A general matter, the law recoils at the idea of allowing the dead hand to destroy property."[91] Here is how two coauthors articulated the common justification for the law's restriction on testamentary destruction: "[D]uring life a person personally suffers the economic consequences, which is a deterrent to foolish decisions ordering property destroyed.... Ordering property destroyed after death imposes no economic consequences upon the testator, who is dead. . . ."[92] This argument is open to the response that it fails to taken into account the testator's opportunity cost in ordering the destruction of his property after death, that is, the foregone opportunity to sell the right to an asset upon his death, the value of which grows as he ages.[93] Whatever we think about these two positions, there still remains the question of the community's capability needs. Everything that I said previously regarding the way in which art contributes to the kind of culture that is necessary for humans to flourish applies here. Of course, at this point the owner is no longer with us and no longer a member of his former communities, so it is not his opportunity to flourish with which we are concerned. But he was a member of communities, and his obligation to them continues to the extent that he owned at death an

89. *See supra* note 88.

90. *See* Strahilevitz, *The Right to Destroy*, *supra* note 1, at 838.

91. *Id.*

92. Jesse Dukeminier & Stanley M. Johanson, Wills, Trusts, and Estates 22–23 (3rd ed. 1984).

93. *See* Strahilevitz, *The Right to Destroy*, *supra* note 1, at. 840–41.

asset that contributed significantly to that cultural life. Think of the obligation as something like a debt that is accrued but unpaid at death. If I owed the state accrued but unpaid taxes at my death, my death does not expunge the obligation; my estate must pay the taxes after I die. By the same token, the owner's obligation to his communities is one that persists beyond his death insofar as he is not free to destroy the asset that is the subject of the obligation. He cannot simply cut off his communities from the basis of their ability to flourish after he dies any more than he could while he was alive.

There is a final scenario to consider—an artist who wishes to destroy a work he considers unworthy of preservation. Sax gives the example of Georges Rouault, who, in the presence of a photographer, threw over three hundred of his own paintings into a furnace. They were all unfinished and unsigned, and he destroyed them in the fear that he would not have the time required to finish them. Or to illustrate another possible reason for artistic destruction, suppose Picasso intended to destroy some twenty paintings he had done earlier in his career because he thought they were no good and might harm his reputation if they were publicly viewed. If one of Picasso's children sought to enjoin him from destroying the paintings, who should prevail? Should artists be given the power to determine who gets to see their work? Sax argued yes on the ground that an "artist should be entitled to decide how the world will remember him or her."[94] Strahilevitz agrees with Sax, although for other reasons. He argues, first, that the artist is in the best position to know which of his works is of inferior quality and so should not form part of his legacy. He also argues that if the artist is denied the right to destroy his works, we are compelling him to speak when he would have preferred to remain silent. This, Strahilevitz suggests, is particularly problematic in cases of works such as "Piss Christ," which are likely to be highly controversial.[95]

Strahilevitz's reasons seem quite compelling, but I want to augment them with capability-related reasons why an artist should have the right to destroy his own works. In the earlier discussion of the Churchill portrait I suggested that in that case the capability most immediately implicated was self-definition, considered as a matter of personal autonomy. For similar reasons, self-definition is also involved where an artist wishes to control which of his works constitute his life's *oeuvre*. Our work and its products do not define who we are as persons, but they form a major part of the tableau of memory that we leave behind. Especially for artists, our surviving works constitute expressions of ourselves, often very deeply so, into indefinitely multiple futures. It is hardly uncommon for people

94. Sax, Playing Darts with a Rembrandt, *supra* note 2, at 200.

95. *See* Strahilevitz, *The Right to Destroy*, *supra* note 1, 833–34.

to carry secrets to the grave with them. The desire to maintain such postmortem secrets is not solely a matter of personal privacy, although it is partly that. Motivated by reasons of vanity, a need to avoid hurting others, or a consideration that something they did in the distant past no longer conforms with the kind of person they later developed, people have many understandable reasons for not exposing every self-perceived wart or blemish to future generations. Such blemishes may include some of their unpublished or unfinished works. An artist may say to himself, with complete honesty, "This [painting/sculture/other work] is not me." Control over which of his works survive him is quite literally a matter of self-definition, a capability that includes but is much more complex than privacy alone.

Closely related to self-definition, another capability involved in the artist's wish to control which of his works survive him is self-expression. Art is quite literally an artist's expression with the outside world, his means of speaking to others. Painters not uncommonly reuse canvasses, painting over old works as if saying, "I don't mean to say that." The canvas wasn't released, the word wasn't published. An artist may wish to have one or more of his works destroyed for the same self-expressive reasons: The work constitutes a statement that he ultimately wishes not to express, for reasons of regret, changes in his personality, concern for the feelings of others, and other reasons. Autonomy, if it is to have any robust meaning, must mean that a person can control what she expresses and, equally important, what she does not express. Members of a person's communities cannot compel a person to speak an unwanted (to that person) statement and still claim to support her self-development as an autonomous agent.

That holds true after a person's death as well as during her life. If she is to experience freedom during her life in a deeply meaningful sense, she must feel secure that her control over her expressions will survive her death.

DISPOSITION OF HUMAN REPRODUCTION MATERIAL

Perhaps the greatest controversy involving the right to destroy in recent years has involved disposition of human procreative material—frozen sperm, eggs, embryos, and pre-embryos. On the question whether an individual has the right to destroy this material, the courts have been strongly in agreement in affirming the right.

One context in which the question has appeared is divorce. A well-known case involved a married couple who, following unsuccessful attempts to conceive a child naturally, tried in vitro fertilization. Some of the ova removed from the wife and fertilized by the husband's sperm were implanted in the wife's uterus. The remaining fertilized embryos were frozen cryogenically for possible subsequent implantation. These efforts at conception failed, and the couple divorced.

The couple, the Davises, disagreed about the disposition of the remaining frozen embryos. Mary Sue wanted to donate them to a childless couple, but Junior wanted them destroyed. The trial court awarded the embryos to Mary Sue. Viewing the embryos as human beings, the court concluded that the decision must be based on the best interests of the children, which in this case meant attempting to bring them to term. The court of appeal reversed, concluding that Junior had a constitutional right not to become a parent against his will. The Tennessee Supreme Court, in *Davis v. Davis*,[96] unanimously ruled in favor of Junior. His interest prevailed, the court reasoned, because "[o]rdinarily the party wishing to avoid procreation should prevail, assuming that the other party has a reasonable possibility of achieving parenthood by [other] means."[97] This result and its reasoning is consistent with the decisional law in other jurisdictions.[98]

The question regarding whether there is a right to destroy human reproduction material also occurs in the postmortem context. For example, in one controversial case, *Hecht v. Superior Court*,[99] a decedent, William Kane, had deposited fifteen vials of his frozen sperm in a cryobank with instructions that upon his death the cryobank should either continue to store the sperm or release it to Kane's executor upon the executor's direction. At the same time Kane executed a will bequeathing "all right, title, and interest that he may have in any specimens of his sperm stored with any sperm bank or similar facility for storage to [Kane's girlfriend] Deborah Ellen Hecht." Shortly thereafter, Kane committed suicide, and Hecht claimed the frozen sperm. His surviving children from a prior marriage, both adults, argued that the probate court should order the sperm destroyed, contending that the court should prevent the birth of a child who would never know its father and prevent further emotional stress on Kane's family members. Their real concern, perhaps, was the possibility of an additional heir who could claim a portion of Kane's $1 million estate. The trial court ordered the frozen sperm destroyed, but the California Court of Appeal vacated the order. It held, first, that Kane had an interest in the sperm that was "in the nature of ownership." It further held that the trial court could not properly order that the frozen sperm be destroyed at the behest of Kane's adult children. Quoting from the *Davis* opinion, the court stated, "[N]o . . . person or entity has an interest sufficient to permit interference with the gamete-providers' decision . . . because no else bears the consequences of these decisions in the way that the gamete-providers do."[100]

96. 842 S.W.2d 588 (Tenn. 1992).

97. *Id.* at 604.

98. *See, e.g.*, J.B. v. M.B., 783 A.2d 707 (N.J. 2001); A.Z. v. B.Z., 725 N.E.2d 1051 (Mass. 2000).

99. 20 Cal. Rptr. 2d 275 (Cal. App. 1993).

100. *Id. quoting* Davis v. Davis, 842 S.W.2d at 602.

In a variation on *Hecht,* a California appellate court has more recently ruled that where a husband's sperm were held by a fertility medical center under a contract, to which the wife expressed assent, expressly giving the husband sole decision-making authority over the sperm and further directing the medical center to destroy the sperm samples in the event of his death, the terms of the contract controlled. In *Estate of Kievernagel,*[101] the contract with the fertility center provided that the sperm sample was Joseph's sole and separate property and that he retained all authority to control its disposition. Following his accidental death, his widow, Iris, sought to compel the fertility clinic to release the sperm, and Joseph's surviving parents sought to block release. The probate court found that the question turned on the decedent's intent regarding use of his sperm, concluding that the contract evidenced the intent of both Iris and Joseph that the sperm be discarded upon his death.

On appeal, Iris argued that the court should not follow the decision in *Hecht* because that decision ignored the fundamental right of a donee spouse to procreate. Instead, Iris suggested, the court should apply the approach of the Tennessee court in *Davis,* balancing the interest of the deceased donor against that of the surviving spouse. The California court of appeal affirmed the lower court's decision. It first agreed with the *Hecht* court that gametic material is a unique type of property and not governed by the general laws governing transfer of personal property upon death. The court also followed *Hecht*'s lead in stating that the person who provided the gametic material had at his death an interest "in the nature of ownership" sufficient to give him decision-making authority as to the use of the gametic material for reproduction. Hence, it concluded, "the disposition of the frozen sperm is governed by the intent of the deceased donor."[102] *Davis*'s balancing approach did not apply here because, unlike in *Davis* where the material in question was a pre-embryo rather than sperm, here there was only one gamete-provider—Joseph. Hence, only he had decisional authority, and only his intent controlled.

Cases like *Hecht* and *Kievernagel,* in which frozen sperm alone rather than pre-embryos are involved, seem relatively easier to resolve. In such cases there is only one gamete-provider, and that person has essential human capabilities at stake. The court in *Kievernagel* touched upon these capabilities in saying: "In this case, there is only one gamete-provider. The material at issue is Joseph's sperm, not a preembryo. Only Joseph had 'an interest, in the nature of ownership, to the extent that he had decisionmaking authority as to the use of his sperm for reproduction.' (*Hecht,* . . . 20 Cal. Rptr. 2d 275.) The disposition of Joseph's frozen sperm

101. 166 Cal. App. 4th 1024 (Cal. Ct. App. 2008).

102. *Id.* at 1027.

does not implicate Iris's right to procreative autonomy."[103] Procreative autonomy is among the most intimate aspects of personal autonomy. The decision whether or not to have a child and the related decisions when to have a child, whether or not to parent the child, and how to parent a child, are among the deeply personal decisions that an individual makes over the entire course of a lifetime. They profoundly affect how one's life goes and affect one's well-being in the most personal sort of way. Personal autonomy requires that an individual is capable of exercising self-direction through practical reasoning. This means that he must be in a position that enables him to imagine future possible life plans and to choose which among those possibilities will enable his life to go maximally well, defined not solely in terms of subjective preference-satisfaction but through realization of objective values including love, friendship, personal dignity, and self-worth.

Control over one's procreative capacity is directly connected to the fulfillment to all of these and other values that collectively constitute what it means objectively to live a well-lived life.

To be sure, Joseph, as the sole gamete-provider, did not live in a vacuum. Other people were affected by his decision regarding the disposition of his frozen sperm. The court in *Kievernagel* seemed wrong in suggesting otherwise as it did in stating, "The disposition of Joseph's frozen sperm does not implicate Iris's right to procreative autonomy."[104] The court took that view because there was no indication that Iris could not have gotten pregnant with another man's sperm.[105] Still, it is not as though Iris was a completely disinterested party in the disposition of his sperm. Joseph was Iris's husband, and it would be entirely plausible that she wanted to have *his* child using *his* sperm. The disposition of Joseph's sperm did affect her life, and we have to take that fact into account. What needs to be said is not that Iris, having provided no gamete, has no interest in the matter or relevant capabilities at stake, but instead that procreative autonomy and, more fundamentally, personal autonomy, play out differently for Joseph and Iris. Autonomy and self-definition are at stake for both Joseph and Iris, but they do not mean the same thing for the two parties. For Joseph, this was a zero-sum situation: He either did or did not control his future as a parent. If his expressed wishes were respected, he would not be a parent, period. If those wishes were not respected, quite possibly, even likely, he would have become a parent under circumstances where he would have completely unable to enjoy any of the benefits of parenthood. Such was not Iris's situation. Here the court was right in observing that the destruction of Joseph's sperm did not necessarily deprive her of the opportunity

103. *Id.*at 1033.

104. *Id.*

105. *Id.*

to experience parenthood, only parenthood with Joseph's child. Seeing how personal autonomy and self-direction have qualitatively different meanings for the two individuals in this sense, it becomes clearer that the well-being of a person who is the sole gamete-provider is so deeply and profoundly affected by the disposition of his sperm (or ova, as the case may be) that it would be an acute mistake to deny him control over such disposition.

One might wish to challenge what I have just said on the basis of the facts of *Kievernagel*. Pointing out that the contract that Joseph and Iris signed that gave Joseph the authority to dispose of his sperm unilaterally only upon his death, one might insist that Joseph's well-being during his life is not really affected by the disposition of his sperm after his death. Contrary to what the court in *Kievernagel* said, Iris, not Joseph, is the one whose autonomy is implicated by the decision of how to dispose of the sperm.

There are several responses to this challenge. One is the obvious point that the facts might be otherwise in a different case. The agreement with the cryobank might give the gamete-provider unilateral authority over the disposition of the reproductive material during life as well as after death, and for various reasons the gamete-provider might change his mind and wish to withdraw and destroy the material during his life. Second, and more directly, even taking the circumstances of *Kievernagel* itself, Joseph's well-being is still deeply at stake in the question whether to recognize his right to destroy the sperm after his death. There is a matter of security here, not in a physical but a psychological sense. Consequences would result from a decision not to destroy Joseph's cryo-preserved sperm after his death but rather to permit his late wife to use it to enable her own pregnancy. One concern that Joseph might have is that if Iris had a child using his sperm, a portion of his estate would have to be set aside for that child, reducing the shares of his living adult children. The law in this area is woefully unclear. In many (most?) states statutes do not address the question of the inheritance rights of children conceived through assisted reproduction. The best law in this general area is the Uniform Probate Code, enacted in less than half the states. Section 2-120 creates, for inheritance purposes, a parent-child relationship between the husband of the child's birth mother "if the husband provided the sperm that the birth mother used *during his lifetime* for assisted reproduction."[106] Subsection k goes on to provide that if an individual is a parent of a child of assisted reproduction who is conceived after that person's death, the child is treated as in gestation at the person's death, and therefore entitled to inherit from his estate as a legal heir, only under two circumstances: (1) if the child was "in utero not later than 36 months after the individual's death," or (2) if the child was "born not later than

106. Unif. Prob. Code §2-120(d) (emphasis added).

45 months after the individual's death."[107] The basic point of these provisions is to place a time limit on how long the sperm donor/husband's estate is kept open to the possibility that additional biological children may be added to his estate following his death.

Someone in Joseph's financial position, who had enough wealth to pay for cryo-preservation, would likely have left a will. Such a will might well have made a disposition to a class such as "my children" or "my descendant," and the question would arise whether the after-born child, conceived using Joseph's sperm, would be included in such a class of beneficiaries. Once again, the law is unclear in most states. The Uniform Probate Code adopts the same approach as it does in cases of intestate estates, that is, a fixed period for closing the class. It provides that if a child of assisted reproduction who is conceived posthumously and the distribution date is the deceased parent's death, the child "is treated as living on the distribution date if the child survives lives 120 hours after birth and was in utero not later than 36 months after the deceased parent's death or born not later than 45 months after the deceased parent's death."[108] So, if Joseph had a will bequeathing a sum of money to his "children," the distribution date would be his death, and a child later conceived with his sperm would receive a portion of that sum only if that child survived by five days and met either of the stated fixed time limits. If not, the child would be excluded from the class gift. Of course, Joseph could relieve his concern over this issue entirely by simply defining the class to exclude any and all posthumously conceived children.

Aside from these estate-planning concerns, Joseph may have deeper anxieties. If Iris uses his sperm successfully to give birth to a child, Joseph will become the biological father of a child whom he will never know. The knowledge of that possibility might cause him considerable anxiety, even emotional pain, over the potential loss of knowing, bonding with, and raising his own child.

Not everyone feels this way, of course; some are very happy at the thought of leaving behind their biological children even though they may never know the child. But others find such a thought quite painful and would prefer to be relieved of any such possibility.[109] That may have been part or even all of the motivation behind the term that Joseph chose in his contract in *Kievernagel* providing that upon his death the sperm was to be discarded rather than donated to his wife.[110]

107. Unif. Prob. Code §2-120(k).

108. *Id.*

109. The court, in *Davis v. Davis*, discussed this problem in some detail. The sperm donor in that case had experienced substantial emotional pain earlier in his life as a result of separation from his birth mother at an early age and for that reason he adamantly opposed permitting his sperm to be used to conceive a child with whom he would have no contact.

110. 166 Cal. App. 4th at 1026.

The assumption that his expressly stated contractual term would be honored and enforced may have been the requisite source of emotional security and support that he needed to commit himself to preserve his sperm in the first place. Given all of these possible consequences, it seems quite clear that Joseph's well-being was not only very much at stake in the question whether to recognize his right to destroy the sperm after his death, but primarily so.

The harder case is *Davis v. Davis,* where both partners rather than just one were the gamete-providers. Recall that in that case, the two parties were now divorced and disagreed about the proper disposition of preserved pre-embryos that had been created with Junior's sperm and Mary Sue's ova. He wanted them discarded, but she wanted to donate them to a childless couple. Unlike the couple in *Kievernagel,* the parties did not sign an agreement at the time of in vitro fertilization. Both parties have real and substantial interests that involve their essential capabilities.

Everything that I said earlier regarding the capabilities at stake for Joseph in *Kievernagel* applies equally to Junior. Privacy, personal security in multiple senses, and self-definition of himself as a person and as a parent are all very much involved in his ability to control the disposition of his own sperm. His situation did differ from Joseph's to the extent that his ex-wife, Mary Sue, did not plan to use his sperm to become pregnant herself. But there still remained the open question whether he was to father a child whom he might never know. There are good reasons why the law recognizes a privacy right to avoid procreating. Mary Sue, as the other gamete-donor, also had a personal interest although perhaps not as strong as if her plan had been to use her ex-husband's sperm to become pregnant herself. The court in *Davis* suggested that the case would have been closer "if Mary Sue Davis were seeking to use the preembryos herself, but only if she could not achieve parenthood by any other reasonable means."[111]

Lior Strahilevitz properly points to what he calls "the libertarian tone" of these opinions. Nowhere do the courts discuss any concerns other than those of the immediate parties—the gamete-donors and their spouses. Strahilevitz suggests that in a case like *Davis,* "society had a powerful interest in permitting the embryos' transfer to a couple that was otherwise unable to conceive."[112] Nevertheless, in these cases the appellate courts make no mention of any interest that the community might have.[113] This is both odd and unfortunate, for members of communities do certainly have legitimate interests in the disposition of the sperm and the

111. *Id.*at 604.

112. Strahilevitz, *The Right to Destroy, supra* note 1, at 836.

113. *See id.* at 837.

pre-embryos. The most obvious interest is enabling couples who are otherwise unable to conceive children on their own to have children. This was the interest that Mary Sue Davis, as a kind of surrogate for childless couples, raised, but the court did not consider the interest of those couples or the broader public's possible interest in facilitating conception. Important capabilities are involved in those interests. For many couples, the ability to have children directly affects their self-definition and self-identification. To be sure, adoption is an alternative, but some couples consider that their fulfillment, both individually and as a couple, can only come through carrying a child to birth. More broadly, society has its own capabilities at stake. A society's procreative policies immediately affect its very self-preservation. To take an extreme example, one thinks of the one-child policy instituted by the state in the People's Republic of China, beginning in 1979 and gradually phased out beginning in 2015. Whatever one's opinion regarding the wisdom or morality of that policy, it was a measure undertaken in the interest of what the government judged China's self-preservation required.

The Chinese one-child policy is illuminating for a different reason, however. It brings into focus the question whether we really want to prioritize society's interests over that of the individual gamete-donor on a matter so deeply personal as procreation and parenthood. The question is not whether society's interests should be taken into account. Society's interests and its capabilities do need to be taken into account, for they certainly affect human flourishing. The real question is what is the best fit between those interests and the interests of the gamete-donor who is immediately involved. This is not a matter of weighing the interests against each other because all of the affected interests involve values that resist weighting. This is why I have framed the question in terms of asking what is the best fit. This is closely related to what Charles Taylor calls "complementarity."[114] We ask how the interests and the affected capabilities of society and the gamete-donor interact with each other such that we might be able to discern an understanding of what human flourishing means in this situation and what it requires. Our perception of society's capability needs might be, for example, that the current birth rate optimizes its resources and, more fundamentally, that adoption is now a means to achieving parenthood that is not only available to couples who are unable to conceive of children themselves but is widely practiced and has become a mainstream social practice. Some couples may not consider it a perfect substitute for having their own biological children, but that choice is not one that is available here. The alternative to adoption in this situation is conceiving a child with the use of another man's sperm, and along a spectrum whose poles are, on the one hand, biological birth using procreative material from both partners, and,

114. *See* Chapter One.

on the other, adoption (in which neither parent contributes genetic material), that alternative immediately moves us some distance away from the couple's preferred pole toward the opposite pole—adoption. The point is that the decision to recognize the gamete-donor's right to control the disposition of his procreative material does not entail a substantial sacrifice in what needs and what capabilities of couples who potentially would use the material for conception or to society as a whole can realistically be met in this situation.

Unlike couples who are potential users of the genetic material, for the gamete-holder this is a zero-sum situation concerning his interests, concerns, and capabilities. Those interests and capabilities either will or will not be realized in full depending on whether we recognize his right to control the disposition of his sperm. And, as I have already discussed, those interests are essential to his ability to experience a life well-lived. His emotional and psychological well-being would be directly and substantially jeopardized were he not in control of his status as a parent. This is precisely why the law regards procreative autonomy a matter meriting particularly strong legal protection. It lies at the very core of what it means to be able to define oneself, one's identity, and one's own life plan.

Viewing the interests and the affected capabilities of society and the gamete-donor this way, it becomes possible to discern what human flourishing means in this situation and what it requires. The relationship between the interests and capabilities of society and the gamete-donor here is less one of conflict than one in which, from an objective viewpoint, deference is due.

Taking into account how deeply a person's capability of defining the very meaning of himself, his identity and the course of his life depends on control of his procreative ability and taking into account the asymmetrical positions of the two sides with respect to alternatives available to them, human flourishing objectively requires that one side's interests defer to the other. The fit between the interests of society and other couples who are potential users of the procreative materials and the interests of the gamete-donor is actually complementary rather than directly in conflict.

Courts tend to frame right-to-destroy disputes in terms of a conflict between respecting individual autonomy and avoiding social waste. That framing unduly obscures what is involved in these cases. Autonomy is a rich value that requires discerned investigation, and social waste masks the existence of community capabilities of legitimate concern. A human flourishing perspective illuminates these multiple values and capabilities. Conflicts involving the right to destroy resist neat categorical solutions, but that does not mean that they cannot be resolved rationally or even with a relatively high degree of predictability, as I have tried to show in this chapter.

9

Race and Property

Georgetown University is an internationally distinguished university with a sizeable capital endowment.[1] It also used to own African slaves. The university, founded in 1789 by Jesuit priest John Carroll,[2] owned slaves from its beginning. The Jesuits first received them as gifts in 1717, and they used them to work on the several farms and plantations that the Jesuits owned throughout Maryland.[3] In 1838, Thomas Mulledy, S.J., sold 272 enslaved men, women, and children belonging to the Jesuits to two individuals in Louisiana. The Jesuits' plantations had become unprofitable, and mounted with debt, the Jesuits sold the slaves for a sizeable profit.[4] Even after the mass sale of slaves, Georgetown continued to use hired slaves for labor.[5] Slavery was not abolished in Maryland until 1864, and

1. As of 2016, Georgetown's capital endowment was $1.484 billion. *See* https://en.wikipedia.org/wiki/Georgetown_University.

2. *See History of Georgetown*, https://www.georgetown.edu/about/history.

3. *See* Guide to the History of Slavery in Maryland (2007).

4. *See* Matthew Quallen, *Slavery Inextricably Tied to Georgetown's Growth*, The Hoya, Oct. 23, 2015.

5. *See College Records Indicate Two Slaves on Campus, available at* http://slavery.georgetown.edu/timeline.

Property and Human Flourishing. Gregory S. Alexander.

the last records of Jesuit-owned slaves were in an 1867 census of emancipated Maryland slaves.[6]

On September 1, 2016, Georgetown University formally announced plans to atone for its past as a slave-owning institution and participant in the slave trade, the profits from which probably saved it from ruin.[7] The plans include the creation of an Institute on the Study of Slavery and Its Legacies, commissioning a memorial to honor the 272 slaves sold, and renaming two campus buildings from the names of two university officials involved in the slave sale to the names of one of the slaves shipped off to Louisiana and a woman who founded a school for black girls in Washington, D.C. The university will also offer to descendants of all the slaves whose labor benefited the university an admissions preference similar to that offered to children and grandchildren of alumni. Historians who have studied slavery and universities state that they are unaware of any other universities whose pasts have been tied to slave ownership that have offered admissions preference to the descendants of slaves.[8]

Reactions to the Georgetown plans have been mixed. Some critics have argued that the university has not gone far enough to atone for its slave-owning and -trading past. Some thought that the university should offer scholarships to descendants.[9] One critic calculated that the $110,000 that the university in 1838 for the sale of its slaves is worth roughly $3.3 million in today's dollars. "Using that purchase as a baseline, at least $50 billion would be owed to the descendants of the 12,000 to 15,000 enslaved people owned by the university's Jesuit priests," the critic argued.[10] She suggested that a more genuine step toward atonement would be establishment of a $1.5 billion endowment for guaranteed admission regardless of income together with full scholarships, including housing and monthly stipends, in perpetuity to the descendants of enslaved people who labored for Georgetown. In an interview with the *New York Times Magazine*, Georgetown professor Michael Eric Dyson suggested individual reparations in

6. *See Slavery Abolished in Maryland, id.*

7. *See* Rachel L. Swarns, *Georgetown University Plans Steps to Atone for Slave Past*, N.Y. TIMES, Sept. 1, 2016, *available at* https://www.nytimes.com/2016/09/02/us/slaves-georgetown-university.html.

8. *See id.*

9. *See id.*

10. Samantha Master, *Georgetown University's "Reparations" Plan Is Worthless White Guilt Repackaged as Justice, available at* http://www.theroot.com/georgetown-university-s-reparations-plan-is-worthless-1790856615.

the form of individual reparations accounts (IRAs), which they would contribute to groups like the United Negro College Fund.[11]

Dyson's suggestion provides an appropriate departure point for this chapter, for what I want to discuss here is what obligations, if any, property owners, both institutional and individual, morally owe to descendants of slaves. This topic is usually framed in terms of reparations, but I wish to reframe it here. I want to consider it from the perspective of the human flourishing concept that I have developed so far. Such an approach has several advantages over a reparations frame of reference. For one, it avoids complicated questions growing out of the demands of reciprocity that commonly accompany reparations analysis. Under the human flourishing theory, the basis of owner obligations is not reciprocity but interdependence, a condition that is ontologically inherent in every person and at all times. A second advantage of the human flourishing theory is that it shifts our primary attention from resources to capabilities. Resources are certainly relevant to certain capabilities, but their role is secondary. The main concern is with providing those to whom we owe obligations the basic abilities without which those persons cannot live what any reasonable person would consider a fulfilling life. How those persons choose to exercise the basic abilities, or whether they choose to exercise those abilities at all, is up to them. But they must have the opportunity to flourish through such capabilities.

My aim in this chapter is not to provide a comprehensive review of the developments in redress for slavery or to develop a complete theory of reparations that responds to all of the many issues that others have raised regarding reparations.[12] Rather the goal is more modest: to conjecture how the human flourishing theory of ownership and its approach to owner obligations might influence moral considerations regarding whether existing white property owners whose direct ancestors economically profited from chattel slavery morally owe obligations to present-day descendants of now-deceased slaves and, if so, and under what theory. I then speculate whether even those whites whose ancestors did not directly profit from slavery or slave trading might owe moral obligations to members of the black community for the myriad injuries that resulted both from chattel slavery and the Jim Crow regime. I offer no definitive theory of which whites owe moral obligations to which members of the black community. That is a very large

11. *See* Interview by Ana Marie Cox, *Michael Eric Dyson Believes in Individual Reparations*, N.Y. Times Magazine, *available at* https://www.nytimes.com/2017/01/04/magazine/michael-eric-dyson-believes-in-individual-reparations.html?rref=collection%2Fsectioncollection%2Fmagazine&action=click&contentCollection=magazine&region=rank&module=package&version=highlights&contentPlacement=7&pgtype=sectionfront.

12. For comprehensive reviews of the arguments, *see* Alfred L. Brophy, Reparations: Pro and Con (2006); John Torpey, Making Whole What Has Been Smashed (2006).

and complex set of issues. I emphasize that I have not fully worked out all aspects of the argument that follows. The discussion is meant to offer some possible ways of thinking and to stimulate discussion. I offer no blueprint for a comprehensive plan of meeting one's moral obligations. The discussion here is more tentative and more speculative in nature. It is one way, for there are certainly are others,[13] of exploring the relationship between ownership of property and race, and looking beyond, between property, race, and citizenship, in modern American society through the lens of a human flourishing theory.

INSTITUTIONS: THE OBLIGATIONS OF GEORGETOWN

Georgetown University is a large and wealthy institution.[14] It is also a member of multiple communities. These include the Roman Catholic Church, the Society of Jesus (the "Jesuits"), and the District of Columbia. It is also a member of the African American community.[15] Its membership in the African American community exists on the basis of several factors, one of which is the sheer fact that it used to own African American slaves. That fact alone is sufficient to establish an immediate and binding relationship between the university and the African American community. Whether or not any of the former Georgetown slaves left descendants surviving today (and they did), Georgetown's ownership of black slaves alone connects it with the black community in ways that other universities and institutions whose pasts do not include ownership of black slaves or immediate profit from the slave trade are not so connected. To be sure, the forced nature of the relationship makes it different from paradigmatic consensual relationships. The fact that the connection was not mutually consensual, however, does not bar the creation of a relationship that is characterized by strongly emotive ties, profound memories that have shaped each side's lives and created conditions of ongoing interdependency. The existence of surviving descendants of those slaves only deepens those communitarian conditions further. Less directly but still relevant, Georgetown is

13. For an outstanding example, *see* Cheryl Harris, *Whiteness as Property*, 106 Harv. L. Rev. (1993).

14. Georgetown's enrollment is 4,793. *See* https://www.georgetown.edu/about/key-facts. Its total capital endowment is $1.484 billion (2016). *See* https://en.wikipedia.org/wiki/Georgetown_University.

15. I fully recognize that these assertions are contestable, the last one especially so. The claim that Georgetown University, as a corporate institution, is itself a member of any community is contestable. I do not wish to get distracted by this question, but I do need to make clear my position that with respect to the question of obligations of property owners, corporate institutions should themselves be considered individuals. In this way I elide the whole debate over methodological individualism. Corporations are generally, including legally, considered as individuals for purposes of being owners (assets are titled in the firm's name), and liability likewise flows to the corporate entity.

tied to the black community by virtue of its black students, faculty, administrators, alumni, and supporters. To be sure, Georgetown historically has been a white institution, and it remains predominantly white. Nevertheless, today its ties to the African American community are very real. Indeed, particularly because it would have failed had it not been for its ownership of slaves, Georgetown has a relationship with the black community that, while not unique, is very special and is not shared by most American universities or other institutions.

From its inception the university has been dependent upon African Americans. The university's status as a slave owner traces to that of the Jesuits, who first landed in Maryland in 1634.[16] The Jesuits received land grants in Maryland, and they managed farms first using indentured servants, then slaves. The first documentation of Jesuit slave ownership in Maryland dates to a 1717 deed of gift from William Hunter.[17] Pope Clement XIV suppressed the Jesuits in 1773. The Jesuits' land and slaves were incorporated 1792 into the corporation of the Roman Catholic Clergy, which managed them. The Society of Jesus was not officially restored until 1814.[18] John Carroll, the first Catholic bishop in the United States, founded Georgetown University in 1789.

Slave ownership came early to the fledging university. One of its first directors, Rev. John Ashton, was a slave owner whose slaves sued him for their freedom. Similarly, one of the early Georgetown College presidents, Rev. Francis Neale, S.J., owned slaves who sued for their freedom.[19] Georgetown used its slaves for the same purpose as other slave owners did, that is, labor. Records from Georgetown College in the late eighteenth century indicate that the college's slaves worked as artisans, cooks, and waitresses.[20] The university's Working Group on Slavery, Memory, and Reconciliation reports that "there was a substantial African-American presence at the school in its early years."[21] There was also a substantial African American presence in the Georgetown neighborhood.

16. *See* Georgetown University Working Group on Slavery, Memory, and Reconciliation, Historical Timeline, *The African-American Presence at Georgetown, available at* http://slavery.georgetown.edu/timeline.

17. *See First Documentation of Jesuit Ownership of Slaves in Maryland*, in *id.*

18. *See The Jesuit Plantation Complex in Maryland*, in *id.*

19. *See* William G. Thomas III, *The Timing of* Queen v. Hepburn: *An Exploration of African American Networks in the Early Republic*, O SAY CAN YOU SEE: EARLY WASHINGTON, D.C., LAW & FAMILY, Aug. 2015, *available at* http://earlywashingtondc.org/stories/queen_v_hepburn.

20. *See The African-American Presence at Georgetown*, Georgetown University Working Group on Slavery, Memory, and Reconciliation, Historical Timeline, *available at* http://slavery.georgetown.edu/timeline.

21. *Id.*

In 1800, the neighborhood of Georgetown had a population of some 5,100, of which over 1,400 were slave and over 270 were freed blacks.[22] Slavery and the slave trade were a reality within Georgetown well into the nineteenth century.[23]

In 1838, Thomas Mulledy, S.J., then the president of Georgetown College, sold 272 enslaved men, women, and children owned by the Maryland Province of the Society of Jesus to Henry Johnson and Jesse Batey, both of Louisiana.[24] The actual event was particularly vicious. Mulledy, fearful of slaves trying to escape, arrived secretly on the Jesuits' Maryland plantation accompanied by sheriffs. Families were split apart, and the slaves were sent to Louisiana where they lived out their lives.[25] Mulledy used the substantial proceeds for building projects, including a new library, a museum, and improvements and to increase the number of students who boarded at the college. The overall effect was not only to clear Georgetown's debts but to begin its transformation into the urban, elite center of higher education that it is today.

Georgetown University's membership in the black community has been extraordinarily important to its ability to flourish as an institution. Indeed, Georgetown literally owes its existence to its ties to the black community. Were it not for the facts that Georgetown gratuitously received slaves and later sold them for a substantial profit, it is likely that the young university in 1838 would not have survived financially. In this most immediate way, the African American community historically has contributed, albeit entirely without its consent, to Georgetown's capability to survive and to flourish. Even beyond this obvious contribution to the university's capability to flourish, the African American community has continued to contribute to the university in various ways, large and small, that have enabled Georgetown's ability to flourish and to become the elite institution that it is today.[26] Among the more obvious contributions, its faculty, staff, and student body include African Americans who come from extraordinarily diverse backgrounds, measured geographically, socioeconomically, politically, and in terms of aspirations. They add a richness to the university community that enhances both the university's reputation and its educational mission.

22. *See* Kathleen Menzie Lesko & Valerie Babb, Black Georgetown Remembered (1991).

23. *See id.*

24. *See The Sale*, Georgetown University Working Group on Slavery, Memory, and Reconciliation, Historical Timeline, *available at* http://slavery.georgetown.edu/timeline.

25. *See* Matthew Quallen, *Slavery Inextricably Tied to Georgetown's Growth*, The Hoya, Oct. 23, 2015, *available at* http://www.thehoya.com/quallen-slavery-inextricably-tied-to-georgetowns-growth.

26. Somewhat along the same lines, Professor Randall Robinson has argued that the basis for reparations is the degree to which African Americans have contributed to American society. *See* Randall Robinson, The Debt: What America Owes Blacks (2000).

One of the more intriguing contributions comes in the form of Patrick Healy, S.J., president of Georgetown University between 1874 and 1882. The university today identifies Father Healy as its first African American president, but that was not always so. Father Healy was born to a white father and a slave mother whose parents also were racially mixed. From the 1880s until the 1950s, the university failed to mention Father Healey's race or the fact that his mother had been a slave. The implicit understanding was that he was white. With the rise of the civil rights movement in the 1960s, the university began to explicitly market Father Healy as a black American. It published a pamphlet entitled, "Patrick Healy, SJ, A Black Man's Dream Come True," apparently part of a concerted effort to shape the university's image as a racially diverse place.[27] Georgetown not only continues to identify Father Healy as African American, but identifies him as the first black president of any major American university in the country.[28] All of this despite the fact that Healy consistently identified himself as white. In a now-somewhat antiquated vernacular, he passed.[29]

Georgetown University and the black community are interdependent and have been so at least since the Maryland Jesuits first received slaves in 1717. The substance of the interdependency and the capabilities that each has enabled the other to develop have changed over time as the relationship between the university and the black community has changed. Georgetown broke the relationship that had existed with the ancestors of present-day descendants of its slaves when it sold those slaves in 1838. To restore a relationship with these descendants—one that rested on an entirely different footing from the one it had with its slaves—Georgetown has now taken steps to create scholarships, and so on, for the present-day descendants of Georgetown slaves. In doing so, it creates a relationship of interdependency between itself and members of the black community.[30]

27. *See On the Record: Georgetown and the Racial Identity of President Patrick Healy*, Interview with Matt Sheptuck, Vox Populi, *available at* https://blog.georgetownvoice.com/2010/04/14/on-the-record-georgetown-and-the-racial-identity-of-president-patrick-healy.

28. *See id.*

29. Passing has a long and complex history, both in the United States and elsewhere. In the United States, the social practice of some Americans of mixed ancestry passing for white dates back at least to the eighteenth century when freedom was often based on rigid binary racial identities, especially in the South. In the eighteenth and even the nineteenth centuries racial identity was based on appearance: If you looked white, you were accepted as white. Of course, matters were often more complex than that. For general discussions, *see* Jeffrey A. Brune & Daniel J. Wilson eds., Disability and Passing: Blurring the Lines of Identity (2013); Randall Kennedy, *Racial Passing*, 62 Ohio St. L.J. 1145 (2001).

30. I am grateful to Bernadette Atuahene for suggesting this to me.

It is that fact and the university's moral obligation to itself that gives rise to its obligation to support the community that has enabled it to flourish.

It would be a mistake to think of these obligations in terms of reparations, although that is the common way of framing the discussion about what, if anything, present property owners owe to descendants of now-deceased slaves.[31] The reason why the obligation that property owners owe to members of the African American community under the human flourishing theory should not be conceived in terms of reparations is that reparations are a matter of remedying past harms. Alfred Brophy explains reparations as "programs that are justified on the basis of past harms and that are designed to assess and correct that harm and/or improve the lives of victims into the future."[32] As Brophy's explanation makes clear, reparations are primarily backward-looking and aimed at giving redress to past victims or their modern day representatives.

In the case of reparations to African Americans, there has been some disagreement about exactly what the harms have been and who the victims have been. Most commentators have assumed that the harm to be remedied by reparations was chattel slavery, but some writers have viewed the harm more broadly. A number of years ago Boris Bittker argued that the harm was much broader. To him, "Black reparations . . . would serve to redress injuries suffered under a legal system that was held by *Brown v. Board of Education* to violate the Constitution."[33] Even more broadly, Harvard law professor Charles Ogletree identifies as the wrongs to be righted by reparations "slavery, Jim Crow laws, and a variety of more or less subtle forms of racism practiced today."[34]

Randall Robinson has taken a different approach to reparations. In his important book *The Debt* he argues that the basis of reparations to African Americans is the contributions that African Americans have made to American society. The advantage of this approach is that it avoids having to identify a specific harm or set of harms. Rather, the perspective shifts from injury to contributions. With this shift in perspective, reparations become less a matter of compensation than avoidance of unjust enrichment.

31. For just a few examples, *see, e.g.*, Brophy, Reparations, *supra* note 12; Randall Robinson, The Debt: What America Owes Blacks (2000); Roy Brooks, Atonement and Forgiveness: A New Model of Black Reparations (2004); Boris I. Bittker, The Case for Black Reparations (1973).

32. Brophy, Reparations, *supra* note 12, at 9.

33. *Id.* at 23.

34. Charles J. Ogletree, Jr., *The Current Reparations Debate*, 36 U.C. Davis L. Rev. 1051, 1052 n.1 (2003).

To the extent that it focuses on the fact that members of the African American community have contributed to the ability of institutions like Georgetown to survive and thrive, Robinson's theory bears some resemblance to the human flourishing theory. It differs in a fundamental respect, however. Robinson's approach views reparations as a matter of reciprocity, repayment for past contributions. Under the human flourishing theory, however, the basis for the moral obligation is not reciprocity, at least not reciprocity alone. Rather, it lies in the fact of interdependence between the individual and the community to which he belongs. To be sure, there is a sense in which interdependence involves reciprocity. But the obligation is not a matter of quid pro quo. As I discussed in Chapter Two, the obligation is more deeply rooted than that. It is ontological, not contractual. The obligation to contribute is an aspect of the obligation to belong and the obligations that we owe to ourselves. Our obligations to ourselves give us an obligation to support the communities and the kind of society that support the culture from which we receive the capabilities necessary for us to flourish. Interdependence not reciprocity, then, is the key to the obligation to make contributions.

Commentators discussing redress to descendants of slaves often claim or assume that the form of justice that is required in cases such as that of Georgetown is corrective or restorative justice.[35] Corrective justice obviously is a possible basis for redress, and it is particularly appropriate when redress takes the form of some specific restitutionary remedy, such as return of wrongfully appropriated property. The case of Georgetown is not such a case, however. What is required here is not corrective justice but a form of social justice that is based on the facts of belonging and inevitable interdependency among members of communities, the form of social justice that I have been tracing so far.

Bernadette Atuahene has developed the concept of "dignity restoration."[36] By that term, she means "material compensation to dispossessed populations through processes that affirm their humanity and establish their agency."[37] This is very close to what I am discussing here. I take Atuahene's compensatory measures to be nonrestitutionary. It aims at something other than, something more than correcting an economic injury. Atuahene discusses the concept in the context of South Africa, where the government has, as she puts it, "tried to move from reparations to the larger more robust task of

35. *See, e.g.*, Eric A. Posner & Adrian Vermeule, *Reparations for Slavery and Other Historical Injustices*, 103 Colum. L. Rev. 689, 691 (2003).

36. *See* Bernadette Atuahene, *Dignity Takings and Dignity Restoration: Creating a New Theoretical Framework for Understanding Involuntary Property Loss and the Remedies Required*, 41 L. & Soc. Inq. 796 (2016).

37. *Id.*

dignity restoration."[38] She emphasizes how dignity restoration looks beyond outcomes by emphasizing process. Restoration can take many forms, occur over an extended length of time, and involve nonstate as well as state actors. It provides not only resources but opportunities. Because it emphasizes process, restoration ideally involves claimants in the process, giving them voice in how restoration proceeds. This process complements the interdependent character of the relationship among the parties. This underscores the difference between dignity restoration and restitution and in that respect is very similar to the sorts of actions that fit best under the human flourishing theory.

This is not to say that slavery and other injuries resulting from various forms of racism practiced over many years are irrelevant under the human flourishing theory. That is not and cannot be the case. It is slavery and other forms of racism that bind Georgetown so closely to the African American community. Those injuries connect Georgetown with the black community in a way that, say, the State University of New York (SUNY) at Stony Brook is not. Whatever problems Stony Brook University may have as an institution with the African American community, the fact is that it was not founded on the backs of slaves. Founded in 1957,[39] it postdated both the end of chattel slavery and the Jim Crow era. It owes its existence and growth to the coffers of the state of New York and the taxpayers of the Empire State. Georgetown, by contrast, owes its existence to slaves and the slave-trade system. These facts, these moral harms, are at the very basis of its obligation to contribute to development of the capabilities necessary for members of that community to flourish.

What, then, are the obligation that Georgetown, as a property owner, owes to the black community? The black reparations debate has stirred up a wide variety of suggested forms of redress. They range from the simple and modest to much more complex and comprehensive plans. Alfred Brophy has usefully categorized all of the various forms of possible remedies into the following types: truth commissions, apologies, civil rights legislation, community-building program, and individual payments.[40] Some of these are voluntary and, so, are moral obligations only; others are legal obligations compelled either by legislation or through litigation. As I will indicate below, legislation and litigation have had limited success, but as the example of Georgetown suggests, there are indications that moral

38. *Id.* at 797.

39. SUNY Stony Brook began as State University College on Long Island, in Oyster Bay, in 1957, and later developed into a major university that was absorbed into the SUNY system. It moved to Stony Brook in 1962. *See* Stony Brook University, https://en.wikipedia.org/wiki/Stony_Brook_University.

40. *See* Brophy, Reparations, *supra* note 12, at 176.

suasion for institutions to take voluntary steps to acknowledge in one way or another their complicity with the moral wrongs of slavery and slave trading is gaining some traction.

One modest step relies on truth commissions. Several universities, including a group of universities called "Universities Studying Slavery" that worked together collaboratively,[41] have already created truth commissions to study their past involvement with slavery and the slave trade.[42] Some state legislatures have also taken the path of study through a truth commission. For example, the Oklahoma state legislature created the Oklahoma Commission to Study the Riot of 1921.[43] The purpose of the commission was to study, in a formal and open manner, the Tulsa Race Riot of 1921.[44] A variation on this remedy is legislation aimed at compelling disclosure of past connections with slavery and/or the slave trade. The City of Chicago, for example, now requires all businesses competing for city contracts to search their records and disclose whether they were involve in the slave trade.[45]

Private litigation has sought more robust forms of remedies. Perhaps the best known of the multiple lawsuits that have been filed against institutions seeking remedies for the firms' past involvement with slavery was the series of lawsuits filed around the country by Deadria Farmer-Paellmann and the Restitution

41. *See* http://slavery.virginia.edu/universities-studying-slavery.

42. *See id.* at 171–72.

43. *See* Okla. Stat. Ann. tit. 74, §8000.1 (2002).

44. Following World War I, the Greenwood District of Tulsa, Oklahoma, was one of the most affluent African American communities in the country. In June 1921, a riot nearly destroyed the entire Greenwood area. A young black man was accused of raping a young white woman who was an elevator operator. After he was taken into custody, rumors spread that he was about to be lynched by a white mob that had gathered outside the police station where he was held. A group of African American men then went to the police station to prevent the lynching. A confrontation between blacks and whites developed, shots were fired, and several people were killed. As news of this event spread throughout the city, mob violence broke out. Thousands of whites rampaged the Greenwood District, burning buildings and indiscriminately killing men and women. At least a dozen private airplanes drop burning balls of turpentine on Greenwood's rooftops. At least three hundred people were killed, and over eight hundred more were injured. Over ten thousand blacks were left homeless. The best account of the entire story is Alfred L. Brophy, Reconstructing the Dreamland: The Tulsa Race Riot of 1921, Race Reparations, and Reconciliation (2002).

45. *See* Sabrina L. Miller & Gary Washburn, *New Chicago Law Requires Firms to Tell Slavery Links*, Chi. Trib., Oct. 3, 2002 (Trib. West), at 1. The Chicago ordinance follows the pattern set by the California Slavery Era Insurance Act, which requires insurance companies in California to disclose past ties to slavery. Unlike the California statute, however, the Chicago ordinance imposes penalties for non-disclosure.

Study Group. The defendant companies were all either in existence at the time slavery existed or successors of such firms. The cases were consolidated in multidistrict litigation in federal court in Chicago. The district court dismissed all the lawsuits with prejudice. On appeal, the U.S. Court of Appeals for the Seventh Circuit modified the district court's judgment to be a dismissal without prejudice, affirmed the majority of the district court's judgment, and reversed the portion of the district court's judgment dismissing the plaintiffs' consumer protection claims, remanding the case for further proceedings consistent with its opinion. In *In re African American Slave Descendants Litigation*,[46] Judge Posner, writing for the court, ruled that the plaintiffs lacked standing to bring derivative injury claims because the plaintiffs showed no evidence that linked them to any of the defendants' behavior. The court also held that the state statutes of limitations precluded relief on the claims that were brought as representatives of slaves' estates. However, the court struck the district court's ruling that the dismissal was with prejudice. Judge Posner left the door open ever so slightly to the plaintiffs:

> If one or more of the defendants violated a state law by transporting slaves in 1850, and the plaintiffs can establish standing to sue, prove the violation despite its antiquity, establish that the law was intended to provide a remedy (either directly or by providing the basis for a common law action for conspiracy, conversion, or restitution) to lawfully enslaved persons or their descendants, identify their ancestors, quantify damages incurred, and persuade the court to toll the statute of limitations, there would be no further obstacle to the grant of relief.[47]

The upshot is, as Alfred Brophy states, that "[t]o achieve reparations for slavery through a lawsuit will be, to put it bluntly, enormously difficult."[48]

Even if litigation succeeded, it is at best an imperfect means of achieving reparations. As a mode of doing politics, it privileges lawyers over citizens.[49] Courtrooms become the fora for political debates, open only to a few, replacing open public deliberations. The remedies are defined by a small group of individuals with their own agendas rather than through a public process of distilling several different options.

46. 471 F.3d 754 (7th Cir. 2006).

47. *Id.* at 759.

48. Brophy, Reparations, *supra* note 12, at 127.

49. *See* John Torpey, Making Whole What Has Been Smashed: On Reparations Politics 108 (2006).

More realistic and effective forms of reparations are community-building programs and direct reparations to individuals.[50] The former include programs aimed at improving education, health care, and other pressing types of need. They are not necessarily directed toward immediate victims of slavery or their representatives but instead concentrate on persons in need. The second form of reparations—direct payments to individuals—are also probably the most controversial. Such payments more overtly appear to be redistributions of wealth, and that alone makes them controversial. Moreover, they entail a variety of difficult questions: Are the recipients entitled on the basis of harm they themselves have suffered or as representatives of now deceased persons who were harmed? Are they designed to prevent unjust enrichment, that is, to disgorge some benefit unjustly received? Must the persons who are obligated to make payments be persons who were unjustly enriched, and if not, were they otherwise somehow sufficiently culpable to render them now liable? All these questions and more have made direct payments probably the least likely form of reparations to be implemented.

Under the human flourishing theory, as I have already explained, contributions that an institution makes to the African American community are not, strictly speaking, reparations. As a result, matters such as identification of specific harms with specific victims and specific perpetrators of such harms are not issues. To return to the example of Georgetown University, its moral obligation is to contribute to the African American community, and this obligation exists by virtue of its membership in that community and interdependence with that community. The obligation is to contribute in ways that enable members of the black community to acquire the capabilities necessary to its members to lead flourishing lives.

So, just what might such obligations include? Because Georgetown's contributions should be ones that are appropriate to it, Georgetown University, as an educational institution, is best suited to enable African Americans to acquire educational capabilities. Specifically, the university is well-suited to enable other members of its community to pursue the educational goals that are increasingly important in modern American society. Those goals obviously include degrees at higher educational institutions, including Georgetown. As I indicated earlier, the university has already announced that it will offer to descendants of all the slaves whose labor benefited the university an admissions preference similar to that offered to children and grandchildren of alumni.

That seems like a good start, but there is no reason to stop there. Some of the descendants of Georgetown slaves criticized the university for failing to take

50. *See* Brophy, Reparations, *supra* note 12, at 176.

further steps. One critic wrote, "If Georgetown is authentically interested in reconciliation and atonement for its history, it should appropriate its $1.5 billion endowment to offer guaranteed admission (or a path to admission) regardless of income or felony status, and full scholarships—including housing, computers and books, and monthly stipends—in perpetuity to the descendants of enslaved people whose labor and bodies built the university."[51] It might be appropriate for the university, as an educational institution, to offer tutoring to black high school students, particularly in the District of Columbia, who hope to attend college. Moreover, some (or perhaps many) of the African American students who are admitted to Georgetown, with or without the benefit of the admissions preference, may not be able bear the freight of the Georgetown tuition plus room and board expenses. Georgetown is an expensive school.[52] A further and important step that the university might take is offering scholarships to black students, especially those who are descendants of Georgetown slaves (difficult as they may be to identify and locate), who attend Georgetown. This would be a direct and meaningful way of contributing to an important capability.

There is no reason why the contributions that Georgetown makes have to be confined to university-level education. Georgetown is an urban school in a city with a large black population, and one form of contribution to education might be through assistance, in cash, kind, or both, to public schools in predominantly black neighborhoods in the District of Columbia. The university might make its students, undergraduate, graduate, or both, available, gratis, as tutors to students in inner-city neighborhood schools at middle school or high school level. It could offer incentives to its students to participate in such a tutoring program through a variety of mechanisms, ranging from course credit to cash compensation.

Other means of enabling members of the African American community to acquire educational skills might be possible. I have sketched only a few obvious candidates. Georgetown perhaps best fulfills its moral obligation if its contributions pertaining to the acquisition of education as a capability. To give agency to those who were dispossessed claimants, Georgetown might allow them to determine how Georgetown should fulfill its obligations to them. Giving them voice in this way advances the human flourishing goal of promoting their autonomy capability. The contributions that any property owner makes in fulfilling his moral obligation to members of his communities should only be those that are

51. Samantha Master, *Georgetown University's "Reparations" Plan Is Worthless White Guilt Repackaged as Justice*, THE ROOT, Sept. 5, 2016, *available at* http://www.theroot.com/georgetown-university-s-reparations-plan-is-worthless-1790856615.

52. Georgetown's tuition and fees for undergraduates currently stands at $50,547. *See College Profile: Georgetown University*, COLLEGE DATA, *available at* http://www.collegedata.com/cs/data/college/college_pg03_tmpl.jhtml?schoolId=1182.

appropriate to that person or institution. Propriety here depends upon a number of considerations, one of which is expertise or specialization that the owner may possess. This is why it makes sense to say that the contributions of Georgetown, an educational institution, should have something to do with education, rather than, say, construction of new low-cost housing.

What is important, indeed crucial, however, to fulfilling an owner's moral obligations is that the owner undertake actions that contribute concretely to enable members of the black community to acquire the capabilities without which those persons cannot hope to experience fulfilling lives. This means that such actions, although they may include strictly symbolic gestures, cannot be limited to symbols alone. Apologies, acknowledgments, plaques and other memorials are a good start, but they are only a start. For an institution that has profited from slavery and the slave trade as Georgetown University did, they are inadequate means of enabling members of the black community, to which it has so long belonged, to acquire any of the basic capabilities that are essential to their leading a fulfilling life—good health, decent education, practical reasoning skills, security, and so on. This is why the measures that Georgetown has taken were appropriate, although, as I have indicated, perhaps not completely so, to satisfy its moral obligation to its community.

Georgetown is hardly the only university to have benefited from slave ownership or slave trading. Brown, Harvard, and Yale, to name only three,[53] all have acknowledged different ties to slavery and taken various steps to atone for these ties. In all three cases, none of the steps approaches what Georgetown has done. The University of Virginia, the College of William and Mary, Columbia University, the University of North Carolina at Chapel Hill, and several other universities have all undertaken efforts to study their respective past involvements with the slave trade and with slavery generally.[54]

Beyond universities, other institutions have also publicly acknowledged that they or their institutional predecessors profited from slavery. For example, New York Life, the nation's third-largest insurance company, disclosed that during the first half of the nineteenth century it sold policies on the lives of slaves. In fact, by 1847, such policies accounted for one-third of all the policies it had sold.[55]

53. *See* Holly Epstein Ojalvo, *Beyond Yale: These Other University Buildings Have Ties to Slavery and White Supremacy*, USA Today, Feb. 13, 2017, *available at* http://college.usatoday.com/2017/02/13/yale-university-buildings-slavery-white-supremacy.

54. *See* Universities Studying Slavery, *available at* http://slavery.virginia.edu/universities-studying-slavery.

55. *See* Rachel L. Swarns, *Insurance Policies on Slaves: New York Life's Complicated Past*, N.Y. Times, Dec. 18, 2016, *available at* https://www.nytimes.com/2016/12/18/us/insurance-policies-on-slaves-new-york-lifes-complicated-past.html.

Company executives state that slave policies generated only about 5 percent of its total revenues during the three fiscal years in which the policies were sold. They claim that the policies were not profitable and did not drive the company's growth. Historians point out, however, that the slave policies did have an impact on the company's growth. The company had two years of revenue to invest before death claims exceeded annual premium payments.[56] In recent years New York Life has provided philanthropic support to the black community, including a $10 million endowment to the Colin Powell Center for Policy Studies at the City College of New York, sponsorship of the National Museum of African American History and Culture, and other initiatives.[57]

The human flourishing theory stresses that contributions owners make should be in a form and to the extent that are appropriate to those owners. For New York Life, its contributions to those members of the African American community who represent the slaves exploited through life insurance policies might take the form of fixed annuities, immediate or deferred. The amount of each annuity should be reasonable to both parties and subject to negotiation. One possible index for the amount, of course, would be the equivalent in today's prices of the insured amount of each slave. That approach seems unduly complex and unfair, however. The insured prices of individual slaves would vary greatly according to time, gender, age, health, and other factors.[58] Hence, the values in today's prices of the individual policy amount would vary greatly.[59] Whatever the index and whatever the amount, New York Life's contribution—and New York Life was not the only insurance firm whose corporate predecessor insured slaves[60]—should take some form that is relevant to its business.

Is the moral obligation confined solely to organizations which themselves or whose predecessors were directly tied to the slave trade? Recall that in the case of Georgetown I suggested that the basis of its moral obligation was the injury, both physical and moral, that it had inflicted on blacks. But in fact the source of that obligation is broader than that. Membership in a community involves obligations. Each of us, including institutions, owes ourselves special responsibilities to

56. *See id.*

57. *See id.*

58. *See* Historical Statistics, Table Bb215-218. Index of slave values, by age, sex, and region: 1850.

59. *See* Samuel H. Williamson & Louis P. Cain, *Measuring Slavery in 2011 Dollars, available at* https://www.measuringworth.com/slavery.php#text11.

60. Aetna, for example, has acknowledged that it, like New York Life, sold policies on the lives of slaves during the antebellum period. *See Aetna Apologies for Slave Insurance*, http://articles.latimes.com/2000/mar/11/business/fi-7637.

ourselves and those responsibilities include an obligation to belong to communities without which we cannot flourish. It is not enough simply to belong, however, for we owe it to ourselves, if we are to develop the capabilities necessary for us to flourish, that we support those communities. This obligation to support, then, is an interpretation of the interdependence that is inherent in our condition.

Given this source of the obligation to support the communities to which we belong, there is no obvious reason why the moral obligation to contribute to the black community, however that obligation is met, must be limited just to those institutions that historically were immediately or directly tied to slavery or the slave trade. Many, perhaps most, organizations and institutions have ties to the black community. They do so, as property owners, by virtue of their dependence upon the black community for development of the capabilities that are necessary for their flourishing. Commercial organizations depend to varying extents upon the black community for their success. The same is true of eleemosynary organizations. The black community has a long history of supporting charitable and religious organizations in small and large ways. A 2012 report by the Kellogg Foundation found that black people are substantially more inclined to make charitable donation than their white counterparts.[61] Nearly two-thirds of African American households donate each year for a total of $11 billion each year.[62] A study in the *Chronicle of Philanthropy* reported that blacks give 25 percent more of their discretionary income to charity than whites do.[63] The objects of black charitable giving is not confined to churches. Groups such as the Boys and Girls Clubs of America receive a disproportionate amount of donations from blacks.

My greater concern is with commercial organizations, especially those more recently established. Consider Apple Inc. Apple was founded in 1976, and, given its recent origin, we can safely assume that it has no ties to slavery or the slave trade. Does Apple owe any moral obligations to make contributions to the black community? If the obligation were owed as reparations for historical injustices, as a measure of corrective justice, Apple might plausibly be able to respond that it owes no such obligations. It was in no way responsible for slavery, nor did it in any way profit from slavery or commercial trafficking in slaves. The case for Apple's responsibility as a matter of corrective justice could be made, but it would be more attenuated and, to many people, less compelling than that of firms like Aetna.

61. *See Cultures of Giving: Energizing and Expanding Philanthropy by and for Communities of Color*, W.K. Kellogg Foundation Report 2012.

62. *Id.*

63. *See* Michael Anft & Harvey Lipman, *How Americans Give*, The Chronicle of Philanthropy, May 1, 2003, *available at* https://www.philanthropy.com/article/How-Americans-Give/188055.

Suppose we look at the question of Apple's moral obligation from the perspectives of its membership in the black community and flourishing. The first point to consider is Apple's membership in the black community. On what basis might Apple be considered a member of the black community? Consent is the obvious basis. Apple might well agree that given the support African Americans have given Apple and its products over the years and given the fact that Apple purports to stand for values of great importance to people of color—inclusivity, nondiscrimination, diversity[64]—Apple might well agree that it is a member of the black community. But, as I have already argued, membership in a community is not premised on consent alone. What matters is a sharing of core values, such that, whatever other differences that may exist between the two parties, they are bonded in some substantial respect and draw from that bond support that enriches their lives. Taking Apple's mission statement at face value, both Apple and the black community share a deep commitment to values that are essential to both of them and bond them together.

Apple's membership in the black community means that a relationship of interdependence exists between the two. It is that relationship that provides the foundation for Apple's obligation to contribute to the black community, a community which facilitates the development of Apple's necessary capabilities, so that members of that community—black Americans—may themselves flourish.

A stark contrast may perhaps help to make the point. Apple is not the Ku Klux Klan. The Klan owes no moral obligation to contribute to the black community. It is in no sense a member of that community. No relationship of dependence exists between the Klan as a property owner and the black community. There is no sharing of value, no support, mutual or otherwise, absolutely nothing connecting the two that might with any plausibility be labeled community. The Klan does not need the black community to make money. Apple does. Apple could not flourish as it has done with the various forms of support it has received from the black community. Moreover, Apple and the black community share core values that are fundamental to the identities of both. Apple is a member; the Klan is not. Of course, the Klan is dependent on the black community for its existence in a sense. Without blacks (and other hated groups), the Klan would not exist. But, again, the Klan's connection with the property community is not property-based in the way that Georgetown's or even Apple's is. Insofar as we limit the moral obligation to persons and entities who are connected with the black communities through property relations, Apple owes moral obligations to enable flourishing; the Klan does not. In the final section of this chapter I will consider whether

64. Apple's mission statement: "The most innovative company must also be the most diverse." *See* https://www.apple.com/diversity.

the limitation of the property basis for the moral obligation should be removed, in which case, the Klan would indeed owe obligations (which doubtless would remain unmet).

Apple might meet its moral obligation to the black community in different ways. Of course, it might make monetary contributions to charitable organizations that serve the needs of the black community. More creatively, it might make more concerted efforts to make good on its mission statement of inclusiveness and diversity by hiring more African American employees. Apple states that 22 percent of its current employees and 27 percent of its new recruits are "underrepresented minorities."[65] But that broad category lumps together blacks, Hispanics, Native Americans, Native Hawaiians, and other Pacific Islanders. Apple's data do not itemize the percentage or number of African Americans specifically. Within the tech industry black representation has historically been low, and Apple's commitment to diversity creates an especially good opportunity for it to meet its moral obligation to contribute to the capabilities of members of the black community by hiring and training additional black computer scientists and engineers. It might augment its efforts through programs that mentor aspiring black computer scientists and engineers while they are in college. These are only a few possibilities. There may be other ways in which Apple could meet its obligation to the black community.

Apple is hardly the only firm to carry this responsibility. If we think about the reasons why Apple is morally obligated to contribute to the development of the capabilities necessary for African Americans to lead flourishing lives, we will quickly realize that many other firms bear the same responsibility. Indeed, it is hard to think of a large firm that does not have this moral obligation.

The main point to stress here is that under the human flourishing theory the contributions that an institution makes are not, strictly speaking, reparations. The basis for the moral obligation to contribute is not reciprocity or any sort of quid pro quo. Rather, it lies in the fact of interdependence between the individual and the community to which it belongs. As I have emphasized, the obligation to contribute to members of a community grows out of the owner's membership in that community and its dependence upon that community for its own ability to flourish.

INDIVIDUALS: WHEN AND WHAT DO INDIVIDUAL PERSONS OWE TO AFRICAN AMERICANS?

My family, my direct ancestors on the Alexander side, arrived in this country from Donegal, Ireland (and before that, Kintyre, Scotland), in 1735. The three

65. *Id.*

Alexander brothers (a fourth Alexander brother remained behind in Donegal) arrived in Pennsylvania and resided in Chester County, Pennsylvania, for ten years before moving to Virginia. There, they all took up residence in what is now Rockbridge County, which is located in southwestern Virginia. My direct ancestor bought land and farmed it.

I know all this about my ancestors because my brother has done extensive genealogical work on our family. When he learned that our direct ancestor, Archibald Alexander, had purchased land in Virginia and farmed it, my brother was concerned that Archibald may have owned slaves. After all, Virginia certainly recognized slavery in the mid-eighteenth century, and landowners commonly owned slaves to farm their land. The possibility was there. My brother's research revealed that Archibald did not own slaves. He and his wife farmed the land themselves. The reasons are not entirely clear, but one possible reason is that Archibald was not wealthy enough to own slaves. Apparently the size of his farm was relatively small, and he had no other source of income or wealth. He was essentially a subsistence farmer. Eventually, he sold the farm and moved, as so many others from that part of Virginia did, west to Kentucky.[66]

Suppose it had been otherwise. Suppose, that is, my direct ancestor, Archibald Alexander, had been a slave owner. Would this mean that I owe moral obligations of some sort to the present-day descendants of those slaves, or if they cannot realistically be identified and located, to the black community generally? The more important question comes if we dispense with the thought experiment that my direct ancestors owned slaves. Do I then no longer owe obligations because there is no property nexus for such obligations? In the thought experiment, my ancestors' status as slave owners provides the nexus with property, in just the same way as it did for firms like Aetna whose predecessors were engaged in slave-trading. But the facts, at least as far as I know, are otherwise. My ancestors did not own slaves, nor were they engaged in the slave-trading business. Is there, then, no property nexus for my moral obligation to members of the black community? If I do owe them obligations, is it merely by virtue of my status as a citizen, in which case the obligations are not endogenous to property ownership itself but are externally imposed by the state? That is one possible answer, but I think it is not necessary to rely on citizenship. I think there is a property nexus here. As a property system, slavery affected not only the slaves themselves, but it also affected and corrupted many other forms of property. Profits from slave trading enabled slave owners to purchase land as well as more slaves. They worked their way into

66. Archibald's descendants continued to press on, moving west to Missouri, where my grandfather, Oscar Alexander, was born and raised in Shelby County. Oscar later moved the Mississippi River to Quincy, Illinois, where he met my grandmother. My parents would later move to Chicago, where I was born and raised.

the corporate system, corrupting property held by large firms such as Aetna. Even after slavery legally ended, its legacy—and very real injuries—continued in the form of Jim Crow, and in that form, the property nexus expanded. The expansion continued as segregation corrupted the property system both formally and informally. An example of this process is chronicled in the recent book by Richard Brooks and Carol Rose, which details how racially restrictive covenants continued to be used, and further entrench segregation in Chicago,[67] even after the Supreme Court had declared them legally unenforceable.[68] This racial corruption of property has become so widespread that it is practically impossible to determine whether any single piece of property has or has not been tainted by the vestiges of slavery and Jim Crow. The reality, then, is that at least some property that I own is racially corrupted property.[69]

Past allocations and holdings of property have lasting consequences. People today, like me, who may think of themselves as innocent are nevertheless using property that has been affected by both the conquest of native nations and slavery and racial discrimination. The obligations that I owe to members of the black community, then, stem from my status as a property owner rather than as a citizen. They are internal to my ownership rather than external from the state.

As a property owner, then, do I owe an obligation to members of the black community?[70] In posing this question, I am not asking whether morally I owe reparations either to the descendants or to the black community. As I have stressed, the moral obligation I have in mind is one that is connected to my membership in the black community, if in fact I am such a member, and the mutual dependency that exists between me and members of that community, if indeed such a relationship of interdependency exists. The immediate question, then, is whether I am a member of the black community. At first blush it might seem strange to ask the question. I am a white person, and as far as my research has disclosed I have no black ancestors or other relatives. The question presents an opportunity to pose a much deeper question, though. What is the basis for membership

67. *See* Richard R.W. Brooks & Carol M. Rose, Saving the Neighborhood: Racially Restrictive Covenants, Law, and Social Norms (2013).

68. *See* Shelley v. Kraemer, 338 U.S. 1 (1948).

69. A comparable argument could be made for Native Americans, much of whose land was taken from them in ways and on terms that were morally, if not legally, corrupt. Their status under the theory I am tentatively offering here, while not identical with that of African Americans, is similar in relevant respects. Because there are differences, however, I confine my discussion only to the case of obligations owed to African Americans.

70. I am only discussing the obligations that white property owners may owe. As to the homeless and those who live in desperate poverty such that effectively they own no property, I would make no such claim.

in a community that is identified by race? What is it that makes a person part of a racial community?

Several observations are in order here. First, as I discussed in Chapter Three, community is a concept that is both contested and protean. Its elasticity, however, does not render it meaningless. However difficult it may be to define, we experience community and being members of communities throughout our lives.

Second, communities come in various stripes, including voluntary and involuntary. I am, at least in a certain familiar sense, a member of my family whether I wish to be or not; I was born into it. On the other hand, I am a member of the community of the Cornell Law School by virtue of my choice and that of my colleagues. This distinction, between voluntary and involuntary communities, however, is less binary than it may appear. Some people do not experience themselves as being members of the group that is their family of origin. Conversely, there are members of what are customarily considered voluntary communities who testify that they experienced themselves as compelled to join their respective community. Perhaps the best we can say in answer to the question, what makes a person a member of a community, particularly a community that is based in something other than contract alone, is that what is important is how one experiences community. Do I experience myself as a member of this community or that? It may not always be necessary that the community accepts me as one of its own. Not all communities are based on agreement, and, again, it matters what the purpose is for asking about membership in a community. Agreement is more important for some purpose than for others. But the really relevant question is whether I experience myself as a member of the community in question.

Third, and related to the point just made, community has different meanings when used in different contexts. Its colloquial meaning—the meaning it has in ordinary conversation when I say I am a member of the Cornell community or the community where I live—may not be the same when I use the term in a different context and for a different purpose. The suggestion that a white person or a predominately white institution may be a member of the black community may give pause. Other terms might seem more suitable. Better, perhaps, to say that I am an ally or a friend of the black community. Despite these concerns, I wish to use the language of community for a specific reason. The language of community of a conceptual/normative language to talk about who is within my circle, rather than always being the layperson's common meaning of community. What I am discussing in this context is not a colloquial expression or even a sociological term but a special signification of particular types of relationships that are based on interdependency such that the persons within those relationships nurture each other's essential capabilities and so, enable each other's flourishing.

Finally, it is important that we not get caught up in binary oppositions in all this. We need to remember what is at stake in asking whether I, or an institution such as Georgetown University, is a member of the black community. In the discussion so far what is at stake has been at stake is the determination of whether I owe moral obligations to members of the black community. But perhaps I owe these persons moral obligations of support whether or not I am a member of the black community. For there may still be a relationship of interdependency of such a kind that we nurture each other's essential capabilities and enable each other's flourishing. That is the real question in the human flourishing calculus, that is, whether a special relationship exists between me and the black community, especially in the sense that we each contribute to each other in ways that enable the development of those capabilities that are essential for us to flourish.

Is it possible, then, that I, a white person, may be a member of the black community? Without essentializing the concept of race, it may be useful—and I am offering this distinction tentatively—to distinguish between being a member of the black community, in the particular sense in which I am using the term, and being a member of the black race. For although I am not a member of the black race (at least let us so stipulate, simply to put aside the very complex questions about the nature of race and whether race even exists[71]), I may indeed be a member of the black community. Here membership in a racial community becomes a matter of whether a relationship of interdependency exists between me and the black community, a relationship in which members of that community and I contribute to one another's necessary capabilities.

There is both a positive, or empirical, and a normative dimension to this matter. Positively, have I or do I use my resources, resources that I own, to contribute in significant ways to the security, autonomy, health, or sociability, for example, of members of the black community? Or do members of the black community use my assets or rely on them in some way that materially contributes to the development of their necessary capabilities? Do I use my resources to contribute to their education, or facilitate development of their ability to engage in practical

71. The literature here is vast. Some notable race skeptics include Anthony Appiah, *The Uncompleted Argument: DuBois and the Illusion of Race*, *in* Overcoming Racism and Sexism (Linda Bell & David Blumenfeld eds., 1995); Anthony Appiah, *Race, Culture, Identity: Misunderstood Connections*, *in* Anthony Appiah & Amy Gutmann, Color Conscious (1996); Naomi Zack, Philosophy of Science and Race (2002); Naomi Zack, Race and Mixed Race (1993). Some race constructivists include Ron Mallon, *Race: Normative, Not Metaphysical or Semantic*, 116 Ethics 525 (2006); Robert Gooding-Williams, *Race, Multiculturalism and Democracy*, 5 Constellations 18 (1998); Paul Taylor, *Appiah's Uncompleted Argument: DuBois and the Reality of Race*, 26 Soc. Theory & Prac. 103 (2000). Finally, there are race population naturalists, a prominent example of whom is Philip Kitchner. *See, e.g.*, Philip Kitchner, *Does "Race" Have a Future?*, 35 Phil. & Pub. Affairs 293 (2007).

reasoning? Do members of the black community contribute to the development of those capabilities that are necessary for my flourishing? Do they enable my sociability? Do they educate me, and so on? The normative dimension of this is that how I view myself and how I view the kind of person I strive to become are matters that are intimately involved with investigating the positive questions. The investigation deeply implicates my moral self-portrait and the moral sketch I am drawing of myself. Seeing oneself as a member of a racial community other than one's own (or what is conventionally taken to be the person's race) is not a question of having black or Asian friends, although that certainly seems like an obviously good idea for such a person. Nor is it a question of atonement for past and present injustices committed against members of that community, liberal white guilt, as it were. Rather, the perception of oneself as a member of that community grows out of living the experience of being *part of* rather than *separate from*. It is a question of having moved beyond Otherness and been able to experience connectedness. As I discussed in Chapter Three, community is based on sharing of values, interests, or experiences. No white person can claim to share the racial experiences that a black person has gone through, but that difference, profound as it is, does not itself prohibit sharing in other important respects between a white person and members of the black community. Deep commitment to justice demands that all human beings be treated with respect and dignity, with the hope that violence between members of different races will end—all of these values and aspirations are ones that can and are shared between many black and white persons. These shared values and commitments provide adequate grounds for establishing a sense of community between white and black persons.

Supposing, then, that white people can be members of the black community, what are the implications for the moral obligations that a white property owner owes to members of the black community? If I consider myself a member of the black community, do I owe moral obligations to that community of the sort that I have described up to this point? More precisely, what are the contours of those obligations?

If I experience myself as a member of the black community, then I think I do morally owe obligations to my fellow community members. Membership in that community, like any community, means that its members and I are interdependent upon each other for developing the capabilities that enable us to live flourishing lives.

I am particularly dependent upon the black community for fostering in me sociability. I grew up in an all-white ethnic neighborhood on the North Side of Chicago. I literally did not know a black person until I entered college, and even then, my contact with members of other races was very limited. My race-consciousness and contact with members of the black community were greatly increased in law school and much more so when I took my first tenure-track

teaching position, in Georgia. Athens, Georgia, in those days (c. 1975–76) was still very much in the midst of the social and political changes of the civil rights movement. Athens society was a palimpsest of the Jim Crow era. Traces of past white- and black-only public drinking fountains, for example, were still visible. The small local Catholic Church that I attended was a locus of civil rights activity and had experienced serious backlash for it. The parish was multiracial and had been active in the civil rights movement in the town, leading at one point to a burning cross on its front lawn. I was active in my church and so became acquainted with a number of African Americans in my parish. In addition, quite of few of my students were black, and during my time in Georgia, I got to know several of them well. The same continued after I moved to Ithaca, New York, and Cornell.

An important aspect of the capability that my membership has enabled me to develop is education about what it means to be white in America. In his recent book, *Between the World and Me*,[72] Ta-Nehisi Coates suggests that it is not his job to educate white people about racism or how to act. That seems quite right to me, but development of education as a capability that I am discussing does not result from tutorial sessions with black friends. Rather, it results from openness, willingness, and sensitivity not only in conversations with black friends and colleagues but also in lectures, public debates, news sources, and the like.

Like many other white Americans, I once assumed that racism was confined strictly to overt acts like racial slurs and exclusions of blacks from restaurants, bars, housing, and other public places. I was entirely ignorant of less transparent but more insidious forms of racism let alone of the inherent advantages of being white. In housing, for example, non-whites are significantly more likely to be evicted than white renters. As the authors of a major recent empirical study state, "One of the most striking geographic relationships we observed is the close parallel of non-white communities and eviction filings."[73] It is no secret that people of color face discrimination in the criminal justice realm as well. In *Floyd v. City of New York*,[74] for example, federal district judge Shira Scheindlin held that the New York City Police Department's application of its stop-and-frisk program discriminated against people of color. She relied in part on data finding that of police stops conducted between 2004 and 2012,

72. Ta-Nehisi Coates, Between the World and Me (2015).

73. J. Revel Sims, Ian Aley, Lexa Dundore, Taylor Laemmli, Sheila Long, & Ruena McFerren, *Evicted in Dane County, Wisconsin: A Collaborative Examination of the Housing Landscape*, University of Wisconsin Department of Urban and Regional Planning (2016), *available at* https://gobigread.wisc.edu/wp-content/uploads/sites/3/2015/06/EvictedInDaneCounty_final.pdf.

74. 959 F. Supp. 2d 540 (S.D.N.Y. 2013).

about 83 percent of the stops were of blacks and Hispanics, while those groups accounted for just half the population.[75] In the workplace, the famous 1991 study by the Urban Institute found that on average white testers were significantly favored over black testers.[76] Subtle racism operates at even more prosaic levels. Eduardo Bonilla-Silva in his widely discussed book *Racism Without Racists*[77] analyzes how white people sometimes deploy various rhetorical moves about colorblindness to mask racist attitudes. For example, using "I am not a racist" or "Some of my best friends are black" as discursive buffers to statements that could be taken as racist.[78] Bonilla-Silva also gives examples of common rhetoric that "otherizes" blacks softly, as he puts it: "these people," "those people."[79] Then there are microaggressions such as "whitesplaining," such as comments aimed at shutting down conversation about race ("You're being divisive"; "There's no such thing as race—we're all human") and comments that deny the legitimacy of a black person's feelings about race ("You're being overly sensitive").[80]

I have also learned about the enduring reality of white privilege in modern America. Most white people have a generally positive relationship with law enforcement authorities. They do not experience the everyday fear of the police that blacks, even wealthy blacks, do. White people do not have violent stereotypes associated with their race. White people can live in any neighborhood in which they choose to live and can afford to do so. Moreover, Cheryl Harris explains how the sheer fact of being white is a form of property: "The wages of whiteness are available to all whites, regardless of class position—even to those whites who are without power, money, or influence. Whiteness, the characteristic that distinguishes them from blacks, serves as compensation even to those who lack material wealth. It is the relative political advantages extended to whites, rather than actual economic gains that are crucial to white workers."[81] All this and more I learned through fellow members of the black community.

75. *Id.* at 558.

76. *See* Melissa Favreault, *Discrimination and Upward Mobility* (Urban Institute, Washington, D.C., 1991).

77. *See* Eduardo Bonilla-Silva, Racism Without Racists: Color-Blind Racism and the Persistence of Racial Inequality in America (4th ed. 2014).

78. *Id.* at 105.

79. *Id.* at 3.

80. *See 6 Ways Well-Intentioned People Whitesplain Racism (And Why They Need to Stop), available at* http://everydayfeminism.com/2016/02/how-people-whitesplain-racism.

81. Harris, *Whiteness as Property, supra* note 13.

More has been involved in this experience than education. Through my interactions with black colleagues, students, fellow parishioners, and others, I have gradually gained a greater capacity to see matters from the perspective of others, to empathize with them, and to gain greater sympathy for people who come from backgrounds very different from my own and who have experienced the world in a far less benign way than I am been privileged to enjoy. This is what sociability involves. It makes the invisible visible, and it has enabled me to cross boundaries that once seemed impermeable. It would be an expression of hubris for me to say that I now understand what it means to be black, but it is certainly the case that my perspective has changed. The capacity to see that not everyone is treated the way that I am treated is not one that I could have developed on my own. Nor could I have developed that capability through conversations with white friends and colleagues. The capability developed only through many conversations, some very uncomfortable at times, with friends, colleagues, and other members of the black community.

Being dependent upon the black community for nurturing my capabilities of education and sociability, what moral obligations do I owe its members? Before venturing some possible answers, let me stress again that whatever obligations I do owe are not by way of reciprocity. As in the case of Georgetown University, my obligations result from the interdependence that exists between me and the black community. Recall that our obligations to ourselves to belong to communities mean that we have the obligation to support those communities and the kind of society that supports the culture from which we receive the capabilities necessary for us to flourish. Understanding that this is the basis for my moral obligations helps frame the available options for meeting those obligations.

The spectrum of possible ways in which I might contribute to the black community so that its members can develop the capabilities necessary for their leading flourishing lives is quite broad. I have colleagues who have adopted black children. This action directly connects their status as property owners with their interdependence with the black community. But adoption is much more than a matter of sharing one's home with a child. It involves a profound commitment to that child as a human being who is worthy of love and dignity. It also represents a connection with the black community and a commitment both to the child and members of that community to nurture the relationships that enable development of one's own capabilities, particularly education and sociability.

At the other end of the spectrum but still connected to property ownership, I might make contributions to the various institutions aimed at improving the lives of African Americans. These institutions range from the NAACP to the United Negro College Fund to the Black Lives Matter Movement. If I am serious about supporting the communities that nurture the capabilities that enable me

to flourish, I need to put my money where my mouth is. Contributions of money seem the minimum way in which I can meet my moral obligation.

Between these two positions range a great variety of possible ways in which I can act upon my moral obligation. Political activism is one such possibility. I might become politically active in causes that disproportionately affect black people. The issues include both national issues such as police violence and more local issues such as lead poisoning in local water supply systems.

Ordinary encounters with others, including friends and family, also may provide me opportunities to act on my responsibilities. White people sometimes make statements or use language in the presence of an all-white audience that they would not make in the presence of African Americans. Rather than remain silent in the face of racist comments or behavior, my obligation is to speak. Even if doing so creates an uncomfortable situation, I have a moral obligation publicly to reject racist talk. As I know from my own experience, silence in these situations may well be taken as assent or at least tolerance of the intolerable.

The discussion in this chapter has been intended as only tentative, simply a beginning of how we might think differently of race, property, and moral obligations to each other. Human flourishing and capabilities as the means to leading a fulfilling life provides, I believe, an illuminating way of viewing very different and controversial questions. I hardly claim to have given the last word. My only hope is that it is a word worth considering.

10

Homelessness and Other Systemic Housing Problems

It is an open secret that a housing crisis exists in the United States today. More accurately, several housing crises exist, for economically distressed Americans face different challenges in their struggles to find adequate housing. The United States faces not one housing crisis but many. Homelessness—actual out-on-the-street homelessness—represents only the most extreme of our housing problems. Other types of impediments stand in the way of the ability of millions of people in this country to enjoy what others take for granted—decent and secure housing.

Decent housing is fundamental to human flourishing. One cannot live a life that by any reasonable standard is well-lived without having available housing that is stable, safe, healthy, and affordable. The constitutions of several other countries recognize how profoundly housing affects human flourishing by making it a matter of constitutional right.[1] I have emphasized the role of communities, both social and spatial, for flourishing throughout this book. It should go without saying that decent housing is integrally tied to the kind of thriving neighborhoods and communities that are required for people to be capable of leading well-lived lives. But the brutal fact is that in America today that tie has been broken for far too many people.

1. *See, e.g.,* Constitution of the Republic of South Africa art. 26. For an analysis of South Africa's experience with its constitutional right to housing, *see* Gregory S. Alexander, The Global Debate over Constitutional Property (2006).

Property and Human Flourishing. Gregory S. Alexander.

My aim in this chapter is not to analyze all of the pathologies that plague the housing scene today, let alone to prescribe remedies for them all. The problems are too vast, too complex to do that within one chapter. Less ambitiously, the aim here is to suggest why these problems elude solutions merely through private law and judicial application of the human flourishing theory of ownership. The reason is that the problems are systemic in nature and require structural solutions that courts are not capable of administering. Courts, using private law principles, can make improvements, but these improvements are marginal and often are only incompletely effective.[2] Structural solutions require legislative and administrative action at all levels of government, federal, state, and local. They begin with, but only begin with, substantial wealth and income redistribution taking several forms including wealth transfer payments, subsidies, tax credits, and enforcement subsidies. These housing problems defy quick solutions. Even with substantial government support, they are likely to persist for some time. But they can be alleviated through concerted government actions that strive for systemic solutions. The human flourishing theory can make a contribution, but it is not a panacea.

In the remainder of this chapter I will briefly sketch the outlines of three especially conspicuous and harmful current housing problems. The problems are not entirely discrete. They are often related to each other sequentially, as one step leading to the next. By showing how housing problems are interconnected in this way, I aim to suggest how the housing crisis that exists today exists on a macro level. I will then indicate why these problems cannot be solved by imposing obligations on private owners on the basis of the human flourishing theory. Systemic, macro-solutions rather than the sort of micro-solutions that the social obligation norm can offer is required in order to eradicate these housing problems.

THREE HOUSING PROBLEMS

Homelessness

"The homeless are homeless, you might say, by choice." Those were the words of President Ronald Reagan.[3] The data do not back up his assessment, however. Few homeless persons want to be homeless.[4]

2. A clear example is the warranty of habitability. Thanks to the work of David Super and others, we now have good reasons to be skeptical of how effective the warranty is in improving the conditions of low-income tenants. *See* David A. Super, *The Rise and Fall of the Implied Warranty of Habitability*, 99 Cal. L. Rev. 389 (2011).

3. E.L. Bassuk, *The Homeless Problem*, 251 Scientific American 40 (1984).

4. *See* G. Morse & R.J. Calsyn, *Mentally Disturbed Homeless People in St. Louis: Needy, Willing, but Underserved*, 14 Int'l J. Mental Health 74 (1986); A.A. Arce, M. Tadlock, M.J. Vergare et al.,

The raw data tell a grim story. As of January 2015, the most recent point-in-time[5] for a count of the homeless population, 564,708 persons were homeless in the United States.[6] The total homeless population includes both those who were unsheltered (173,268)[7] and those who were sheltered (391,440).[8]

The largest homeless subpopulation was individuals, constituting of nearly 63 percent of the total homeless population. The next cohort were people in families, constituting 37 percent of the homeless population.[9] Individuals who were chronically homeless[10] represented about 15 percent of the relevant population (83,170), while families who were chronically homeless represented a much lower percentage, about 2 percent (13,105).[11] Veterans constitute about 8 percent (47,725) of the homeless population, and children and unaccompanied youth make up about 6.5 percent (36,907), although this latter number is unlikely to be accurate.[12]

Homelessness has decreased since 2014, both overall and in every counted subpopulation.[13] This extends national trends since 2007.[14] The greatest decreases have been among veterans (35 percent decrease since 2009), the unsheltered homeless (32 percent decrease since 2007), and people who are chronically homeless (31 percent since 2007).

These trends, however, do not reflect an entirely accurate picture of homelessness in America. Unsurprisingly, larger and more populous areas of the country, such as New York City, Chicago, and Los Angeles, see larger numbers of

A Psychiatric Profile of Street People Admitted to an Emergency Shelter, 34 Hosp. Comm. Psych. 812 (1982).

5. Point-in-time counts are the only measures that capture sheltered and unsheltered homeless populations.

6. Homelessness Research Institute, National Alliance to End Homelessness, The State of Homelessness in America 7 (2016).

7. Unsheltered homelessness refers to persons who live in the streets, in a car, in abandoned buildings, or generally in places unsuited for human habitation.

8. *See* The State of Homelessness in America, *supra* note 6.

9. *See id.*

10. Chronic homelessness is defined as "homelessness among people who have a disability—including serious mental illness, chronic substance use disorders, or chronic medical issues—and who are homeless repeatedly or for long periods of time." *Id.* at 21.

11. *See id.*

12. *See id.* at 6 n.4.

13. *See id.* at 3.

14. *See id.* at 9.

homeless people, but the objective numbers of homeless people do not necessarily translate into higher rates. But rates tell us much about the trends in homelessness in relation to the size of and trends in the general population of the nation or in individual states.[15]

Equally unsurprising is the fact that rates of homelessness vary among states. So, increases in homeless populations were concentrated in the West and the Northeast, with the largest increases occurring in New York and California.[16] Large decreases occurred in three states with large homeless populations, Florida (13.6 percent decrease), Texas (nearly 17 percent decrease), and Georgia (16.5 percent decrease). In these three states the decreases were especially significant among unsheltered homeless persons.[17]

Most people who become homeless are in financial straits. For lower-income persons housing typically demands a larger percentage of their income. What often precedes homelessness is "doubling-up" living with family or friends.[18] Lack of affordable housing is a pressing issue that creates the looming specter of homelessness for many people and too often leads to reality.

Several factors contribute to the economic dimension of homelessness. For one, recovery from the Great Recession has been very uneven, with nagging persistency of poverty. In 2014, the national poverty rate was 15.5 percent.[19] This figure was not appreciably higher than it was the previous year, but it was significantly higher than it was in 2007, just before the Great Recession. Although the number of unemployed people has steadily decreased since 2009, the number of people living in poverty has steadily increased.[20] The number of poor renter households paying more than 50 percent of their income toward housing increased by 2.1 percent to total 6.5 million.[21] The increase is likely due to the fact that while incomes for this group have remained flat, rents have continued to increase.

Poverty rates correlate only incompletely with homelessness. So, the 2015 report of the Homeless Research Institute shows that although the poverty rate

15. *See id.* at 11.

16. *See id.* at 14.

17. *See id.* at 16.

18. According to the 2014 Annual Homeless Assessment Report to Congress (AHAR) Part II (December 2015), 74.3 percent of people who had housing prior to becoming sheltered homeless person were living in the home of a family or friend.

19. *See* The State of Homelessness in America, *supra* note 6, at 37.

20. *See id.*

21. *See id.*

in Mississippi is more than double that in New Hampshire, the homelessness rate in Mississippi is almost half of that in New Hampshire.[22] One likely reason is the significantly higher cost of housing in New Hampshire.[23] Although housing costs do vary considerably by state, the national picture is one of lack of affordability. In its 2014 report, the National Low Income Housing Coalition developed a metric it called the annual Housing Wage—the hourly wage a full-time worker must earn to afford a decent two-bedroom rental home at HUD-estimated Fair Market Rent while spending no more than 30 percent of income on housing costs.[24] The report found:

> In the United States, the 2014 two-bedroom Housing Wage is $18.92. This national average is more than two-and-a-half times the federal minimum wage, and 52% higher than it was in 2000. In no state can a full-time minimum wage worker afford a one-bedroom or a two-bedroom rental unit at Fair Market Rent.[25]

The greatest need is among the lowest-income households. On the supply side, today only a very small percentage of the rental market is affordable for this cohort. For every one hundred extremely low income (ELI) renter households,[26] there are just thirty-one affordable and available units.[27] Most newly constructed units are for high- or higher-income renters, and the supply of subsidized rental housing has been steadily shrinking. On the demand side, one out of every four renter households today is an extremely low-income household. In 2010, there was a need for 6.8 million units affordable and available to ELI households; this figure rose to 7 million by 2012.[28]

Another factor contributing to homelessness is unemployment. The unemployment rate has dropped nationally since 2008, but the unemployment rate

22. *See id.* at 42.

23. In 2014, a two-bedroom apartment in Mississippi would require that a household make $13.67 per hour in a full-time job; in New Hampshire the household would need to earn $20.50 an hour. Althea Arnold, Sheila Crowley, Elina Bravve, Sarah Brundage, & Christine Biddlecombe, Out of Reach 2014, National Low Income Housing Coalition, *available at* http://nlihc.org/oor/2014.

24. *See id.*

25. *See id.* at 4.

26. ELI households are defined as those with incomes at or below 30 percent of area median income (AMI). The AMI itself is set by family size and varies by region. *See id.*

27. *Id.*

28. *Id.*

alone can be deceiving. It does not reflect, for example, people who have given up looking for employment and are no longer counted in the workforce.

Loss of a job is especially likely to lead to homelessness in households that spend a disproportionate amount of income on housing. A household in which more than 50 percent of its income is devoted to rent is one that is experiencing what is known as severe housing cost burden.[29] Such households live in a financially perilous state, and a sudden unexpected financial reversal such as job loss or major medical expense can be the trigger that leads to homelessness.

Homelessness strongly correlates with mental disorders.[30] According to the 2014 Point-In-Time Count, on a given night in 2014, approximately 20 percent of the homeless population had severe mental illness or conditions related to chronic substance abuse.[31] The most common mental disorders are alcohol and drug dependence.[32] Lesser mental disorders have also been associated with homelessness.[33]

This very brief survey hardly provides a complete or comprehensive picture, let alone analysis, of the problem of homelessness. It is a snapshot. But snapshots can reveal what we might otherwise miss. Homelessness has been with us for so long that it is on the verge of becoming ordinary. Once ordinary, it slides into acceptable. The purpose of my snapshot is to remind us that it is not ordinary for human beings to live on streets, on benches, or in cars, and it is certainly not acceptable. In the final part of this chapter I ask whether the private law of property is the appropriate or efficacious vehicle for mounting a serious response to this unacceptable problem.

Eviction

Eviction and homelessness are not entirely discrete problems. Eviction from an apartment or other form of rental housing is often the last step into the street. But the problems are not identical either. Many people who are evicted do not become homeless, at least not directly.

29. *See id.* at 48.

30. *See, e.g.,* Seena Fazel, Vivek Khosla, Helen Doll, & John Geddes, *The Prevalence of Mental Disorders Among the Homeless in Western Countries: Systemic Review and Meta-Regression Analysis*, PLOS MED, Dec. 2, 2008, *available at* https://doi.org/10.1371/journal.pmed.0050225.

31. *See* The State of Homelessness in America, *supra* note 6.

32. *See* Fazel et al., *The Prevalence of Mental Disorders, supra* note 30.

33. *See* Lisa Stand, *Homelessness and Mental Health: Moving Past Stereotypes*, Nat'l Alliance to End Homelessness, Oct. 10, 2013, *available at* http://www.endhomelessness.org/blog/entry/homelessness-and-mental-health-moving-past-stereotypes1#.WTCQo9xlCpo.

Some double up with family or friends; others manage to find alternative, cheaper housing, although this is becoming increasingly difficult as the supply of low-income housing continues to lag far behind demand.

Thanks to inspired social science research, particularly Matthew Desmond's justly praised book *Evicted*,[34] we know a good deal about eviction in America today. Desmond's book provided an in-depth study of eviction in one city, Milwaukee, Wisconsin.[35] He found that in Milwaukee, which has fewer than 105,000 renter households, landlords evict approximately 16,000 adults and children each year. That represents sixteen families evicted through judicial process.[36] Of course, eviction occurs through nonjudicial means as well. Indeed, landlords typically prefer informal methods of evictions as these are cheaper than court-supervised removal. Apparently, nearly half of all evictions in Milwaukee occur through informal means.[37]

Desmond further found that between 2009 and 2011, roughly one-quarter of all moves that Milwaukee's poorest renters made were done involuntarily.[38] Looking at eviction court records in other cities, he found similar numbers in other urban areas, including New York, Chicago, Cleveland, and Kansas City.[39]

Eviction creates ripple effects, none of which are good. Evicted people commonly are unable to qualify for public housing because officials count eviction as a strike against applicants when they review the large number of applications. The upshot is, as Desmond puts it, that "people who have the greatest need for housing assistance—the rent-burdened and evicted—are systematically denied it."[40] Further, evictions may lead to unemployment. The probability of being laid off is 15 percent higher for workers who have been evicted than for those who have not. Stress and the demands of trying to avoid eviction undermine many workers' job performance.[41] Eviction often exacerbates the very problem that leads to eviction in the first place, high rents. This is especially true where a tenant has been evicted from a rent-regulated apartment, and the landlord may

34. Matthew Desmond, Evicted: Poverty and Profit in the American City (2016).

35. Desmond points out that there is nothing unique or unusual about Milwaukee in this respect. Similar numbers exist for Chicago, Cleveland, Kansas City, and other cities. *See id.* at 5.

36. *See id.* at 4.

37. *See id.*

38. *See id.* at 296.

39. *See id.*

40. *Id.* at 297 (footnote omitted).

41. *See id.* at 296–97.

then charge market-level prices. It may also be true for tenants evicted from non-regulated premises because in a rising market landlords can use eviction as the opportunity to capture the higher market price.[42] Eviction can damage a tenant's credit record.[43] Families who find subsequent housing commonly move into premises with substandard conditions and often in poorer, more dangerous neighborhoods.[44]

Eviction can destroy communities and lead to higher crime rates. As more people in neighbors are displaced, neighbors become strangers to each other and no longer watch out for each other. Desmond found that Milwaukee neighborhoods with high eviction rates have higher violent crime rates the following year, even after controlling for past crime rates and other relevant factors.[45] Finally, we should not overlook the toll that eviction mentally takes on a person. Eviction depresses people and saps them of their spirit, sending them even further into a downward spiral.

How did we get here? Obviously, the Great Recession played a role, but it was not the sole reason. The rise in eviction is not recent, and there are multiple reasons for it. Some of these have to do with the housing market itself, others with the economy generally, still others with noneconomic factors. Here is a brief survey of some of these factors.

Begin with the supply side. The supply of low-cost housing has fallen significantly in recent years. Nationwide, the vacancy rate for units renting at $300 to $349, for example, fell from nearly 16 percent in 2004 to less than 6 percent in 2011.[46] The same pattern holds more broadly. Between 2010 and 2013, the national apartment vacancy rate fell by half, from 8 percent to 4.3 percent.[47] Add to that the fact that public housing is practically unavailable for most people

42. In San Francisco, Ellis Act evictions, which are used to convert rent-regulated apartments to market-price apartments, increased by 170 percent between March 2010 and February 2013. Marisa Lagos, *San Francisco Evictions Surge, Report Finds*, San Francisco Gate, Nov. 5, 2013. *See* Desmond, Evicted, *supra* note 34, at 392 n.12.

43. *See* D. James Greiner, Cassandra Wolos Pattanayak, & Jonathan Hennessy, *The Limits of Unbundled Legal Assistance: A Randomized Study in a Massachusetts District Court and Prospects for the Future*, 126 Harv. L. Rev. 901 (2013).

44. See Matthew Desmond & Nathan Wilmers, *Is Housing the Poor Lucrative? The Profit Margins of Urban Landlords*, Working Paper: Harvard University, 2016.

45. *See* Desmond, Evicted, *supra* note 34, at 298.

46. *See id.* at 349 n.4.

47. *See* Todd Sinai, *The Rent Affordability Crisis*, 2 Issue Brief no. 3, March 2014, Penn Wharton Public Policy Initiative, *available at* http://repository.upenn.edu/cgi/viewcontent.cgi?article=1017&context=pennwhartonppi.

who need it. In larger cities throughout the country the waiting lists for public housing are long, sometimes in decades. As a result, three in four families who qualify for housing assistance get nothing.[48]

Developers use subsidies from government programs like the federal Low-Income Housing Tax Credit program, the largest affordable housing program, to finance construction of new low-income apartments. However, the cost of development has been increasing, due to higher construction and labor costs. These rising costs cause the amount of affordable housing that developers can build to decline.[49] New multifamily housing built is mostly priced for the luxury market, and new affordable rental housing is harder to find. Also, more housing communities are being built for people with lower incomes, which can increase the cost to develop a property.

The supply/demand imbalance has led to bursts of rent growth, pricing low-income renters out of many markets, especially urban markets. Rents have been growing rapidly over the last several years. Between 2008 and 2011, in the middle of the Great Recession, rent growth trailed inflation in most major cities. During the same period, however, rent growth exceeded inflation everywhere—and in some cities, by as much as 3 percent per year. This recent rent growth undid the prior rent declines in many cities. Combined with the rent growth between 1990 and 2007, the result has been higher housing costs.

Many people do not realize that most low-income households pay market rents.[50] The facts are that most low-income families receive no government housing assistance and live in private, not public, housing.[51] In 2015, of the 9.6 million households below the poverty line in the United States 1.3 million households lived in public housing, 1 million living in Section 8 projects, 1.4 million using housing vouchers, 300,000 in low-income tax credit housing, and 800,000 living in other subsidized housing programs.[52] That leaves 4.8 million households (50 percent of the households living in poverty) renting at market levels. With

48. *See* Desmond, Evicted, *supra* note 34, at 59.

49. *See* Bendix Anderson, *New Affordable Housing Development Under Threat as Construction Costs Rise*, Nat'l Real Est. Investor, Sept. 6, 2016.

50. *See* Gerard Mildner, *The Gentrification Plan for Metro Portland*, Portland State University Center for Real Estate Quarterly Report, Fall 2015, p. 7, *available at* https://www.pdx.edu/syndication/sites/www.pdx.edu.syndication/files/Quarterly%202015-11.pdf.

51. *See* Matthew Desmond & Carl Gerschenson, *Who Gets Evicted? Assessing Individual, Neighborhood, and Network Factors*, 30 Soc. Sci. Res. 1 (2016) (in press), *available at* http://dx.doi.org/10.1016/j.ssresearch.2016.08.017.

52. *See* U.S. Department of Housing and Urban Development, 2015, U.S. Census Bureau, 2015.

rents growing at higher rates, low-income tenants are caught in an impossible squeeze.

Rent growth alone does not tell the whole story of lack of affordability. Compounding the problem has been stagnation or slippage in income levels. Nationally, between 2000 and 2011, for example, rent growth exceeded the growth in median renter income by one percentage point each year on average, primarily because real median income declined during that period. The usual metric of affordability is 30 percent of income. The great majority of lowest-income households have long exceeded that percentage of income paid on rent. Rents have exceeded 30 percent of income for more than two-thirds of the lowest income households since at least 1980.[53] What has been striking is the spread of unaffordability both geographically and among income levels. Using the 30 percent metric, rents in marquee cities such as New York and San Francisco have long been unaffordable. Lack of affordability has spread to nearly all other major American cities and smaller cities as well. Decline in affordability has also spread among income levels. As a Wharton study reports, "In many cities, the shares of households in middle-income brackets paying more than 30 percent of their incomes in rent have been rising to levels comparable to the lowest-income categories."[54] In fact, the same study finds that the greatest decline in affordability has occurred among low-to-middle-income households.

Individual discrimination also factors into eviction. Strikingly, only one study to date has examined discrimination in the eviction decision, and that study focused on the role of children.[55]

Analyzing survey and administrative data of tenants appearing in housing court, that study found that families with children were far more likely to receive an eviction judgment, controlling for arrears. The discrepancy reflected landlord discretion. One study found that low-income women, especially those who live in black and brown neighborhoods, have also been subject to discrimination.[56]

In the one study to date that has examined whether racial minorities who fall behind on rent are more likely to be evicted, compared with whites who also fall behind, Desmond and his coauthor found no evidence that black, Latino, or female tenants were more likely to be evicted.[57] The explanation seems to be

53. *See* Sinai, *The Rent Affordability Crisis, supra* note 47.

54. *See id.*

55. *See* Matthew Desmond, Weihua An, Richelle Winkler, & Thomas Ferris, *Evicting Children*, 92 Soc. Forces 303 (2013).

56. *See* Matthew Desmond, *Eviction and the Reproduction of Urban Poverty*, 118 Am. J. Soc. 88 (2012).

57. *See* Desmond & Gerschenson, *Who Gets Evicted?, supra* note 51.

that prejudiced landlords realize that any replacement renters will share the same demographic characteristics as the displaced renters. Desmond and Gerschenson state, "Operating in certain neighborhoods largely entails renting exclusively to certain demographic groups."[58] What fluctuates in the landlord's tenant base, they surmise, is not its racial or economic composition but family composition and size. Landlords have incentives to replace large households with smaller ones, and families with children with childless tenants.

Discrimination on the basis of familial status is proscribed by the federal Fair Housing Act,[59] but landlords have incentives nevertheless.

Personal misfortunes also may lead to or increase the probability of eviction. Critical misfortunes include job losses, major unexpected medical expenses, and other sudden and unexpected costs that place the tenant's financial stability in serious jeopardy. Any of these critical events can trigger a cascade of events that ends with eviction, especially for a tenant who has high rent-to-income ratios and no savings to cover a sudden income loss.

Neighborhood characteristics are another explanatory factor. Gentrification is the obvious example. The social science literature has long argued that gentrification leads to the systematic displacement of low-income residents.[60] Yet other studies have found no evidence that gentrification displaces poor families.[61] In their study, Desmond and Gerschenson examined whether gentrified or ungentrified neighborhoods experience higher rates of eviction than wealthier neighborhoods that are considered ineligible for gentrification.[62] They found "no significant effect for any of our indicators of gentrification, suggesting that renters living in racially or economically transitioning neighborhoods do not have a higher likelihood of eviction than renters living in racially and economically homogeneous areas (conditional on other covariates)." Desmond and Gerschenson did find that "renters' chances of eviction increase with their neighborhood's crime and eviction rates."[63] They speculate that tenants living in

58. *Id.*

59. 42 U.S.C. §3604(a).

60. *See, e.g.*, Peter Marcuse, *Gentrification, Abandonment, and Displacement: The Linkages in New York City*, *in* Gentrification and the City 153 (Neil Smith & Peter Williams eds., 1986); Kathe Newman & Elvin Wyly, *The Right to Stay Put, Revisited: Gentrification and Resistance to Displacement in New York City*, 43 Urb. Stud. (2006).

61. *See* Jacob Vigdor, *Does Gentrification Harm the Poor?*, Wharton Papers Urb. Aff. 133 (2002).

62. *See* Desmond & Gerschenson, *Who Gets Evicted?*, *supra* note 51.

63. *Id.*

high-crime areas might put up less of a fight when facing eviction than similar tenants in more desirable neighborhoods.

A final factor that social scientists have considered in studying what contributes to eviction is a tenant's social network. In their study, Desmond and Gerschenson studied tenants with "downward ties"—those who had either experienced what they call "poverty shocks" (e.g., eviction, incarceration, teenage pregnancy) or who were presently disadvantaged (e.g., jobless, addicted to drugs, in an abusive relationship). They found that such tenants had a higher likelihood of eviction, all other things being equal.[64] At the same time, they found no evidence that upward ties—to homeowners, the gainfully employed, or the college educated—made tenants less likely to be evicted. They explain the apparent anomaly on the basis of two factors at work. First, landlords may view tenants embedded in disadvantaged networks as undesirable. If the tenant's friends and family, who visit the tenant's apartment, are involved in criminal or violent activities, landlords are apt to be upset. Second, a tenant who has downward ties may view eviction as another hardship to endure rather than a change to resist. Even if they wanted to resist, tenants with downward ties may lack knowledge and resources to resist.[65]

The upshot of this social scientific work is that eviction is a complex problem with multiple, overlapping causes. It is not a recent phenomenon but has been developing for several decades. As it has developed, the causation story has changed. It is, in short, a dynamic social problem.

Foreclosure

Some background about the mortgage crisis will illuminate the current foreclosure scene. Over the past three decades, the market for home loan mortgage financing has been dramatically transformed. Until the mid-1980s, a typical purchaser would go to a local savings and loan association and borrow money to purchase her home. The association would make the loan from money in customer savings accounts, would secure the loan with a mortgage, and would hold the promissory note and the mortgage until the loan was fully repaid or otherwise terminated.

Thus, the flow of mortgage money was geographically constrained, with some areas—particularly rapidly growing areas—facing shortages of funds and relatively high interest rates.

64. *See id.*

65. *See id.*

The walls that segmented mortgage markets by state or locality began to crack a bit when Congress established the Federal National Mortgage Association (Fannie Mae) in 1938 and the Federal Home Loan Mortgage Corporation (Freddie Mac) in 1970. These government-sponsored enterprises were created to establish a secondary market in which mortgages could be bought and sold much like stocks, thereby evening out credit flows across the nation. In the 1980s, Fannie Mae and Freddie Mac were instrumental in creating mortgage-backed securities (MBS).

Hundreds of mortgage loans were purchased and pooled together; securities representing the pool were issued to investors, who received payments of principal and interest as they were made by homeowners. The securities, typically guaranteed by Fannie Mae and Freddie Mac, appealed to many investors who would otherwise have found home mortgage loans unattractive investments, thereby increasing the supply of capital and reducing interest rates. For loans that did not meet the credit requirements or size limitations of Fannie Mae and Freddie Mac, similar MBS markets were created by private investors and investment banks. They were often called "private label" MBS.[66]

Accompanying the growth of an efficient secondary mortgage market was a change in the types of mortgage loans offered to borrowers. For years, the only type in the United States was a fully amortizing fixed interest rate mortgage. With this type of loan, typical borrowers make a constant payment each month that includes both a component for interest and one for principal. The amount of each payment stays the same for the life of the loan—typically fifteen to thirty years—but as the principal is gradually paid off, the part of each payment attributable to interest declines and the part attributable to principal increases. At the end of the loan term, the debt is completely paid off.

In the early 1980s, when interest rates on home mortgage loans went up to 16 percent and more, financial institutions began to experiment with adjustable rate loans. Such loans, still widely used, feature an initial below-market interest rate that gradually increases according to an index based on debt issued by the Federal Reserve Bank. Typically, an adjustable rate mortgage loan can go up or down by a limited amount each year and has a lifetime cap.

Beginning in the late 1990s, there were tremendous and sometimes convulsive changes in the home loan mortgage market. Increasing automation, the growth of the secondary mortgage market, the increasing detachment between origination and investment in mortgage debt, a desire to extend homeownership to underserved groups, and increasing competition in the industry led to a profusion of

66. For a description of the transformation of the secondary mortgage market, *see* Michael H. Schill, *Uniformity or Diversity: Residential Real Estate Finance Law in the 1990s and the Implications of Changing Financial Markets*, 64 S. Cal. L. Rev. 1261 (1991).

mortgage instruments. Only three decades ago, home mortgage lending was a "one-size-fits-all" industry where would-be borrowers either qualified for a loan or did not, and if they did, were given a standard fixed rate or adjustable rate loan at a set interest rate. But by 2005, risk-based lending was in full swing and seemingly no matter how risky one's profile, a mortgage loan of some sort could be obtained . . . at a price.

This increasingly risky segment of the mortgage market is often categorized as the "subprime" market or the Alt-A market. The "prime" market provides loans to people with high credit scores, fairly typical loan-to-value ratios of 80 or 90 percent, and characteristics that meet standard underwriting criteria. The subprime and Alt-A markets, on the other hand, made loans available to people with low credit scores and sometimes unverifiable income. Loan instruments often combined low "teaser" rates for two years with much higher rates for the remainder of the term. Oftentimes, borrowers were allowed to borrow 100 percent or more of the value of the properties they were purchasing. In some instances, they paid less than the full interest accruing on the debt, which led to the growth rather than the decline of mortgage principal (sometimes referred to as "negative amortization"). As described later in this chapter, the economic slowdown and then the deep recession that the United States experienced beginning in 2007 led this house of cards to collapse and resulted in unprecedented waves of mortgage default and foreclosure, the collapse and bailout of Fannie Mae and Freddie Mac, and, ultimately, the deepest recession since the Great Depression of the 1930s.

These changes in the mortgage market were a contributing factor to the housing "bubble" that affected the United States in the first decade of the twenty-first century. According to the widely cited twenty-city Case-Shiller repeat-sales housing price index, from 2001 to 2006 house prices skyrocketed by 70 percent in real terms. Over the next five years, they fell back to earth, declining by over 40 percent.[67] A complete understanding of the housing bubble may never be achieved, but the combination of historically low interest rates, "irrational exuberance," and diminishing credit quality seem to be the primary culprits. Old underwriting principles such as minimum down payments, income verifications, and careful appraisal policies were abandoned as borrowers frequently purchased homes they could not afford, either for their own use or as speculative investments. As the economy slowed and interest rates increased, borrowers increasingly had trouble making payments, and defaults rose. The wave of foreclosures that occurred further depressed prices, leaving many homeowners with homes

67. *See* Edward L. Glaeser & Todd Sinai, *Postmortem for a Housing Crash, in* Housing and the Financial Crisis 1 (Edward L. Glaeser & Todd Sinai eds., 2013).

worth less than their mortgage loan balances. These owners were unable to sell their homes and, with no equity left, many stopped paying their mortgages to avoid "throwing good money after bad." This magnified the foreclosure problem and, in turn, intensified the decline in prices. Before prices started stabilizing in 2012, more than five million homeowners had lost their homes to foreclosure, and an additional eleven million (one out of every four households with a mortgage) were underwater.[68]

We might well ask why lenders made loans to borrowers who could not afford them and why borrowers ultimately wanted these loans. Clearly, the low interest rate environment that the Federal Reserve Bank maintained provided many investors with an incentive to seek out vehicles that would provide higher rates of return for their money. Mortgage-backed securities (MBS) became one of these investments and were pursued by everyone from individual investors and hedge funds to pension funds and government-sponsored enterprises such as Fannie Mae and Freddie Mac. Loan originators came under great pressure to increase their volumes of loans to feed the MBS pipeline, leading to deterioration in quality and more and more subprime and Alt-A (no documentation) loans. The number of subprime mortgages originated almost doubled from 1.1 million in 2003 to 1.9 million in 2005.[69] Almost one-third of all mortgage debt that originated in 2005 was in the form of either subprime or Alt-A loans, three times their share of the market only two years earlier. Over three-quarters of subprime loans had short-term teaser rates that reset to much higher rates after two or three years. Median credit scores for these borrowers were almost one hundred points lower than for Alt-A borrowers, who themselves had lower scores than those in the prime market. Over one-third of subprime loans and two-thirds of Alt-A loans did not require that borrowers document their income.[70]

It is unclear to what extent federal policies are responsible for financial institutions taking on too much risk. A variety of federal policies and statutes promote homeownership among American households, ranging from the favorable treatment of homeownership under the tax code to laws specifically incentivizing banks to lend to low- and moderate-income homebuyers such as the Community Reinvestment Act and the statutorily mandated affordable housing goals governing Fannie Mae and Freddie Mac. Several commentators have suggested that these latter regulations led banks to make imprudent loans to buyers who should

68. *See* Jesse Dukeminier, James E. Krier, Gregory S. Alexander, Michael H. Schill, & Lior Jacob Strahilevitz, Property 660 (8th ed. 2014).

69. *See id.*

70. *See* Christopher Mayer et al., *The Rise in Mortgage Defaults*, 23 J. Econ. Perspectives 27 (2009).

never have become homebuyers.[71] Other studies have refuted these claims by arguing that while Fannie Mae and Freddie Mac certainly purchased their share of poorly underwritten loans, private, unregulated investors did the same as they pooled loans into "private label" MBS.[72]

What about borrowers? Why did so many individuals borrow money and purchase homes that they could not afford? There is no doubt that some buyers sought to leverage low-cost debt to make potentially lucrative investments. Some committed fraud by submitting inflated property appraisals and/or inaccurate personal financial disclosures to loan underwriters. Some expected to flip their homes within one or two years before the below-market "teaser" rates adjusted to much higher market rates. But many others were uninformed and became victims. The idea that homeownership is an essential part of the American Dream is a powerful American ideology creating a predisposition among many to want to become homeowners. When the individual desire of an unsophisticated person to become a homeowner interacts with strong market pressures by mortgage bankers and financial institutions to originate loans, the results can be—and were—combustible.

As the housing bubble burst, mortgage loan defaults ballooned, and millions of homeowners found themselves "underwater." Foreclosure filings skyrocketed, and allegations of mortgage foreclosure irregularities such as robo-signing (i.e., the process of lenders and their agents quickly signing affidavits and other foreclosure documents without personally verifying their accuracy) became commonplace. Other problems disclosed by one exhaustive federal investigation included disparities in or absence of necessary documentation such as the note or assignment of the mortgage, improper imposition of fees, and, in some instances, foreclosure actions against properties whose borrowers were not delinquent.[73] Some members of the financial community suggested that the public outcry and ensuing litigation was a bit overblown.[74] Other commentators took the opposite stance. For example, David Dana argues that adherence to formalities does indeed matter since it could result in a homeowner retaining his home. Following the law also demonstrates the law's equal treatment of people who are not wealthy or powerful, it reflects society's emphasis on the importance of the

71. *See, e.g.*, Peter J. Wallison, Dissent from the Majority Report of the Financial Crisis Inquiry Commission 2–3 (2011).

72. *See* U.S. Dept. of Housing and Urban Development, Report to Congress on the Root Causes of the Foreclosure Crisis 41–43 (2010).

73. *See* U.S. Federal Reserve System et al., Interagency Review of Foreclosure Policies and Practices 3–4 (2011).

74. *See, e.g.*, Editorial, *The Politics of Foreclosure*, Wall St. J., Oct. 9, 2010, at A14.

home, and it may prevent the occurrence of another foreclosure crisis by increasing lender precautions.[75]

As a result of the collapse of housing prices between 2007 and 2011, approximately one out of four homeowners had mortgage balances that exceeded the value of their properties.[76] These "underwater" borrowers were unable to sell their homes because no purchaser would want to buy a house encumbered by a mortgage in excess of its value. Many were unable to refinance their mortgages to take advantage of low market interest rates because they had no equity in their homes. These underwater borrowers had only unappealing options available to them. Beginning in 2009 as part of the Troubled Asset Relief Program, the federal government created a series of programs to provide lenders with financial incentives to modify mortgages. These programs initially reduced the interest rates and lengthened the amortization terms of mortgages. Ultimately, the programs also provided subsidies to enable mortgagees to forgive principal.

When the federal mortgage modification initiatives were originally announced, they were expected to benefit three to four million homeowners. The actual number of mortgages that are in active permanent modification thus far, however, has been far smaller.[77] One reason is that Congress provided sunset limits for some of these programs. For example, the Home Affordable Modification Program, which enabled struggling homeowners to modify their mortgages by reducing the interest rate, fix the interest rate, and extend the term of the mortgage, terminated in 2016 with no renewal.

Nevertheless, mortgage foreclosures have steadily declined since 2009. In 2009, the number of filings was 3,457,643 with completions totaling 2,920,000.[78] In 2013, the comparable numbers were 1,369,405 and 921,064. As of 2016, the number of filings had dropped to 956,864, with 427,997 foreclosures completed.[79]

There is empirical evidence that the foreclosure crisis was patterned strongly along racial lines.[80] Black, Latino, and racially integrated neighborhoods had

75. *See* David A. Dana, *Why Mortgage "Formalities" Matter*, 24 Loy. Consumer L. Rev. 505 (2012); *see also* Nestor M. Davidson, *New Formalism in the Aftermath of the Housing Crisis*, 93 B.U. L. Rev. 389 (2013).

76. *See* Dukeminier et al., Property, *supra* note 68, at 684.

77. *See* Office of the Special Inspector General for the Troubled Asset Relief Program, *Quarterly Report to Congress* 63–64 (Apr. 2013).

78. Home Foreclosure Statistics 2016, *available at* http://www.statisticbrain.com/home-foreclosure-statistics/.

79. *Id.*

80. *See* Matthew Hall, Kyle Crowder, & Amy Spring, *Neighborhood Foreclosures, Racial/Ethnic Transitions, and Residential Segregation*, 80 Am. Soc. Rev. 526 (2015).

exceptionally high foreclosure rates. Using data on nearly all foreclosure events in the United States between 2005 and 2009, one study showed that the foreclosure crisis was structured strongly along racial/ethnic lines and likely spawned racially selective migration patterns that hardened racial/ethnic boundaries between neighborhoods and increased residential segregation beyond what it otherwise would have been.[81] Jacob Rugh and Douglas Massey argue that residential segregation created a unique niche of minority borrowers to whom lenders differentially marketed highly risky loans. Testing this hypothesis by regressing foreclosure actions in the top one hundred metropolitan areas on measures of black, Hispanic, and Asian segregation (controlling for relevant factors such as creditworthiness), they found that black residential isolation and dissimilarity are powerful predictors of foreclosures in large U.S. metropolitan areas.[82] Surprisingly, perhaps, other data reveal that the most racially diverse neighborhoods experienced exceedingly high rates of foreclosure, with nearly one-third of these neighborhoods falling into the very high range.[83] The upshot is that foreclosures became a common occurrence in neighborhoods in which black and Latino households lived and, especially, where they shared space with members of other groups.

Despite the fact that the number of foreclosures has continued to decrease since 2009, the facts remain that large numbers of people continue to lose their homes because of foreclosure, that questionable mortgage practices continue among some lenders, and that foreclosure is racially skewed to a significant extent. In view of these facts it surely cannot be said that the foreclosure problem is over.

SOLVING THE HOUSING CRISIS AND OTHER STRUCTURAL PROBLEMS AFFECTING PROPERTY: WHAT CAN THE HUMAN FLOURISHING THEORY CONTRIBUTE?

What, if any, contribution can the human flourishing theory of property make toward eliminating these and other housing problems? Answering this question provides an opportunity to identify both the limits of the human flourishing theory and what it does add to policy analyses of structural problems such as homelessness, tenant eviction, and mortgage foreclosure. It also provides an

81. *See id.*

82. *See* Jacob S. Rugh & Douglas S. Massey, *Racial Segregation and the American Foreclosure Crisis*, 75 Am. Soc. Rev. 629 (2010).

83. *See* Paul S. Calem, Kevin Gillen, & Susan Wachter, *The Neighborhood Distribution of Subprime Mortgage Lending*, 29 J. Real Est. Fin. & Econ. 393 (2004).

opportunity to discuss the relationship between the human flourishing theory that I have developed here and progressive property theory more broadly.

It is important to be clear at the outset about what the human flourishing theory is and what it isn't. At its core, it is a conceptual theory. It is a theory about the concept of private ownership, its nature and its value foundations. The analysis of private ownership's value foundations is what connects it both to capabilities theory and to Charles Taylor's social thesis. I explained this in Chapters One and Two. It is not in and of itself a solution to every socioeconomic problem that concerns or involves property. What it can do—and this is a very important contribution not to be underestimated—is to lay the necessary theoretical foundation for solutions. Not all property-related problems are simply a matter of recognizing the existence of an entitlement, but some are. This is one reason why I discussed the right to exclude in Chapter Six. Lack of public access to resources, ranging from beaches to hotels to lunch counters, is a matter of entitlement distribution. The problem stems from a mistaken conception of private ownership, which undergirds the view that owners have a nearly absolute right to exclude anyone save for a few clearly delineated exceptions. Once we recognize, however, that this is not what ownership means, then it becomes possible to resolve access problems such as beach access and public accommodations through recognition of an entitlement. This can be done either as a matter of private law, as in the beach cases, or public law, as in the public accommodation context. The human flourishing theory itself is the vehicle for entitlement recognition of that sort.

Other sorts of problems that involve property elude such solution. Problems of this sort are structural or systemic in nature. That is, they inhere not simply in discrete entitlement recognition or arrangement but in social and cultural structures and patterned arrangements embedded in society. Their origins lie in institutions, social networks, and social norms. They are deeply entrenched, and they are complex. They defy any single or simple solution.

Consider the warranty of habitability. That rule basically involved recognition of an entitlement. The landlord's ownership interest did not include the entitlement to ignore the care and condition of the premises during the rental period. Rather the tenant holds the entitlement to the landlord's maintaining the premises in safe, decent conditions. But we now know that legal recognition of the tenant's right to habitable conditions did little to ameliorate the problem that too many poor tenants live in decrepit housing units.[84] Few tenants who need it know about it. Those who do often lack the legal sophistication to assert their rights under the doctrine. They lack legal advice and legal representation. Plus, if moving costs are relatively low, tenants may prefer to move rather than go

84. *See* Super, *Warranty of Habitability*, *supra* note 2.

through litigation at the risk of losing. Moreover, the new defenses available to tenants required substantially more judicial resources than the old regime did. Few courts were prepared to do the work required of them, work that was more efficaciously handled by administrative agencies through enforcement of housing codes. The net result of all these and other impediments is, as David Super states, that "the new regime of landlord-tenant law inaugurated four decades ago has failed at achieving any of its major goals."[85]

If entitlement recognition and entitlement enforcement are not solutions to the problems of homelessness, eviction, and foreclosure, then what other, broader solutions might be more effective? Matthew Desmond offers some possibilities toward the end of his book. He observes, correctly, I think, that "[a] problem as big as the affordable-housing crisis calls for a big solution."[86] The solution actually has several increments. One is establishing publicly funded legal services for low-income families in housing courts. Desmond suggests that this would be a "cost-effective measure that would prevent homelessness, decrease evictions, and give poor families a fair shake."[87] Judging from the evidence of various researchers, including both Desmond and David Super, this change would very likely have some positive effects. Most landlords are repeat players and are well represented in court. Poor tenants, on the other hand, are largely ignorant of the legal system. Desmond's idea would level the playing field to some degree and give poor tenants a fighting chance at avoiding eviction, and possibly the streets. It would not, on the other hand, address the problem of lack of housing code enforcement. Poor tenants might be able to remain, but remain in what? A real solution requires that they have available to them premises that are decent and habitable, and that requires more than a housing court alone can accomplish.

Desmond's much more ambitious proposal is a universal housing voucher. Every family below a specified income level would be eligible for a housing voucher which they could use to live anywhere they choose within certain constraints. Premises would be required to be decent, modest, and fairly priced. Desmond suggests that program administrators could develop finely grained analyses to prevent landlords from overcharging and families from selecting excessively large premises. Families would spend no more than 30 percent of their own income toward housing, with the voucher picking up the difference.[88] Desmond asserts that this program would "change the face of poverty in this country." "Evictions

85. *See id.* at 458.

86. Desmond, Evicted, *supra* note 34, at 303.

87. *Id.*

88. *See id.* at 308.

would plummet and become rare occurrences. Homelessness would almost disappear."[89] Although a universal housing voucher would surely make a significant difference in the several housing problems, it overstates the case, I think, to say that as a result homelessness would almost disappear.[90] Homelessness is a complex problem with several causes. One of these lies on supply side, the strong imbalance between demand and supply of decent and affordable housing. We need to know to what extent a universal housing voucher would stimulate construction of or conversion to low-income housing. A further source of homelessness is noneconomic. It is well known that many who are now on the streets (or in cars, etc.) suffer from serious emotional and mental disorders that contribute to their homeless condition. The 2015 point-in-time HUD Homeless Assessment Report found that 25 percent of the homeless (140,000 of the 564,708 people were homeless on a given night in the United States) were seriously mentally ill at any given point in time. Forty-five percent of the homeless had a mental illness.[91] The problem of inadequate treatment for mental illness must be addressed simultaneously with problems of supply and inadequate income if we are to truly eliminate homelessness.

The systemic nature of the problem is such that there is little or no mechanism for coordinating the several dimensions of homelessness. Desmond points out that to be workable, a universal housing voucher problem would best be handled on a national scale. While true, the problem is not simply geographic or federal-state in nature, but, more systematically, that responsible agencies, including federal agencies alone, lack a central office that coordinates all efforts and resources aimed at eliminating homelessness. There is a federal Interagency Council on Homelessness, established in 2010, which created a plan to end homelessness by 2015. In its 2015 report to the president, the target date was pushed ahead to 2017. That council lacks the necessary authority and resources,

89. *Id.*

90. Desmond addresses two further problems with a universal housing voucher. One is moral hazard. It might create a disincentive for tenants to work. Desmond acknowledges that some data indicate some support for the claim, but he points out that other studies have found no effect. He argues, "By and large, the poor do not want some small life." *Id.* at 310. A second problem is that landlords use the voucher program as an opportunity to increase their profits by raising rents. Desmond's proposed solution is rent control regulation. "Making a universal housing program as efficient as possible would require regulating costs," he states. "Expanding housing vouchers without stabilizing rent would be asking taxpayers to subsidize landlords' profits." *Id.* at 311.

91. *See* The 2015 Annual Homeless Assessment Report (AHAR) to Congress, U.S. Department of Housing and Urban and Urban Department, Office of Community Planning and Development, *available at* https://www.hudexchange.info/resources/documents/2015-AHAR-Part-1.pdf. *See also* https://mentalillnesspolicy.org/consequences/homeless-mentally-ill.html.

however, to meet its stated goal. Not only affordability and supply problems, but mental health issues, veterans' issues, racial and ethnic discrimination and segregation problems, substance abuse problems all need to be addressed and addressed simultaneously, and this can only be accomplished through effective coordination under the umbrella of a single federal agency with the powers and resources to implement the deep changes that need to be made to end homelessness and evictions.

No super-agency can end evictions either, for the problem is structural as well as systemic. The structure of the residential housing market creates incentives for both landlords and tenants that perpetuate the cycle that leads to eviction of low-income tenants. The drastic imbalance between supply of and demand for low-cost housing nationally, the dearth of public assistance for low-income tenants (meaning that they pay market-level rent), the professionalization of property management, coupled with the screening practices of landlords, discrimination by landlords, and nonenforcement of housing codes all create an entrenched structure within which low-income tenants have no leverage whatsoever. Desmond observes that even during the Depression the number of eviction was a fraction of what it is now.[92] A major part of the explanation is that the structure of the residential housing market, especially the low-income market, was very different then. Real change, then, must be structural.

This is certainly not to say that programs such as Desmond's universal housing vouchers are not worth pursuing. Much to the contrary, they are exactly what we need in the absence of any sort of more structural approach to the problems of eviction and homelessness. If well planned and implemented, a voucher program may well decrease homelessness and evictions to a substantial extent. Moreover, the voucher accords with the human flourishing theory in its aim to provide low-income tenants with essential capabilities, including not only access to decent housing but also individual autonomy over where to live.[93] Theoretically, this might lead to breaking up concentrations of low-income tenants, but we know from the experience of Section 8 tenants that the actual result might be otherwise. Section 8 voucher recipients tend to remain in areas that are familiar to them.[94] Partly this is due to several features of the Section 8 program that act as

92. *See* Desmond, Evicted, *supra* note 34, at 3–4.

93. Zach Bray correctly observes that Section 8 better fits "the values and ends of the new progressive-property approach . . . than rent control." Zachary Bray, *The New Progressive Property and the Low-Income Housing Conflict*, 2012 BYU L. Rev. 1109, 1127 (2012). But, as I have indicated, Section 8, is a highly flawed program. The voucher program that Desmond proposes offers great improvements.

94. *See* Alana Semuels, *How Housing Policy Is Failing America's Poor*, The Atlantic, June 24, 2015.

incentives for continuing segregation.[95] Partly it is due to landlords discriminating against low-income tenants.[96] The universal housing voucher program must be designed in such a way as to avoid these problems.

Although the mortgage foreclosure rate has been declining, it, too, remains an entrenched problem, especially for lower-income families. Some remedies have been attempted, but none has been adequate. Again, the problem is systemic and structural with many aspects. To pick only one example, it is very difficult for delinquent borrowers to modify their loans. There are several reasons for this. The transaction costs of loan modifications are substantial. Also complicating matters, sometimes second mortgage liens exist that need to be extinguished for modification. A major problem is identifying the mortgage holder. It is frequently difficult or impossible for borrowers to identify the entity with which they should negotiate. The use of MERS—the Mortgage Electronic Registration Systems, Inc.—has contributed substantially to the problem. MERS is a private organization formed by mortgage lenders who wanted to trade mortgages more cheaply and quickly. MERS holds the mortgages for the benefit of the mortgagees, but it does not own the mortgage and lacks authority to act on behalf of the lender. Usually, the real owner of the mortgage is not listed in the public land records, making it difficult to impossible for borrowers to identify their creditor so that they can renegotiate the loan.

MERS amounts to a usurpation of the state public recording system. That system has well-known flaws and is highly imperfect, but it does facilitate renegotiation by making it possible for borrowers to identify who owns their mortgages. A well-run title registration system would be superior to recording and certainly fairer than MERS, but registration is not popular in this country for multiple reasons. Scholars have called for a national public registry of land titles,[97] but the problem is deeper than land titles alone. MERS was created to facilitate the transfer of mortgages. The need to be able to transfer mortgages quickly and cheaply itself arose as a result of the emergence of mortgage-backed securities. The securitization of home mortgage is itself a long story, and there are multiple competing narratives accounting for it.

Partly it has to do with changes in federal law that were pushed by large institutional lenders. Another part is the role played by Fannie Mae and Freddie

95. *See* Philip Tegeler, *Continuing Barriers to Housing Choice and Integration in HUD's Section 8 Voucher Program*, Poverty & Race Research Action Council, Dec. 14, 2010, *available at* http://www.prrac.org/pdf/Section_8_fair_housing_barriers_12-15-10.pdf.

96. *See* Semuels, *Housing Policy, supra* note 94.

97. *See* Tanya Marsh, *Foreclosures and the Failure of the American Land Title Recording System*, 111 Colum. L. Rev. Sidebar 19 (2011).

Mac. More deeply, Neil Fligstein and Adam Goldstein argue that the development and internalization by large financial firms of a conception of firm organization and control is at the root of the story of mortgage finance.[98] The model was "predicated on securing a supply of raw mortgages in order to fill the firm's vertically integrated pipeline and thereby guarantee itself fees at all parts of the process."[99] This account shows how the problems stemming from securitization of mortgages were systemic and structural in nature.

One of the more interesting solutions to the foreclosure problem involved the use of the government's eminent domain power. First developed by Robert Hockett and Mortgage Resolution Partners,[100] the idea is for a city to force a sale of underwater mortgages by paying mortgage holders 80 percent of the home's current value, enough to satisfy the constitutional requirement of just compensation. The mortgage holders will thus not receive the face value of the mortgages as compensation for the local government taking the property, but an amount that is heavily discounted. The city then converts the acquired mortgages into Federal Housing Association loans with smaller principals that correspond with the current value of the home. Several cities considered using the plan but then backed off for various reasons including concerns about its legal footing. The city of Richmond, California, however, has adopted it and successfully fended off court challenges.[101]

The obvious benefit of this idea is that it enables homeowners to remain in their homes and restructure their debt. It does not address, however, the deeper systemic and structural problems that led to the foreclosure problem in the first place. Such changes would involve lending practices ranging from robo-signing to mortgage assignments, including securitization itself. Structural changes such as these rather than the clearly inadequate procedural reforms such as minimum notice periods[102] and uniform mortgage servicing

98. *See* Neil Fligstein & Adam Goldstein, *The Transformation of Mortgage Finance and the Industrial Roots of the Mortgage Meltdown*, U.C. Berkeley Dept. of Sociology, Oct. 2012, *available at* http://sociology.berkeley.edu/sites/default/files/faculty/fligstein/The%20Transformation%20of%20Mortgage%20Fi nance2.pdf.

99. *Id.*

100. *See* Christopher Matthews, *Should Eminent Domain Be Used to Save Underwater Homes*, Time, July 12, 2012.

101. *See* Michael E. Reyen, *Eminent Domain Mortgage Seizures Down But Not Out*, American Banker, June 16, 2014, *available at* https://www.americanbanker.com/opinion/eminent-domain-mortgage-seizures-down-but-not-out.

102. *See* Frank S. Alexander et al., *Legislative Responses to the Foreclosure Crisis in Nonjudicial Foreclosure States*, 31 Rev. Banking Fin. L. 341, 357–409 (2011).

standards[103] are what is necessary to match the type of problem involved. The old chestnut about bringing back Glass-Steagall keeps being tossed around, but that is a very questionable idea, as others have pointed out.[104] Perhaps even more fundamental changes would be needed, included restructuring large banks and the banking system.

Even if changes of that magnitude are not necessary, the changes that are necessary finally to eliminate the foreclosure problem go far beyond what the human flourishing theory in and of itself can accomplish. That theory alone cannot make systemic or structural changes. As I have already indicated, what it can do is to effect legal recognition of property entitlements in persons who are not titleholders. Doing so, it lays the foundation for other, broader changes as well.

Although the human flourishing theory proper is not capable itself of effecting deep systemic or structural changes relating to property, progressive property theory is. The human flourishing theory is only one part of the broader body of work that is progressive property. This includes work that is more programmatic in nature, that is, work whose aim is changing or advocating for particular policies or programs. Examples of this sort of progressive property work include Zachary Bray's article on Section 8 housing vouchers.[105] It also includes work such as Thomas Mitchell's proposals to reform inheritance of black farm land,[106] Christopher Odinet's article on the Puerto Rican debt crisis,[107] and Rashmi Dyal-Chand's paper on the incompatibility between entrepreneurship and community economic development.[108] The principle goal of all of this scholarship is to find solutions to practical property-related problems that oppress the lives of poor or powerless people. In this sense, all of the work shares the ultimate goal of advancing human flourishing. The work offers proposals that affect entitlements but require changes that go beyond entitlement recognition and entitlement enforcement. Some of the changes, like Odinet's, are more structural in nature, and others, like Dyal-Chand's, are cultural.

103. *See* Mortgage Servicing Rules Under the Real Estate Settlement Procedures Act (Regulation X), 78 Fed. Reg. 10696 (codified at 12 C.F.R. §1024) (Feb. 14, 2013).

104. For a persuasive argument against restoring Glass-Steagall, *see* Barry Eichengreen, *Why No Glass-Steagall II?*, Project Syndicate, Jan. 10, 2013.

105. *See* Bray, *The Low-Income Housing Conflict*, *supra* note 93.

106. *See* Thomas W. Mitchell, *Reforming Property Law to Address Devastating Land Loss*, 66 Ala. L. Rev. 1 (2014).

107. *See* Christopher K. Odinet, *Of Progressive Property and Public Debt*, 51 Wake Forest L. Rev. 1101 (2016).

108. *See* Rashmi Dyal-Chand & James V. Rowan, *Developing Capabilities, Not Entrepreneurs: A New Theory for Community Economic Development*, 42 Hofstra L. Rev. 839 (2013).

What makes property scholarship such as these pieces progressive are three characteristics: (1) their shared goal of human flourishing, (2) their understanding of property as based on a pluralistic value foundation that includes but is far from limited to preference-satisfaction, and (3) their commitment to improving the lives of those who live on the margins of society. Using property to help the lives of marginalized people is, after all, what makes progressive property *progressive.*

Bibliography

Books, Monographs

Abbey, Ruth (ed.). 2004. *Charles Taylor*. Cambridge: Cambridge University Press.

Adler, Matthew D. & Posner, Eric A. 2006. *New Foundations of Cost-Benefit Analysis*. Cambridge, MA: Harvard University Press.

Anaya, S. James. 2004. *Indigenous Peoples in International Law*. 2nd ed. New York: Oxford University Press.

Andersen, Benedict. 1983. *Imagined Communities*. London: Verso.

Anderson, Elizabeth. 1993. *Value in Ethics and Economics*. Cambridge, MA: Harvard University Press.

Annas, Julia. 1993. *The Morality of Happiness*. New York: Oxford University Press.

Annual Homeless Assessment Report (AHAR) to Congress. 2015. U.S. Department of Housing and Urban and Urban Department, Office of Community Planning and Development, available at https://www.hudexchange.info/resources/documents/2015-AHAR-Part-1.pdf.

Aristotle, 1962. *Niomachean Ethics*, trans. Martin Ostwald. Indianapolis: Bobbs-Merrill.

Arnold, Althea, Crowley, Sheila, Bravve, Elina, Brundage, Sarah, & Biddlecombe, Christine. 2014. *Out of Reach*. National Low Income Housing Coalition, available at http://nlihc.org/oor/2014.

Banner, Stuart. 2008. *Who Owns the Sky? The Struggle to Control Airspace from the Wright Brothers On*. Cambridge, MA: Harvard University Press.

Bell, Colin & Newby, Howard. 1973. *Community Studies: An Introduction to the Sociology of the Local Community*. New York: Praeger Publishers.

Berger, Alan S. 1978. *The City: Urban Communities and Their Problems*. Dubuque: Brown.

Berlin, Ira. 2008. *A Guide to the History of Slavery in Maryland*. Annapolis: Maryland State Archives.

Bittker, Boris I. 1973. *The Case for Black Reparations*. New York: Vintage Books.

Blackstone, William. 1766. *Commentaries on the Laws of England*. 4 vols. Reprinted 1979, Chicago: University of Chicago Press.

Bonilla-Silva, Eduardo. 2014. *Racism Without Racists: Color-Blind Racism and the Persistence of Racial Inequality in America*. 4th ed. Lanham: Rowman & Littlefield Publishers, Inc.

Property and Human Flourishing. Gregory S. Alexander.

Brandt, Richard. 1979. *A Theory of the Good and the Right*. New York: Oxford University Press.

Brooks, Richard R.W. & Rose, Carol M. 2013. *Saving the Neighborhood: Racially Restrictive Covenants, Law and Social Norms*. Cambridge, MA: Harvard University Press.

Brooks, Roy. 2004. *Atonement and Forgiveness: A New Model of Black Reparations*. Berkeley: University of California Press, 2004.

Brophy, Alfred L. 2003. *Reconstructing the Dreamland: The Tulsa Riot of 1921, Race, Reparations and Reconciliation*. New York: Oxford University Press.

Brophy, Alfred L. 2006. *Reparations: Pro and Con*. New York: Oxford University Press.

Brown, Ray A. 1975. *The Law of Personal Property*. 3rd ed. Chicago: Callahan.

Brudner, Alan. 1995. *The Unity of the Common Law*. Berkley: University of California Press.

Brune, Jeffrey A. & Wilson, Daniel J. (eds.). 2013. *Disability and Passing: Blurring the Lines of Identity*. Philadelphia: Temple University Press.

Buckland, William W. 1963. *A Textbook of Roman Law from Augustus to Justinian*. 3rd ed. Cambridge: University Press.

Care, Norman S. 2000. *Decent People*. Lanham: Rowman & Littlefield Publishers.

Coates, Ta-Nehisi. 2015. *Between the World and Me*. New York: Spiegel & Grau.

Coleman, Jules. 1992. *Risks and Wrongs*. New York: Cambridge University Press.

Dagan, Hanoch. 2011. *Property: Values and Institutions*. New York: Oxford University Press.

Dagan, Hanoch. 2013. *Reconstructing American Legal Realism & Rethinking Private Law Theory*. New York: Oxford University Press.

Daly, Herman E. 1996. *Beyond Growth: The Economics of Sustainable Development*. Boston: Beacon Press.

Davis, Shelton. 1988. *Land Rights and Indigenous Peoples*. Cambridge, MA: Cultural Survival.

Desmond, Matthew. 2016. *Evicted: Poverty and Profit in the American City*. New York: Crown.

De Shalit, Avner. 1995. *Why Prosperity Matters: Environmental Policies and Future Generations*. New York: Routledge.

Dickens, Charles. 2009. *A Christmas Carol*. New York: Everyman's Library.

Doss, Erika. 1995. *Spirit Poles and Flying Pigs: Public Art and Cultural Democracy in American Communities*. Washington, D.C.: Smithsonian Institution Press.

Duguit, León. 1978. *Las Transformaciones del Derecho Pùblico y Privado*. Buenos Aires: Editorial Heliasta S.R.L.

Dukeminier, Jesse, Krier, James E., Alexander, Gregory S., Schill, Michael H., & Strahilevitz, Lior Jacob. 2014. *Property*. 8th ed. New York: Wolters Kluwer Law & Business.

Dukeminier, Jesse & Johanson, Stanley M. 1984. *Wills, Trusts, and Estates*. 3rd ed. Boston: Little Brown.

Dukeminier, Jesse, Krier, James E., Alexander, Gregory S., & Schill, Michael H. 2010. *Property*. 7th ed. New York: Aspen Publishers.

Dukeminier, Jesse, Sitkoff, Robert, & Lindgren, James. 2009. *Wills, Trusts and Estates*. 8th ed. New York: Aspen Publishers.

Dworkin, Ronald. 2011. *Justice for Hedgehogs*. Cambridge, MA: Belknap Press of Harvard University Press.

Dworkin, Ronald. 1977. *Taking Rights Seriously*. Cambridge, MA: Harvard University Press.

Elster, Jon. 1983. *Sour Grapes*. New York: Cambridge University Press.

Epstein, Richard A. 1985. *Takings*. Cambridge, MA: Harvard University Press.

Freyfogle, Eric T. 2003. *The Land We Share: Private Property and the Common Good*. Washington, D.C.: Island Press/Shearwater Books.

Fox O'Mahony, Lorna. 2007. *Conceptualizing Home: Theories, Law, and Policies*. Oxford: Hart Publishing.

Gallanis, Thomas P. 2011. *Family Property Law: Cases and Materials on Wills, Trusts and Future Interests*. 5th ed. New York: Foundation Press.

Galston, William A. 1980. *Justice and the Human Good*. Chicago: University of Chicago Press.

Garner, Bryan A. & Black, Henry Campbell. 1999. *Black's Law Dictionary*. 7th ed. St. Paul: West Group.

Geertz, Clifford. 2000. *Local Knowledge*. New York: Basic Books.

Glaeser, Edward. 2011. *Triumph of the City: How Our Greatest Invention Makes Us Richer, Smarter, Greener, Healthier, and Happier*. New York: Penguin Press.

Gordley, James. 2006. *Foundations of Private Law: Property, Tort, Contract, Unjust Enrichment*. Oxford: Oxford University Press.

Gray, John Chipman. 1942. *The Rule Against Perpetuities*. 4th ed. Boston: Little Brown.

Gray, Kevin & Gray, Susan Francis. 2009. *Elements of Land Law*. 5th ed. New York: Oxford University Press.

Green, T.H. 1967 (orig. pub. 1882). *Lectures on the Principles of Political Obligation*. Ann Arbor: University of Michigan Press.

Griffin, James. 1986. *Well-being*. New York: Oxford University Press.

Griffin, James. 1996. *Value Judgment: Improving Our Ethical Beliefs*. New York: Oxford University Press.

Hare, Richard M. 1963. *Freedom in Reason*. Oxford: Clarendon Press.

Harris, J.W. 1996. *Property and Justice*. Oxford: Clarendon Press.

Hart, H.L.A. 1961. *The Concept of Law*. Oxford: Oxford University Press.

Haybron, Dan. 2008. *The Pursuit of Unhappiness*. Oxford: Oxford University Press.

Hayek, Friedrich A. von. 2005. *The Road to Serfdom*. London: Institute of Economic Affairs.

Hegel, G.W.F. 1952. *The Philosophy of Right*, trans. T.M. Knox. New York: Oxford University Press.

Hesse, Konrad. 1995. *Grundzüge des Verfassungsrecht der Bundesrepublik Deutschland*. 20th ed. Heidelberg: C.F. Muller.

Holmes, Stephen & Sunstein, Cass. *The Cost of Rights: Why Liberty Depends on Taxes*. New York: W.W. Norton.

Homelessness Research Institute, National Alliance to End Homelessness. 2016. *The State of Homelessness in America*.

Hursthouse, Rosalind. 1999. *On Virtue Ethics*. Oxford: Oxford University Press.

Hyland, Richard. 2009. *Gifts: A Study in Comparative Law*. New York: Oxford University Press.

Ivison, Duncan. 2002. *Postcolonial Liberalism*. Cambridge: Cambridge University Press.

Jones, Martin et al. 2015. *An Introduction to Political Geography*. 2nd ed. New York: Routledge.

Kagan, Shelley. 1998. *Normative Ethics*. Boulder, CO: Westview Press.

Kant, Immanuel. 1991. *The Metaphysics of Morals*, trans. M. Gregor. Cambridge: Cambridge University Press.

Kaplow, Louis & Shavell, Steven. 2003. *Fairness Versus Welfare*. Cambridge, MA: Harvard University Press.

Kraut, Richard. 2002. *Aristotle: Political Philosophy*. New York: Oxford University Press.

Ladd, Everett Carll. 1999. *The Ladd Report*. New York: Free Press.

Leopold, Aldo. 1949. *A Sand County Almanac*. New York: Oxford University Press.

Lesko, Kathleen Menzie, Babb, Valiere, & Gibbs, Carroll R. 1991. *Black Georgetown Remembered*. Washington, D.C.: Georgetown University Press.

Locke, John. 1988. *Two Treatises of Government*, ed. Peter Laslett. Cambridge: Cambridge University Press.

Lukes, Steven. 1973. *Individualism*. Oxford: Basil Blackwell.

Lyons, David. 1965. *The Forms and Limits of Utilitarianism*. Oxford: Clarendon Press.

MacIntyre, Alasdair. 1981. *After Virtue*. Notre Dame: University of Notre Dame Press.

MacIntyre, Alasdair. 1999. *Dependent Rational Animals: Why Human Beings Need the Virtues*. Chicago: Open Court.

Mason, Anthony. 2000. *Community, Solidarity and Belonging: Levels of Community and Their Normative Significance*. New York: Cambridge University Press.

Massey, Doreen B. 2005. *For Space*. London: SAGE.

Meisels, Tamar. 2009. *Territorial Rights*. 2nd ed. Dordrecht: Springer.

Miller, David. 1995. *On Nationality*. Oxford: Clarendon Press.

Minow, Martha. 1998. *Between Vengeance and Forgiveness*. Boston: Beacon Press.

Moore, G.E. 1903. *Principa Ethica*. Cambridge: Cambridge University Press.

Nine, Cara, 2012. *Global Justice and Territory*. Oxford: Oxford University Press.

Nozick, Robert. 1974. *Anarchy, State and Utopia*. New York: Basic Books.

Nussbaum, Martha C. 1986. *The Fragility of Goodness*. Cambridge: Cambridge University Press.

Nussbaum, Martha C. 2000. *Women and Human Development: The Capabilities Approach*. Cambridge: Cambridge University Press.

Office of the Special Inspector General for the Troubled Asset Relief Program. April 2013. *Quarterly Report to Congress*.

O'Neill, John. 1993. *Ecology, Policy and Politics*. London: Routledge.

Parfit, Derek. 1984. *Reasons and Persons*. Oxford: Clarendon Press.

Penner, J.E. 1997. *The Idea of Property in Law*. Oxford: Clarendon Press.

Posner, Richard A. 1995. *Aging and Old Age*. Chicago: University of Chicago Press.

Posner, Richard A. 2003. *Economic Analysis of Law*. 6th ed. New York: Aspen Publishers.

Putnam, Robert D. 2000. *Bowling Alone: The Collapse and Revival of American Government*. New York: Simon & Schuster.

Putnam, Robert D. 1993. *Making Democracy Work: Civic Traditions in Modern Italy*. Princeton, NJ: Princeton University Press.

Rawls, John. 1971. *A Theory of Justice*. Cambridge, MA: Belknap Press of Harvard University Press.

Rawls, John. 1993. *Political Liberalism*. New York: Columbia University Press.

Raz, Joseph. 1986. *The Morality of Freedom*. New York: Oxford University Press.

Reynold, Susan. 2010. *Before Eminent Domain: Toward a History of Exploration of Land for the Common Good*, eds. Daniel Ernst & Thomas A. Green. Chapel Hill: University of North Carolina Press.

Rheingold, Howard. 2000. *The Vertical Community: Homesteading on the Electronic Frontier*. Cambridge, MA: MIT Press.

Ripstein, Arthur. 2009. *Force and Freedom: Kant's Legal and Political Philosophy*. Cambridge, MA: Harvard University Press.

Robinson, Randall. 2000. *The Debt: What America Owes Blacks*. New York: Dutton.

Rupp, George. 2006. *Globalization Challenged: Conviction, Conflict, Community*. New York: Columbia University Press.

Sandel, Michael. 1982. *Liberalism and the Limits of Justice*. New York: Cambridge University Press.

Sax, Joseph. 1999. *Playing Darts with a Rembrandt: Public and Private Rights in Cultural Treasures*. Ann Arbor: University of Michigan Press.

Scanlon, Thomas. 1998. *What We Owe to Each Other*. Cambridge, MA: Belknap Press of Harvard University Press.

Selznick, Philip. 1992. *The Moral Commonwealth: Social Theory and the Promise of Community*. Berkeley, CA: University of California Press.

Sen, Amartya. 1999. *Commodities and Capabilities*. 3rd ed. Delhi: Oxford University Press.

Sen, Amartya. 1999. *Development as Freedom*. New York: Knopf.

Sen, Amartya. 1987. *On Ethics and Economics*. Oxford: B. Blackwell.

Simes, Lewis. 1955. *Public Policy and the Dead Hand*. Ann Arbor: University of Michigan Press.

Sims, J. Revel, Aley, Ian, Dundore, Lexa, Laemmli, Taylor, Long, Sheila, Lutz, E., & McFerren, Ruena. 2016. *Evicted in Dane County, Wisconsin: A Collaborative Examination of the Housing Landscape*. University of Wisconsin Department of Urban and Regional Planning, available at https://gobigread.wisc.edu/wp-content/uploads/sites/3/2015/06/EvictedInDaneCounty_final.pdf.

Skurbaty, Zelim. 2000. *As If Peoples Mattered*. Boston: Martinus Nijhoff Publishers.

Singer, Joseph William. 2000. *Entitlement: The Paradoxes of Property*. New Haven, CT: Yale University Press.

Slote, Michael. 1983. *Goods and Virtues*. Oxford: Clarendon Press.

Smith, Nicholas H. 2002. *Charles Taylor: Meaning, Morals and Modernity*. Malden, MA: Blackwell Publishers.

Stewart, John A. 1973. *Notes on the Niomachean Ethics of Aristotle*. New York: Arno Press.

Styron, William. 1979. *Sophie's Choice*. New York: Random House.

Taylor, Charles. 1985. *Human Agency and Language*. New York: Cambridge University Press.

Taylor, Charles. 1989. *Sources of the Self: The Making of the Modern Identity*. Cambridge, MA: Harvard University Press.

Taylor, Charles. 1964. *The Expectation of Behavior*. New York: Humanities Press.

Taylor, Robert R. 1974. *The World in Stone: The Role of Architecture in the National Socialist Ideology*. Berkeley: University of California Press.

Teitel, Ruti G. 2000. *Transitional Justice*. New York: Oxford University Press.

Thompson, Janna. 2009. *Intergenerational Justice: Rights and Responsibilities in an Intergenerational Polity*. Oxford: Oxford University Press.

Tönnies, Ferdinand. 1963. *Community and Society*. Cambridge: Cambridge University Press.

Torpey, John. 2006. *Making Whole What Has Been Smashed*. Cambridge, MA: Harvard University Press.

Turkle, Sherry. 2015. *Reclaiming Conversation: The Power of Talk in the Digital Age.* New York: Penguin Press.

Ullrich, Volker. 2016. *Hitler: Ascent 1889–1939.* New York: Alfred A. Knopf.

Unger, Roberto Mangabeira. 1975. *Knowledge and Politics.* New York: Free Press.

U.S. Department of Housing and Urban Development. 2015. US Census Bureau.

U.S. Department of Housing and Urban Development. 2010. *Report to Congress on the Root Causes of the Foreclosure Crisis.*

U.S. Federal Reserve System et al. 2011. *Interagency Review of Foreclosure Policies and Practices.*

Van der Walt, Andre. 1999. *Constitutional Property Clauses.* Cambridge, MA: Kluwer Law International.

Van der Walt, Andre. 2011. *Constitutional Property Law.* 3rd ed. Cape Town: Juta Law.

Waldron, Jeremy. 1998. *The Right to Private Property.* Oxford: Clarendon.

Wallison, Peter J. 2011. *Dissent from the Majority Report of the Financial Crisis Inquiry Commission.* Washington, D.C.: American Enterprise Institute.

Walzer, Michael. 1983. *Spheres of Justice.* New York: Basic Books.

Williams, Bernard. 1985. *Ethics and the Limits of Philosophy.* Cambridge, MA: Harvard University Press.

Williams, Bernard. 1981. *Moral Luck.* Cambridge: Cambridge University Press.

Williams, Raymond. 1976. *Keywords: A Vocabulary of Culture and Society.* New York: Oxford University Press.

Wittgenstein, Ludwig. 1953. *Philosophical Investigations.* Oxford: Blackwell.

Wolff, Jonathan 1991. *Property, Justice and the Minimal State.* Cambridge: Polity Press.

Wollheim, Richard. 1984. *The Thread of Life.* Cambridge, MA: Harvard University Press.

Zack, Naomi. 2002. *Philosophy of Science and Race.* New York: Routledge.

Zack, Naomi. 1993. *Race and Mixed Race.* Philadelphia: Temple University Press.

Book Chapters

Anderson, Elizabeth. 1997. Practical Reason and Incommensurable Goods. In *Incommensurability, Incomparability, and Practical Reason,* ed. Ruth Chang, 90, 101, 102, 103. Cambridge, MA: Harvard University Press.

Appiah, Anthony. 1996. Race, Culture, Identity: Misunderstood Connections. In Appiah, Anthony & Gutmann, Amy, *Color Conscious.* Princeton: Princeton University Press.

Appiah, Anthony. 1995. The Uncompleted Argument: DuBois and the Illusion of Race. In *Overcoming Racism and Sexism,* eds. Linda Bell & David Blumenfeld. Lanham: Rowman & Littlefield.

Barry, Brian. 1978. Circumstances of Justice and Future Generations. In *Obligations to Future Generations,* eds. R.I. Sikora & Brian Barry, 204, 243. Philadelphia: Temple University Press.

Brownlie, Ian. 1988. The Rights of Peoples in Modern International Law. In *The Rights of Peoples,* ed. James Crawford, 1–16. Oxford: Clarendon Press.

Callahan, Daniel. 1981. What Obligations Do We Have to Future Generations? In *Responsibilities to Future Generations,* ed. Ernest Partridge, 73. Buffalo: Prometheus Books.

Chang, Ruth. 1997. Introduction. In *Incommensurability, Incomparability, and Practical Reason,* ed. Ruth Chang, 1, 2, 14–16, 34. Cambridge, MA: Harvard University Press.

Christopherson, Susan. 1994. The Fortress City: Privatized Spaces, Consumer Citizenship. In *Post-Fordism: A Reader*, ed. Ash Amin, 409. Cambridge, MA: Blackwell.

Davis, Christopher G. & Lehman, Darrin R. 1995. Counterfactual Thinking and Coping with Traumatic Life Events. In *What Might Have Been: The Social Psychology of Counterfactual Thinking*, eds. Neal J. Roese & James M. Olson, 353–74. Mahwah, NJ: Lawrence Erlbaum Associates.

Feinberg, Joel. 1974. The Rights of Animals and Unborn Generations. In *Philosophy and Environmental Crisis*, ed. William T. Blackstone, 4, 64–65. Athens: University of Georgia Press.

Garbarion, J. & Kastelny, K. 2005. Neighborhood and Community Influences on Parenting. In *Parenting: An Ecological Perspective*, eds. Tom Luster & Lynn Okagaki. Mahwah: Lawrence Erlbaum Associates.

Glaeser, Edward L. & Sinai, Todd. 2013. Postmortem for a Housing Crash. In *Housing and the Financial Crisis* 1, eds. Edward L. Glaeser & Todd Sinai. Chicago: University of Chicago Press.

Golding, Martin P. 1981. Obligation to Future Generations. In *Responsibilities to Future Generations*, ed. Ernest Partridge, 61–62. Buffalo: Prometheus Books.

Gray, Kevin & Gray, Susan Francis. 1999. Private Property and Public Property. In *Property and the Constitution*, ed. Janet McLean, 11, 15. Portland, OR: Hart.

Heathwood, Chris. 2015. Monism and Pluralism About Value. In *The Oxford Handbook of Value Theory*, eds. Iwao Hirose & Jonas Olson, 136, 140. New York: Oxford University Press.

Ivison, Duncan, Patton, Paul, & Sanders, Will. 2000. Introduction. In Duncan Ivison & Paul Patton, *Political Theory and the Rights of Indigenous Peoples*. Cambridge: Cambridge: Cambridge University Press.

Kant, Immanuel. 1996. Groundwork of the Metaphysic of Morals. In *The Cambridge Edition of the Works of Immanuel Kant: Practical Philosophy*, ed. & trans. Mary J. Gregor, 37, 78. Cambridge: Cambridge University Press.

Kavka, Gregory. 1981. The Futurity Problem. In *Responsibilities to Future Generations*, ed. Ernest Partridge 109, 112–13, 114. Buffalo: Prometheus Books.

Kerr, Fergus. 2004. The Self and the Good: Taylor's Moral Ontology. In *Charles Taylor*, ed. Ruth Abbey, 84, 88. Cambridge: Cambridge University Press.

Kollock, Peter & Smith, Marc A. 1999. Communities in Cyberspace. In *Communities in Cyberspace*, eds. Mark A. Smith & Peter Kollock, 3, 17. London: Routledge.

Laitinen, Arto. 2004. A Critique of Charles Taylor's Notions of "Moral Sources" and "Constitutive Goods." In *Moral Realism*, eds. Jussi Kotkavirta & Michael Quante, 73–104. Helsinki: Philosophical Society of Finland.

Makinson, David. 1988. Rights of Peoples: Point of View of a Logician. In *The Rights of Peoples*, ed. James Crawford, 69–92. Oxford: Clarendon Press.

Marcuse, Peter. 1986. Gentrification, Abandonment, and Displacement: The Linkages in New York City. In *Gentrification of the City*, eds., Neil Smith & Peter Williams, 153. Boston: Allen & Unwin.

McCaffery, Edward J. 2001. Must We Have the Right to Waste? In *New Essay in the Legal and Political Theory of Property*, ed. Stephen R. Munzer, 76. Cambridge: Cambridge University Press.

Michalska, Anna. 1991. Rights of Peoples to Self-Determination in International Law. In *Issues of Self-Determination*, ed. William Twining, 71–90. Aberdeen: Aberdeen University Press.

Michelman, Frank I. 1982. Ethics, Economics, and the Law of Property. In *Nomos XXIV: Ethics, Economics & the Law*, eds. J. Roland Pennock & John W. Chapman, 3. New York: New York University Press.

Mulhall, Stephen. 2004. Articulating the Horizons of Liberalism. In *Charles Taylor*, ed. Ruth Abbey, 105, 115. Cambridge: Cambridge University Press.

Nadler, Janice & Seidman Diamond, Sheri. 2008. Government Takings of Private Property: Kelo and the Perfect Storm. In *Public Opinion and Constitutional Controversy*, ed. Nathaniel Persity et al., 287. New York: Oxford University Press.

Nedelsky, Jennifer. 1996. Should Property Be Constitutionalized? A Relational and Comparative Approach. In *Property Law on the Threshold of the 21st Century*, eds. G.E. van Maanen & A.J. van der Walt, 417–32. Antwerp: Maklu.

Nettheim, Garth. 1988. "Peoples" and "Populations"—Indigenous Peoples and Rights of Peoples. In *The Rights of Peoples*, eds. James Crawford & Hans Kruuk. Oxford: Clarendon Press.

Papier, H.J. 1990. Art. 14. In *Grudgesetz Kommentar*, 28th ed., eds. T. Maunz et al., 253. Munich: C.H. Beck.

Partridge, Ernest. 2001. Future Generations. In *A Companion to Environmental Philosophy*, ed. Dale Jamieson, 377. Malden, MA: Blackwell Publishers.

Raz, Joseph. 1997. Incommensurability and Agency. In *Incommensurability, Incomparability, and Practical Reason*, ed. Ruth Chang, 110, 111. Cambridge, MA: Harvard University Press.

Roese, Neal J. & Olson, James M. 1995. Counterfactual Thinking: A Critical Overview. In *What Might Have Been: The Social Psychology of Counterfactual Thinking*, eds. Neal J. Roese & James M. Olson, 1–55. Mahwah, NJ: Lawrence Erlbaum Associates.

Roux, Theunis. 2008. Land Restitution and Reconciliation in South Africa. In *Justice and Reconciliation in Post-Apartheid South Africa*, eds. François du Bois & Antié du Bois-Pedain, 144–71. Cambridge: Cambridge University Press.

Salsich Jr., Peter W. 2000. Toward a Property Ethic of Stewardship: A Religious Perspective. In *Property and Values: Alternatives to Public and Private Ownership*, eds. Charles Geisler & Gail Daneker, 21. Washington, D.C.: Island Press.

Sen, Amartya. 1993. Capability and Well-Being. In *The Quality of Life*, eds. Martha Nussbaum & Amartya Sen, 30, 32–33. New York: Oxford University Press.

Sherman, Steven & McConnell, Allen R. 1995. Dysfunctional Implications of Counterfactual Thinking: When Alternatives to Reality Fail Us. In *What Might Have Been: The Social Psychology of Counterfactual Thinking*, eds. Neal J. Roese & James M. Olson, 199–231. Mahwah, NJ: Lawrence Erlbaum Associates, Publishers.

Singer, Joseph William. 2010. How Property Norms Construct the Externalities of Ownership. In *Property and Community*, eds. Gregory S. Alexander & Eduardo M. Peñalver, 57, 59. New York: Oxford University Press.

Smith, Nicholas H. Taylor and the Hermeneutic Tradition. In *Charles Taylor*, ed. Ruth Abbey, 24, 31. Cambridge: Cambridge University Press.

Stocker, Michael. 1997. Abstract and Concrete Value: Plurality, Conflict, and Maximization. In *Incommensurability, Incomparability, and Practical Reason*, ed. Ruth Chang, 196, 203. Cambridge, MA: Harvard University Press.

Stolzenberg, Nomi. 2009. Facts on the Ground. In *Property and Community*, eds. Gregory S. Alexander & Eduardo M. Peñalver, 107–39. New York: Oxford University Press.

Tan, Kok-Chor. 2007. Colonialism, Reparations, and Global Justice. In *Reparations: Interdisciplinary Inquiries*, eds. Jon Miller & Rahul Kumar, 280–306. Oxford: Oxford University Press.

Taylor, Charles. 1985. Atomism. In *Philosophical Papers: Philosophy and the Human Sciences, Vol. 2*, ed. Charles Taylor, 187, 189, 190–91, 204–05, 207, 209. Cambridge: Cambridge University Press.

Taylor, Charles. 1995. Cross Purposes: The Liberal-Communitarian Debate. In *Charles Taylor, Philosophical Arguments*, 181. Cambridge, MA: Harvard University Press.

Taylor, Charles. 1997. Leading a Life. In *Incommensurability, Incomparability, and Practical Reason*, ed. Ruth Chang, 170, 176, 178–82, 183. Cambridge, MA: Harvard University Press.

Taylor, Charles. 1985. Social Theory in Practice. In *Philosophical Papers: Philosophy and the Human Sciences, Vol. 2*, ed. Charles Taylor, 96. Cambridge: Cambridge University Press.

Taylor, Charles. 1985. The Nature and Scope of Distributive Justice. In *Taylor: Philosophical Papers, Vol. 2*, 289–317. Cambridge: Cambridge University Press.

Taylor, Charles. 1985. The Person. In *The Category of the Person: Anthropology, Philosophy, History*, eds. M. Carrithers, S. Collins, & S. Lukes, 257, 259. New York: Cambridge University Press.

Waldron, Jeremy. Historic Injustice: Its Remembrance and Supersession. In *Justice, Ethics and New Zealand Society*, eds. Graham Odde & Roy W. Perrett, 139–170. New York: Oxford University Press.

Wellman, Barry & Gulia, Milena. 1999. Virtual Communities as Communities: Net Surfers Don't Ride Alone. In *Communities in Cyberspace*, eds. Mark A. Smith & Peter Kollock, 167, 169. London: Routledge.

Wiggins, David. 1980. Deliberation and Practical Reason. In *Essays on Aristotle's Ethics*, ed. Amélie Oksenberg Rorty, 221. Berkley: University of California Press.

Wiggins, David. 1997. Four Proposals. In *Incommensurability, Incomparability, and Practical Reason*, ed. Ruth Chang, 52. Cambridge, MA: Harvard University Press.

Articles

Alexander, Frank S. et al. 2011. Legislative Responses to the Foreclosure Crisis in Nonjudicial Foreclosure States. *Review of Banking Finance Law* 31:341.

Alexander, Gregory S. 1989. Dilemmas of Group Autonomy: Residential Associations and Community. *Cornell Law Review* 75:1.

Alexander, Gregory S. 2013. Ownership and Obligations: The Human Flourishing Theory of Property. *Hong Kong Law Journal* 43:451.

Alexander, Gregory S. 2009. The Social-Obligation Norm in American Property Law. *Cornell Law Review* 94:745.

Anaya, S. James. 2004. International Human Rights and Indigenous Peoples: The Move Toward the Multicultural State. *Arizona Journal of International and Comparative Law* 21:13.

Andersen, Robert, Grabb, Edward, & Curtis, James. 2006. Trends in Civic Association Activity in Four Democracies: The Special Case of Women in the United States. *American Sociological Review* 71:376.

Arce, A.A., Tadlock, M., Vergare, M.J. et al. 1982. A Psychiatric Profile of Street People Admitted to an Emergency Shelter. *Hospital Community Psychiatry* 34:812.

Arneson, Richard J. 1999. Human Flourishing Versus Desire Satisfaction. *Social Philosophy and Policy* 116:113.

Atuahene, Bernadette. 2016. Dignity Takings and Dignity Restoration: Creating a New Theoretical Framework for Understanding Involuntary Property Loss and the Remedies Required. *Law and Social Inquiry* 41:796.

Bales, R.E. 1971. Act-Utilitarianism: Account of Right-Making Characteristics or Decision- Making Procedures? *American Philosophical Quarterly* 8:261.

Been, Vicki, Gould, Ingrid, Gedal, Michael, Glaeser, Edward, & McCabe, Brian. 2016. Preserving History or Restricting Development? The Heterogeneous Effects of Historic Districts on Local Housing Markets in New York City. *Journal of Urban Economics* 92:16.

Berger, Lawrence. 1978. The Public Use Requirement in Eminent Domain. *Oregon Law Review* 57:203.

Bolanos, Omaira. 2011. Redefining Identities, Redefining Landscapes: Indigenous Identity and Land Rights Struggles in the Brazilian Amazon. *Journal of Cultural Geography* 28:45.

Bray, Zachary. 2012. The New Progressive Property and the Low-Income Housing Conflict. *Brigham Young University Law Review* 2012:1109.

Byrne, J.P. 2012. Historic Preservation and Its Cultured Despisers: Reflections on the Contemporary Role of Preservation Law in Urban Development. *George Mason Law Review* 19:665.

Calabresi, Guido & Melamed, A. Douglas. 1972. Property Rules, Liability Rules, and Inalienability: One View of the Cathedral. *Harvard Law Review* 85:1089.

Calem, Paul S., Gillen, Kevin & Wachter, Susan. 2004. The Neighborhood Distribution of Subprime Mortgage Lending. *Journal of Real Estate Finance and Economics* 29:393.

Callahan, Joan C. 1987. On Harming the Dead. *Ethics* 97:341.

Care, Norman S. 1982. Future Generations, Public Policy and the Motivation Problem. *Environmental Ethics* 4:195.

Cassady, Julie. 1998. Sovereignty of Aboriginal Peoples. *Indiana International & Comparative Law Review* 9:65.

Chang, Ruth. Emphatic Comparability and Constitutive Incommensurability, or Buying and Selling Friends, 3 (unpublished manuscript).

Chaskin, Robert J. 1997. Perspectives on Neighborhood and Community: A Review of the Literature. *Social Service Review* 71:521.

Choi, Naomi. 2015. Liberalism and the Interpretive Turn. *Review of Politics* 77:243.

Choi, Naomi. Practice Dependence: Social Explanation as Normative Justification. 12–15 (unpublished paper).

Claeys, Eric R. 2011. Exclusion and Exclusivity in Gridlock. *Arizona Law Review* 53:9.

Clowney, Stephen. 2013. Landscape Fairness: Removing Discrimination from the Built Environment. *Utah Law Review* 2013:1.

Cohen, Felix S. 1954. Dialogue on Private Property. *Rutgers Law Review* 9:357.

Cohen, Morris R. 1927. Property and Sovereignty. *Cornell Law Quarterly* 13:8.

Craswell, Richard. 1998. Incommensurability, Welfare, Economics, and the Law. *University of Pennsylvania Law Review* 146:1424.

Crisp, Roger. 2013. Well-Being. *Stanford Encyclopedia of Philosophy*. https://plato.stanford.edu/entries/well-being.

Dagan, Hanoch. 2012. Pluralism and Perfection in Private Law. *Columbia Law Review* 112:1409.

Dagan, Hanoch. 2007. Re-Imagining Takings Law. *Tel Aviv University Law Faculty Papers* 7–8.

Dagan, Hanoch. 1999. Takings and Distributive Justice. *Virginia Law Review* 86:741.

Dagan, Hanoch. 2008. The Limited Autonomy of Private Law. *The American Journal of Comparative Law* 56:809.

Dagan, Hanoch. 2007. The Social Responsibility of Ownership. *Cornell Law Review* 92:1255.

Dana, David A. 2012. Why Mortgage "Formalities" Matter. *Loyola Consumer Law Review* 24:505.

Davidson, Nestor M. 2013. New Formalism in the Aftermath of the Housing Crisis. *Boston University Law Review* 93:389.

Davis, Lawrence. 1976. Comments on Nozick's Entitlement Theory. *The Journal of Philosophy* 73:839.

Demsetz, Harold. 1967. Toward a Theory of Property Rights. *The American Economic Review* 57:347.

Desmond, Matthew & Gerschenson, Carl. 2016. Who Gets Evicted? Assessing Individual, Neighborhood, and Network Factors. *Social Science Research* 30:1. Available at http://dx.doi.org/10.1016/j.ssresearch.2016.08.017.

Desmond, Matthew, An, Weihua, Winkler, Richelle, & Ferris, Thomas. 2013. Evicting Children. *Social Forces* 92:303.

Desmond, Matthew. 2012. Eviction and the Reproduction of Urban Poverty. *American Journal of Sociology* 118:88.

Dickinson, Kelvin H. 1985. Mistaken Improvers of Real Estate. *North Carolina Law Review* 64:37.

Dworkin, Ronald. 1996. Objectivity and Truth: You'd Better Believe It. *Philosophy and Public Affairs* 25:87.

Dyal-Chand, Rashmi & Rowan, James V. 2013. Developing Capabilities, Not Entrepreneurs: A New Theory for Community Economic Development. *Hofstra Law Review* 42:839.

Eagle, Steven J. 2000. The Rise and Rise of "Investment-Backed Expectations." *The Urban Lawyer* 32:437.

Ederington, Benjamin. 1997. Property as a Natural Institution: The Separation of Property from Sovereignty in International Law. *American University International Law Review* 13:263.

Ellickson, Robert C. 1986. Adverse Possession and Perpetuities Law: Two Dents in the Libertarian Model of Property Rights. *Washington University Law Quarterly* 64:723.

Ellickson, Robert C. 2014. The Affirmative Duties of Property Owners. *Brigham-Kanner Property Rights Conference Journal* 3:7.

Epstein, Richard A. 1986. Past and Future: The Temporal Dimension in the Law of Property. *Washington University Law Quarterly* 64:667.

Epstein, Richard A. 1979. Possession as the Root of Title. *Georgia Law Review* 13:1221.

Epstein, Richard A. 2014. Public Accommodations Under the Civil Rights Act of 1964: Why Freedom of Association Counts as a Human Right. *Stanford Law Review* 66:1241.

Fazel, Seena, Khosla, Vivek, Doll, Helen, & Geddes, John. 2008. The Prevalence of Mental Disorders Among the Homeless in Western Countries: Systemic Review and Meta-Regression Analysis. *PLOS MED* Dec. 2, 2008. Available at https://doi.org/10.1371/journal.pmed.0050225.

Foot, Philippa. 1995. Does Moral Subjectivism Rest on a Mistake? *Oxford Journal of Legal Studies* 15:1.

Frederick, Shane et al. 2002. Time Discounting and Time Preference: A Critical Review. *Journal of Economic Literature* 40:351.

Freeman, James. 2002. Democracy and Danger on the Beach: Class Relations in the Public Space of Rio de Janeiro. *Space and Culture* 5:9.

Freyfogle, Eric T. 1996. Ethic, Community and Private Land. *Ecology Law Quarterly* 23:631.

Freyfogle, Eric T. 2006. Goodbye to the Public-Private Divide. *Environmental Law* 36:101.

Freyfogle, Eric. T. 2007. The Enclosure of America. *Illinois Public Law and Legal Theory Research Paper Series* (Research Paper No. 07-10, University of Illinois). http://ssrn.com/abstract=1024846.

Gallie, W.B. 1956. Essentially Contested Concepts. *Proceeding of the Aristotelian Society* 56:167.

Gooding Williams, Robert. 1998. Race, Multiculturalism, and Democracy. *Constellations* 5:18.

Gray, Kevin & Gray, Susan Francis. 1999. Civil Rights, Civil Wrongs and Quasi-Public Space. *European Human Rights Law Review* 4:46.

Greiner, D. James, Pattanayak, Cassandra Wolos, & Hennessy, Jonathan. 2013. The Limits of Unbundled Legal Assistance: A Randomized Study in a Massachusetts District Court and Prospects for the Future. *Harvard Law Review* 126:901.

Grey, Thomas C. 1986. The Malthusian Constitution. *University of Miami Law Review* 41:21.

Gruber, Jonathan. 2008. Covering the Uninsured in the United States. *Journal of Economic Literature* 46:571.

Hale, Matthew. 1670. De Portibus Maris. *Hargraves Law Tracts* 1:78.

Hall, Matthew, Crowder, Kyle, & Spring, Amy. 2015. Neighborhood Foreclosures, Racial/Ethnic Transitions, and Residential Segregation. *American Sociological Review* 80:526.

Harris, Cheryl. 1993. Whiteness as Property. *Harvard Law Review* 106:1707.

Harris, Judith Rich. 1995. Where Is the Child's Environment? A Group Socialization Theory of Development. *Psychological Review* 102:458.

Hausman, Daniel M. & McPherson, Michael S. 2009. Preference Satisfaction and Welfare Economics. *Economics and Philosophy* 25:1.

Heller, Michael A. & Krier, James E. 1999. Deterrence and Distribution in the Law of Takings. *Harvard Law Review* 112:997.

Hillery, George. 1955. Definitions of a Community: Areas of Agreement. *Rural Sociology* 20:111.

Hirsch, Adam J. 1999. Bequests for Purposes: A Unified Approach. *Washington & Lee Law Review* 56:69.

Holmes, Oliver Wendell. 1897. The Path of the Law. *Harvard Law Review* 10:457.

Hursthouse, Rosalind. 2003. Virtue Ethics. *Stanford Encyclopedia of Philosophy*. https://plato.stanford.edu/entries/ethics-virtue/.

Kahneman, Daniel & Miller, D.T. 1982. Norm Theory: Comparing Reality to Its Alternatives. *Psychological Review* 93:136.

Kaplow, Louis. 2007. Primary Goods, Capabilities, . . . or Well-Being? *Philosophical Review* 116:603.

Katz, Larissa. 2008. Exclusion and Exclusivity in Property Law. *University of Toronto Law Journal* 58:275.

Katz, Larissa. 2012. Governing Through Owners: How and Why Formal Private Property Rights Enhance State Power. *University of Pennsylvania Law Review* 160:2029.

Kennedy, Randall. 2001. Racial Passing. *Ohio State Law Journal* 62:1145.

Kingsbury, Ben. 1992. Competing Conceptual Approaches to Indigenous Group Issues in New Zealand Law. *University of Toronto Law Journal* 52:101.

Kitcher, Philip. 2007. Does "Race" Have a Future? *Philosophy and Public Affairs* 35:293.

Klass, Alexandra B. 2006. Modern Public Trust Principles: Recognizing Rights and Integrating Standards. *Notre Dame Law Review* 82:699.

Kumar, Rahul. Responsibility and Rectification for Past Injustice: The Case of American Chattel Slavery (typescript, February 2004).

Kutz, Christopher. 2004. Justice in Reparations: The Cost of Memory and the Value of Talk. *Philosophy & Public Affairs* 32:277.

Kysar, Douglas A. 2007. Discounting . . . on Stilts. *University of Chicago Law Review* 74:119.

Langbein, John H. 2004. Mandatory Rule in the Law of Trusts. *Northwestern University Law Review* 98:1105.

Lehavi, Amnon. 2009. How Property Can Create, Maintain, or Destroy Community. *Theoretical Inquiries in Law* 10:43.

Lewinsohn-Zamir, Daphne. 2003. The Objectivity of Well-Being and the Objectives of Property Law. *New York University Law Review* 78:1669.

Mallon, Ron. 2006. "Race": Normative, Not Metaphysical or Semantic. *Ethics* 116:525.

Marsh, Tanya. 2011. Foreclosures and the Failure of the American Land Title Recording System. *Columbia Law Review Sidebar* 111:19.

Mason, Elinor. 2011. Value Pluralism. *Stanford Encyclopedia of Philosophy*. https://plato.stanford.edu/entries/value-pluralism/.

Matthews, Eric. 1973. Objectivity, Values, and History. *American Philosophical Quarterly* 10:213.

Mautner, Menachem. 1991. "The Eternal Triangles of the Law": Toward a Theory of Priorities in Conflicts Involving Remote Parties. *Michigan Law Review* 90:95.

Mayer, Christopher et al., 2009. The Rise in Mortgage Defaults. *Journal of Economic Perspectives* 23:27.

Merrill, Thomas W. 1998. Property and the Right to Exclude. *Nebraska Law Review* 77:730.

Merrill, Thomas W. 2014. Property and the Right to Exclude II. *Brigham-Kanner Property Rights Conference Journal* 3:1.

Merrill, Thomas W. 1986. The Economics of Public Use. *Cornell Law Review* 72:61.

Merrill, Thomas W. 2000. The Landscape of Constitutional Property. *Virginia Law Review* 86:885.

Merrill, Thomas W. 2012. The Property Strategy. *University of Pennsylvania Law Review* 160:2061.

Merrill, Thomas W. & Smith, Henry E. Optimal Standardization in the Law of Property: The Numerus Clausus Principle. *Yale Law Journal* 110:1.

Merrill, Thomas W. & Smith, Henry E. 2001. The Property/Contract Interface. *Columbia Law Review* 101:773.

Merrill, Thomas W. & Smith, Henry E. 2001. Whatever Happened to Property in Law and Economics? *Yale Law Journal* 111:357.

Merryman, John Henry. 1959. Improving the Lot of the Trespassing Improver. *Stanford Law Review* 11:456.

Mildner, Gerard. 2015. The Gentrification Plan for Metro Portland. *Portland State University Center for Real Estate Quarterly Report* Fall 2015. Available at https://www.pdx.edu/syndication/sites/www.pdx.edu.syndication/files/Quarterly%20 2015-11.pdf.

Miller, D.T. & Gunasegaram S. 1990. Temporal Order and the Perceived Mutability of Event: Implications for Blame Assignment. *Journal of Personality & Social Psychology* 59:1111.

Mirow, M.C. 2010. The Social-Obligation Norm of Property: Duguit, Hayem, and Others. *Florida Journal of International Law* 22:191.

Mitchell, Thomas W. 2014. Reforming Property Law to Address Devastating Land Loss. *Alabama Law Review* 66:1.

Morris, J.N., Clayton, D.G., Everitt, M.G., Semmence, A.M., & Burgess, E.H. 1990. Exercise in Leisure Time: Coronary Attack and Death Rates. *British Heart Journal* 63:235.

Morse, G. & Calsyn, R.J. 1986. Mentally Disturbed Homeless People in St. Louis: Needy, Willing, but Underserved. *International Journal of Mental Health* 14:74.

Moyes, Patrick & Gravel, Nicholas. 2011. Utilitarianism or Welfarism: Does It Make a Difference? *Cahier du GREThA no. 2011-30*. Available at http://www.ite.univ-mrs.fr/pp/Gravel/UtilWelf%20DT%20version.pdf.

Newman, Kathe & Wyly, Elvin. 2006. The Right to Stay Put, Revisited: Gentrification and Resistance to Displacement in New York City. *Urban Studies*. 43.

Odinet, Christopher K. 2016. Of Progressive Property and Public Debt. *Wake Forest Law Review* 51:1101.

Ogletree, Charles. 2003. The Current Reparations Debate. *University of California Davis Law Review* 36:1051.

Olafson, Frederick A. 1994. Comments on Sources of the Self by Charles Taylor. *Philosophy and Phenomenological Research* 54:191.

Oliveri, Rigel C. 2010. Discriminatory Housing Advertisements Online. *Indiana Law Review* 43:1125.

Patton, Paul. 2005. Historic Injustice and the Possibility of Supersession. *Journal of Intercultural Studies* 26:255.

Peñalver, Eduardo M. 2009. Land's Virtues. *Cornell Law Review* 94:821.

Peñalver, Eduardo M. 2011. Property's Memories. *Fordham Law Review* 80:1071.

Pitcher, George. 1984. The Misfortunes of the Dead. *American Philosophical Quarterly* 21:183.

Posner, Eric A. & Vermeule, Adrian. 2003. Reparations for Slavery and Other Historical Injustices. *Columbia Law Review* 103:689.

Radin, Margaret J. 1982. Property and Personhood. *Stanford Law Review* 34:957.

Radin, Margaret J. 1986. The Consequences of Conceptualism. *University of Miami Law Review* 41:239.

Rose, Carol M. 1985. Possession as the Origin of Property. *The University of Chicago Law Review* 52:73.

Rose, Carol M. 1981. Preservation and Community: New Direction in the Law of Historic Preservation. *Stanford Law Review* 33:473.

Rose, Carol M. 2003. Romans, Roads and Romantic Creators: Traditions of Public Property in the Information Age. *Law and Contemporary Problems* 66:89.

Rose, Carol M. 1986. The Comedy of the Commons: Custom, Commerce, and Inherently Public Property. *The University of Chicago Law Review* 53:711.

Rosenblum, Nancy L. 2015. Good Neighbors: The Democracy of Everyday Life in America 7, 9, 10, 13, 22, 24 (unpublished manuscript, July 24, 2015).

Rugh, Jacob S. & Massey, Douglas S. 2010. Racial Segregation and the American Foreclosure Crisis. *American Sociological Review* 75:629.

Samitz, G., Egger, M., & Zwahlen, M. 2011. Domains of Physical Activity and All-Cause Mortality: Systematic Review and Dose-Response Meta-Analysis of Cohort Studies. *International Journal of Epidemiology* 40:1382.

Sax, Joseph L. 1970. The Public Trust Doctrine in Natural Resource Law: Effective Judicial Intervention. *Michigan Law Review* 68:471.

Scheffler, Samuel. 2017. Membership and Political Obligation. *Journal of Political Philosophy* 25:1.

Schill, Michael H. 1991. Uniformity or Diversity: Residential Real Estate Finance Law in the 1990s and the Implications of Changing Financial Markets. *Southern California Law Review* 64:1261.

Schweikard, David P. 2004. On and Beyond Taylor's Moral Realism. *Redescriptions: Political Thought, Conceptual History and Feminist Theory* 8:254.

Sen, Amartya. 1979. Utilitarianism and Welfarism. *Journal of Philosophy* 76:474.

Sen, Amartya. 1985 Well-Being, Agency and Freedom: The Dewey Lectures. *The Journal of Philosophy* 82:169.

Shiffrin, Seana V. 2010. Inducing Moral Deliberation: On the Occasional Virtues of Fog. *Harvard Law Review* 123:1214.

Sinai, Todd. 2014. The Rent Affordability Crisis, *Issue Brief* 2, no. 3 (March 2014). Penn Wharton Public Policy Initiative. Available at http://repository.upenn.edu/cgi/viewcontent.cgi?article=1017&context=pennwhartonppi.

Singer, Joseph William. 1996. No Right to Exclude: Public Accommodations and Private Property. *Northwestern University Law Review* 90:1283.

Singer, Joseph William. 1988. The Reliance Interest in Property. *Stanford Law Review* 40:611.

Sinnot-Armstrong, Walter. 2006. Consequentialism. *Stanford Encyclopedia of Philosophy*. https://plato.stanford.edu/entries/consequentialism/.

Smith, Henry E. 2004. Exclusion and Property Rules in the Law of Nuisance. *Virginia Law Review* 90:965.

Smith, Henry E. 2002. Exclusion Versus Governance: Two Strategies for Delineating Property Rights. *The Journal of Legal Studies* 31:S453.

Smith, Henry E. 2009. Mind the Gap: The Indirect Relation Between Ends and Means in American Property Law. *Cornell Law Review* 94:959.

Smith, Henry E. 2004. Property and Property Rules. *New York University Law Review* 79:1719.

Smith, Henry E. 2005. Self-Help and the Nature of Property. *Journal of Law, Economics and Property* 1:69.

Smith, Peter M. 1997. Valediction to Market Overt. *American Journal of Legal History* 41:225.

Stephan, Paul B. 2002. Redistributive Litigation: Judicial Innovation, Private Expectations, and the Shadow of International Law. *Virginia Law Review* 88:789.

Stern, Stephanie M. 2008. Residential Protectionism and the Legal Mythology of Home. *Michigan Law Review* 107:1093.

Strahilevitz, Lior J. 2016. Historic Preservation and Its Even Less Authentic Alternative (unpublished manuscript, Sept. 2016).

Strahilevitz, Lior J. 2006. Information Asymmetries and the Right to Exclude. *Michigan Law Review* 104:1835.

Strahilivetz, Lior J. 2005. The Right to Destroy. *Yale Law Journal* 114:781.

Sugden, Robert. 1993. Welfare, Resources and Capabilities. *Journal of Economic Literature* 31:1947.

Summers, James. 2004. The Idea of the People: The Right of Self-Determination, Nationalism and Legitimacy in International Law (doctoral dissertation, University of Helsinki). http://ethesis.helsinki.fi/julkaisut/oik/julki/vk/summers/theideao.pdf.

Symposium. 2011. The Social Function of Property: A Comparative Perspective. *Fordham Law Review* 80:1003.

Taylor, Paul. 2000. Appiah's Uncompleted Argument: W.E.B. Du Bois and the Reality of Race. *Social Theory and Practice* 26:103.

Thompson, Judith J. 1997. The Right and the Good. *Journal of Philosophy* 94:275.

Tversky, Amos & Kahneman, Daniel. 1986. Rational Choice and the Framing of Decisions. *Journal of Business* 59:S251.

Vigdor, Jacob. *Does Gentrification Harm the Poor?* Wharton Papers Urban Affairs 133 (2002).

Waldron, Jeremy. 2009. Community and Property—For Those Who Have Neither. *Theoretical Inquiries in Law* 10:161.

Waldron, Jeremy. 2000. Homelessness and Community. *University of Toronto Law Journal* 50:371.

Waldron, Jeremy. 1991. Homelessness and the Issue of Freedom. *University of California Los Angeles Law Review* 39:295.

Waldron, Jeremy. 2003. Indigeneity? First Peoples and Last Occupancy. *New Zealand Journal of Public & International Law* 1:55.

Waldron, Jeremy. 2010. Secularism and the Limits of Community. 8 (unpublished paper, Dec. 2010).

Waldron, Jeremy. 2004. Settlement, Return, and the Supersession Thesis. *Theoretical Inquiries in Law* 5:237.

Waldron, Jeremy. 1992. Superseding Historic Injustice. *Ethics* 103:4.

Walzer, Michael. 1990. What Does It Mean to Be an "American"? *Social Research* 57:591.

Ward, Geoffrey C. 2001. Mongrel Nation. *Smithsonian* (Nov. 2001).

Washburn, Robert M. 1996. "Reasonable Investment-Backed Expectations" as a Factor in Defining Property Interest. *Washington University Urban Law Annual; Journal of Urban and Contemporary Law* 49:63.

Wenar, Leif. 2006. Reparation for the Future. *Journal of Social Philosophy* 37:396.

Wood, Alan. 2001. The Objectivity of Value. *New Literary History* 32:859.

Cases

Amalgamated Food Employees Union Local 590 v. Logan Valley Plaza, 391 U.S. 308 (1968).

A.Z. v. B.Z., 725 N.E.2d 1051 (Mass. 2000).

Batchelder v. Allied Stores Int'l, Inc., 445 N.E.2d 590 (Mass. 1983).

Bell v. Wells, 557 A.2d 168 (Me. 1989).

Berman v. Parker, 348 U.S. 26 (1954).

Blundell v. Catterall, 106 Eng. Rep. 1190 (1821).

Borough of Neptune City v. Borough of Avon-by-the-Sea, 294 A.2d 47 (N.J. 1972).

Boy Scouts of America v. Dale, 530 U.S. 640 (2000).

BVerfGE 89, 1 (*Besitzrecht des Mieters*) (1993).

BVerfGE 52, 1 (1979).

BVerfGE 66, 248 (1984).

BVerfGE 74, 264 (1987).

BVerfGE 100, 226 (*Denkmalschutz*) (1999).

City of Daytona Beach v. Tona-Rama, Inc., 294 So. 2d 73 (Fla. 1974).

Concerned Citizens of Brunswick County Taxpayers Ass'n v. State, 404 S.E.2d 677 (N.C. 1991).

Dale v. BSA, 734 A.2d 1196 (N.J. 1999).

Davis v. Davis, 842 S.W.2d 588 (Tenn. 1992).

Dolan v. City of Tigard, 512 U.S. 374 (1994).

Duke of Norfolk's Case, 22 Eng. Rep. 931 (Ch. 1681).

Estate of Kievernagel, 166 Cal. App. 4th 1024 (Cal. Ct. App. 2008).

Eyerman v. Mercantile Trust Co., N.A., 524 S.W.2d 210 (Mo. Ct. App. 1975).

Floyd v. City of New York, 959 F.Supp.2d 540 (S.D.N.Y. 2013).

Gion v. City of Santa Cruz, 465 P.2d 50 (Cal. 1970).

Glass v. Goeckel, 703 N.W.2d 58 (Mich. 2005).

Government of the Republic of South Africa v. Grootboom, 2001 (1)SA 46(CC).

Goulding v. Cook, 661 N.E.2d 1322 (Mass. 1996).

Hecht v. Superior Court, 20 Cal. Rptr. 2d 275 (Cal. App. 1993).

Hixon v. Public Service Comm'n, 146 N.W.2d 577 (Wis. 1966).

Hollified v. Monte Vista Biblical Gardens, 553 S.E.2d 662 (Ga. Ct. App. 2001).

Home for Incurables of Baltimore City v. University of Maryland. Medical System Corp., 797 A.2d 746 (Md. 2002).
Howard v. Kunto, 477 P.2d 210 (Wash. Ct. App. 1970).
Hudgens v. NLRB, 424 U.S. 507 (1976).
In re African American Slave Descendants Litigation, 471 F.3d 754 (7th Cir. 2006).
Jacobs v. Major, 132 Wis.2d 82 (Or. App. 1986).
Jacque v. Steenberg Homes, Inc., 563 N.W.2d 154 (Wis. 1997).
J.B. v. M.B., 783 A.2d 707 (N.J. 2001).
J.C. & Assocs. v. D.C. Bd. Of Appeals & Review, 778 A.2d 296 (D.S. 2001).
Just v. Marinette County, 201 N.W.2d 761 (Wis. 1972).
Kaiser Aetna v. United States, 444 U.S. 164 (1979).
Kanak v. Minister for Land & Water Conservation, 180 ALR 489, at 31 (NSW) (2000).
Kelo v. City of New London, 843 A.2d 500 (Conn. 2004).
Kelo v. City of New London, 545 U.S. 469 (2005).
Keystone Bituminous Coal Ass'n v. DeBendictis, 480 U.S. 470 (1987).
Loretto v. Teleprompter Manhattan CATV Corp., 458 U.S. 419 (1982).
Lucas v. South Carolina Coastal Council, 505 U.S. 1003 (1992).
Matthews v. Bay Head Improv. Ass'n., 471 A.2d 355 (N.J. 1984), cert. denied, 459 U.S. 821 (1984).
Matter of Pulitzer, 249 N.Y.S. 87 (Sur. Ct. 1931), aff'd mem., 260 N.Y.S. 975 (App. Div. 1932).
Meksras Estate, 63 Pa. D. & C.2d 371 (C.P. Phila. Co. 1974).
Montana Coalition for Stream Access v. Curran, 682 P.2d 163 (Mont. 1984).
Munn v. Illinois, 94 U.S. 113, 126 (1877).
National Organization of Women v. Little League Baseball, Inc., 338 A.2d 198 (1974).
N.J. Coalition Against War in the Middle East v. J.M.B. Realty Corp., 650 A.2d 757 (N.J 1994).
Nollan v. California Coastal Comm'n, 483 U.S. 825 (1987).
Opinion of the Justices, 313 N.E.2d 561 (Mass. 1974).
Penn Central Transportation Co. v. New York City, 438 U.S. 104 (1978).
Pennsylvania Coal Co. v. Mahon, 260 U.S. 393 (1922).
People ex rel. Marbro Corp. v. Ramsey, 171 N.E.2d 246 (Ill. App. 1960).
Ploof v. Putnam, 71 A. 188 (Vt. 1908).
PruneYard Shopping Center v. Robbins, 447 U.S. 74 (1980).
Pullen v. Ulmer, 923 P.2d 54 (Alaska 1996).
Raleigh Ave. Beach Ass'n v. Atlantis Beach Club, 879 A.2d 112 (N.J. 2005).
R.A.V. v. St. Paul, 505 U.S. 377 (1992).
Regina v. Pratt, 119 Eng. Rep. 319 (1855).
Shelley v. Kraemer, 334, U.S. 1 (1948).
State ex rel. Thornton v. Hay, 462 P.2d 671 (Or. 1969).
State v. DeCoster, 653 A.2d 891 (Me. 1995).
State v. Schaeffer, 117 N.E. 220 (Ohio 1917).
State v. Schmid, 423 A.D.2d 615 (N.J. 1980).
State v. Shack, 277 A.2d 369 (N.J. 1971).
Stevens v. City of Cannon Breach, 854 P.2d 449 (Or. 1993).
Uston v. Grand Resorts, Inc., 564 F.2d 1217 (9th Cir. 1977).

Uston v. Resorts Int'l Hotel, Inc., 445 A.2d 370 (N.J. 1982).
Williams v. Lubbering, 63 Atl. 90 (N.J. 1906).

Working Papers

Desmond, Matthew & Wilmers, Nathan. 2016. Is Housing the Poor Lucrative? The Profit Margins of Urban Landlords, Working Paper: Harvard University.

Fligstein, Neil & Goldstein, Adam. 2012. The Transformation of Mortgage Finance and the Industrial Roots of the Mortgage Meltdown. U.C. Berkeley Dept. of Sociology. Available at http://sociology.berkeley.edu/sites/default/files/faculty/fligstein/The%20Transformation%20of%20Mortgage%20Finance2.pdf.

Fried, Barbara H. 2011. Does Nozick Have a Theory of Property Rights? *Stanford Public Law and Legal Theory Working Papers Series* (Research Paper No. 1272031, Stanford University). http://ssrn.com.abstract+1782031.

Tegeler, Philip. 2010. Continuing Barriers to Housing Choice and Integration in HUD's Section 8 Voucher Program, Poverty & Race Research Action Council, Dec. 14, 2010. Available at http://www.prrac.org/pdf/Section_8_fair_housing_barriers_12-15-10.pdf.

Waldron, Jeremy. 2010. Vagueness and the Guidance of Action (NYU Public Law & Legal Theory Research Paper Series Working Paper No. 10-81, Oct. 29, 2010). Available at http://ssrn.co,/abstract+1699963.

Statutory Materials

42 U.S.C. §§2000a et seq.
42 U.S.C. §3603(b)(2).
42 U.S.C. §3604(a).
Basic Law of the Federal Republic of Germany art. 14.2. Basic Law of the Federal Republic of Germany art. 14.3.1. German Civil Code (BGB) §932(1).
Hawaii Rev. Stat. § 6E-1—43 (2009).
Mortgage Servicing Rules Under the Real Estate Settlement Procedures Act (Regulation X), 78 Fed. Reg. 10696 (codified at 12 C.F.R. §1024) (Feb. 14, 2013).
N.J. Stat. Ann. 2A:170-31—2A:170-41, repealed by L.1978, c. 95, § 2C:98-2, eff. Sept. 1, 1979.
Ohio Gen. Code §12603.
Okla. Stat. Ann. tit. 74, §8000.1 (2002).
Restatement (Second) of Torts § 197 cmt. h.
Restatement (Second) of Torts § 204.
Restatement (Third) of Trusts § 27(2).
Restatement (Third) of Trusts § 67 (2003-12).
S. Afr. Const. 1996 § 25(2).
S. Afr. Const. 1996 § 25(4).
S. Afr. Const. 1996 § 36(1).
Uniform Commercial Code § 2-403(2).
Uniform Probate Code § 2-120(d).
Uniform Probate Code § 2-120(k).
Uniform Trust Code § 404.
Uniform Trust Code § 105(b)(3).

Uniform Trust Code § 412 (2010).
Uniform Trust Code § 413 (2010).

Newspapers, Magazines, Etc.

Anderson, Bendix. 2016. New Affordable Housing Development Under Threat as Construction Costs Rise. *National Real Est. Investor*, Sept. 6, 2016.

Anft, Michael & Lipman, Harvey. 2003. How Americans Give. *The Chronicle of Philanthropy*, May 1, 2003. Available at https://www.philanthropy.com/article/How-Americans-Give/188055.

Associated Press. 2000. Aetna Apologizes for Slave Insurance. *Los Angeles Times*, March 11, 2000. Available at http://articles.latimes.com/2000/mar/11/business/fi-7637.

Banks, David. 2012. Sherry Turkle's Chronic Digital Dualism Problem. *The Society Pages, Cyborgology* (April 23, 2012). Available at http://thesocietypages.org/cyborgology/2012/04/23/sherry-turkles-chronic-digital-dualism-problem.

Columbia Journalism School. *The Pulitzer Prizes*. Available at http://www.journalism.columbia.edu/page/164-pulitzer (last visited Dec. 14, 2013).

Cox, Ana Marie. 2017. Michael Eric Dyson Believes in Individual Reparations. *New York Times Magazine*, Jan. 4, 2017. Available at https://www.nytimes.com/2017/01/04/magazine/michael-eric-dyson-believes-in-individual-reparations.html?rref=collection%2Fsectioncollection%2Fmagazine&action=click&contentCollection=magazine&region=rank&module=package&version=highlights&contentPlacement=7&pgtype=sectionfront.

Davis, Lauren Cassani. 2015. The Flight from Conversation. *The Atlantic* (Oct. 7, 2015). Available at http://www.theatlantic.com/technology/archive/2015/10/reclaiming-conversation-sherry-turkle/409273 (last visited Oct. 22, 2015).

Editorial. 2010. The Politics of Foreclosure. *Wall Street Journal*, Oct. 9, 2010.

Eichengreen, Barry. 2013. Why No Glass-Steagall II? *Project Syndicate*, Jan. 10, 2013.

Edvinsson, Rodney. Portal for Historical Statistics. *Historicalstatistics.org*. Available at http://www.historicalstatistics.org/.

Favreault, Melissa. 1991. Discrimination and Upward Mobility. *The Urban Institute*.

Georgetown University. 2017. *Wikipedia*. Available at https://enwikipedia.org/wiki/Georgetown_University.

Georgetown University Working Group on Slavery, Memory and Reconciliation, Historical Timeline, *College Records Indicate Two Slaves on Campus*. Available at http://slavery.georgetown.edu/timeline/.

Georgetown University Working Group on Slavery, Memory and Reconciliation, Historical Timeline, *First Documentation of Jesuit Ownership of Slaves in Maryland*. Available at http://slavery.georgetown.edu/timeline/.

Georgetown University Working Group on Slavery, Memory and Reconciliation, Historical Timeline, *Slavery Abolished in Maryland*. Available at http://slavery.georgetown.edu/timeline./.

Georgetown University Working Group on Slavery, Memory and Reconciliation, Historical Timeline, *The African-American Presence at Georgetown*. Available at http://slavery.georgetown.edu/timeline./.

Georgetown University Working Group on Slavery, Memory and Reconciliation, Historical Timeline, *The Jesuit Plantation Complex in Maryland*. Available at http://slavery.georgetown.edu/timeline/.

Georgetown University Working Group on Slavery, Memory and Reconciliation, Historical Timeline, *The Sale*. Available at http://slavery.georgetown.edu/timeline/.

History of Georgetown, *Georgetown University*. Available at https://www.georgetown.edu/about/history/.

Home Foreclosure Statistics. 2016. Available at http://www.statisticbrain.com/home-foreclosure-statistics.

Hopluch, Amanda. 2012. Andres Serrano's Controversial Piss Christ Goes on View in New York. *The Guardian*, Sept. 28, 2012. Available at https://www.theguardian.com/artanddesign/2012/sep/28/andres-serrano-piss-christ-new-york.

Inclusion and Diversity. *Apple*. Available at https://www.apple.com/diversity.

Interview, On the Record: Georgetown and the Racial Identity of President Patrick Healy, Interview with Max Sheptuck, *Vox Populi*. Available at https://blog.georgetownvoice.com/2010/04/14/on-the-record-georgetown-and-the-racial-identity-of-president-patrick-healy.

Johnson, Maisha Z. 2016. Six Ways Well-Intentioned People Whitesplain Racism (And Why They Need to Stop). *Everyday Feminism*, Feb. 7, 2016. Available at http://everydayfeminism.com/2016/02/how-people-whitesplain-racism./.

Key Facts, *Georgetown University*. Available at https://www.georgetown.edu/about/key-facts.

Lemann, Nicholas. 1996. Kicking in Groups. *The Atlantic Online* (April 1996).

Margalit, Avishai. 2001. Settling Scores. *New York Review of Books*, Sept. 20, 2001, 14.

Mason, Randall. 2005. Economics and Historic Preservation: A Guide and Review of the Literature. *Brookings Institution*. Available at https://www.brookings.edu/wp-content/uploads/2016/06/20050926_preservation.pdf.

Master, Samantha. 2016. Georgetown University's "Reparations" Plan Is Worthless White Guilt Repackaged as Justice. *The Root*, Sept. 5, 2016. Available at http://www.theroot.com/georgetown-university-s-reparations-plan-is-worthless-1790856615.

Matthews, Christopher. 2012. Should Eminent Domain Be Used to Save Underwater Homes. *Time*, July 12, 2012.

Miller, Sabrina R. & Washburn, Gary. 2002. New Chicago Law Requires Firms to Tell Slavery Links. *Chicago Tribune*, Oct. 3, 2002 (Trib. West), p.1.

Ojalvo, Holly Epstein 2017. Beyond Yale: These Other University Buildings Have Ties to Slavery and White Supremacy. *USA Today*, Feb. 13, 2017. Available at http://college.usatoday.com/2017/02/13/yale-university-buildings-slavery-white-supremacy/.

Quallen, Matthew. 2015. Slavery Inextricably Tied to Georgetown's Growth. *The Hoya*. Oct. 23, 2015.

Quenqua, Douglas. 2011. Dress Codes in New York Clubs: Will This Get Me In? *New York Times*, July 27, 2011, p. E1.

Reyen, Michael E. 2014. Eminent Domain Mortgage Seizures Down But Not Out. *American Banker*, June 16, 2014. Available at https://www.americanbanker.com/opinion/eminent-domain-mortgage-seizures-down-but-not-out.

Russell, John. 1978. Critic's Notebook: The Art of Finding a Met President. *New York Times*, Jan. 16, 2011, p. F13.

Semuels, Alana. 2015. How Housing Policy Is Failing America's Poor. *The Atlantic*, June 24, 2015.

Stony Brook University, 2017. *Wikipedia*. Available at https://en.wikipedia.org/wiki/Stony_Brook_University.

Swarns, Rachel L. 2016. Georgetown University Plans Steps to Atone for Slave Past. *N.Y. Times*, Sept. 1, 2016. Available at https://www.nytimes.com/2016/09/02/us/slaves-georgetown-university.html.

Swarns, Rachel L. 2016. Insurance Policies on Slaves: New York Life's Complicated Past, *N.Y. Times*, Dec. 18, 2016. Available at https://www.nytimes.com/2016/12/18/us/insurance-policies-on-slaves-new-york-lifes-complicated-past.html.

Thomas III, William G. 2015. The Timing of Queen v. Hepburn: An Exploration of African American Networks in the Early Republic. *O Say Can You See: Early Washington D.C., Law & Family*, Aug. 2015. Available at http://earlywashingtondc.org/stories/queen_v_hepburn.

University of Virginia, President's Commission on Slavery and the University, *Universities Studying Slavery*. Available at http://slavery.virginia.edu/universities-studying-slavery/.

William K. Kellogg Foundation. 2012. Cultures of Giving: Energizing and Expanding Philanthropy By and For Communities of Color, *W.K. Kellogg Foundation Report*.

Williamson, Samuel H. & Cain, Louis P. Measuring Slavery in 2011 Dollars. *Measuring Worth*. Available at https://www.measuringworth.com/slavery.php#text11.

Websites

http://repository.upenn.edu/cgi/viewcontent.cgi?article=1017&context=pennwhartonppi (trened in national apartment vacancy rate, cited in Chapter 10).

https://www.pdx.edu/syndication/sites/www.pdx.edu.syndication/files/Quarterly%202015-11.pdf (low-income households pay market rates, cited in Chapter 10).

http://dx.doi.org/10.1016/j.ssresearch.2016.08.017 (reference to paper by Desmond and Gerschenson on who gets evicted, cited in Chapter 10).

http://www.statisticbrain.com/home-foreclosure-statistics (data on foreclosure filings, cited in Chapter 10).

https://www.hudexchange.info/resources/documents/2015-AHAR-Part-1.pdf (data on mental illness among the homeless population, cited in Chapter 10).

https://mentalillnesspolicy.org/consequences/homeless-mentally-ill.html (data on mental illness among the homeless population, cited in Chapter 10).

http://www.prrac.org/pdf/Section_8_fair_housing_barriers_12-15-10.pdf (reference to fair housing problems with Section 8, cited in Chapter 10).

http://sociology.berkeley.edu/sites/default/files/faculty/fligstein/The%20Transformation%20of%20Mortgage%20Finance2.pdf (paper by Neil Fligstein and Adam Goldstein, cited in Chapter 10).

https://www.americanbanker.com/opinion/eminent-domain-mortgage-seizures-down-but-not-out-https://www.brookings.edu/wp-content/uploads/2016/06/

20050926_preservation.pdf (reference to article about eminent domain and underwater mortgages, cited in Chapter 10).

https://www.theguardian.com/artanddesign/2012/sep/28/andres-serrano-piss-christ-new-york.

https://en.wikipedia.org/wiki/Georgetown_University (reference to Georgetown capital endowment, cited in Chapter 9).

https://www.georgetown.edu/about/history (reference to Georgetown University history, cited in Chapter 9).

http://slavery.georgetown.edu/timeline (reference to slaves on Georgetown campus), cited in Chapter 9).

https://www.nytimes.com/2016/09/02/us/slaves-georgetown-university.html (reference to Georgetown reparation plans, cited in Chapter 9).

http://www.theroot.com/georgetown-university-s-reparations-plan-is-worthless-1790856615 (article critizing Georgetown reparations plan, cited in Chapter 9).

https://www.nytimes.com/2017/01/04/magazine/michael-eric-dyson-believes-in-individual-reparations.html?rref=collection%2Fsectioncollection%2Fmagazine&action=click&contentCollection=magazine&region=rank&module=package&version=highlights&contentPlacement=7&pgtype=sectionfront (article on Michael Eric Dyson's views on slavery reparations, cited in Chapter 9).

https://www.georgetown.edu/about/key-facts (article giving data about Georgetown University, cited in Chapter 9).

https://enwikipedia.org/wiki/Georgetown_University (reference to Georgetown University's capital endowment, cited in Chapter 9).

http://earlywashingtondc.org/stories/queen_v_hepburn (reference to Georgetown University president owning slaves, cited in chapter 9).

https://web.archive.org/web/20160303172633/http://blog.georgetownvoice.com/2010/04/14/on-the-record-georgetown-and-the-racial-identity-of-president-patrick-healy (reference to mixed racial identity of early Georgetown president, cited in Chapter 9).

https://en.wikipedia.org/wiki/Stony_Brook_University (data about Stony Brook University, cited in chapter 9).

http://slavery.virginia.edu/universities-studying-slavery/ (reference to "Universities Studying Slavery," cited in Chapter 9).

http://college.usatoday.com/2017/02/13/yale-university-buildings-slavery-white-supremacy/ (reference to article about university buildings with ties to slavery, cited in Chapter 9).

https://www.nytimes.com/2016/12/18/us/insurance-policies-on-slaves-new-york-lifes-complicated-past.html (article about New York Life Insurance Co.'s past connections with slavery, cited in Chapter 9).

https://www.measuringworth.com/slavery.php#text11 (index of slave values, cited in Chapter 9).

http://articles.latimes.com/2000/mar/11/business/fi-7637 (reference to Aetna Life Insurance and slavery, cited in Chapter 9).

https://www.philanthropy.com/article/How-Americans-Give/188055 (report on charitable giving data, cited in Chapter 9).

https://www.apple.com/diversity (reference to Apple's corporate statement, cited in Chapter 9).

http://everydayfeminism.com/2016/02/how-people-whitesplain-racism./ (reference to whitesplain racism, cited in Chapter 9).

https://gobigread.wisc.edu/wp-content/uploads/sites/3/2015/06/EvictedInDaneCounty_final.pdf (reference to close parallel of non-white communities and eviction filings, cited in Chapter 9).

http://thesocietypages.org/cyborgology/2012/04/23/sherry-turkles-chronic-digital-dualism-problem (reference to David Banks, Sherry Turkle's Chronic Digital Dualism Problem, cited in Chapter 3).

https://doi.org/10.1371/journal.pmed.0050225.

http://repository.upenn.edu/cgi/viewcontent.cgi?article=1017&context=pennwhartonppi.

https://www.pdx.edu/syndication/sites/www.pdx.edu.syndication/files/Quarterly%202015-11.pdf; http://www.journalism.columbia.edu/page/164-pulitzer.

https://plato.stanford.edu/entries/well-being (reference to article by Roger Crisp, cited in Chapter 1).

http://www.theatlantic.com/technology/archive/2015/10/reclaiming-conversation-sherry-turkle/409273 (reference to Lauren Cassani Davis, The Flight from Conversation, cited in Chapter 3).

http://ssrn.com/abstract=1024846 (reference to Eric T. Freyfogle, The Enclosure of America, cited in Chapter 2).

http://ssrn.com.abstract+1782031 (reference to Barbara Fried, Does Nozick Have a Theory of Property Rights?, cited in Chapter 1).

https://plato.stanford.edu/entries/ethics-virtue/ (reference to Rosalind Hursthouse, Value Pluralism, cited in Chapter 1).

https://plato.stanford.edu/entries/value-pluralism/ (reference to Elinor Mason, Value Pluralism, cited in Chapter 1).

http://www.vcharite.univ-mrs.fr/pp/Gravel/UtilWelf%20DT%20version.pdf (paper by Patrick Moyes & Nicolas Gravel, cited in Chapter 1).

https://plato.stanford.edu/entries/consequentialism/ (reference to Walter Sinnott-Armstrong, Consequentialism, cited in Chapter 1).

http://ethesis.helsinki.fi/julkaisut/oik/julki/vk/summers/theideao.pdf (Ph.D. dissertation by James Summers, The Idea of the People, cited in Chapter 5).

http://ssrn.co,/abstract+1699963 (paper by Jeremy Waldron, Vagueness and the Guidance of Action, cited in Chapter 6).

Index

Property and Human Flourishing. Gregory S. Alexander.